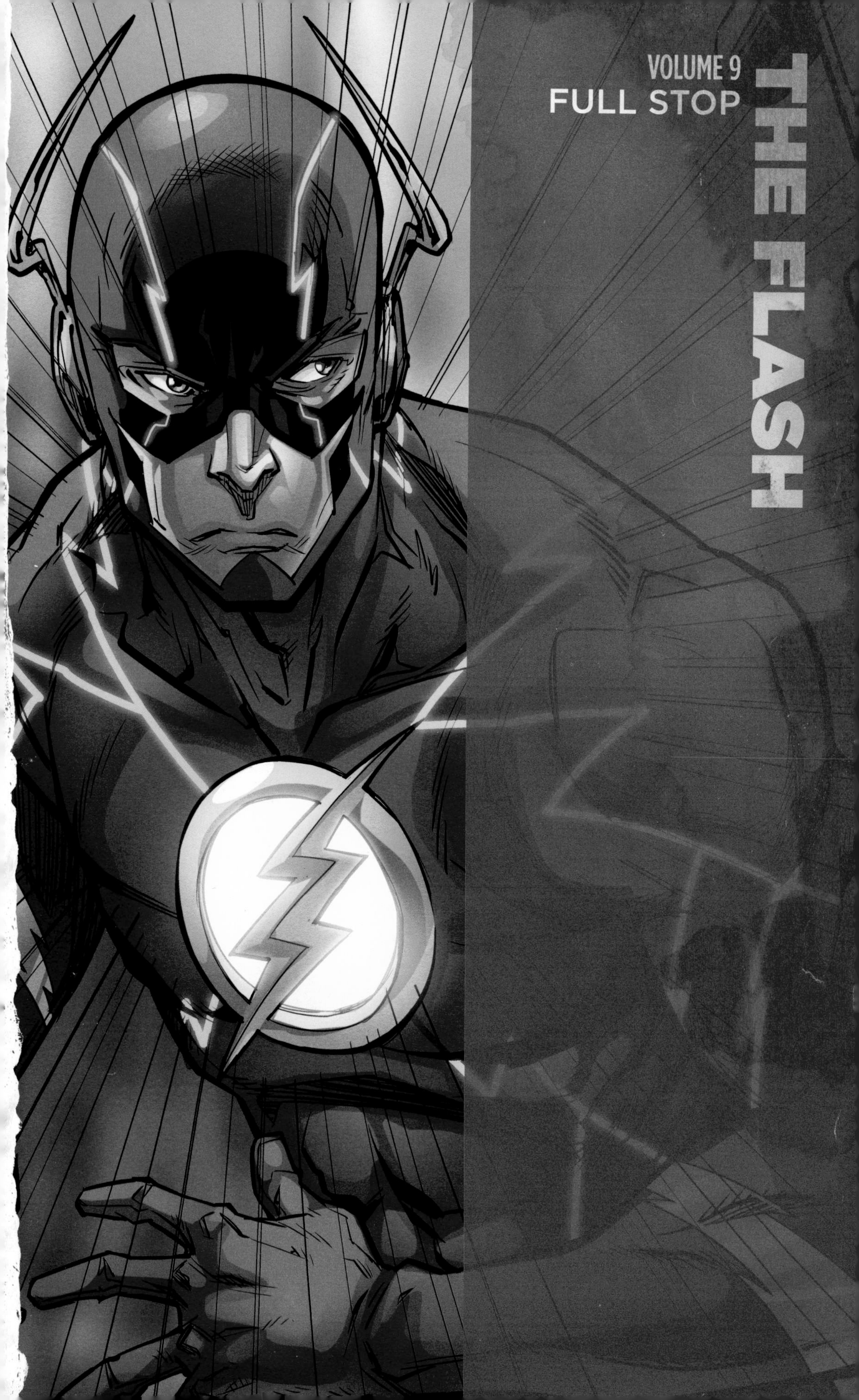
VOLUME 9
FULL STOP
THE FLASH

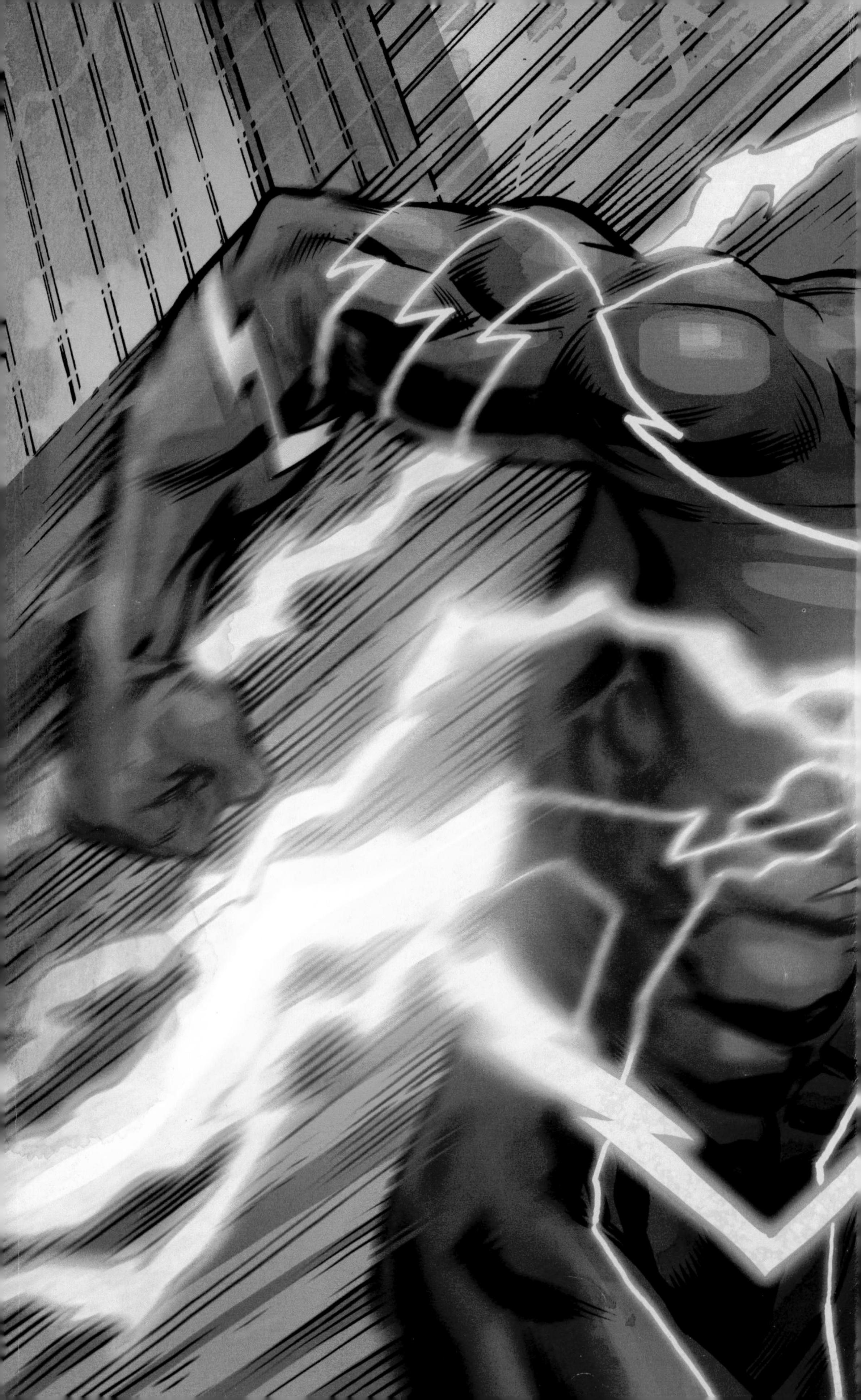

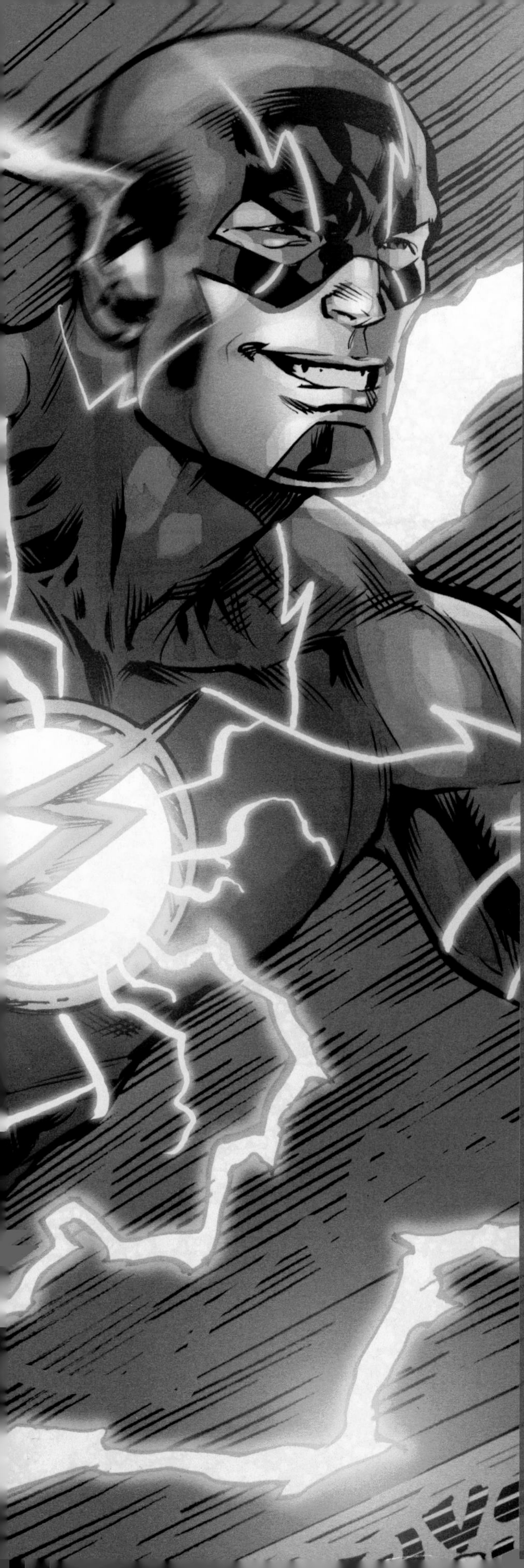

THE FLASH

VOLUME 9
FULL STOP

WRITTEN BY
VAN JENSEN
ROBERT VENDITTI

PENCILS BY
PHIL BRIONES
JOE EISMA
JESÚS MERINO
PAUL PELLETIER
GUS VAZQUEZ

INKS BY
PHIL BRIONES
JOE EISMA
WAYNE FAUCHER
SCOTT HANNA
TONY KORDOS
JESÚS MERINO
GUS VAZQUEZ

COLOR BY
GUY MAJOR
PETE PANTAZIS

LETTERS BY
PAT BROSSEAU

COLLECTION COVER ART BY
JOE PRADO
IVAN REIS

BRIAN CUNNINGHAM Editor – Original Series
AMEDEO TURTURRO Assistant Editor – Original Series
JEB WOODARD Group Editor – Collected Editions
SUZANNAH ROWNTREE Editor – Collected Edition
STEVE COOK Design Director – Books
DAMIAN RYLAND Publication Design

BOB HARRAS Senior VP – Editor-in-Chief, DC Comics

DIANE NELSON President
DAN DiDIO Publisher
JIM LEE Publisher
GEOFF JOHNS President & Chief Creative Officer
AMIT DESAI Executive VP – Business & Marketing Strategy, Direct to Consumer & Global Franchise Management
SAM ADES Senior VP – Direct to Consumer
BOBBIE CHASE VP – Talent Development
MARK CHIARELLO Senior VP – Art, Design & Collected Editions
JOHN CUNNINGHAM Senior VP – Sales & Trade Marketing
ANNE DePIES Senior VP – Business Strategy, Finance & Administration
DON FALLETTI VP – Manufacturing Operations
LAWRENCE GANEM VP – Editorial Administration & Talent Relations
ALISON GILL Senior VP – Manufacturing & Operations
HANK KANALZ Senior VP – Editorial Strategy & Administration
JAY KOGAN VP – Legal Affairs
THOMAS LOFTUS VP – Business Affairs
JACK MAHAN VP – Business Affairs
NICK J. NAPOLITANO VP – Manufacturing Administration
EDDIE SCANNELL VP – Consumer Marketing
COURTNEY SIMMONS Senior VP – Publicity & Communications
JIM (SKI) SOKOLOWSKI VP – Comic Book Specialty Sales & Trade Marketing
NANCY SPEARS VP – Mass, Book, Digital Sales & Trade Marketing

THE FLASH VOLUME 9: FULL STOP

DC Comics, 2900 West Alameda Ave., Burbank, CA 91505
Printed by LSC Communications, Salem, VA, USA. 10/14/16. First Printing.
ISBN: 978-1-4012-6925-8

Library of Congress Cataloging-in-Publication Data is available.

PEFC Certified

Printed on paper from
sustainably managed
forests, controlled
sources

PEFC/29-31-337   www.pefc.org

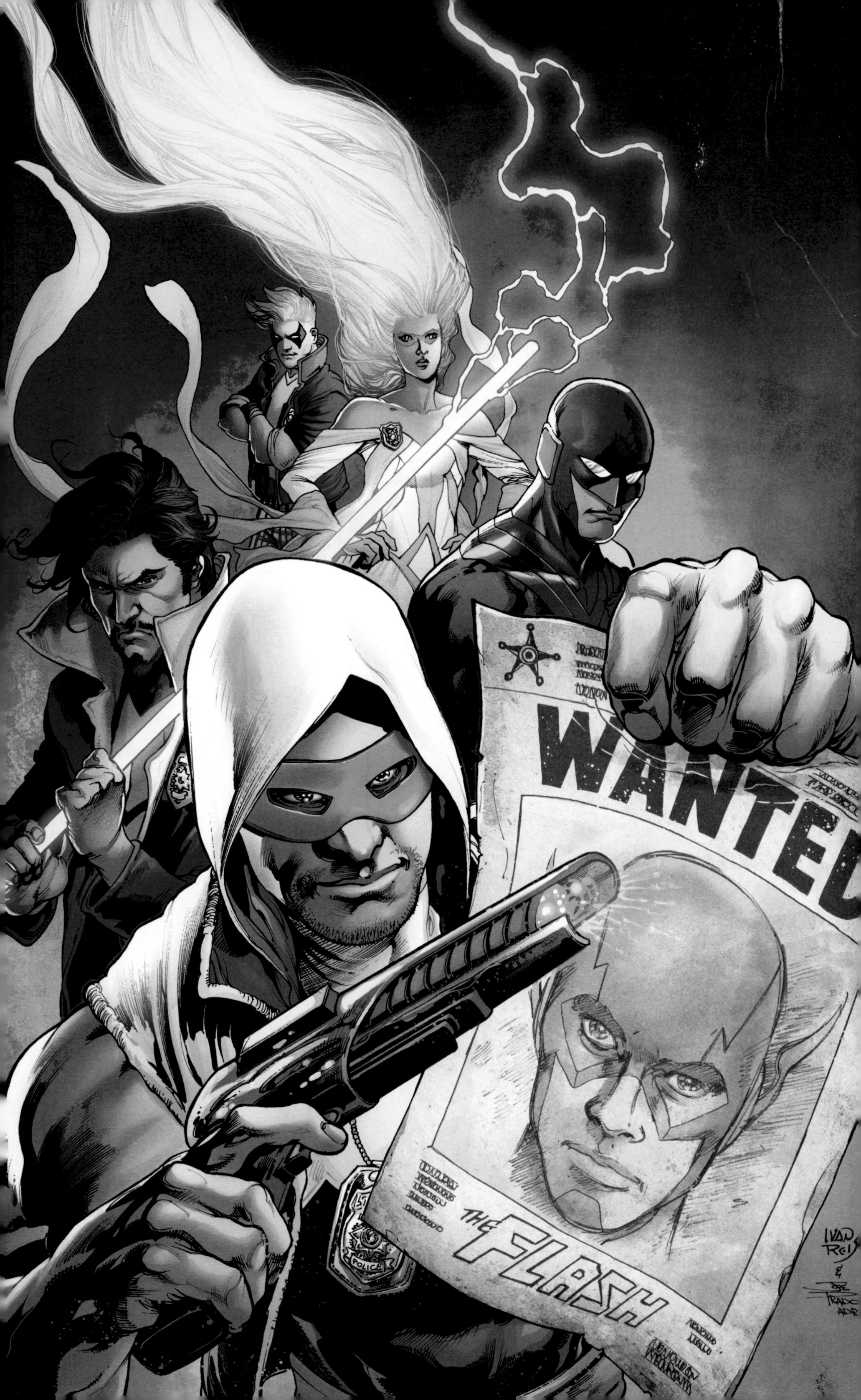
WANTE
THE FLASH
POLICE

PUBLIC ENEMY

ROBERT VENDITTI VAN JENSEN writers JESÚS MERINO artist GUY MAJOR colorist PAT BROSSEAU letterer IVAN REIS JOE PRADO cover

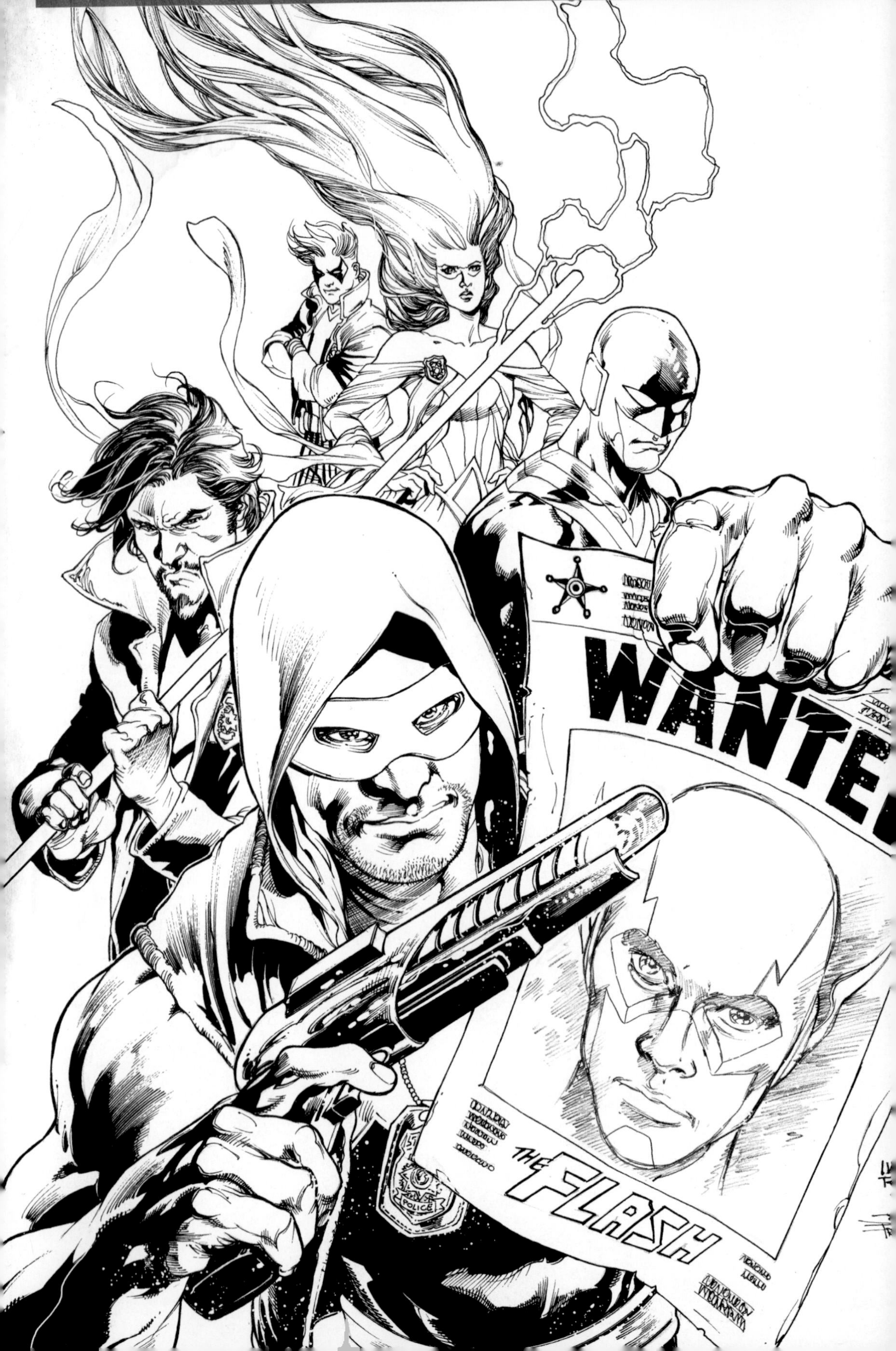

WANTED
THE FLASH
POLICE

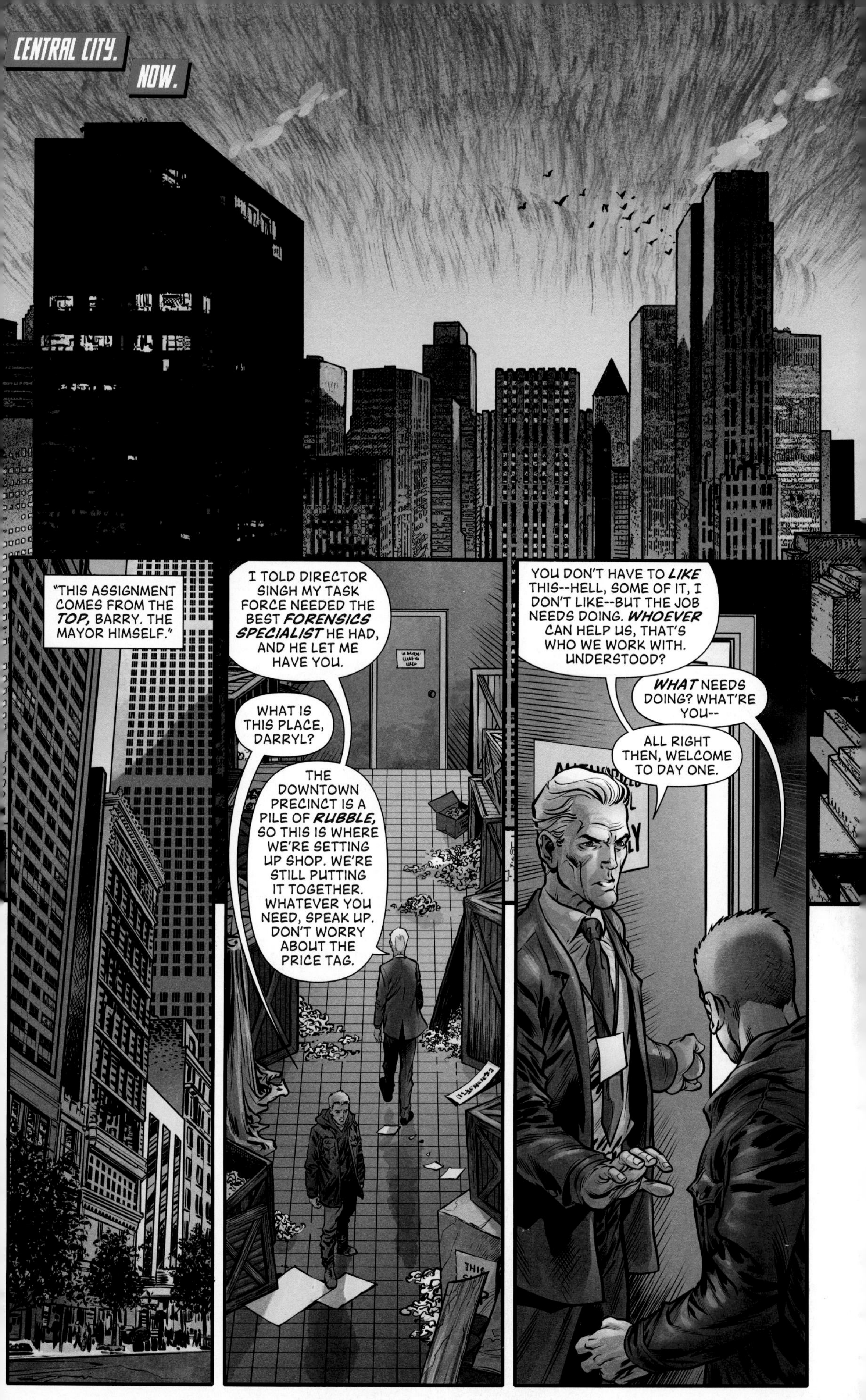
CENTRAL CITY.
NOW.
"THIS ASSIGNMENT COMES FROM THE TOP, BARRY. THE MAYOR HIMSELF."
I TOLD DIRECTOR SINGH MY TASK FORCE NEEDED THE BEST FORENSICS SPECIALIST HE HAD, AND HE LET ME HAVE YOU.
WHAT IS THIS PLACE, DARRYL?
THE DOWNTOWN PRECINCT IS A PILE OF RUBBLE, SO THIS IS WHERE WE'RE SETTING UP SHOP. WE'RE STILL PUTTING IT TOGETHER. WHATEVER YOU NEED, SPEAK UP. DON'T WORRY ABOUT THE PRICE TAG.
YOU DON'T HAVE TO LIKE THIS--HELL, SOME OF IT, I DON'T LIKE--BUT THE JOB NEEDS DOING. WHOEVER CAN HELP US, THAT'S WHO WE WORK WITH. UNDERSTOOD?
WHAT NEEDS DOING? WHAT'RE YOU--
ALL RIGHT THEN, WELCOME TO DAY ONE.

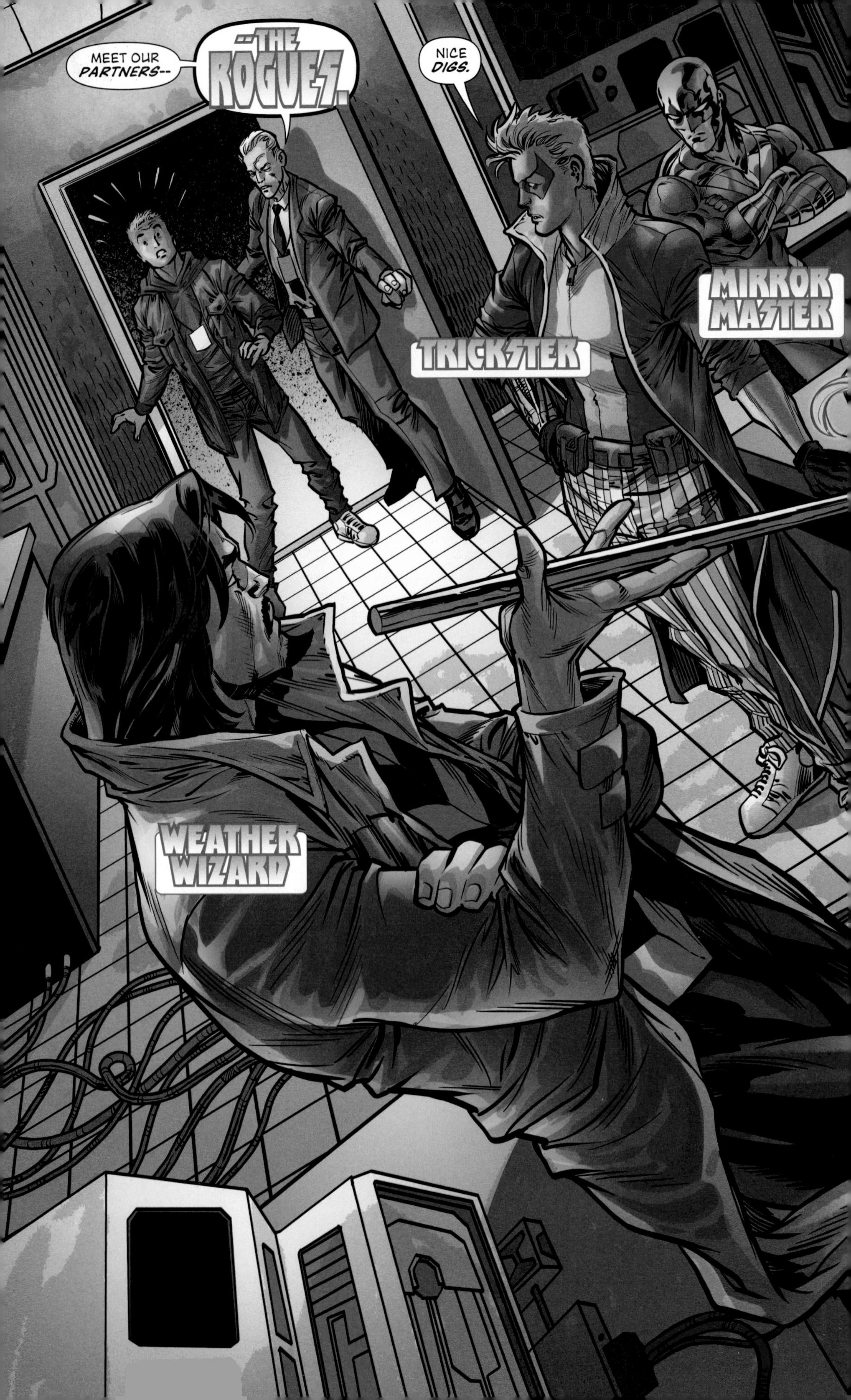
MEET OUR PARTNERS--
--THE ROGUES.
NICE DIGS.
TRICKSTER
MIRROR MASTER
WEATHER WIZARD

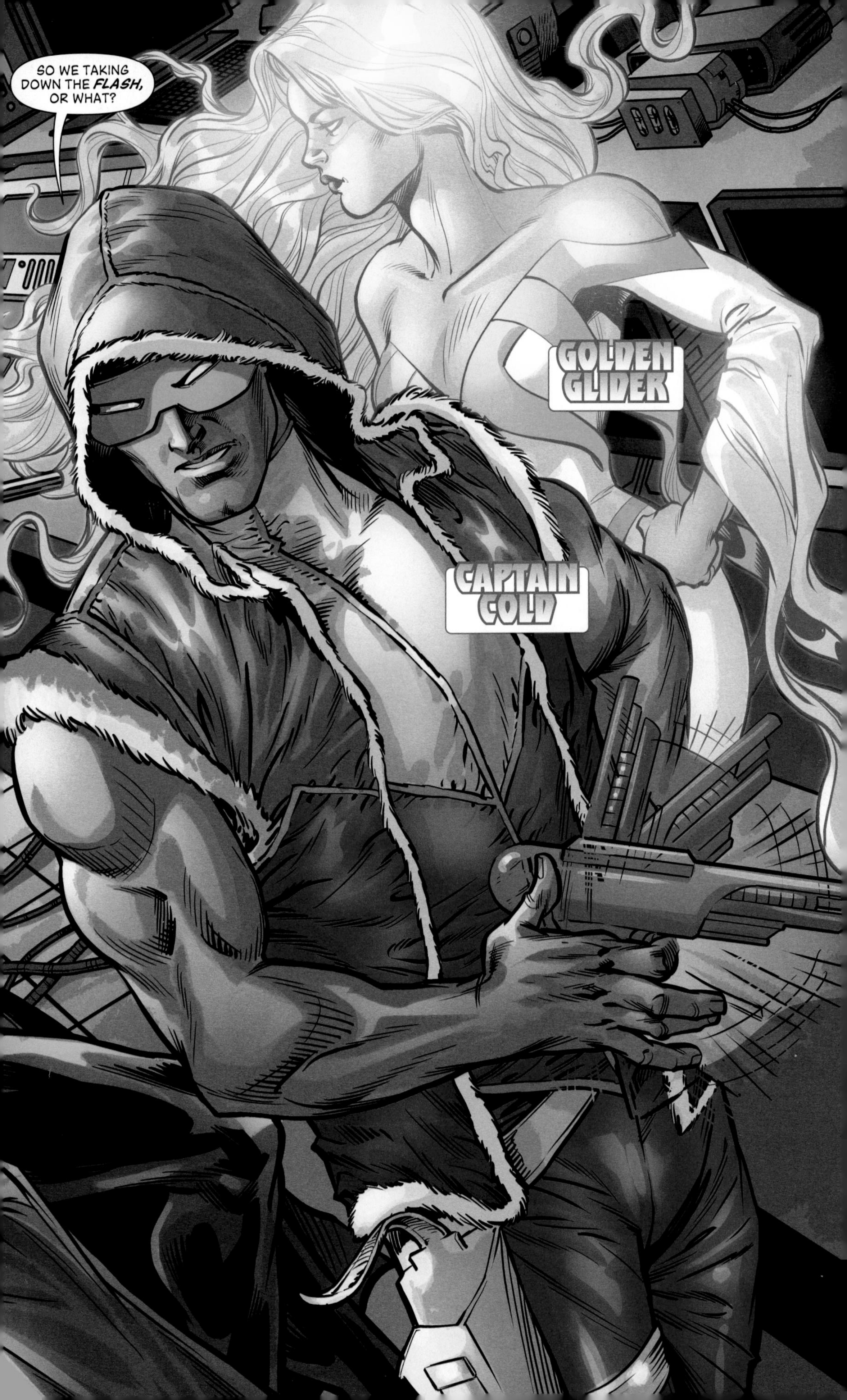
SO WE TAKING DOWN THE FLASH, OR WHAT?
GOLDEN GLIDER
CAPTAIN COLD

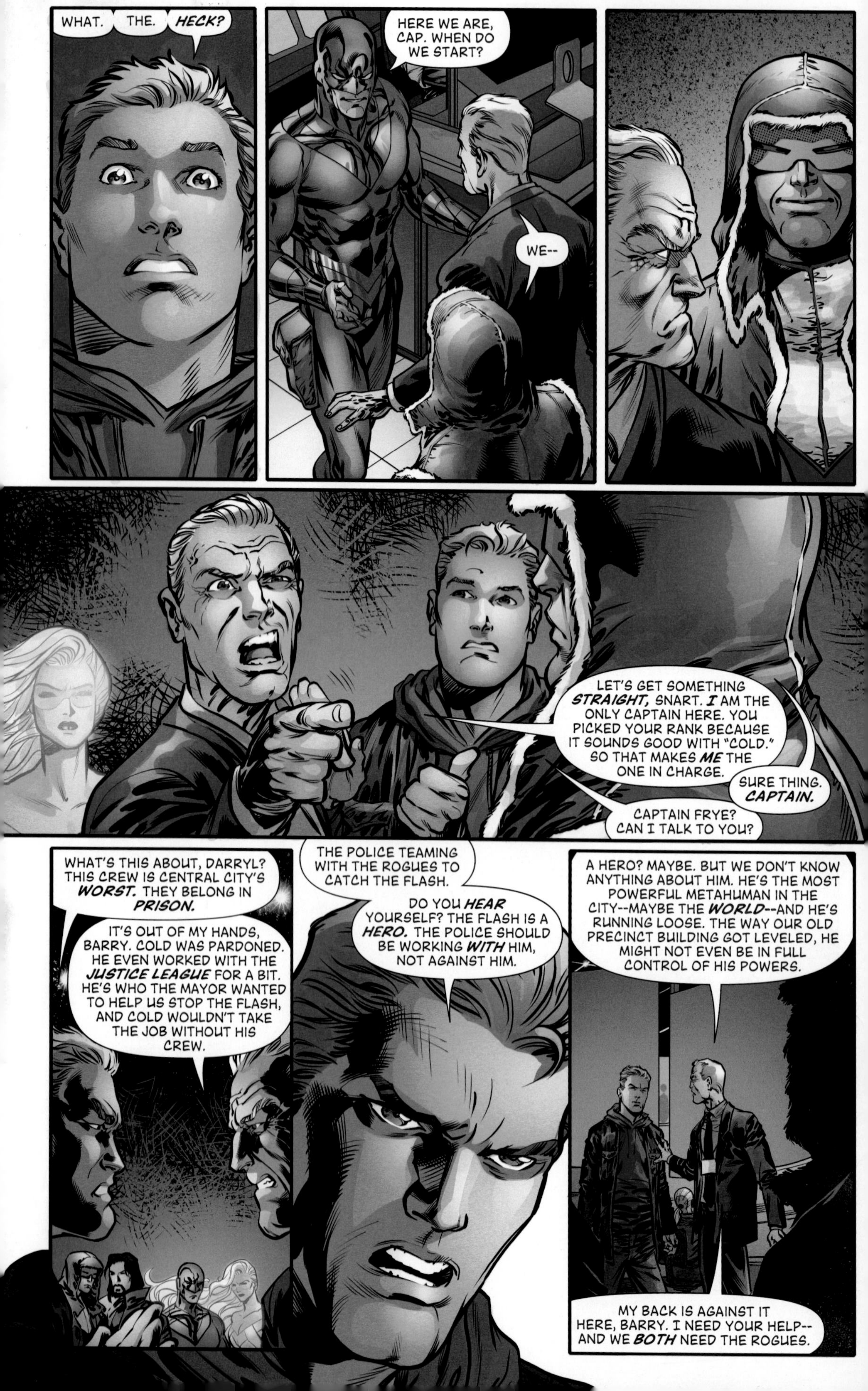
WHAT. THE. *HECK?*
HERE WE ARE, CAP. WHEN DO WE START?
WE--
LET'S GET SOMETHING *STRAIGHT,* SNART. *I* AM THE ONLY CAPTAIN HERE. YOU PICKED YOUR RANK BECAUSE IT SOUNDS GOOD WITH "COLD." SO THAT MAKES *ME* THE ONE IN CHARGE.
SURE THING. *CAPTAIN.*
CAPTAIN FRYE? CAN I TALK TO YOU?
WHAT'S THIS ABOUT, DARRYL? THIS CREW IS CENTRAL CITY'S *WORST.* THEY BELONG IN *PRISON.*
IT'S OUT OF MY HANDS, BARRY. COLD WAS PARDONED. HE EVEN WORKED WITH THE *JUSTICE LEAGUE* FOR A BIT. HE'S WHO THE MAYOR WANTED TO HELP US STOP THE FLASH, AND COLD WOULDN'T TAKE THE JOB WITHOUT HIS CREW.
THE POLICE TEAMING WITH THE ROGUES TO CATCH THE FLASH.
DO YOU *HEAR* YOURSELF? THE FLASH IS A *HERO.* THE POLICE SHOULD BE WORKING *WITH* HIM, NOT AGAINST HIM.
A HERO? MAYBE. BUT WE DON'T KNOW ANYTHING ABOUT HIM. HE'S THE MOST POWERFUL METAHUMAN IN THE CITY--MAYBE THE *WORLD*--AND HE'S RUNNING LOOSE. THE WAY OUR OLD PRECINCT BUILDING GOT LEVELED, HE MIGHT NOT EVEN BE IN FULL CONTROL OF HIS POWERS.
MY BACK IS AGAINST IT HERE, BARRY. I NEED YOUR HELP-- AND WE *BOTH* NEED THE ROGUES.

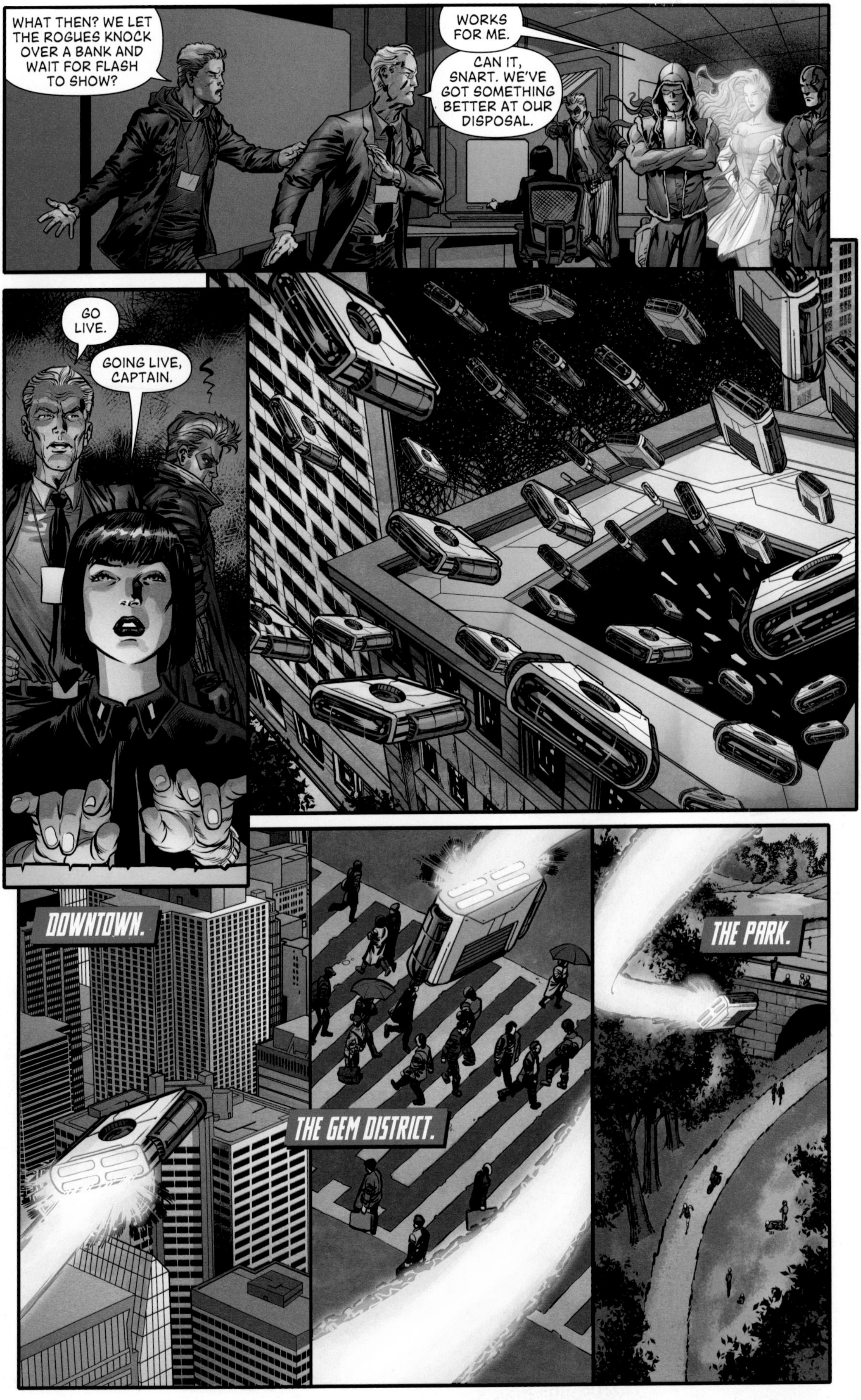
WHAT THEN? WE LET THE ROGUES KNOCK OVER A BANK AND WAIT FOR FLASH TO SHOW?
WORKS FOR ME.
CAN IT, SNART. WE'VE GOT SOMETHING BETTER AT OUR DISPOSAL.
GO LIVE.
GOING LIVE, CAPTAIN.
DOWNTOWN.
THE GEM DISTRICT.
THE PARK.

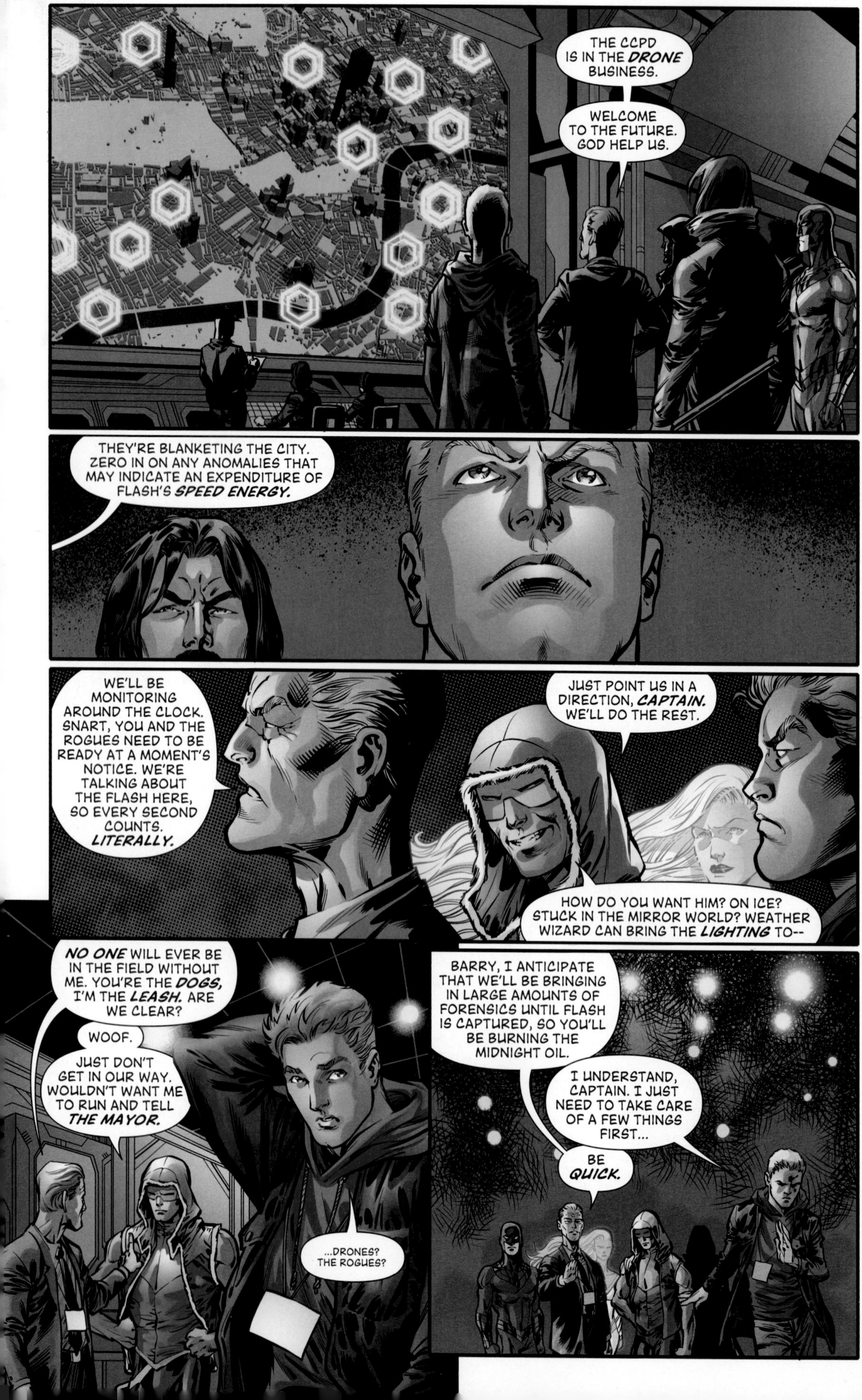
THE CCPD IS IN THE DRONE BUSINESS.
WELCOME TO THE FUTURE. GOD HELP US.
THEY'RE BLANKETING THE CITY. ZERO IN ON ANY ANOMALIES THAT MAY INDICATE AN EXPENDITURE OF FLASH'S SPEED ENERGY.
WE'LL BE MONITORING AROUND THE CLOCK. SNART, YOU AND THE ROGUES NEED TO BE READY AT A MOMENT'S NOTICE. WE'RE TALKING ABOUT THE FLASH HERE, SO EVERY SECOND COUNTS. LITERALLY.
JUST POINT US IN A DIRECTION, CAPTAIN. WE'LL DO THE REST.
HOW DO YOU WANT HIM? ON ICE? STUCK IN THE MIRROR WORLD? WEATHER WIZARD CAN BRING THE LIGHTING TO--
NO ONE WILL EVER BE IN THE FIELD WITHOUT ME. YOU'RE THE DOGS, I'M THE LEASH. ARE WE CLEAR?
WOOF.
JUST DON'T GET IN OUR WAY. WOULDN'T WANT ME TO RUN AND TELL THE MAYOR.
...DRONES? THE ROGUES?
BARRY, I ANTICIPATE THAT WE'LL BE BRINGING IN LARGE AMOUNTS OF FORENSICS UNTIL FLASH IS CAPTURED, SO YOU'LL BE BURNING THE MIDNIGHT OIL.
I UNDERSTAND, CAPTAIN. I JUST NEED TO TAKE CARE OF A FEW THINGS FIRST...
BE QUICK.

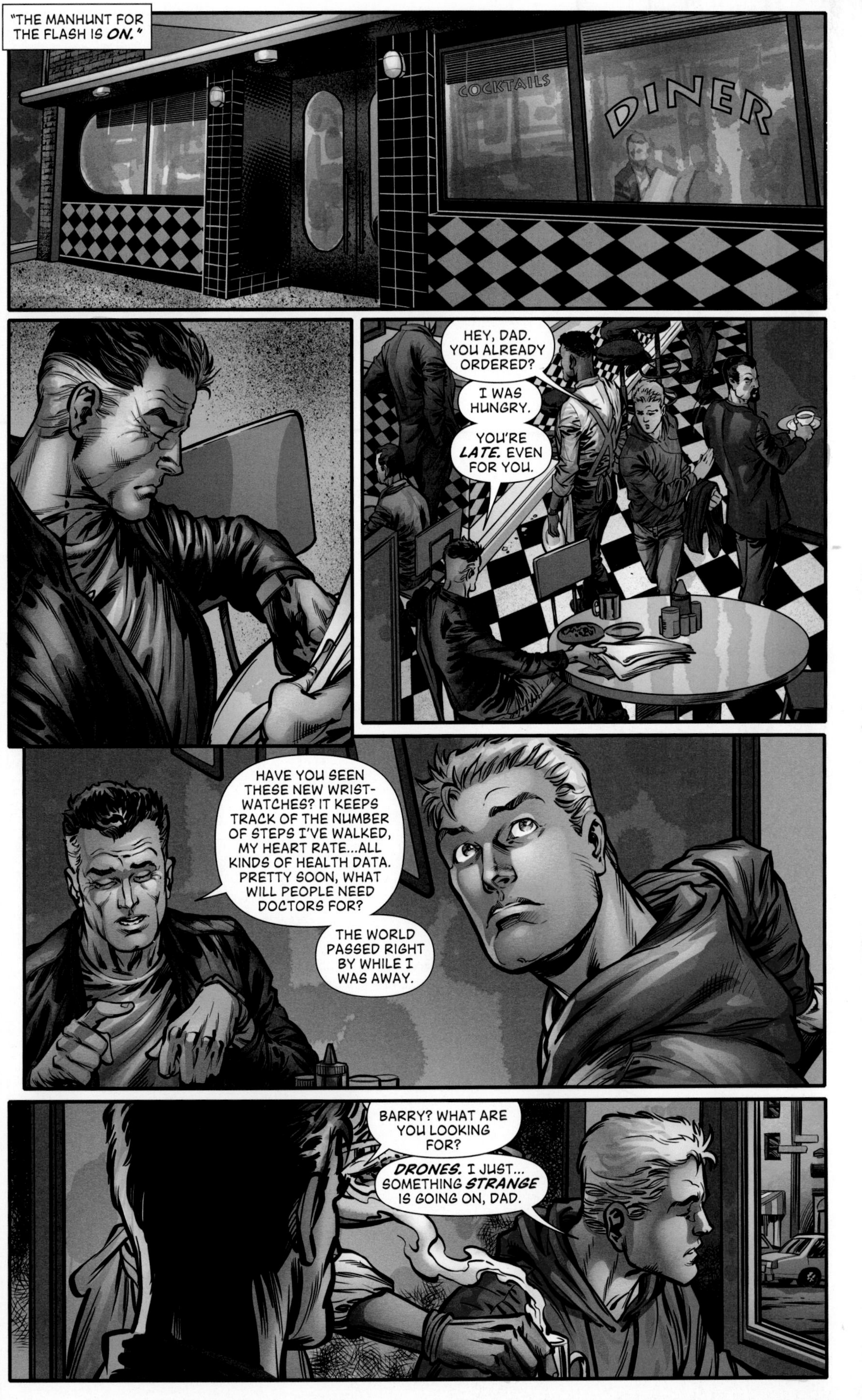
"THE MANHUNT FOR THE FLASH IS ON."
COCKTAILS
DINER
HEY, DAD. YOU ALREADY ORDERED?
I WAS HUNGRY.
YOU'RE LATE. EVEN FOR YOU.
HAVE YOU SEEN THESE NEW WRIST-WATCHES? IT KEEPS TRACK OF THE NUMBER OF STEPS I'VE WALKED, MY HEART RATE...ALL KINDS OF HEALTH DATA. PRETTY SOON, WHAT WILL PEOPLE NEED DOCTORS FOR?
THE WORLD PASSED RIGHT BY WHILE I WAS AWAY.
BARRY? WHAT ARE YOU LOOKING FOR?
DRONES. I JUST... SOMETHING STRANGE IS GOING ON, DAD.

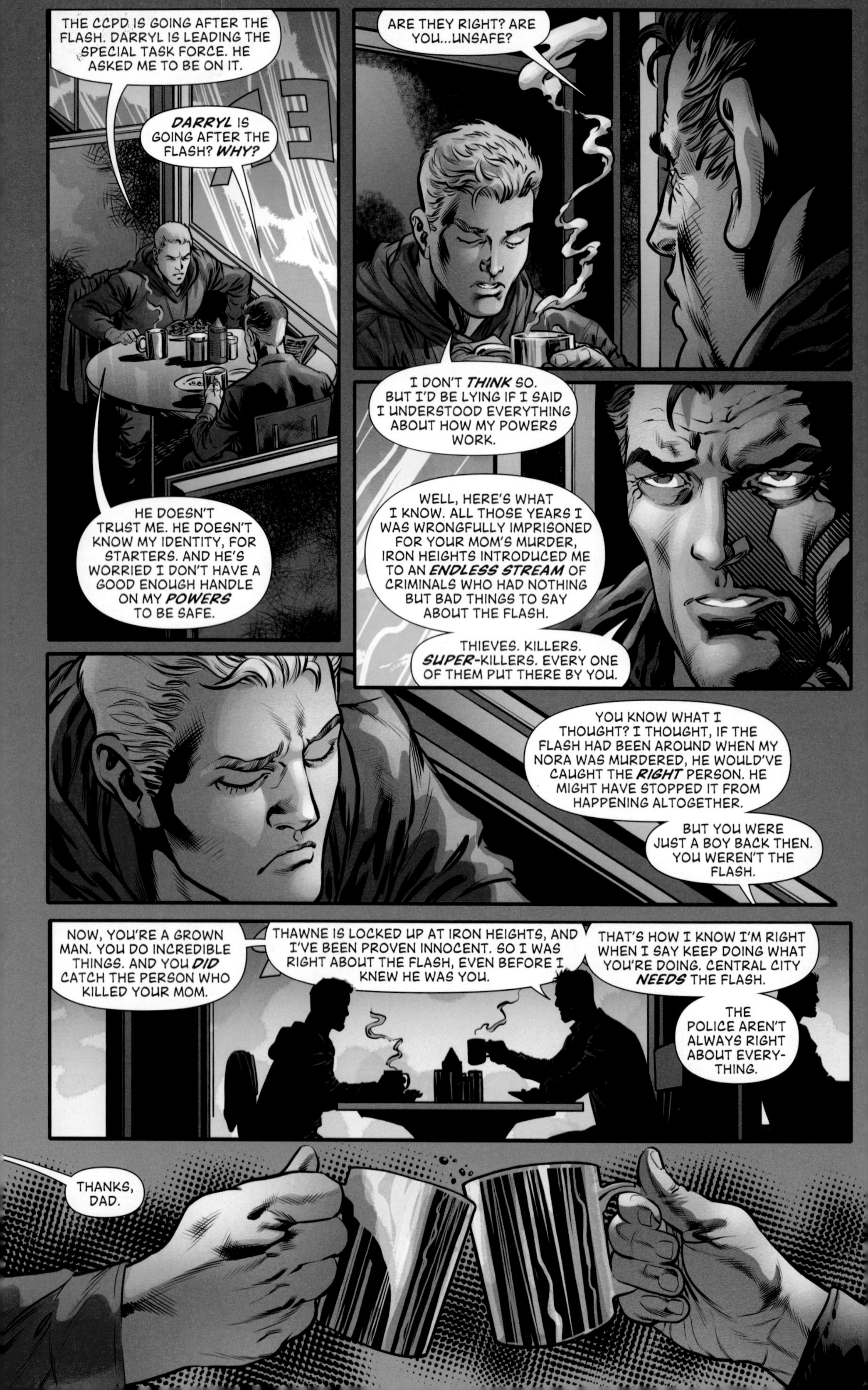
THE CCPD IS GOING AFTER THE FLASH. DARRYL IS LEADING THE SPECIAL TASK FORCE. HE ASKED ME TO BE ON IT.
DARRYL IS GOING AFTER THE FLASH? WHY?
HE DOESN'T TRUST ME. HE DOESN'T KNOW MY IDENTITY, FOR STARTERS. AND HE'S WORRIED I DON'T HAVE A GOOD ENOUGH HANDLE ON MY POWERS TO BE SAFE.
ARE THEY RIGHT? ARE YOU...UNSAFE?
I DON'T THINK SO. BUT I'D BE LYING IF I SAID I UNDERSTOOD EVERYTHING ABOUT HOW MY POWERS WORK.
WELL, HERE'S WHAT I KNOW. ALL THOSE YEARS I WAS WRONGFULLY IMPRISONED FOR YOUR MOM'S MURDER, IRON HEIGHTS INTRODUCED ME TO AN ENDLESS STREAM OF CRIMINALS WHO HAD NOTHING BUT BAD THINGS TO SAY ABOUT THE FLASH.
THIEVES. KILLERS. SUPER-KILLERS. EVERY ONE OF THEM PUT THERE BY YOU.
YOU KNOW WHAT I THOUGHT? I THOUGHT, IF THE FLASH HAD BEEN AROUND WHEN MY NORA WAS MURDERED, HE WOULD'VE CAUGHT THE RIGHT PERSON. HE MIGHT HAVE STOPPED IT FROM HAPPENING ALTOGETHER.
BUT YOU WERE JUST A BOY BACK THEN. YOU WEREN'T THE FLASH.
NOW, YOU'RE A GROWN MAN. YOU DO INCREDIBLE THINGS. AND YOU DID CATCH THE PERSON WHO KILLED YOUR MOM.
THAWNE IS LOCKED UP AT IRON HEIGHTS, AND I'VE BEEN PROVEN INNOCENT. SO I WAS RIGHT ABOUT THE FLASH, EVEN BEFORE I KNEW HE WAS YOU.
THAT'S HOW I KNOW I'M RIGHT WHEN I SAY KEEP DOING WHAT YOU'RE DOING. CENTRAL CITY NEEDS THE FLASH.
THE POLICE AREN'T ALWAYS RIGHT ABOUT EVERY-THING.
THANKS, DAD.

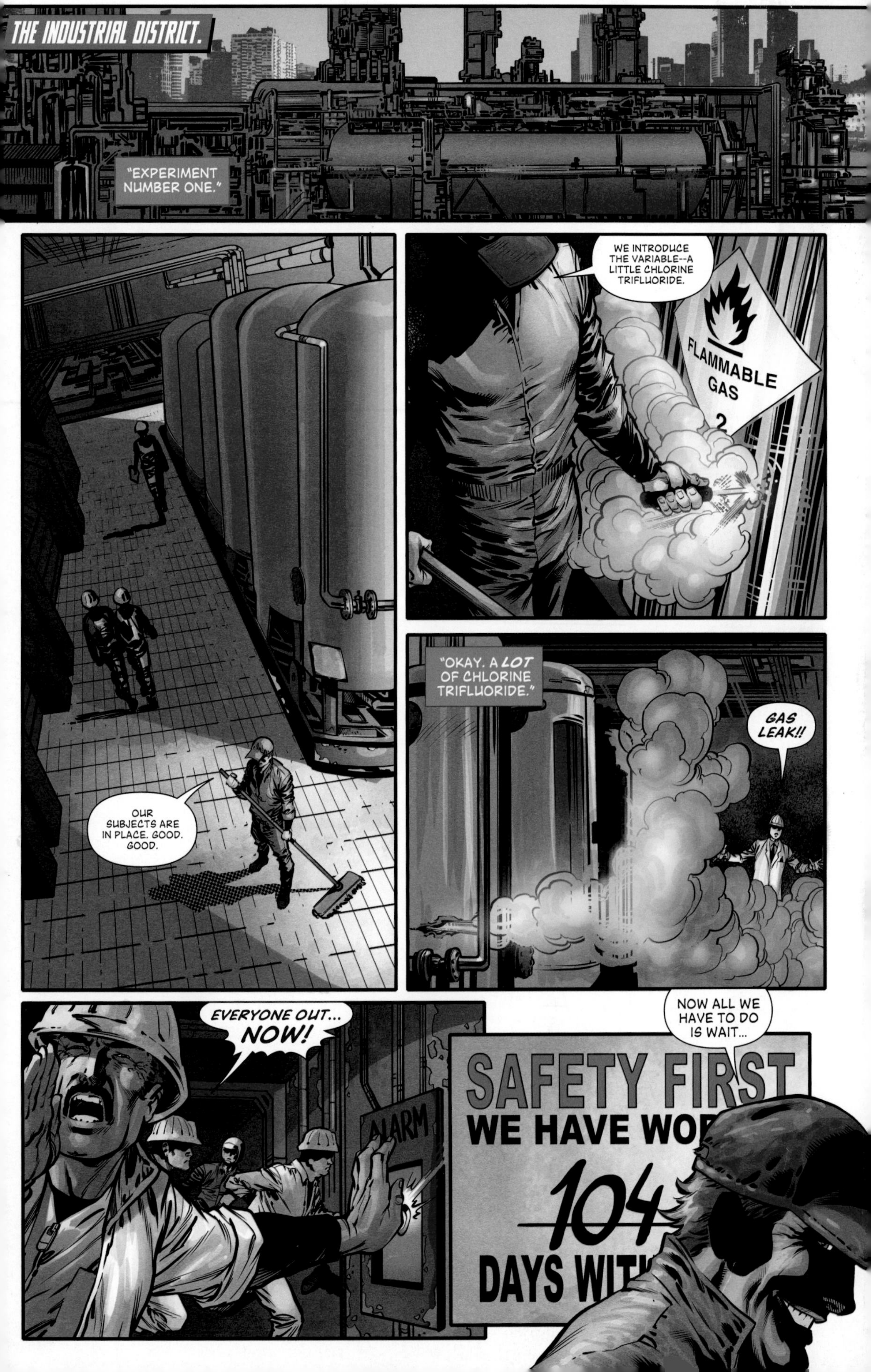
THE INDUSTRIAL DISTRICT.
"EXPERIMENT NUMBER ONE."
OUR SUBJECTS ARE IN PLACE. GOOD. GOOD.
WE INTRODUCE THE VARIABLE--A LITTLE CHLORINE TRIFLUORIDE.
FLAMMABLE GAS
2
"OKAY. A LOT OF CHLORINE TRIFLUORIDE."
GAS LEAK!!
EVERYONE OUT... NOW!
ALARM
NOW ALL WE HAVE TO DO IS WAIT...
SAFETY FIRST
WE HAVE WO
104
DAYS WIT

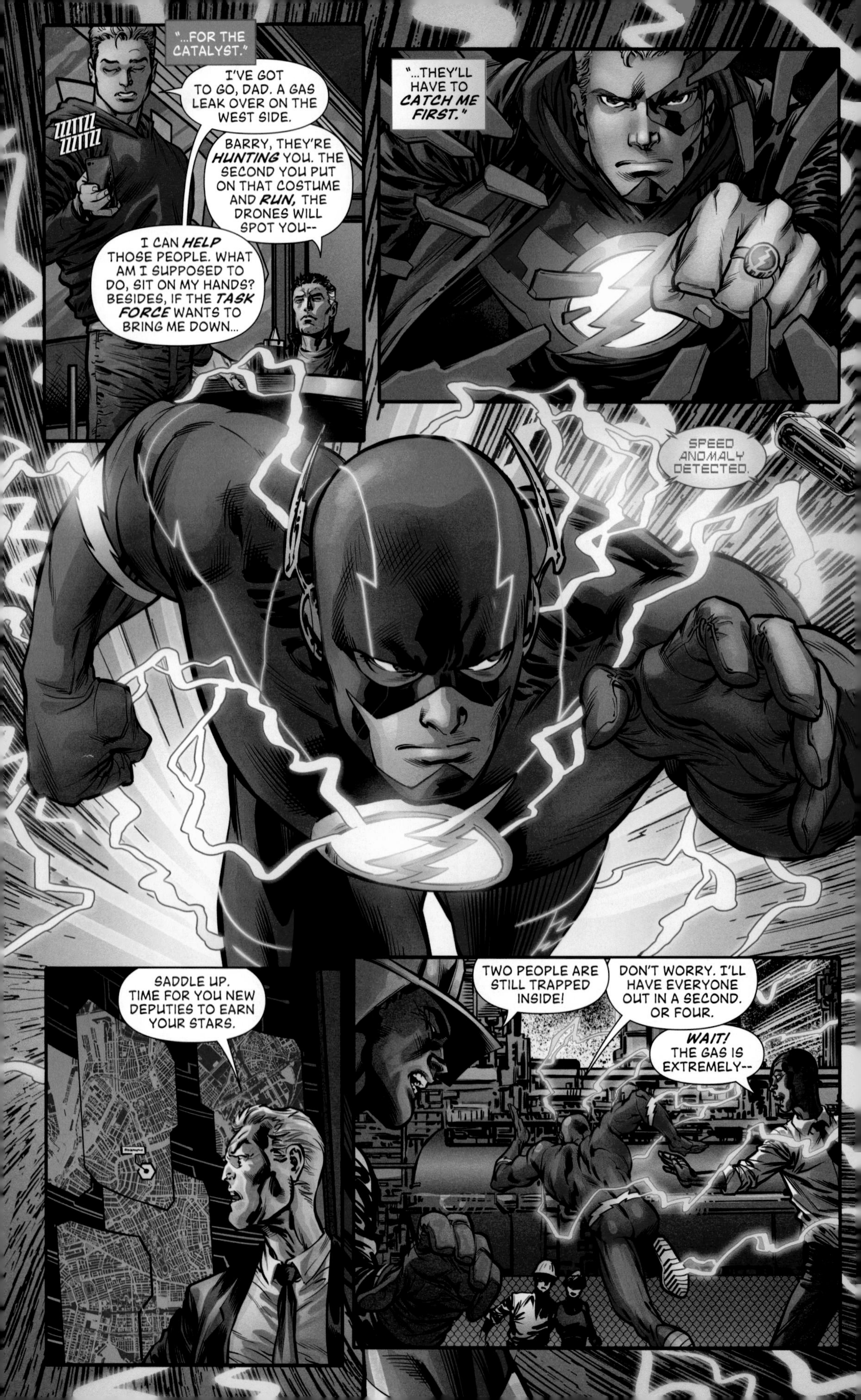
"...FOR THE CATALYST."
ZZZTZZZ ZZZTZZZ
I'VE GOT TO GO, DAD. A GAS LEAK OVER ON THE WEST SIDE.
BARRY, THEY'RE *HUNTING* YOU. THE SECOND YOU PUT ON THAT COSTUME AND *RUN,* THE DRONES WILL SPOT YOU--
I CAN *HELP* THOSE PEOPLE. WHAT AM I SUPPOSED TO DO, SIT ON MY HANDS? BESIDES, IF THE *TASK FORCE* WANTS TO BRING ME DOWN...
"...THEY'LL HAVE TO *CATCH ME FIRST.*"
SPEED ANOMALY DETECTED.
SADDLE UP. TIME FOR YOU NEW DEPUTIES TO EARN YOUR STARS.
TWO PEOPLE ARE STILL TRAPPED INSIDE!
DON'T WORRY. I'LL HAVE EVERYONE OUT IN A SECOND. OR FOUR.
WAIT! THE GAS IS EXTREMELY--

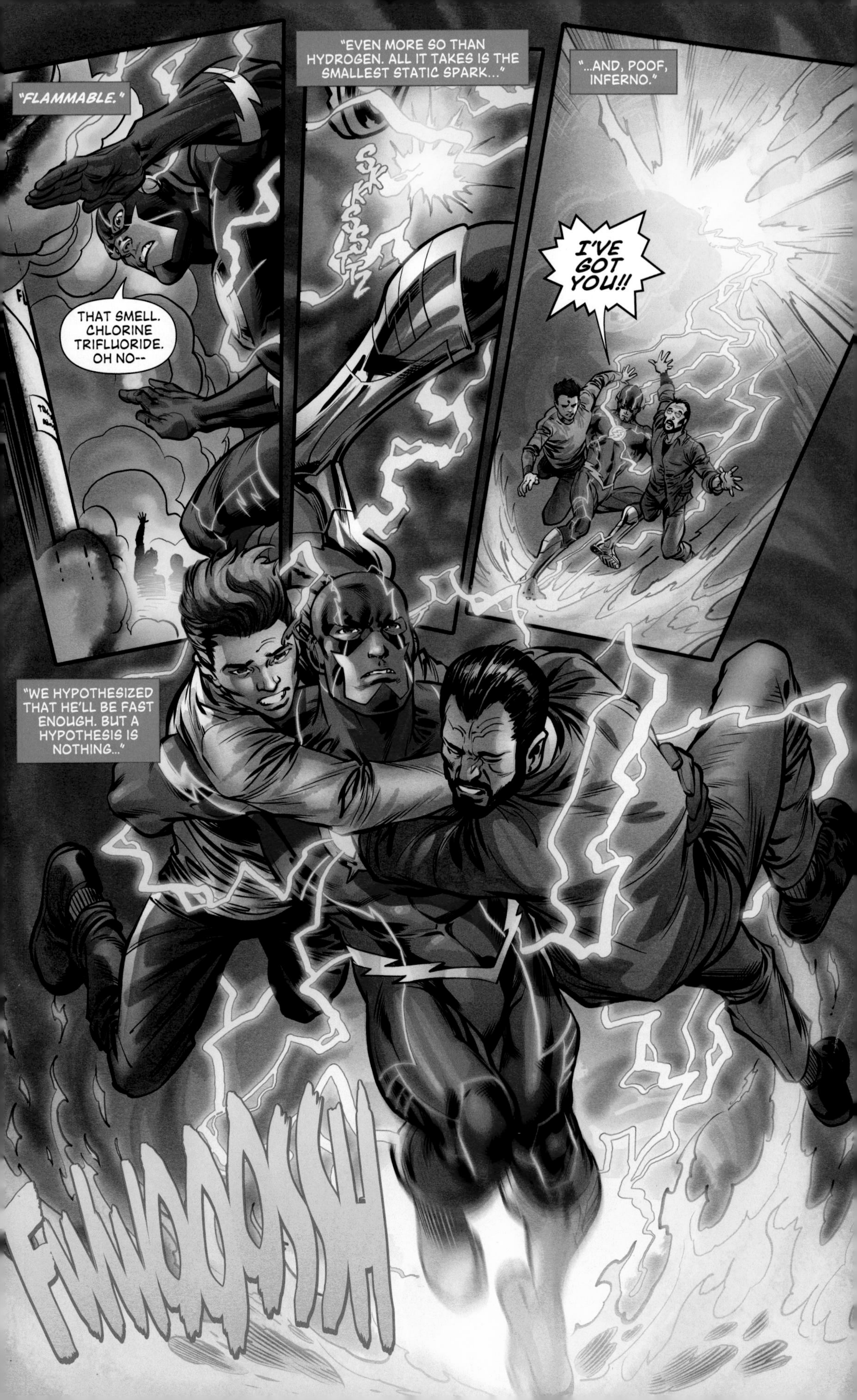
"FLAMMABLE."
THAT SMELL. CHLORINE TRIFLUORIDE. OH NO--
"EVEN MORE SO THAN HYDROGEN. ALL IT TAKES IS THE SMALLEST STATIC SPARK..."
SKKSSTT
"...AND, POOF, INFERNO."
I'VE GOT YOU!!
"WE HYPOTHESIZED THAT HE'LL BE FAST ENOUGH. BUT A HYPOTHESIS IS NOTHING..."
FWWOOSH

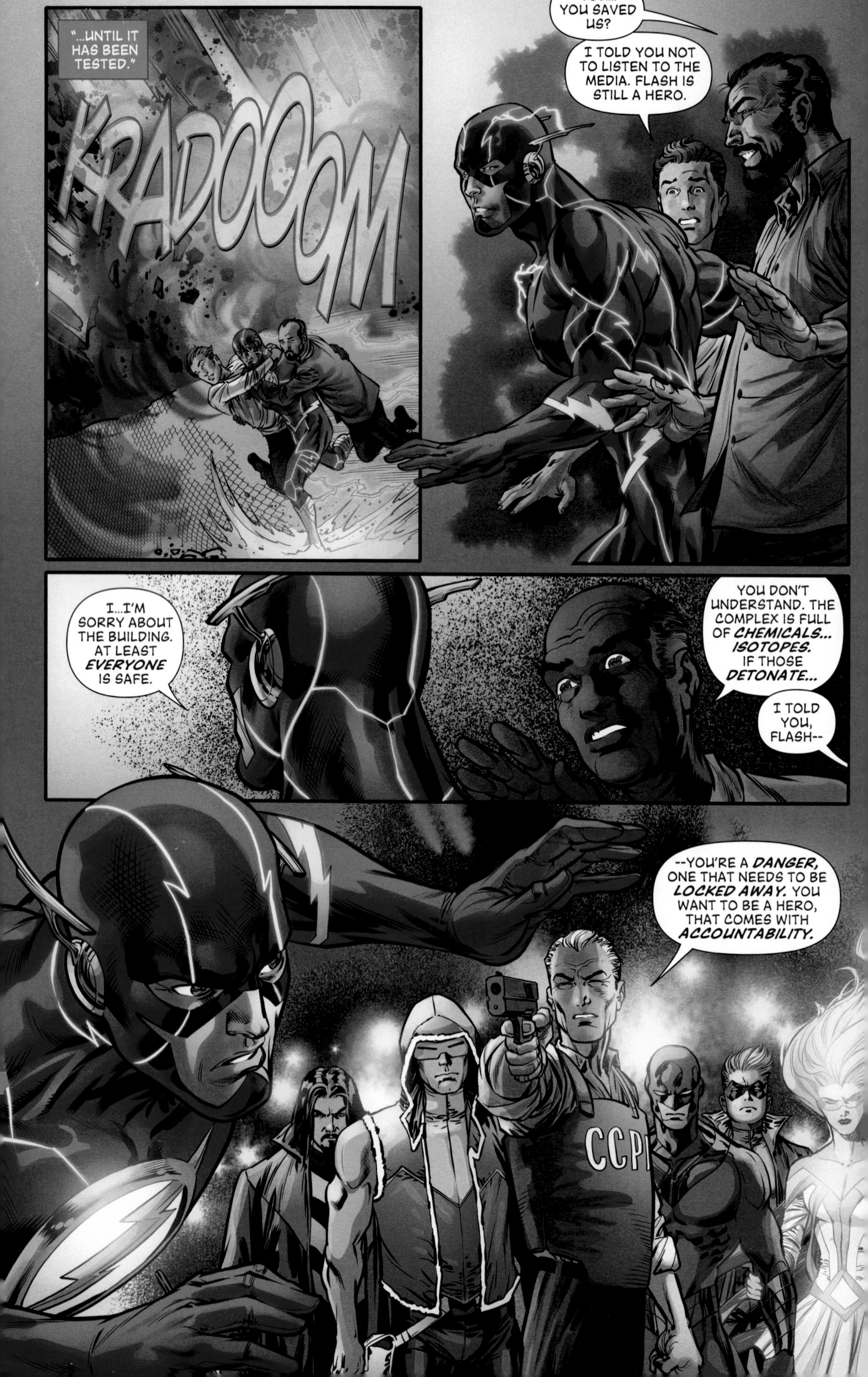
"...UNTIL IT HAS BEEN TESTED."
KRADOOOM
YOU... YOU SAVED US?
I TOLD YOU NOT TO LISTEN TO THE MEDIA. FLASH IS STILL A HERO.
I...I'M SORRY ABOUT THE BUILDING. AT LEAST EVERYONE IS SAFE.
YOU DON'T UNDERSTAND. THE COMPLEX IS FULL OF CHEMICALS... ISOTOPES. IF THOSE DETONATE...
I TOLD YOU, FLASH--
--YOU'RE A DANGER, ONE THAT NEEDS TO BE LOCKED AWAY. YOU WANT TO BE A HERO, THAT COMES WITH ACCOUNTABILITY.
CCPD

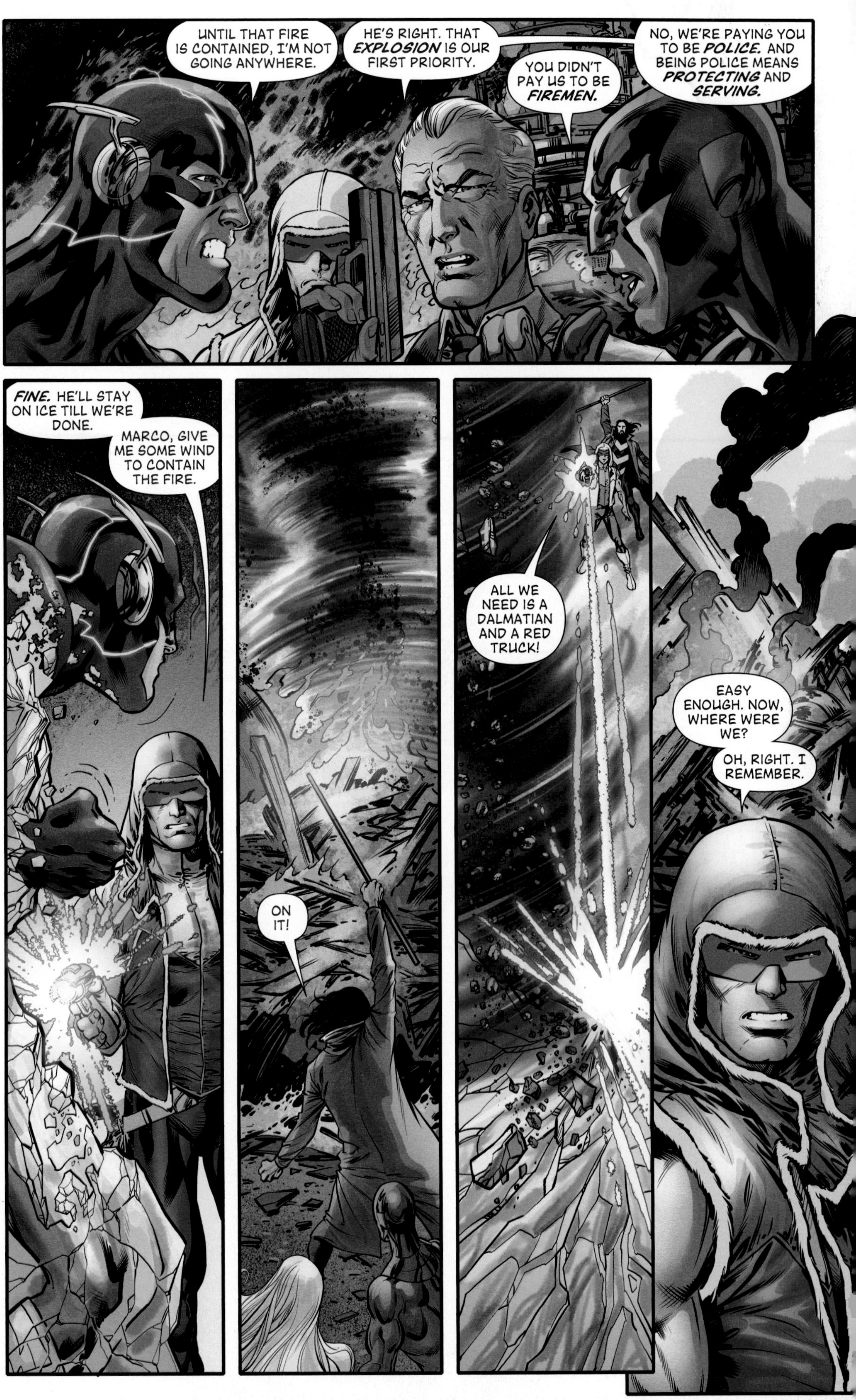
UNTIL THAT FIRE IS CONTAINED, I'M NOT GOING ANYWHERE.
HE'S RIGHT. THAT EXPLOSION IS OUR FIRST PRIORITY.
YOU DIDN'T PAY US TO BE FIREMEN.
NO, WE'RE PAYING YOU TO BE POLICE. AND BEING POLICE MEANS PROTECTING AND SERVING.
FINE. HE'LL STAY ON ICE TILL WE'RE DONE.
MARCO, GIVE ME SOME WIND TO CONTAIN THE FIRE.
ON IT!
ALL WE NEED IS A DALMATIAN AND A RED TRUCK!
EASY ENOUGH. NOW, WHERE WERE WE?
OH, RIGHT. I REMEMBER.

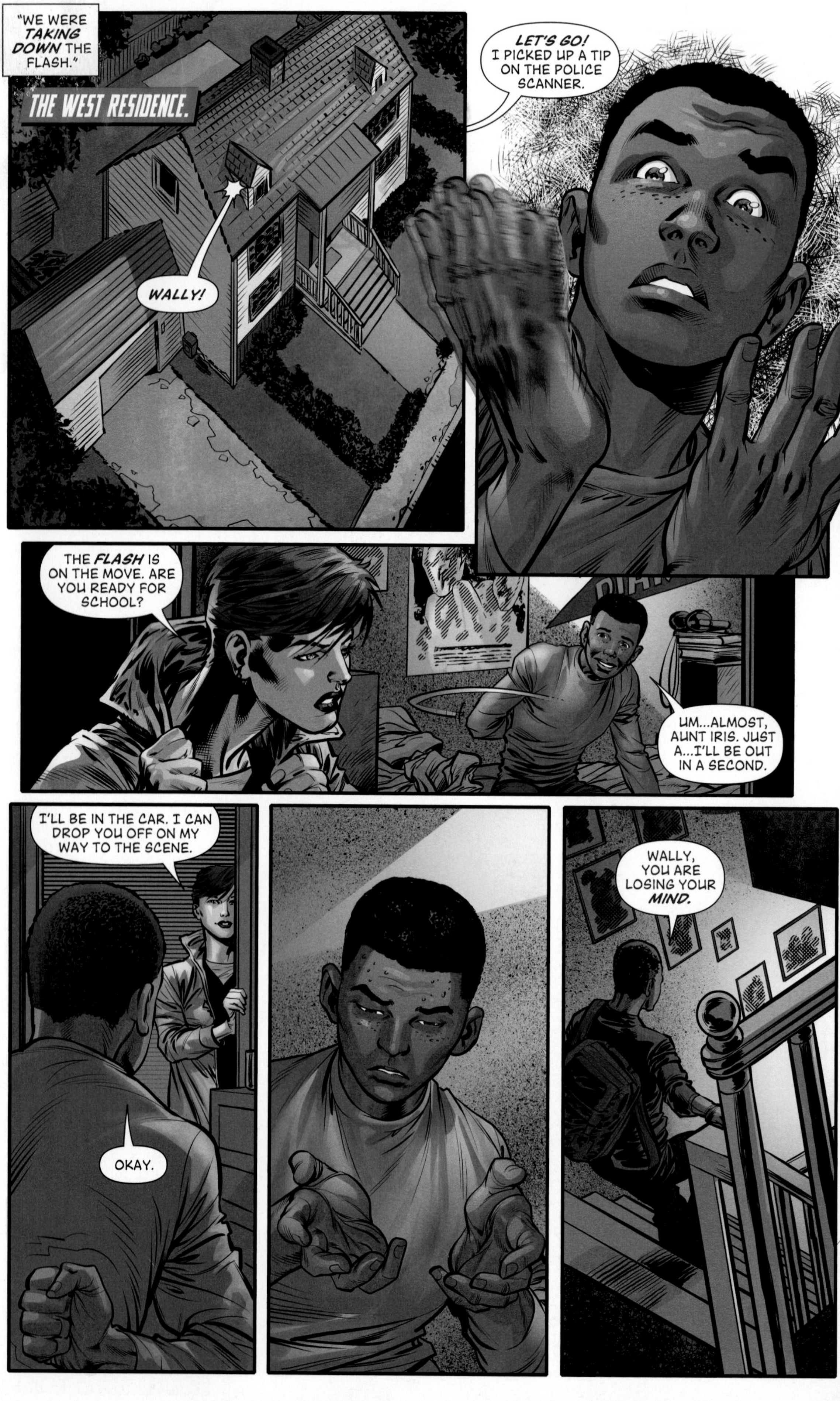
"WE WERE TAKING DOWN THE FLASH."
THE WEST RESIDENCE.
WALLY!
LET'S GO! I PICKED UP A TIP ON THE POLICE SCANNER.
THE FLASH IS ON THE MOVE. ARE YOU READY FOR SCHOOL?
UM...ALMOST, AUNT IRIS. JUST A...I'LL BE OUT IN A SECOND.
I'LL BE IN THE CAR. I CAN DROP YOU OFF ON MY WAY TO THE SCENE.
OKAY.
WALLY, YOU ARE LOSING YOUR MIND.

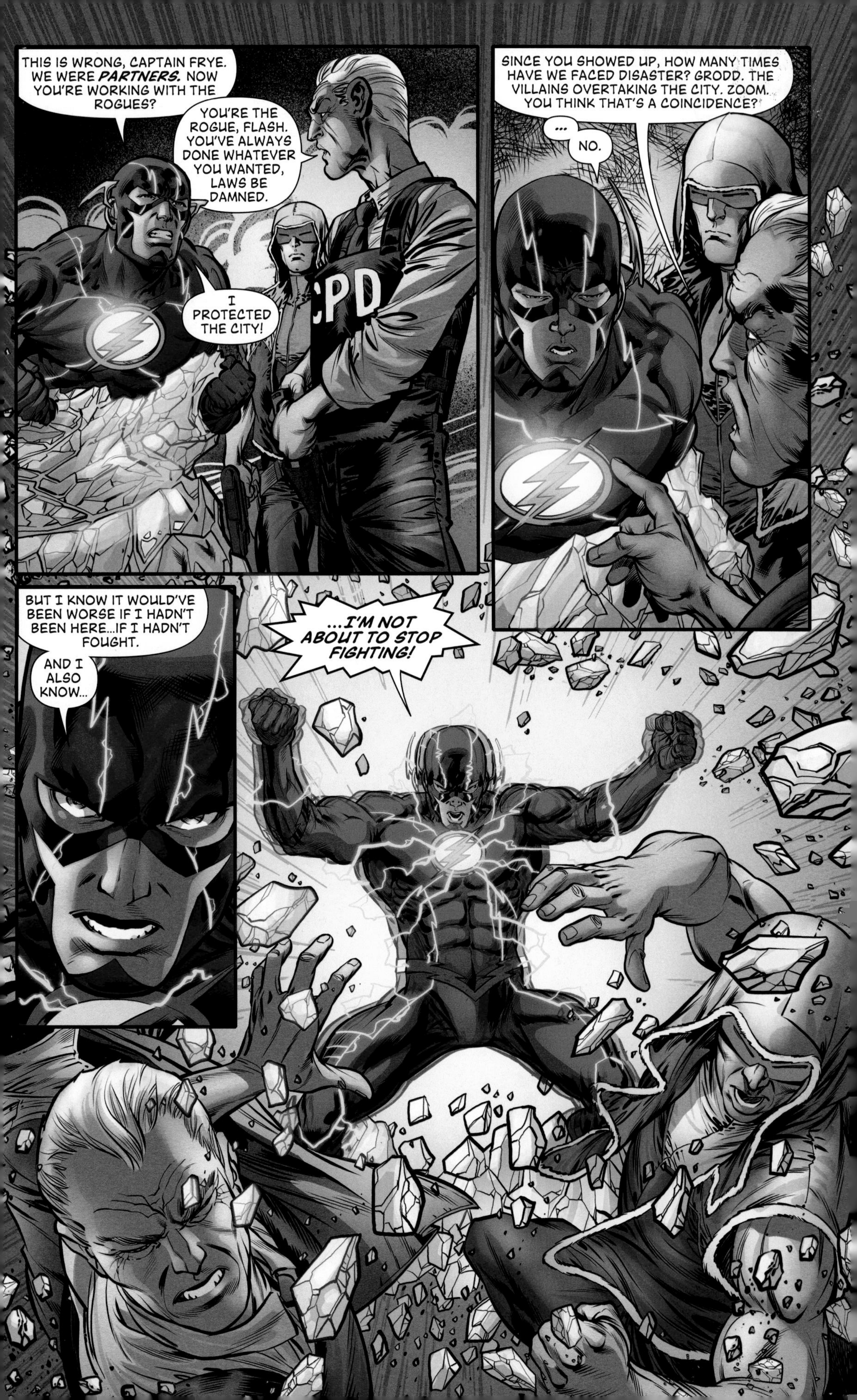
THIS IS WRONG, CAPTAIN FRYE. WE WERE *PARTNERS.* NOW YOU'RE WORKING WITH THE ROGUES?
YOU'RE THE ROGUE, FLASH. YOU'VE ALWAYS DONE WHATEVER YOU WANTED, LAWS BE DAMNED.
I PROTECTED THE CITY!
CPD
SINCE YOU SHOWED UP, HOW MANY TIMES HAVE WE FACED DISASTER? GRODD. THE VILLAINS OVERTAKING THE CITY. ZOOM. YOU THINK THAT'S A COINCIDENCE?
...
NO.
BUT I KNOW IT WOULD'VE BEEN WORSE IF I HADN'T BEEN HERE...IF I HADN'T FOUGHT.
AND I ALSO KNOW...
...I'M NOT ABOUT TO STOP FIGHTING!

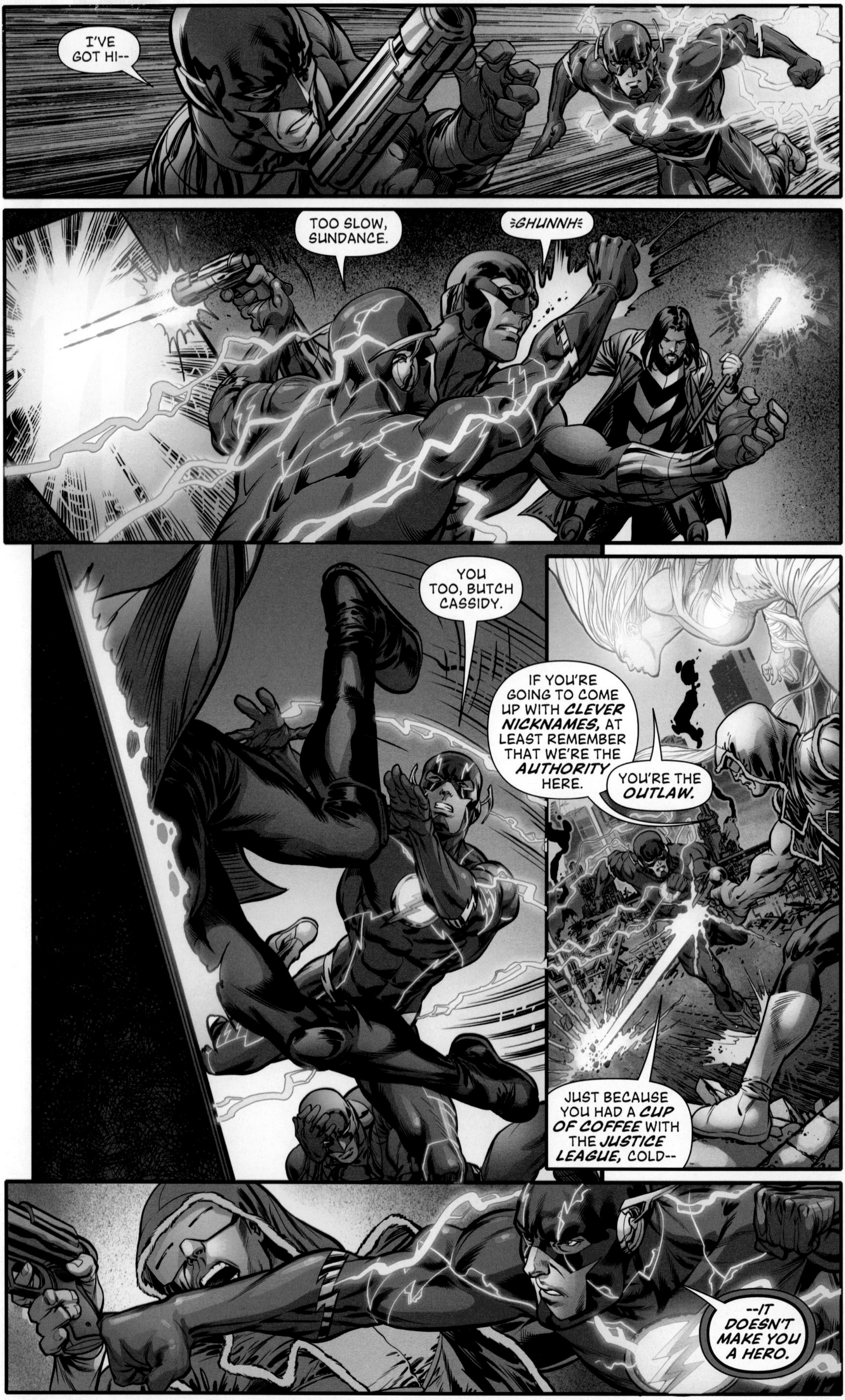
I'VE GOT HI--
TOO SLOW, SUNDANCE.
GHUNNH
YOU TOO, BUTCH CASSIDY.
IF YOU'RE GOING TO COME UP WITH *CLEVER NICKNAMES,* AT LEAST REMEMBER THAT WE'RE THE *AUTHORITY* HERE.
YOU'RE THE *OUTLAW.*
JUST BECAUSE YOU HAD A *CUP OF COFFEE* WITH THE *JUSTICE LEAGUE,* COLD--
--IT DOESN'T MAKE YOU A HERO.

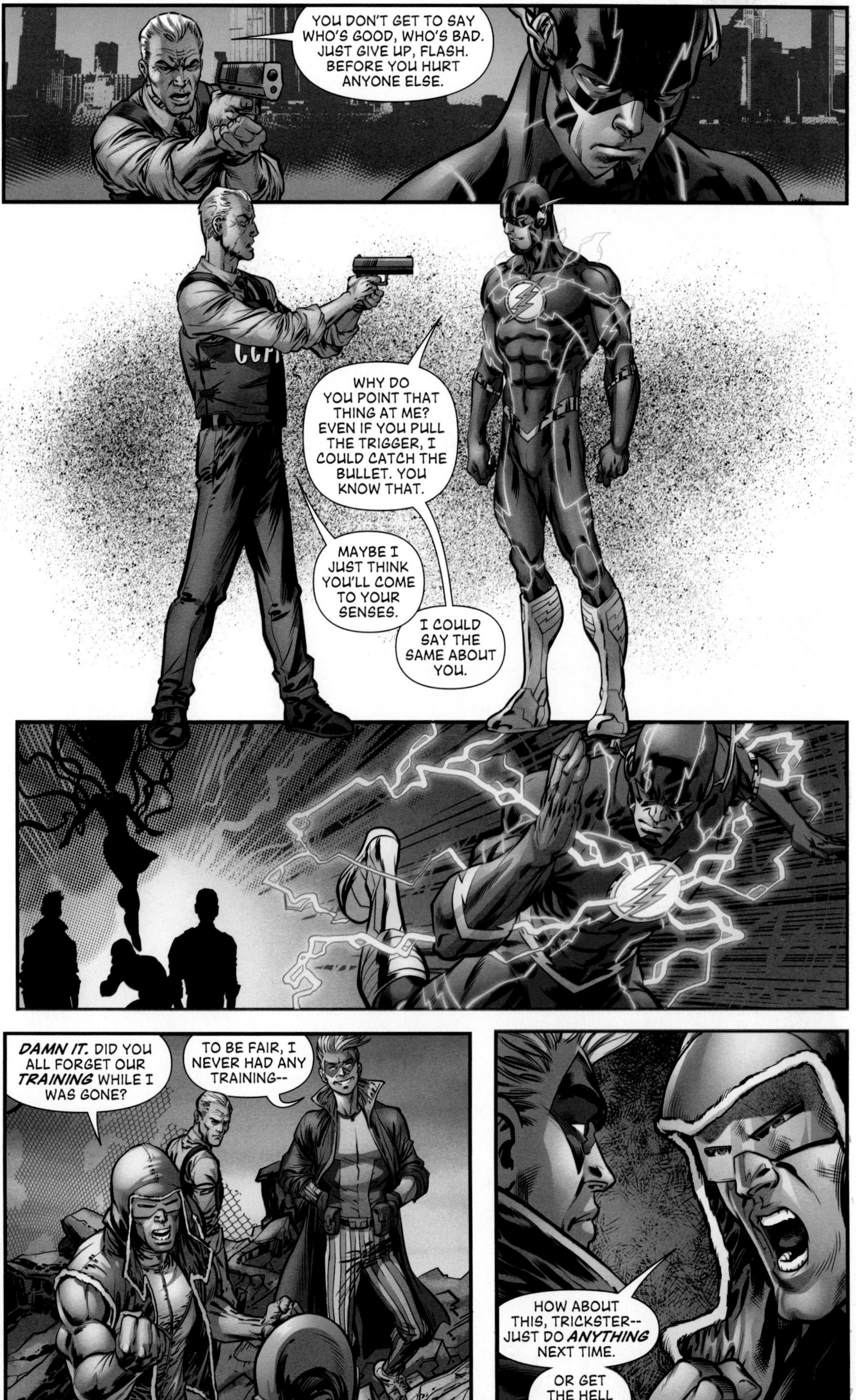
YOU DON'T GET TO SAY WHO'S GOOD, WHO'S BAD. JUST GIVE UP, FLASH. BEFORE YOU HURT ANYONE ELSE.
CCPD
WHY DO YOU POINT THAT THING AT ME? EVEN IF YOU PULL THE TRIGGER, I COULD CATCH THE BULLET. YOU KNOW THAT.
MAYBE I JUST THINK YOU'LL COME TO YOUR SENSES.
I COULD SAY THE SAME ABOUT YOU.
DAMN IT. DID YOU ALL FORGET OUR TRAINING WHILE I WAS GONE?
TO BE FAIR, I NEVER HAD ANY TRAINING--
HOW ABOUT THIS, TRICKSTER-- JUST DO ANYTHING NEXT TIME.
OR GET THE HELL OUT OF THE WAY.

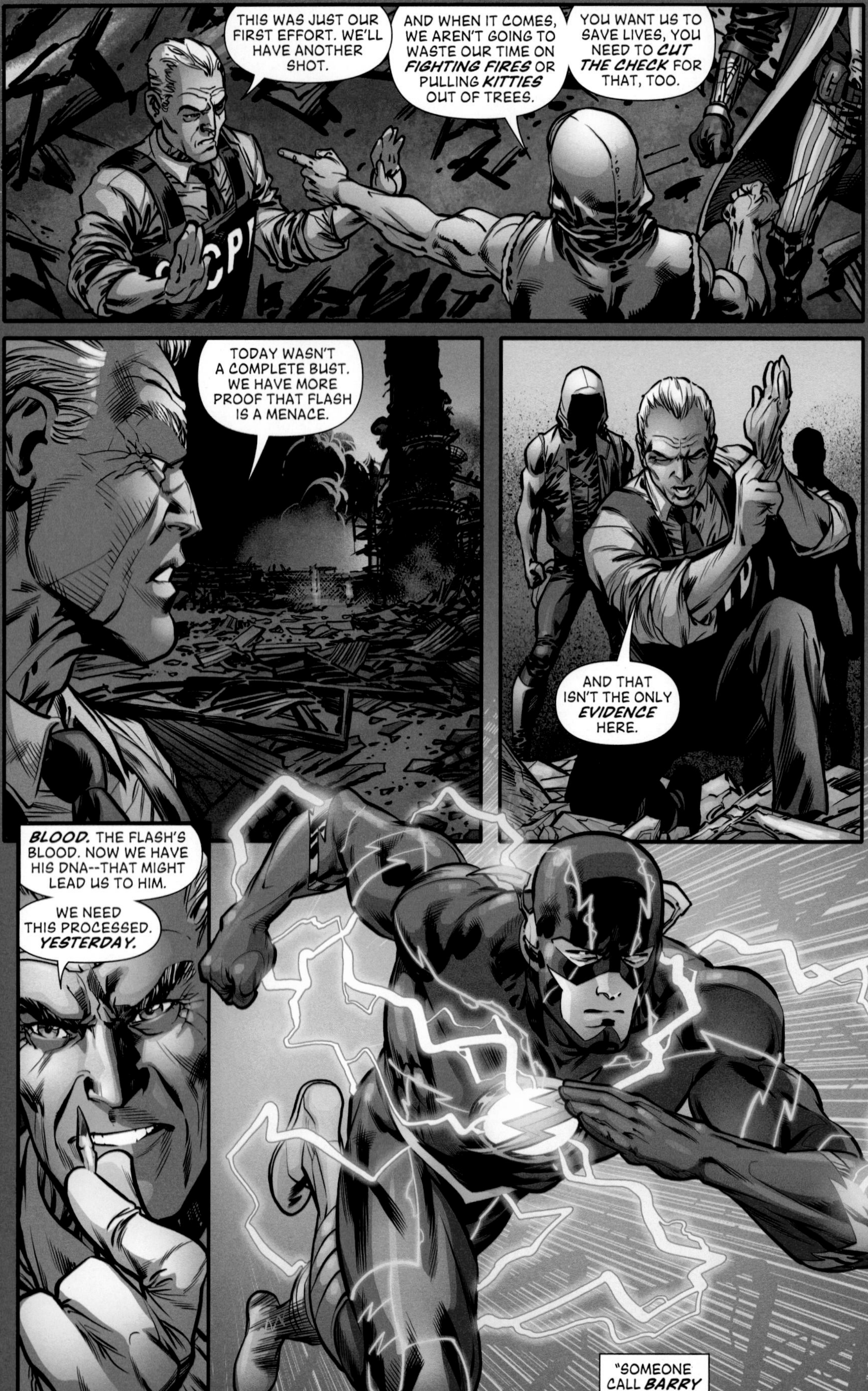
THIS WAS JUST OUR FIRST EFFORT. WE'LL HAVE ANOTHER SHOT.
AND WHEN IT COMES, WE AREN'T GOING TO WASTE OUR TIME ON *FIGHTING FIRES* OR PULLING *KITTIES* OUT OF TREES.
YOU WANT US TO SAVE LIVES, YOU NEED TO *CUT THE CHECK* FOR THAT, TOO.
TODAY WASN'T A COMPLETE BUST. WE HAVE MORE PROOF THAT FLASH IS A MENACE.
AND THAT ISN'T THE ONLY *EVIDENCE* HERE.
BLOOD. THE FLASH'S BLOOD. NOW WE HAVE HIS DNA--THAT MIGHT LEAD US TO HIM.
WE NEED THIS PROCESSED. *YESTERDAY.*
"SOMEONE CALL *BARRY ALLEN.*"

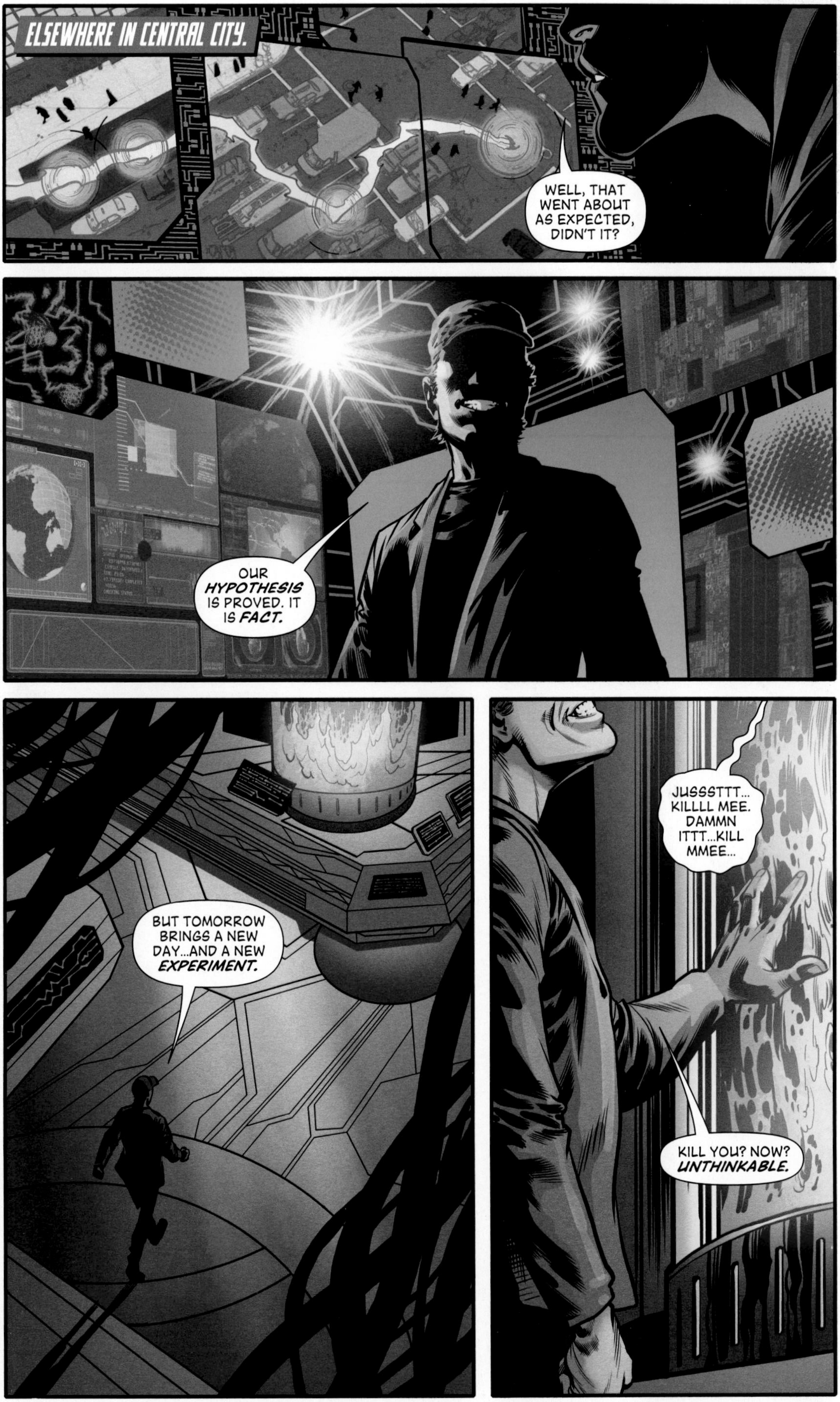
ELSEWHERE IN CENTRAL CITY.
WELL, THAT WENT ABOUT AS EXPECTED, DIDN'T IT?
OUR *HYPOTHESIS* IS PROVED. IT IS *FACT.*
BUT TOMORROW BRINGS A NEW DAY...AND A NEW *EXPERIMENT.*
JUSSSTTT... KILLLL MEE. DAMMN ITTT...KILL MMEE...
KILL YOU? NOW? *UNTHINKABLE.*

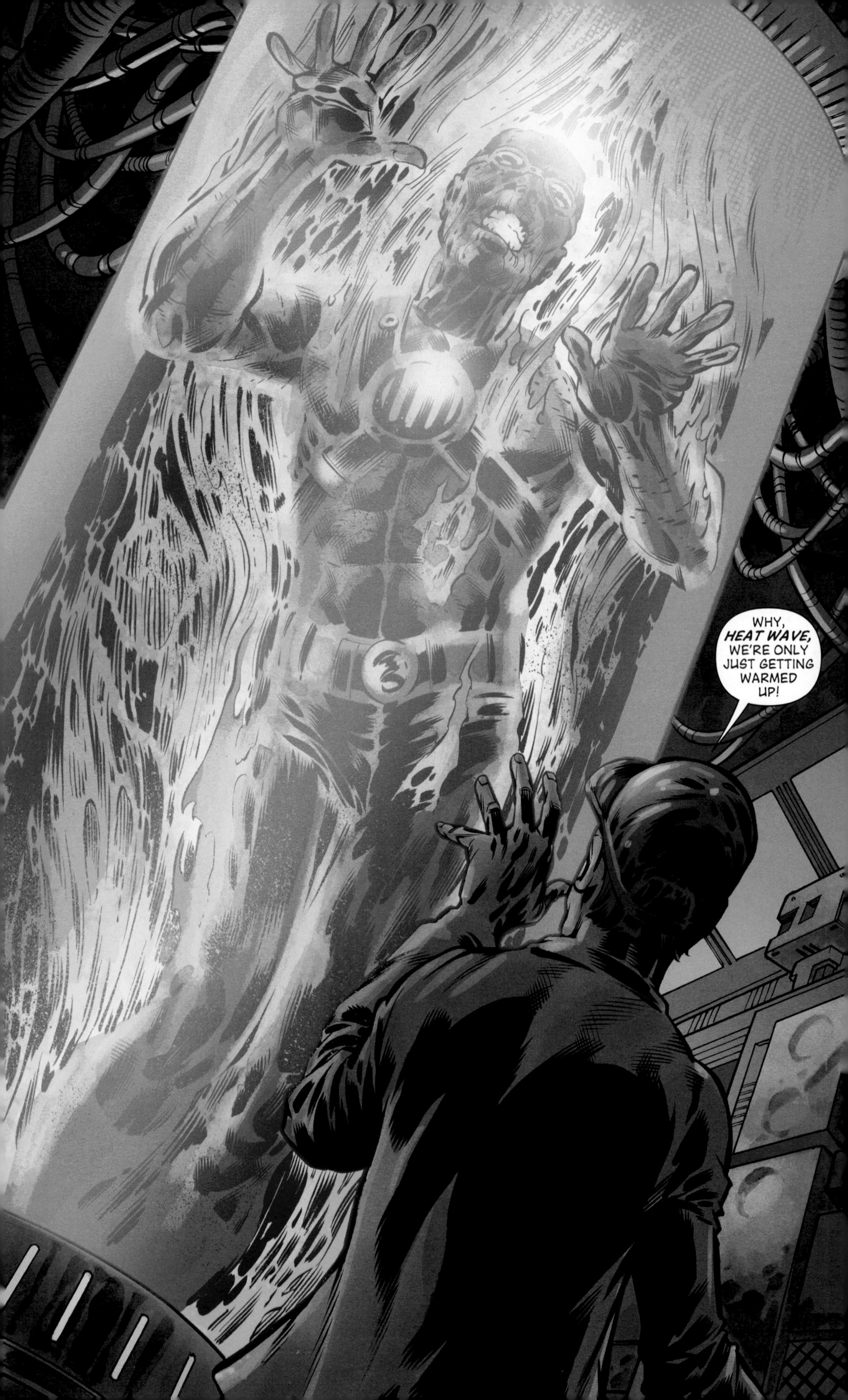
WHY, HEAT WAVE, WE'RE ONLY JUST GETTING WARMED UP!

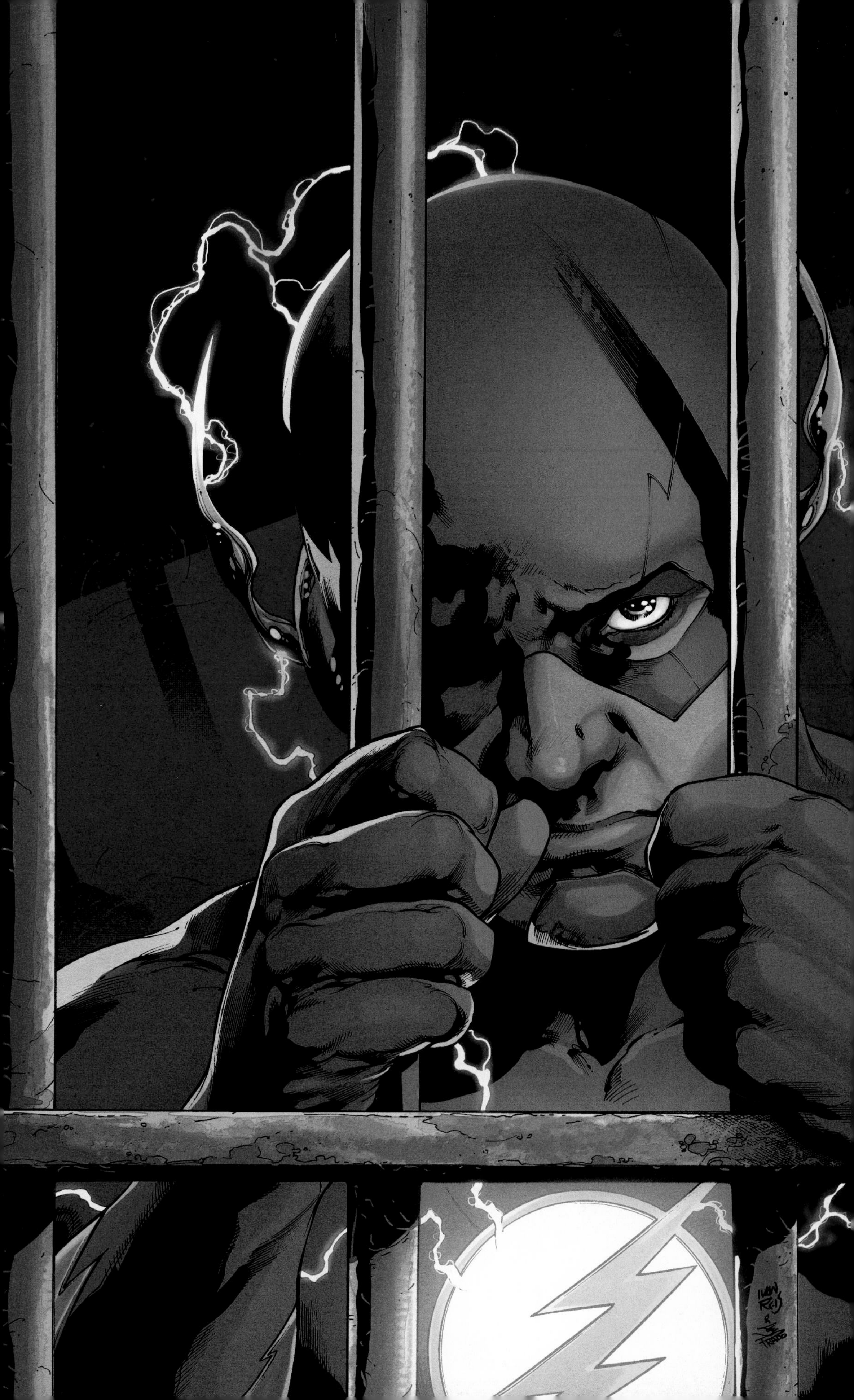

NEW BLOOD

ROBERT VENDITTI VAN JENSEN writers PHIL BRIONES artist GUY MAJOR colorist PAT BROSSEAU letterer IVAN REIS JOE PRADO ADRIANO LUCAS cover

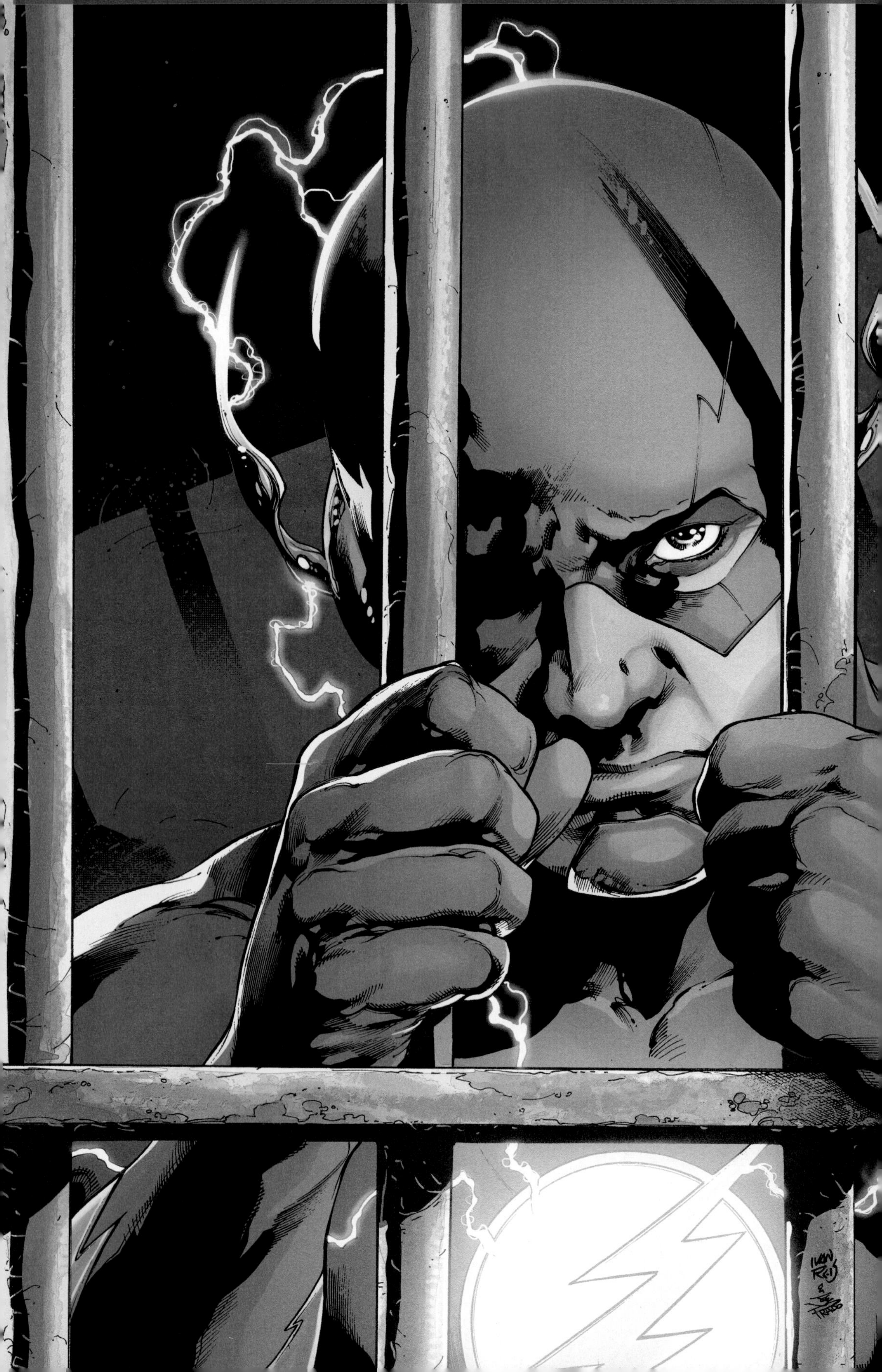

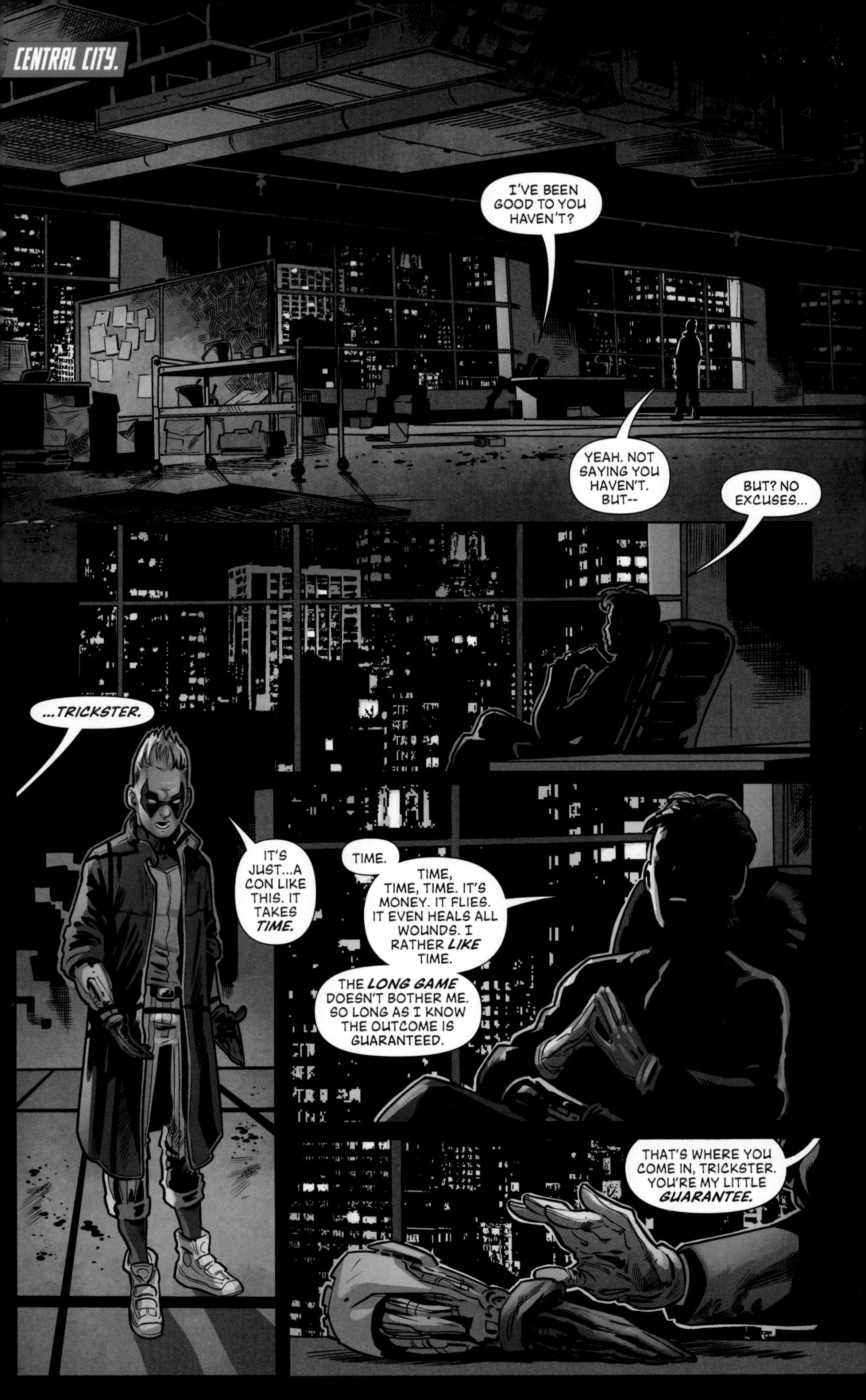
CENTRAL CITY.
I'VE BEEN GOOD TO YOU HAVEN'T?
YEAH. NOT SAYING YOU HAVEN'T. BUT--
BUT? NO EXCUSES...
...TRICKSTER.
IT'S JUST...A CON LIKE THIS. IT TAKES *TIME.*
TIME.
TIME, TIME, TIME. IT'S MONEY. IT FLIES. IT EVEN HEALS ALL WOUNDS. I RATHER *LIKE* TIME.
THE *LONG GAME* DOESN'T BOTHER ME. SO LONG AS I KNOW THE OUTCOME IS GUARANTEED.
THAT'S WHERE YOU COME IN, TRICKSTER. YOU'RE MY LITTLE *GUARANTEE.*

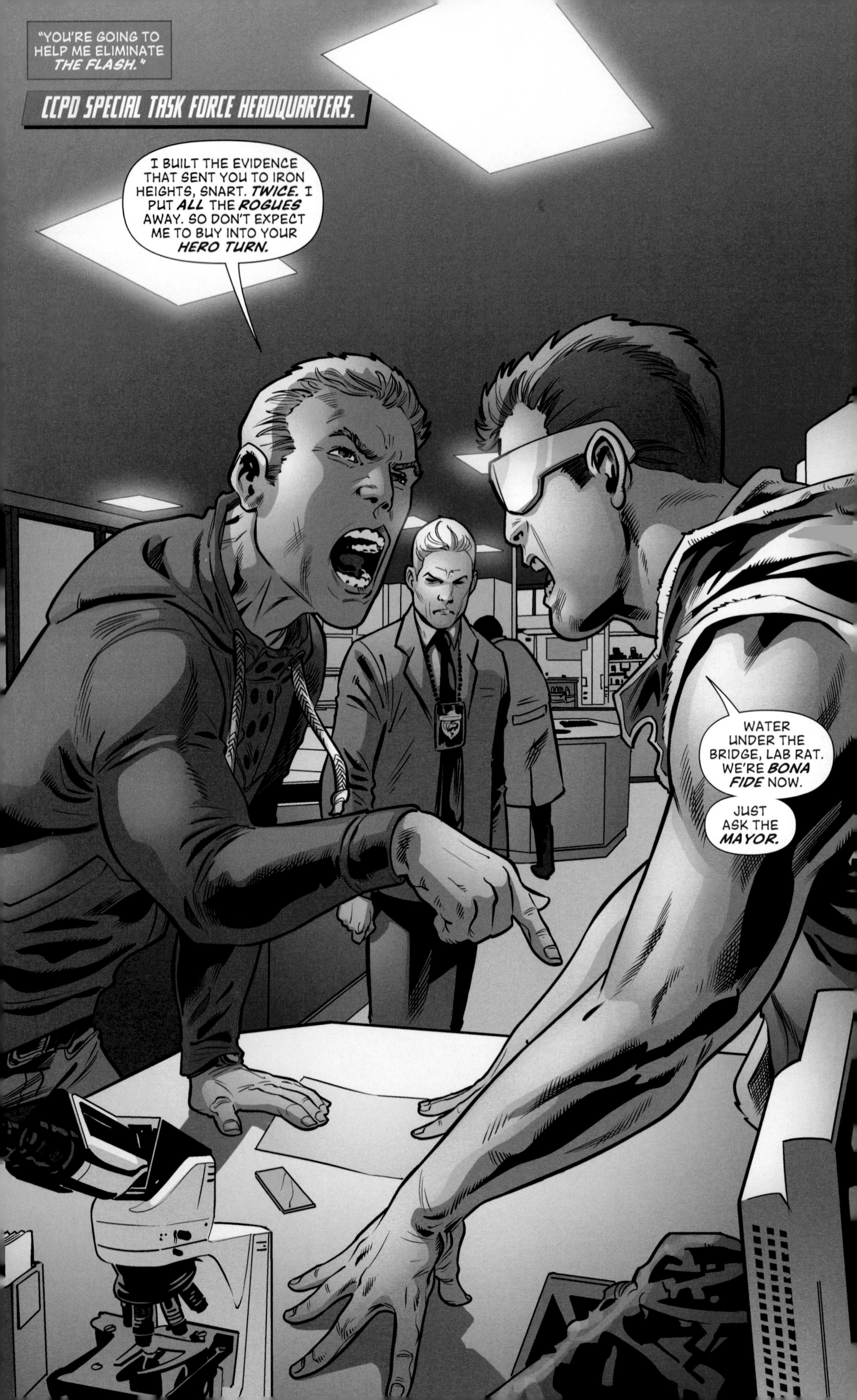
"YOU'RE GOING TO HELP ME ELIMINATE *THE FLASH.*"
CCPD SPECIAL TASK FORCE HEADQUARTERS.
I BUILT THE EVIDENCE THAT SENT YOU TO IRON HEIGHTS, SNART. *TWICE.* I PUT *ALL* THE *ROGUES* AWAY. SO DON'T EXPECT ME TO BUY INTO YOUR *HERO TURN.*
WATER UNDER THE BRIDGE, LAB RAT. WE'RE *BONA FIDE* NOW.
JUST ASK THE *MAYOR.*

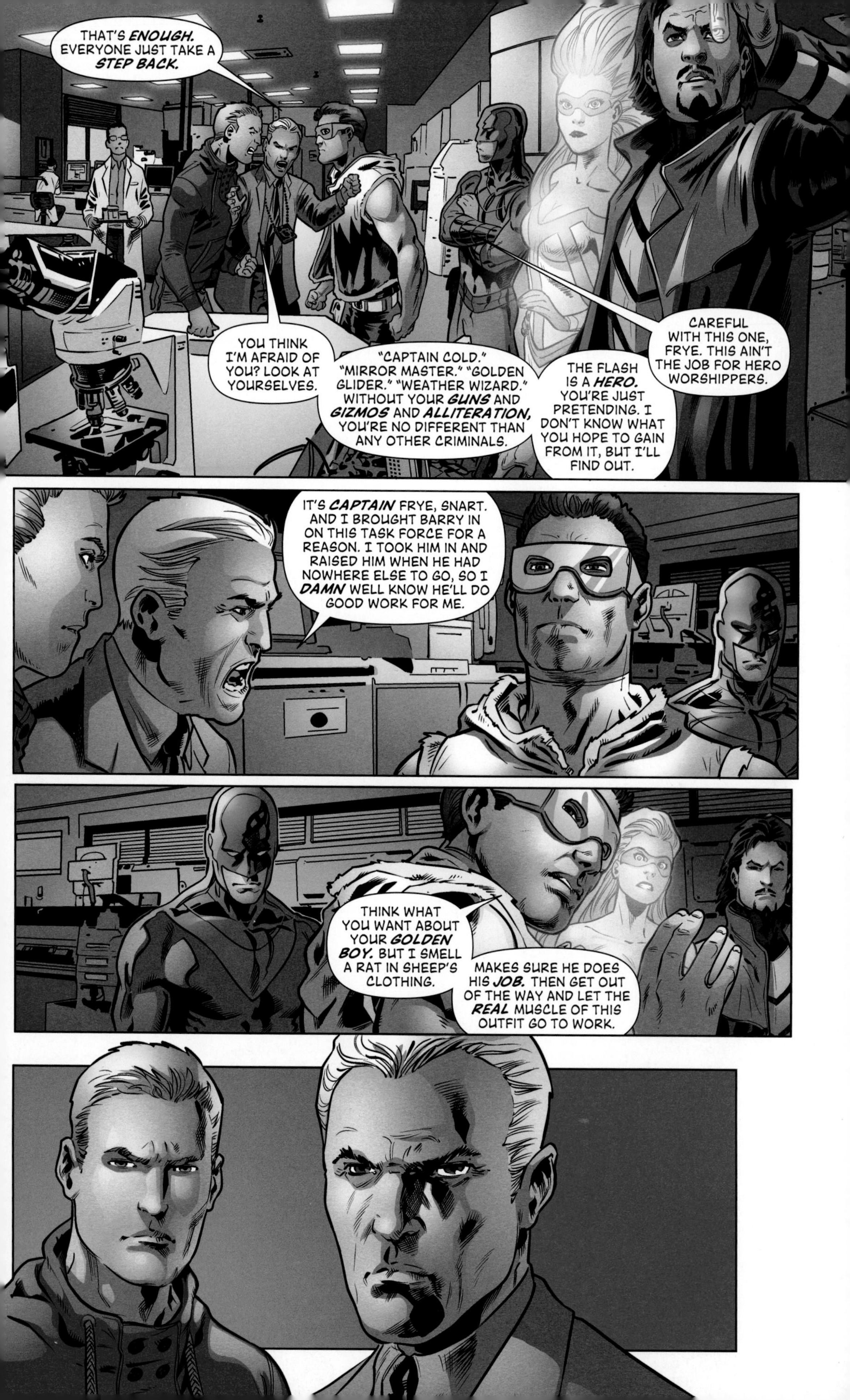
THAT'S ENOUGH. EVERYONE JUST TAKE A STEP BACK.
YOU THINK I'M AFRAID OF YOU? LOOK AT YOURSELVES.
"CAPTAIN COLD." "MIRROR MASTER." "GOLDEN GLIDER." "WEATHER WIZARD." WITHOUT YOUR GUNS AND GIZMOS AND ALLITERATION, YOU'RE NO DIFFERENT THAN ANY OTHER CRIMINALS.
THE FLASH IS A HERO. YOU'RE JUST PRETENDING. I DON'T KNOW WHAT YOU HOPE TO GAIN FROM IT, BUT I'LL FIND OUT.
CAREFUL WITH THIS ONE, FRYE. THIS AIN'T THE JOB FOR HERO WORSHIPPERS.
IT'S CAPTAIN FRYE, SNART. AND I BROUGHT BARRY IN ON THIS TASK FORCE FOR A REASON. I TOOK HIM IN AND RAISED HIM WHEN HE HAD NOWHERE ELSE TO GO, SO I DAMN WELL KNOW HE'LL DO GOOD WORK FOR ME.
THINK WHAT YOU WANT ABOUT YOUR GOLDEN BOY. BUT I SMELL A RAT IN SHEEP'S CLOTHING.
MAKES SURE HE DOES HIS JOB. THEN GET OUT OF THE WAY AND LET THE REAL MUSCLE OF THIS OUTFIT GO TO WORK.

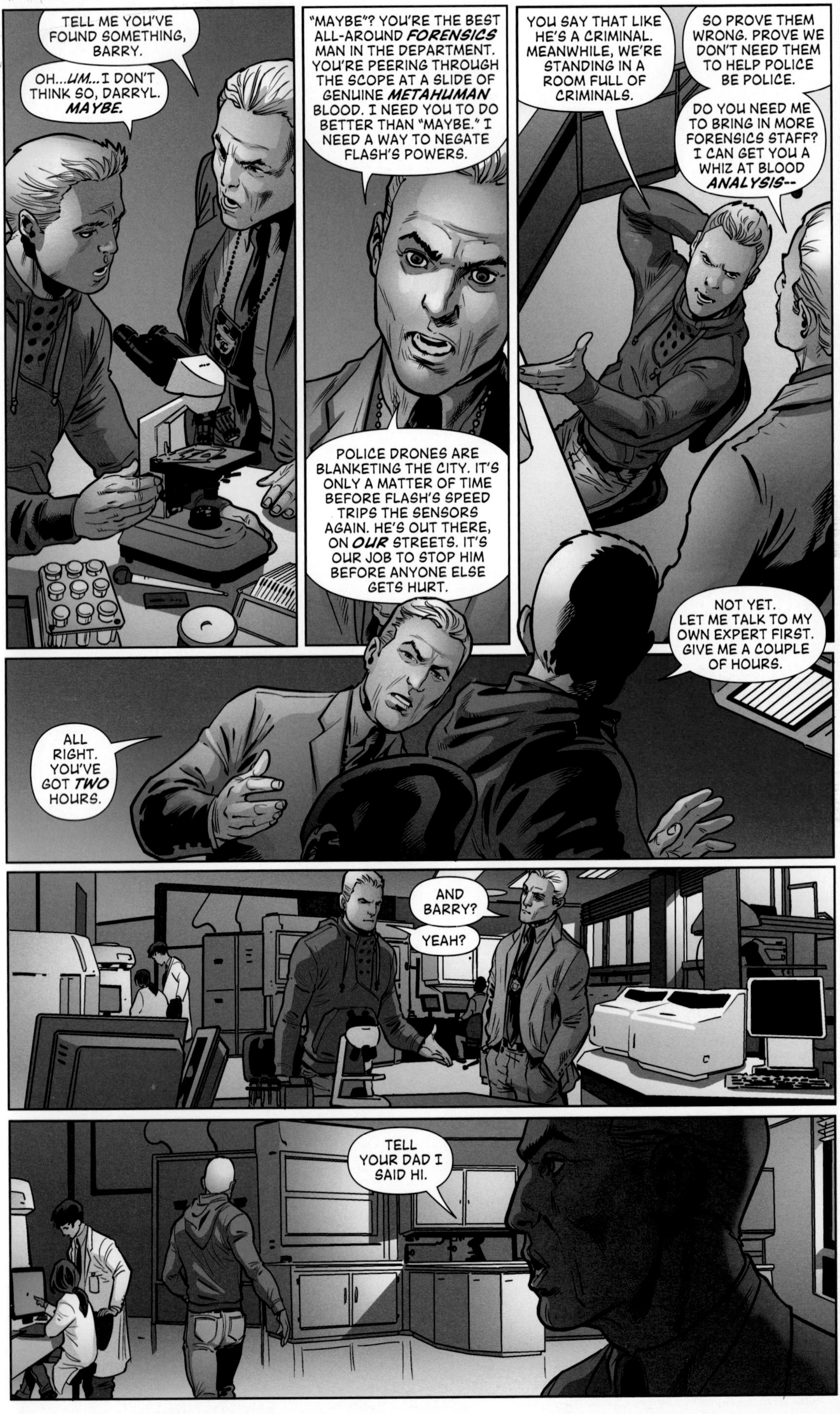
TELL ME YOU'VE FOUND SOMETHING, BARRY.
OH...*UM...* I DON'T THINK SO, DARRYL. ***MAYBE.***
"MAYBE"? YOU'RE THE BEST ALL-AROUND ***FORENSICS*** MAN IN THE DEPARTMENT. YOU'RE PEERING THROUGH THE SCOPE AT A SLIDE OF GENUINE ***METAHUMAN*** BLOOD. I NEED YOU TO DO BETTER THAN "MAYBE." I NEED A WAY TO NEGATE FLASH'S POWERS.
POLICE DRONES ARE BLANKETING THE CITY. IT'S ONLY A MATTER OF TIME BEFORE FLASH'S SPEED TRIPS THE SENSORS AGAIN. HE'S OUT THERE, ON ***OUR*** STREETS. IT'S OUR JOB TO STOP HIM BEFORE ANYONE ELSE GETS HURT.
YOU SAY THAT LIKE HE'S A CRIMINAL. MEANWHILE, WE'RE STANDING IN A ROOM FULL OF CRIMINALS.
SO PROVE THEM WRONG. PROVE WE DON'T NEED THEM TO HELP POLICE BE POLICE.
DO YOU NEED ME TO BRING IN MORE FORENSICS STAFF? I CAN GET YOU A WHIZ AT BLOOD ***ANALYSIS--***
NOT YET. LET ME TALK TO MY OWN EXPERT FIRST. GIVE ME A COUPLE OF HOURS.
ALL RIGHT. YOU'VE GOT ***TWO*** HOURS.
AND BARRY?
YEAH?
TELL YOUR DAD I SAID HI.

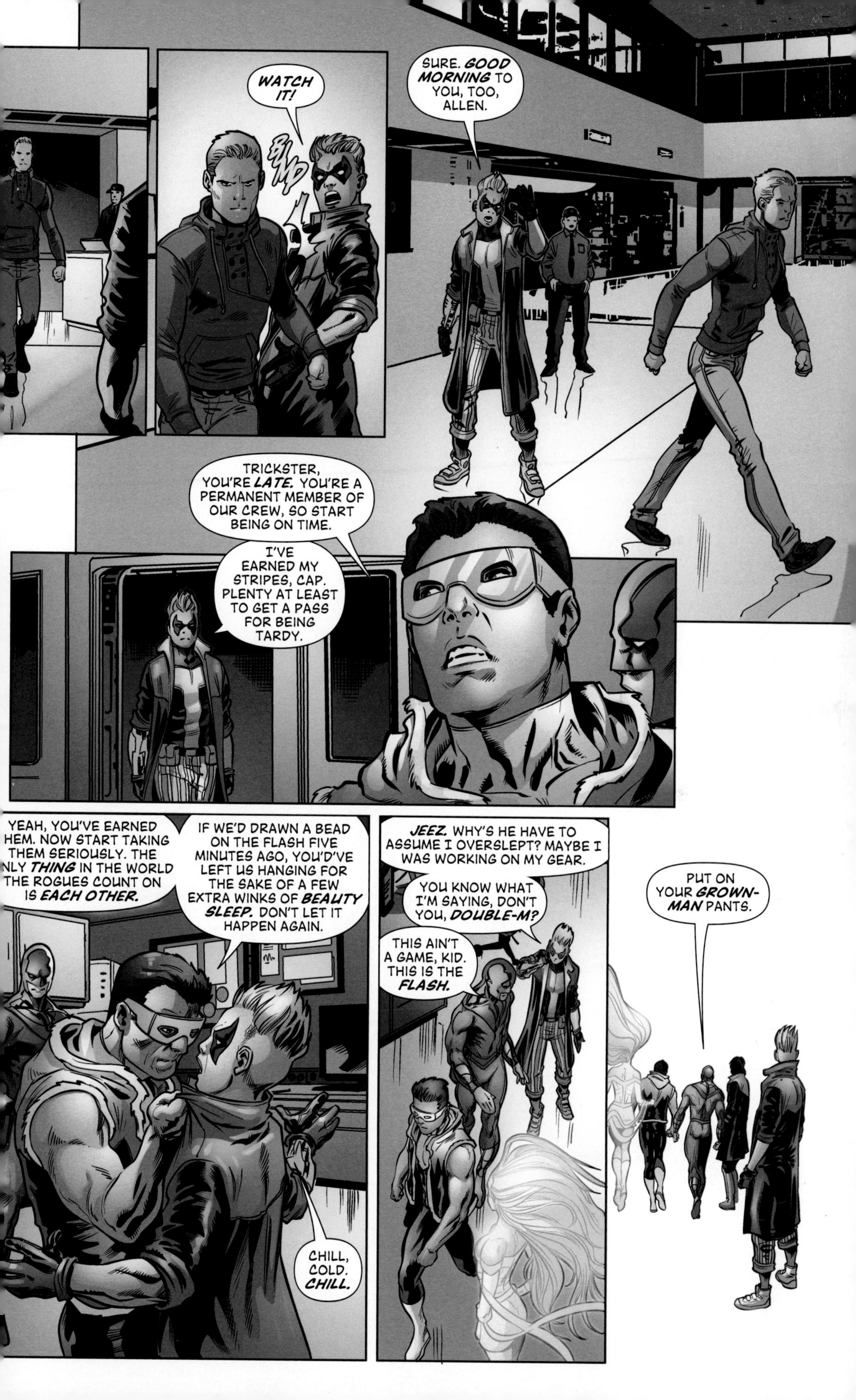
WATCH IT!
BUMP
SURE. GOOD MORNING TO YOU, TOO, ALLEN.
TRICKSTER, YOU'RE LATE. YOU'RE A PERMANENT MEMBER OF OUR CREW, SO START BEING ON TIME.
I'VE EARNED MY STRIPES, CAP. PLENTY AT LEAST TO GET A PASS FOR BEING TARDY.
YEAH, YOU'VE EARNED HEM. NOW START TAKING THEM SERIOUSLY. THE NLY THING IN THE WORLD THE ROGUES COUNT ON IS EACH OTHER.
IF WE'D DRAWN A BEAD ON THE FLASH FIVE MINUTES AGO, YOU'D'VE LEFT US HANGING FOR THE SAKE OF A FEW EXTRA WINKS OF BEAUTY SLEEP. DON'T LET IT HAPPEN AGAIN.
CHILL, COLD. CHILL.
JEEZ. WHY'S HE HAVE TO ASSUME I OVERSLEPT? MAYBE I WAS WORKING ON MY GEAR.
YOU KNOW WHAT I'M SAYING, DON'T YOU, DOUBLE-M?
THIS AIN'T A GAME, KID. THIS IS THE FLASH.
PUT ON YOUR GROWN-MAN PANTS.

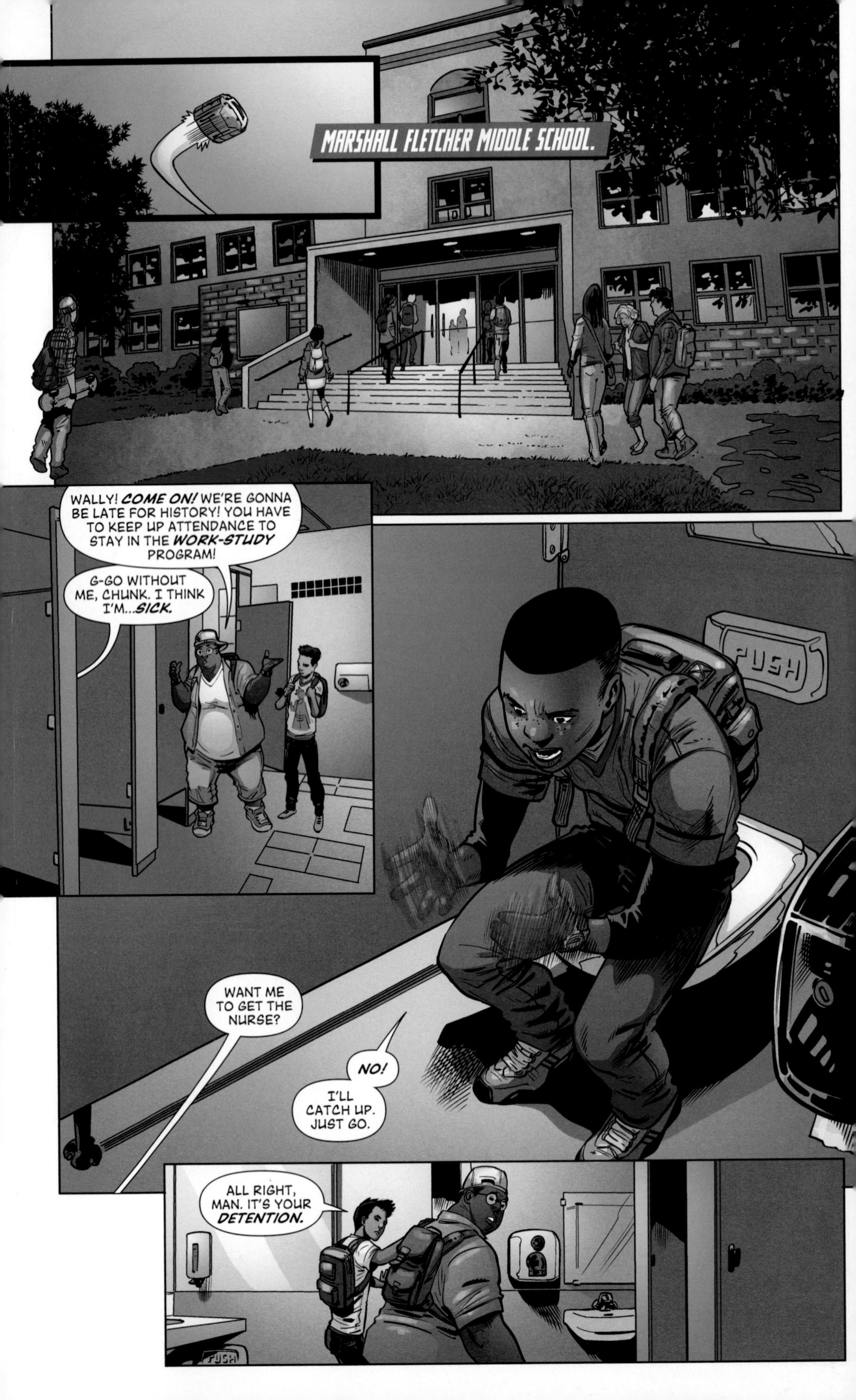
MARSHALL FLETCHER MIDDLE SCHOOL.
WALLY! COME ON! WE'RE GONNA BE LATE FOR HISTORY! YOU HAVE TO KEEP UP ATTENDANCE TO STAY IN THE WORK-STUDY PROGRAM!
G-GO WITHOUT ME, CHUNK. I THINK I'M...SICK.
PUSH
WANT ME TO GET THE NURSE?
NO!
I'LL CATCH UP. JUST GO.
ALL RIGHT, MAN. IT'S YOUR DETENTION.

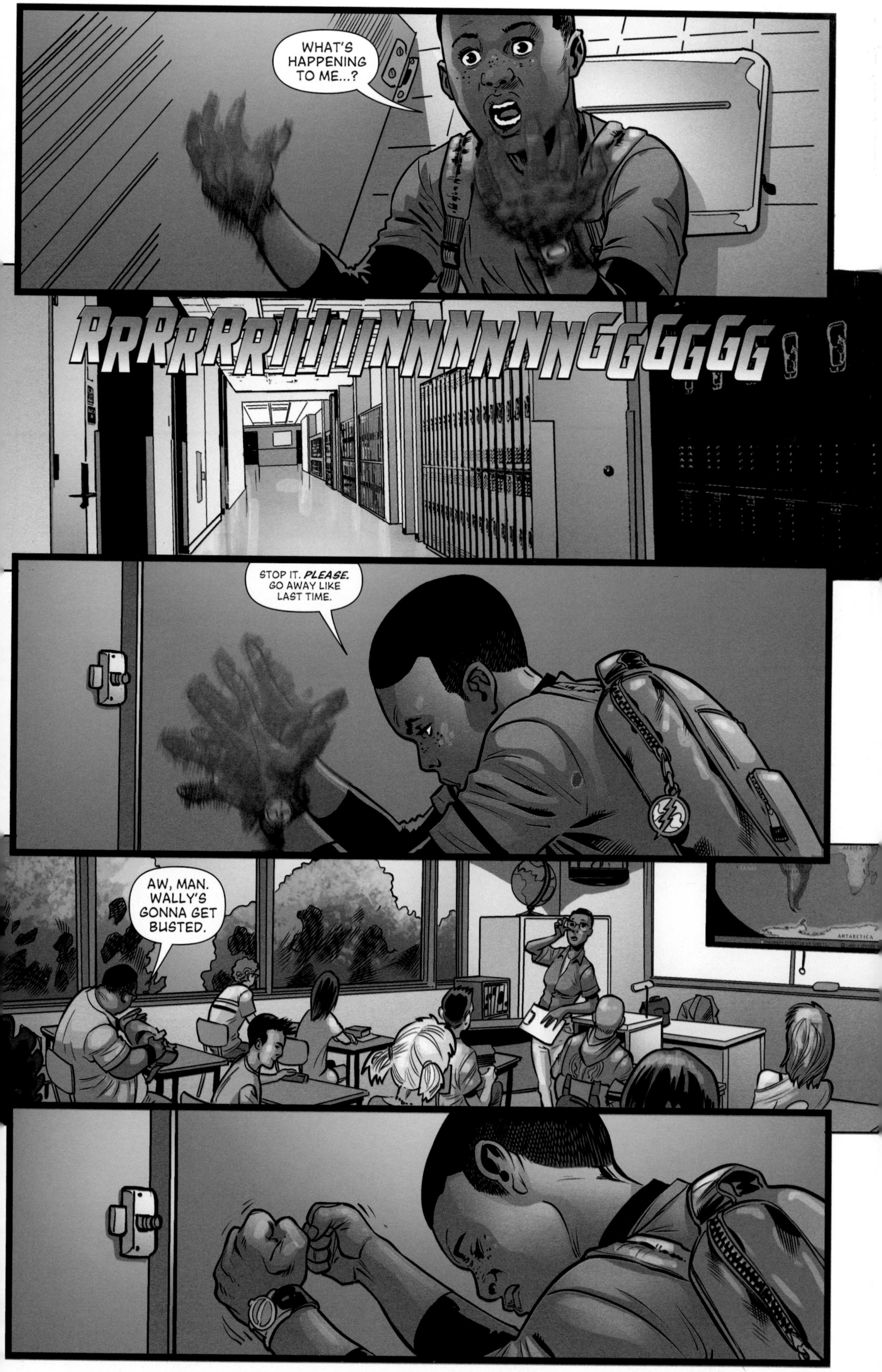
WHAT'S HAPPENING TO ME...?
RRRRRIIIIIINNNNNNGGGGGG
STOP IT. PLEASE. GO AWAY LIKE LAST TIME.
AW, MAN. WALLY'S GONNA GET BUSTED.

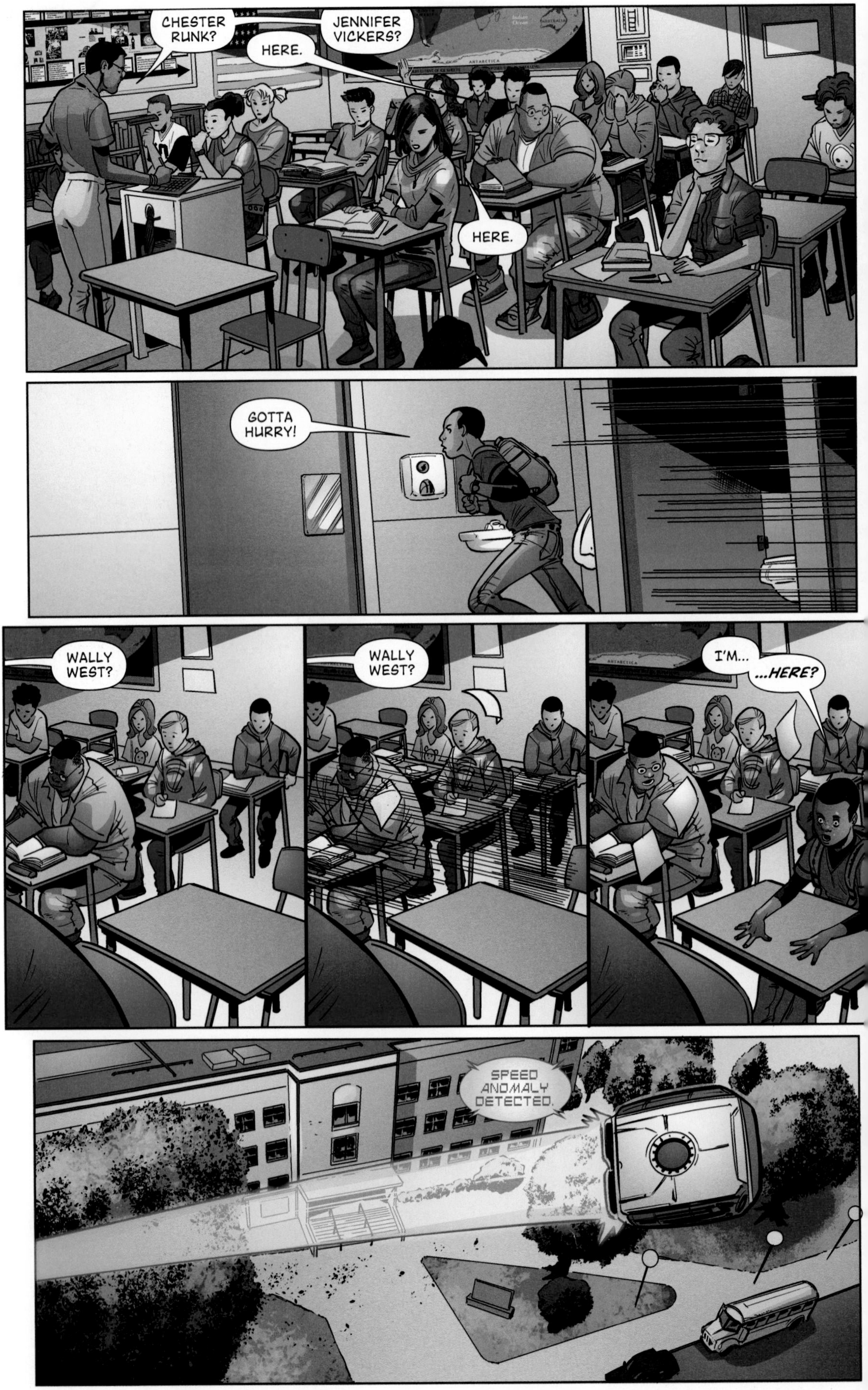
CHESTER RUNK?
JENNIFER VICKERS?
HERE.
HERE.
GOTTA HURRY!
WALLY WEST?
WALLY WEST?
I'M...
...HERE?
SPEED ANOMALY DETECTED.

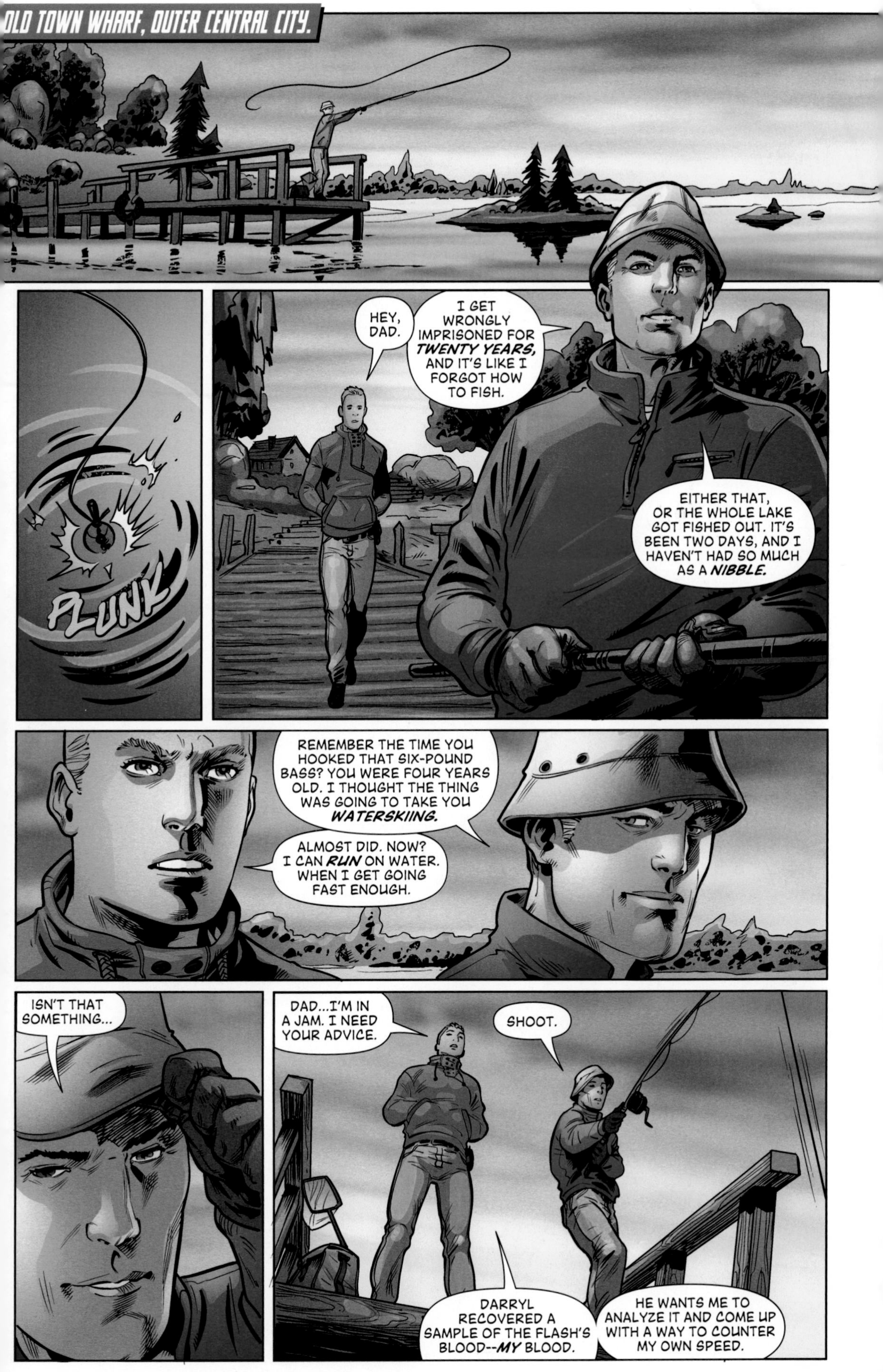
OLD TOWN WHARF, OUTER CENTRAL CITY.
PLUNK
HEY, DAD.
I GET WRONGLY IMPRISONED FOR TWENTY YEARS, AND IT'S LIKE I FORGOT HOW TO FISH.
EITHER THAT, OR THE WHOLE LAKE GOT FISHED OUT. IT'S BEEN TWO DAYS, AND I HAVEN'T HAD SO MUCH AS A NIBBLE.
REMEMBER THE TIME YOU HOOKED THAT SIX-POUND BASS? YOU WERE FOUR YEARS OLD. I THOUGHT THE THING WAS GOING TO TAKE YOU WATERSKIING.
ALMOST DID. NOW? I CAN RUN ON WATER. WHEN I GET GOING FAST ENOUGH.
ISN'T THAT SOMETHING...
DAD...I'M IN A JAM. I NEED YOUR ADVICE.
SHOOT.
DARRYL RECOVERED A SAMPLE OF THE FLASH'S BLOOD--MY BLOOD.
HE WANTS ME TO ANALYZE IT AND COME UP WITH A WAY TO COUNTER MY OWN SPEED.

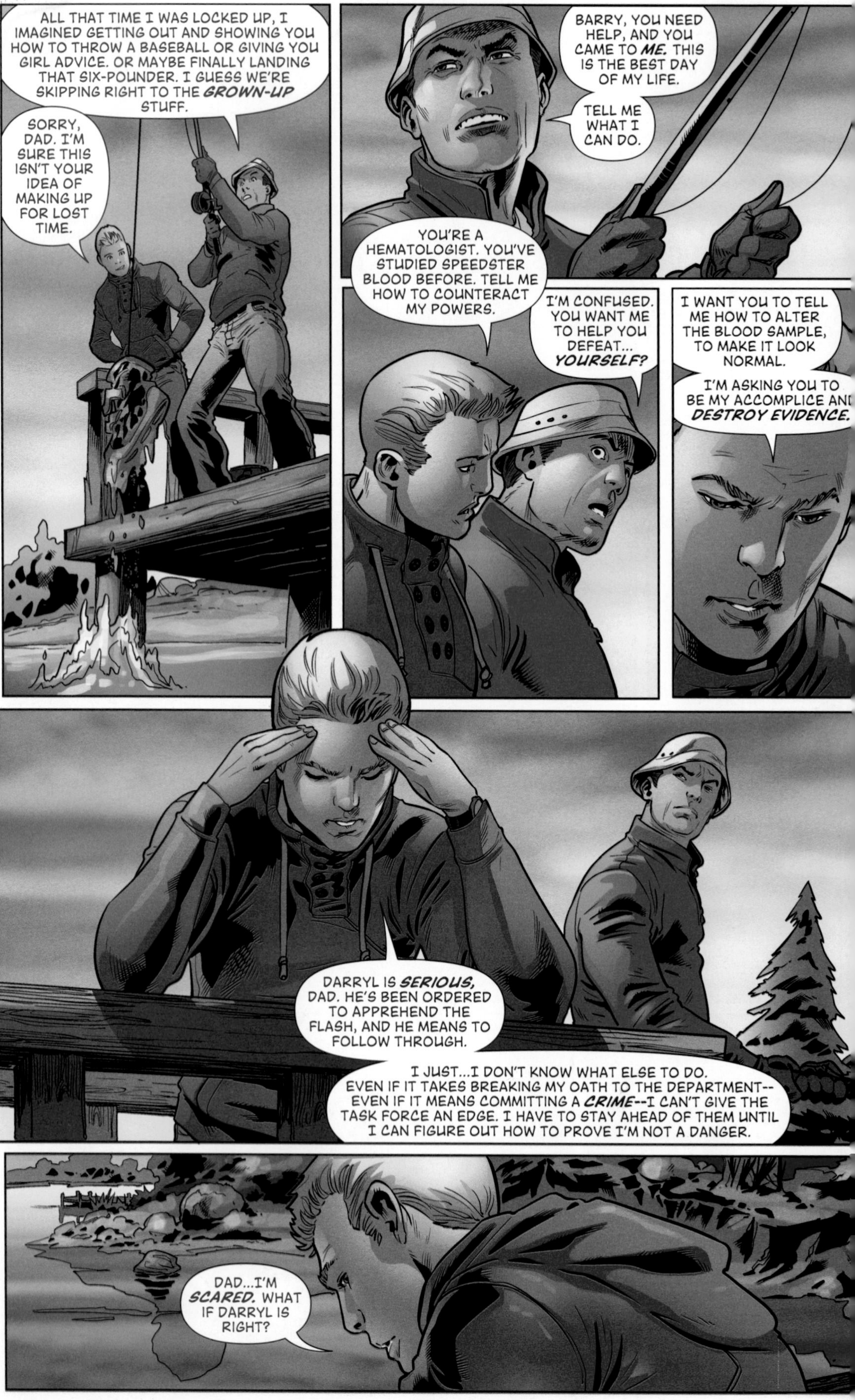
ALL THAT TIME I WAS LOCKED UP, I IMAGINED GETTING OUT AND SHOWING YOU HOW TO THROW A BASEBALL OR GIVING YOU GIRL ADVICE. OR MAYBE FINALLY LANDING THAT SIX-POUNDER. I GUESS WE'RE SKIPPING RIGHT TO THE *GROWN-UP* STUFF.
SORRY, DAD. I'M SURE THIS ISN'T YOUR IDEA OF MAKING UP FOR LOST TIME.
BARRY, YOU NEED HELP, AND YOU CAME TO *ME.* THIS IS THE BEST DAY OF MY LIFE.
TELL ME WHAT I CAN DO.
YOU'RE A HEMATOLOGIST. YOU'VE STUDIED SPEEDSTER BLOOD BEFORE. TELL ME HOW TO COUNTERACT MY POWERS.
I'M CONFUSED. YOU WANT ME TO HELP YOU DEFEAT... *YOURSELF?*
I WANT YOU TO TELL ME HOW TO ALTER THE BLOOD SAMPLE, TO MAKE IT LOOK NORMAL.
I'M ASKING YOU TO BE MY ACCOMPLICE AND *DESTROY EVIDENCE.*
DARRYL IS *SERIOUS,* DAD. HE'S BEEN ORDERED TO APPREHEND THE FLASH, AND HE MEANS TO FOLLOW THROUGH.
I JUST...I DON'T KNOW WHAT ELSE TO DO. EVEN IF IT TAKES BREAKING MY OATH TO THE DEPARTMENT-- EVEN IF IT MEANS COMMITTING A *CRIME*--I CAN'T GIVE THE TASK FORCE AN EDGE. I HAVE TO STAY AHEAD OF THEM UNTIL I CAN FIGURE OUT HOW TO PROVE I'M NOT A DANGER.
DAD...I'M *SCARED.* WHAT IF DARRYL IS RIGHT?

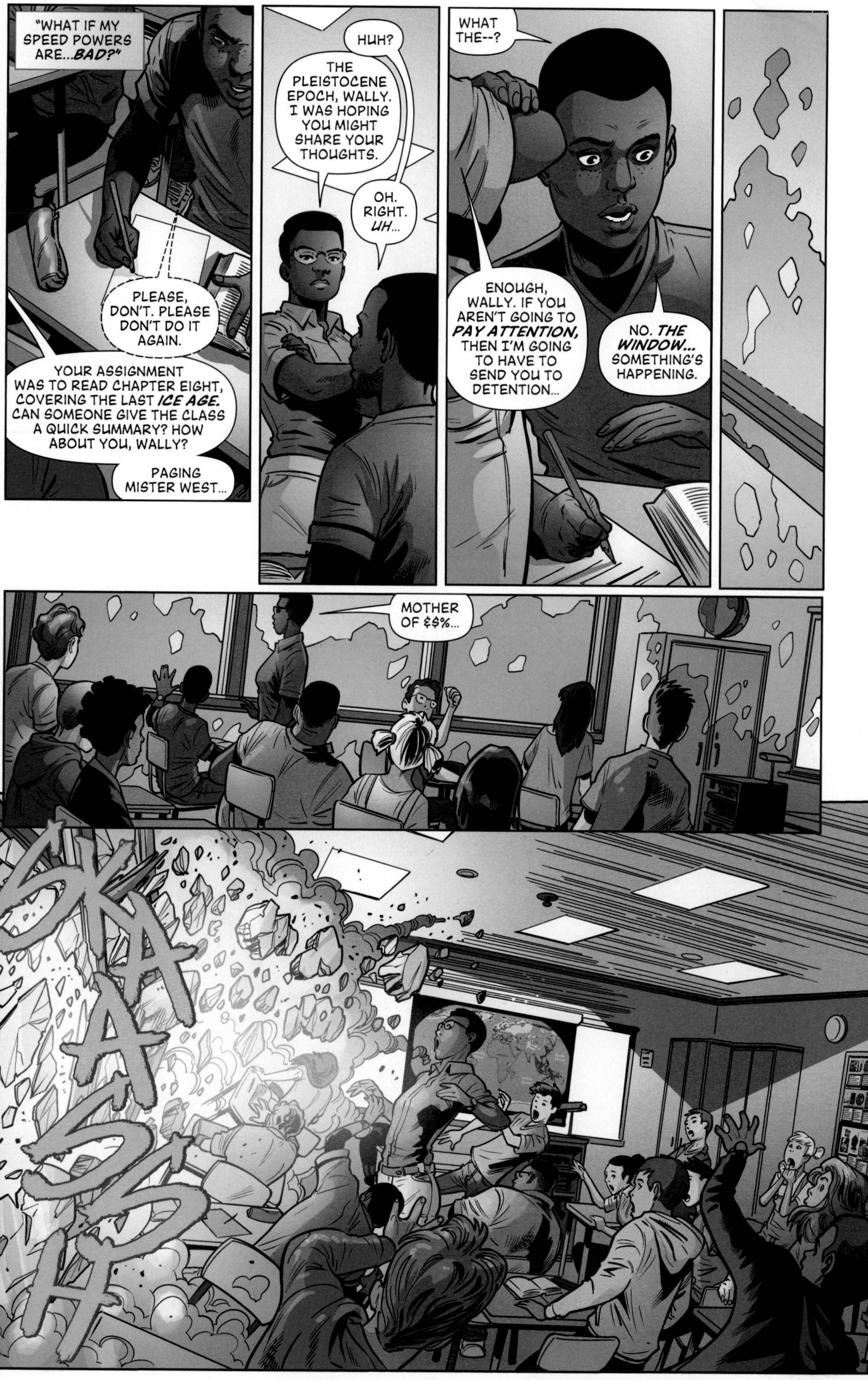
"WHAT IF MY SPEED POWERS ARE...BAD?"
PLEASE, DON'T. PLEASE DON'T DO IT AGAIN.
YOUR ASSIGNMENT WAS TO READ CHAPTER EIGHT, COVERING THE LAST ICE AGE. CAN SOMEONE GIVE THE CLASS A QUICK SUMMARY? HOW ABOUT YOU, WALLY?
PAGING MISTER WEST...
HUH?
THE PLEISTOCENE EPOCH, WALLY. I WAS HOPING YOU MIGHT SHARE YOUR THOUGHTS.
OH. RIGHT. UH...
WHAT THE--?
ENOUGH, WALLY. IF YOU AREN'T GOING TO PAY ATTENTION, THEN I'M GOING TO HAVE TO SEND YOU TO DETENTION...
NO. THE WINDOW... SOMETHING'S HAPPENING.
MOTHER OF $$%...
SKAASSH

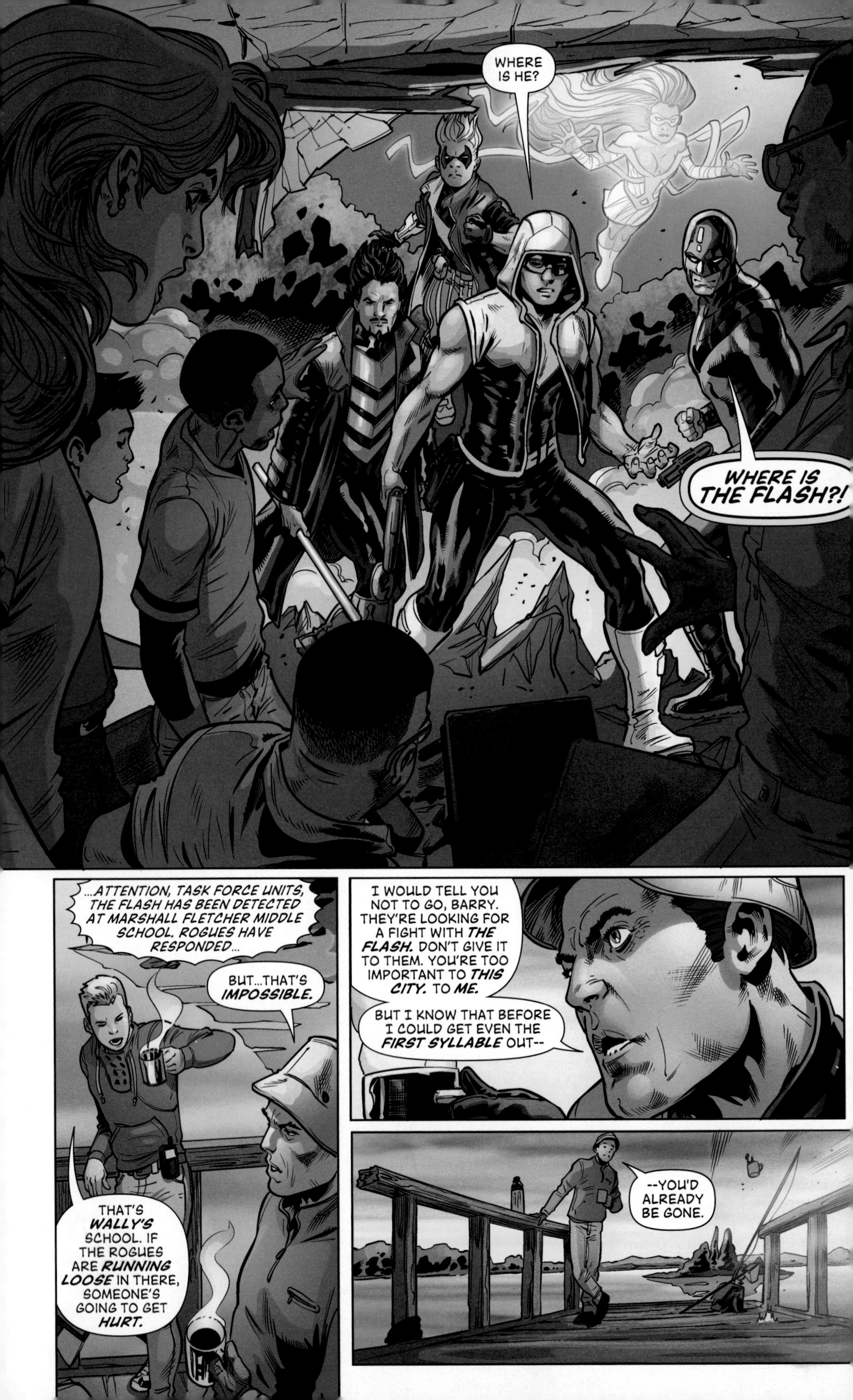
WHERE IS HE?
WHERE IS THE FLASH?!
...ATTENTION, TASK FORCE UNITS, THE FLASH HAS BEEN DETECTED AT MARSHALL FLETCHER MIDDLE SCHOOL. ROGUES HAVE RESPONDED...
BUT...THAT'S IMPOSSIBLE.
THAT'S WALLY'S SCHOOL. IF THE ROGUES ARE RUNNING LOOSE IN THERE, SOMEONE'S GOING TO GET HURT.
I WOULD TELL YOU NOT TO GO, BARRY. THEY'RE LOOKING FOR A FIGHT WITH THE FLASH. DON'T GIVE IT TO THEM. YOU'RE TOO IMPORTANT TO THIS CITY. TO ME.
BUT I KNOW THAT BEFORE I COULD GET EVEN THE FIRST SYLLABLE OUT--
--YOU'D ALREADY BE GONE.

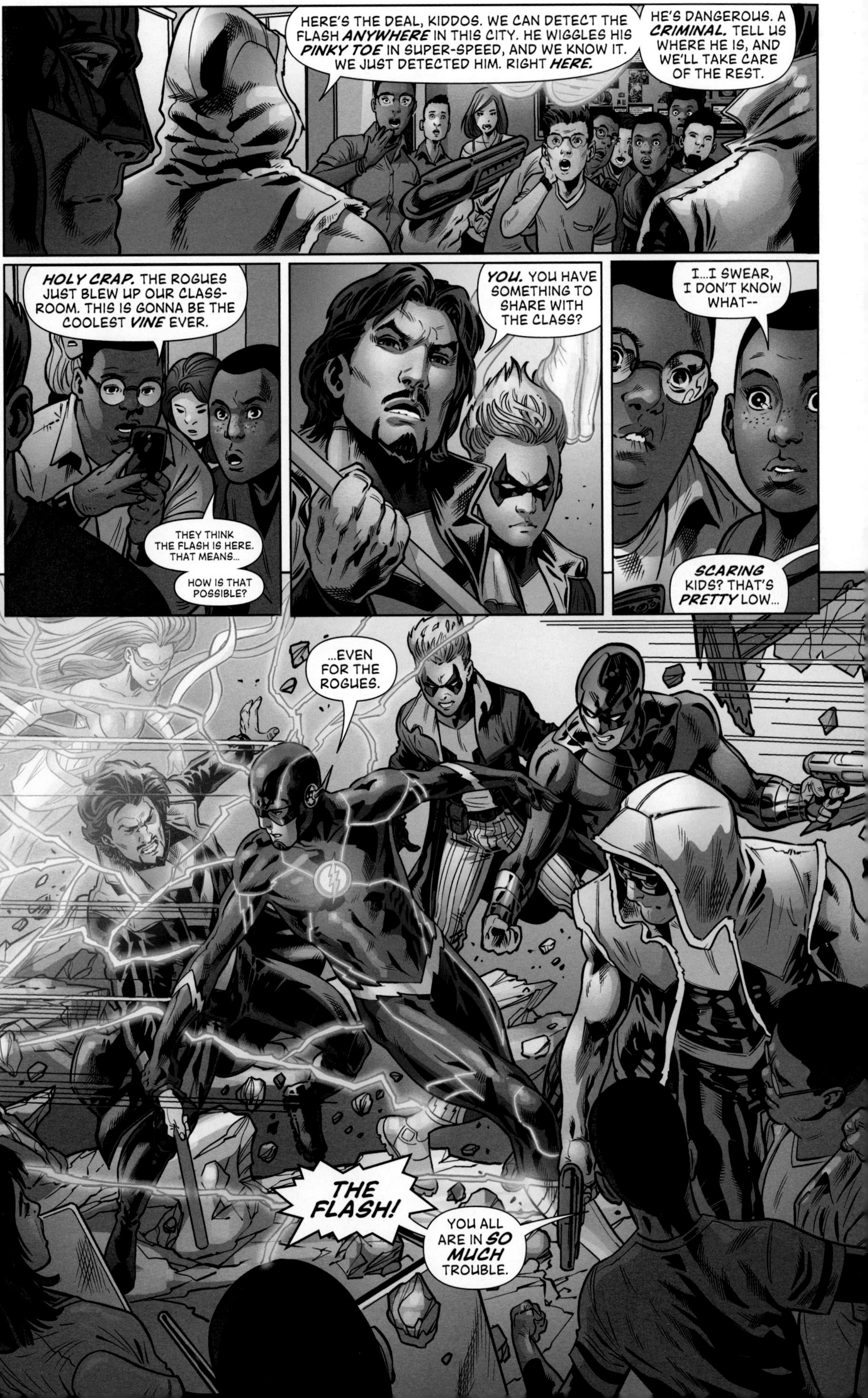
HERE'S THE DEAL, KIDDOS. WE CAN DETECT THE FLASH ANYWHERE IN THIS CITY. HE WIGGLES HIS PINKY TOE IN SUPER-SPEED, AND WE KNOW IT. WE JUST DETECTED HIM. RIGHT HERE.
HE'S DANGEROUS. A CRIMINAL. TELL US WHERE HE IS, AND WE'LL TAKE CARE OF THE REST.
HOLY CRAP. THE ROGUES JUST BLEW UP OUR CLASS-ROOM. THIS IS GONNA BE THE COOLEST VINE EVER.
THEY THINK THE FLASH IS HERE. THAT MEANS...
HOW IS THAT POSSIBLE?
YOU. YOU HAVE SOMETHING TO SHARE WITH THE CLASS?
I...I SWEAR, I DON'T KNOW WHAT--
SCARING KIDS? THAT'S PRETTY LOW...
...EVEN FOR THE ROGUES.
THE FLASH!
YOU ALL ARE IN SO MUCH TROUBLE.

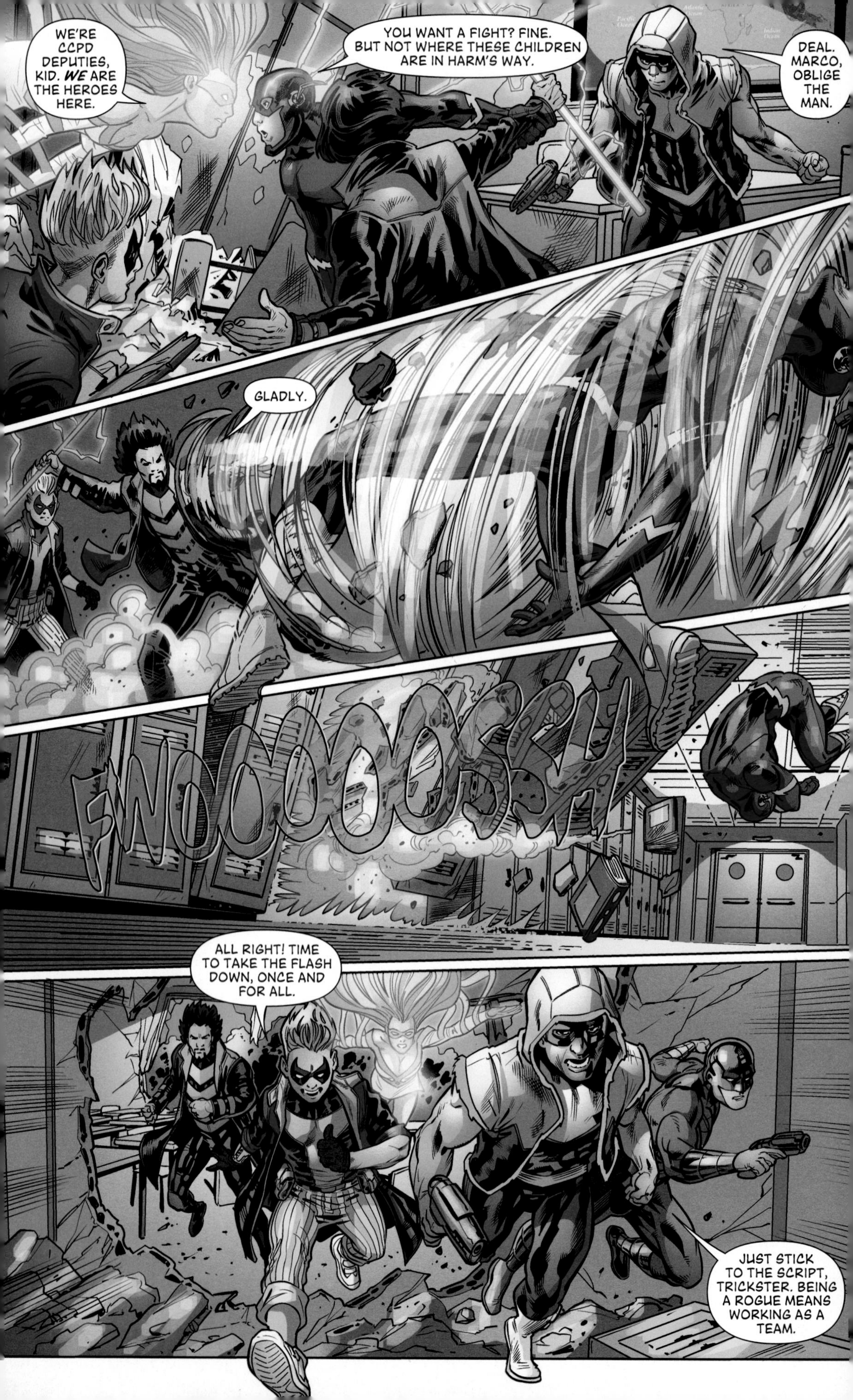
WE'RE CCPD DEPUTIES, KID. WE ARE THE HEROES HERE.
YOU WANT A FIGHT? FINE. BUT NOT WHERE THESE CHILDREN ARE IN HARM'S WAY.
DEAL. MARCO, OBLIGE THE MAN.
GLADLY.
FWOOOOOOSH!
ALL RIGHT! TIME TO TAKE THE FLASH DOWN, ONCE AND FOR ALL.
JUST STICK TO THE SCRIPT, TRICKSTER. BEING A ROGUE MEANS WORKING AS A TEAM.

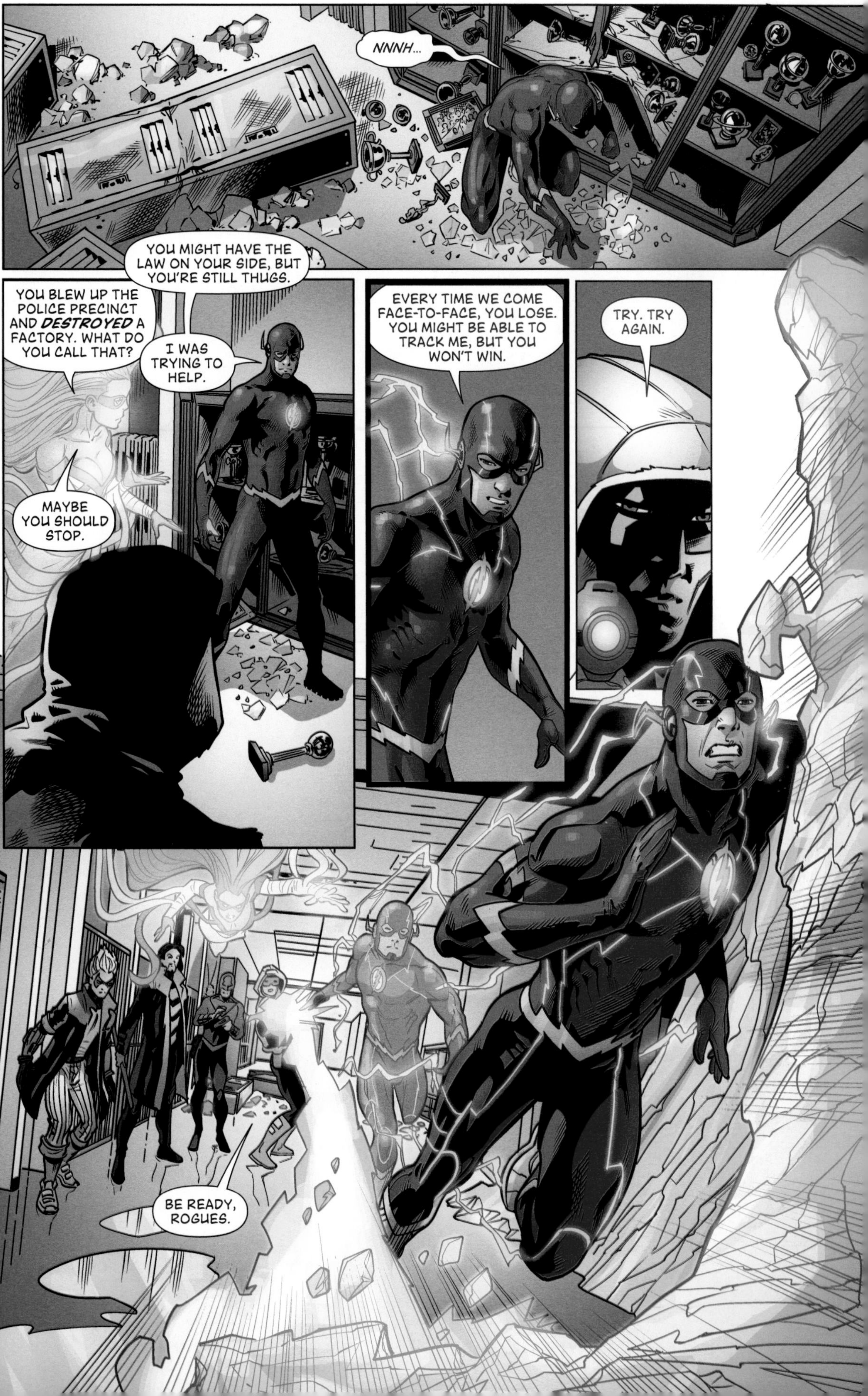

NNNH...
YOU MIGHT HAVE THE LAW ON YOUR SIDE, BUT YOU'RE STILL THUGS.
YOU BLEW UP THE POLICE PRECINCT AND *DESTROYED* A FACTORY. WHAT DO YOU CALL THAT?
I WAS TRYING TO HELP.
MAYBE YOU SHOULD STOP.
EVERY TIME WE COME FACE-TO-FACE, YOU LOSE. YOU MIGHT BE ABLE TO TRACK ME, BUT YOU WON'T WIN.
TRY. TRY AGAIN.
BE READY, ROGUES.

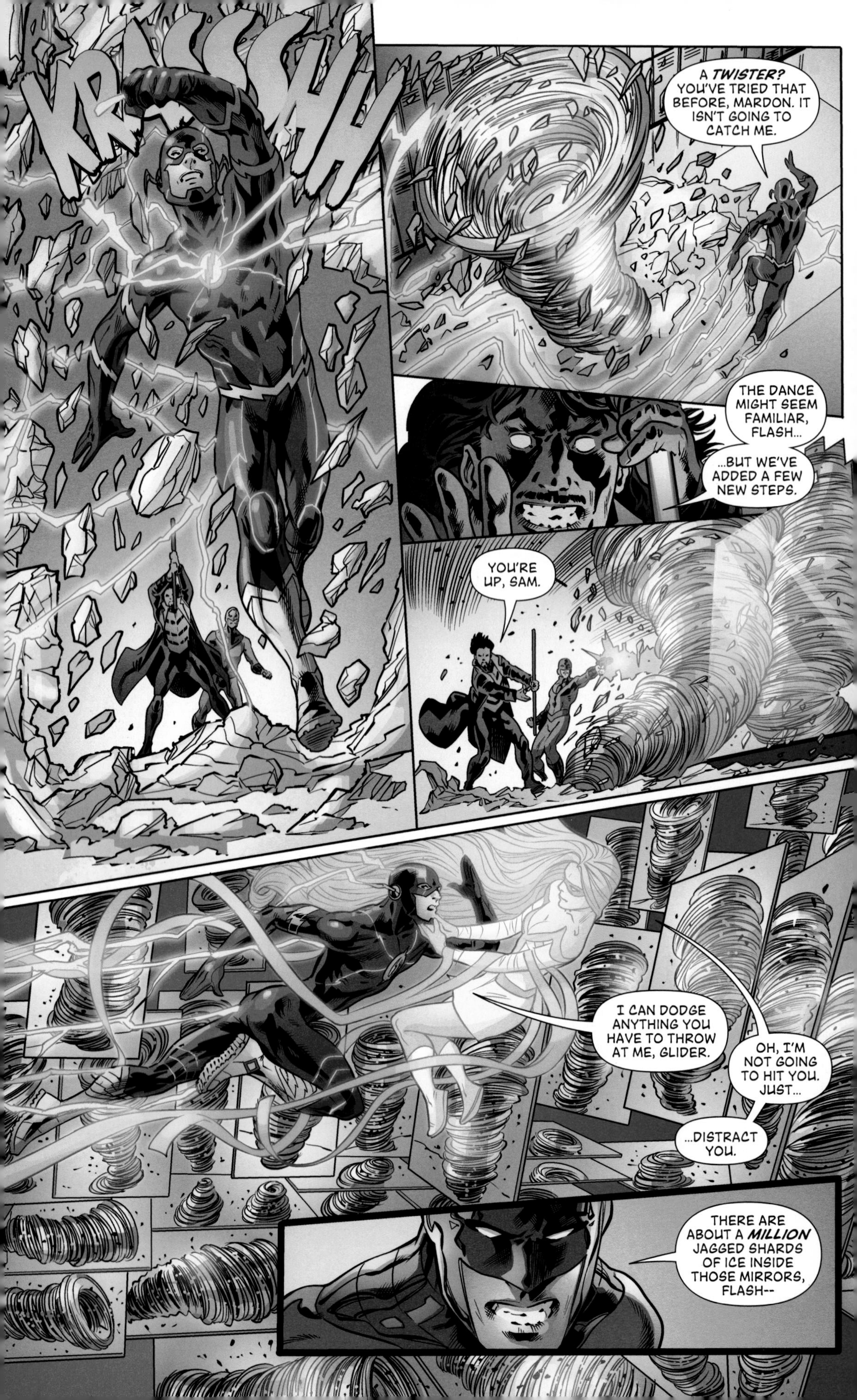
KRASSHH
A *TWISTER?* YOU'VE TRIED THAT BEFORE, MARDON. IT ISN'T GOING TO CATCH ME.
THE DANCE MIGHT SEEM FAMILIAR, FLASH...
...BUT WE'VE ADDED A FEW NEW STEPS.
YOU'RE UP, SAM.
I CAN DODGE ANYTHING YOU HAVE TO THROW AT ME, GLIDER.
OH, I'M NOT GOING TO HIT YOU. JUST...
...DISTRACT YOU.
THERE ARE ABOUT A *MILLION* JAGGED SHARDS OF ICE INSIDE THOSE MIRRORS, FLASH--

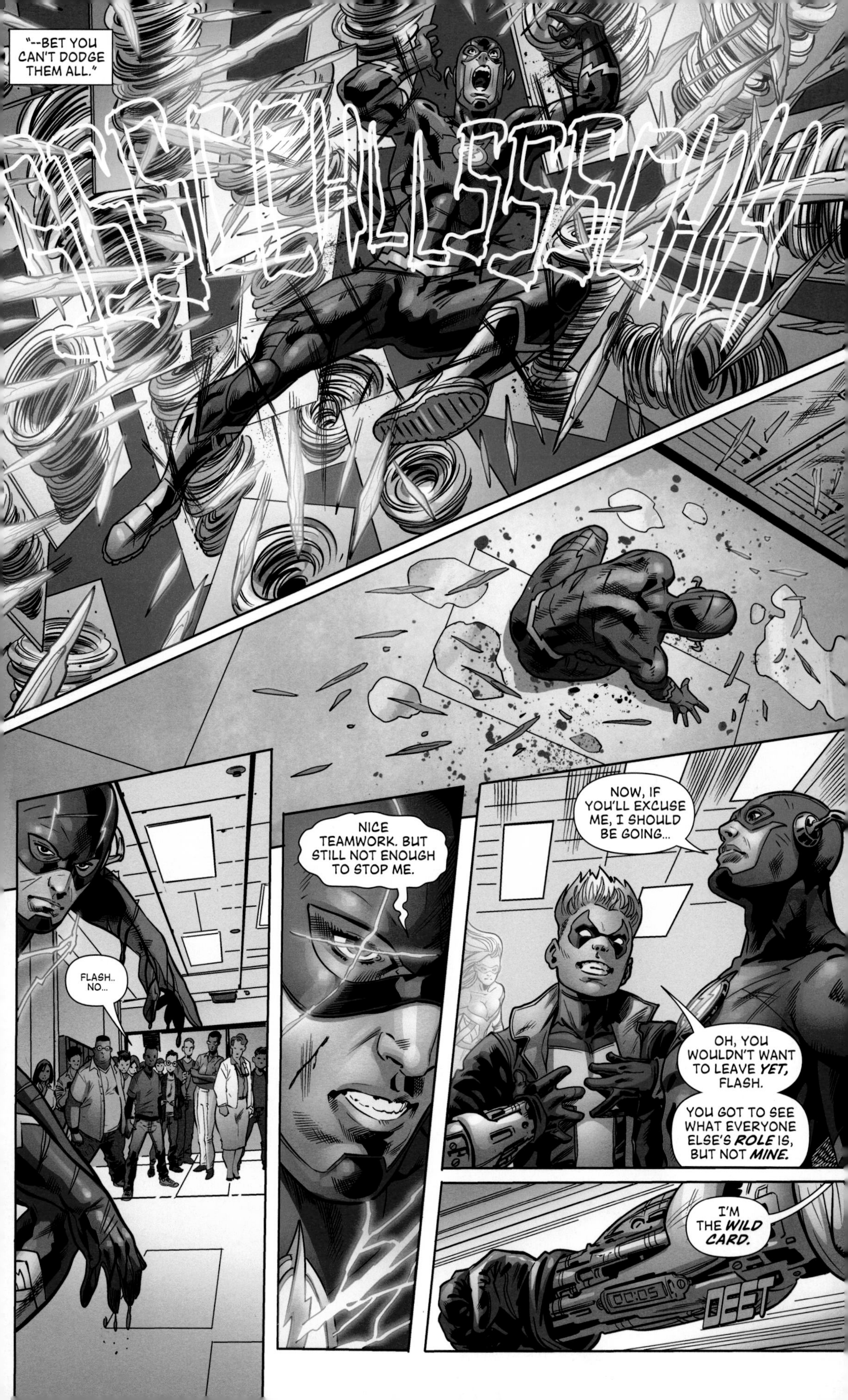
"--BET YOU CAN'T DODGE THEM ALL."
SSSCHLLSSSCHH
FLASH.. NO...
NICE TEAMWORK. BUT STILL NOT ENOUGH TO STOP ME.
NOW, IF YOU'LL EXCUSE ME, I SHOULD BE GOING...
OH, YOU WOULDN'T WANT TO LEAVE *YET,* FLASH.
YOU GOT TO SEE WHAT EVERYONE ELSE'S *ROLE* IS, BUT NOT *MINE.*
I'M THE *WILD CARD.*
00:05
BEET

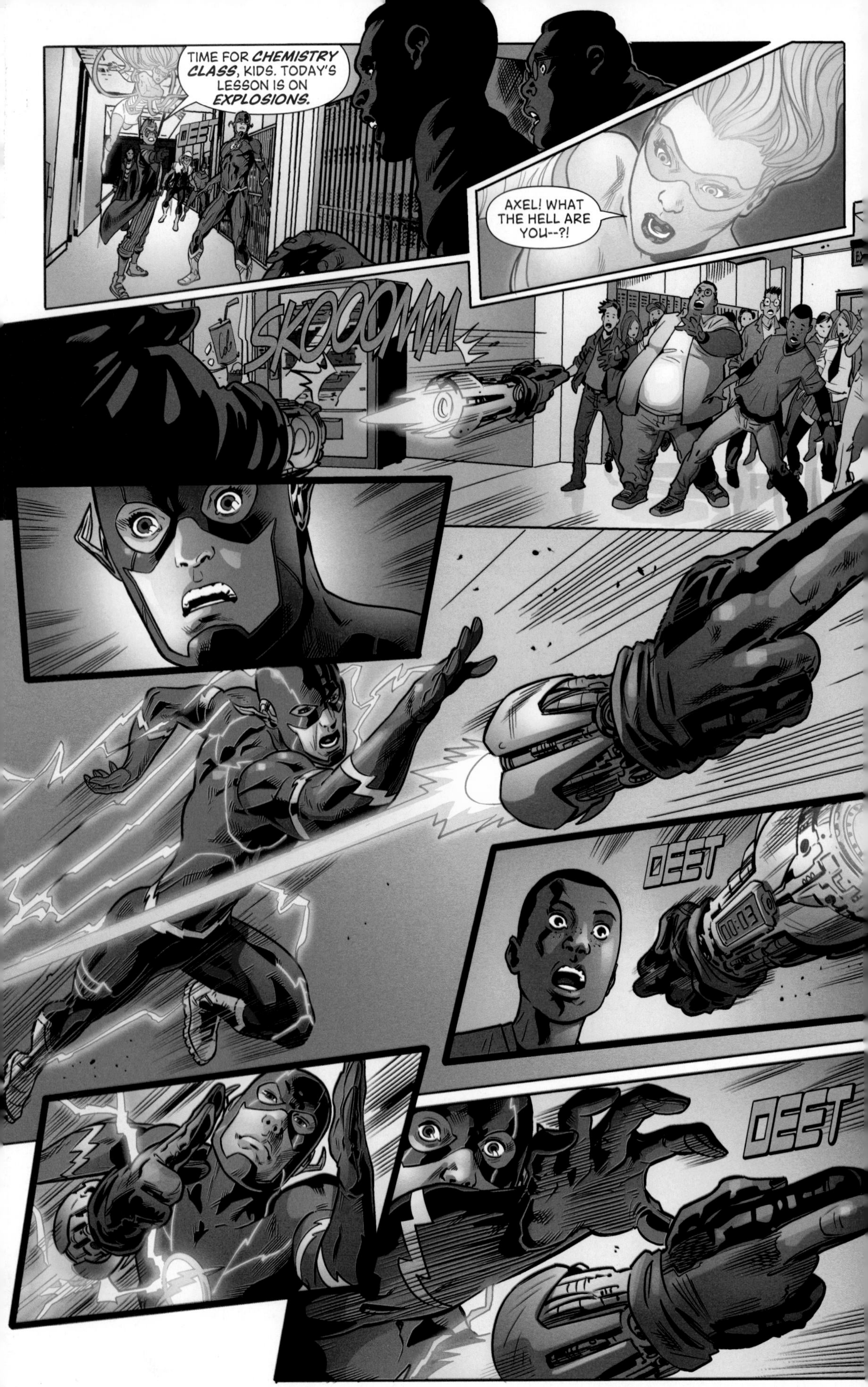
TIME FOR CHEMISTRY CLASS, KIDS. TODAY'S LESSON IS ON EXPLOSIONS.
DEET
AXEL! WHAT THE HELL ARE YOU--?!
SKOOOMM
DEET
00:03
DEET

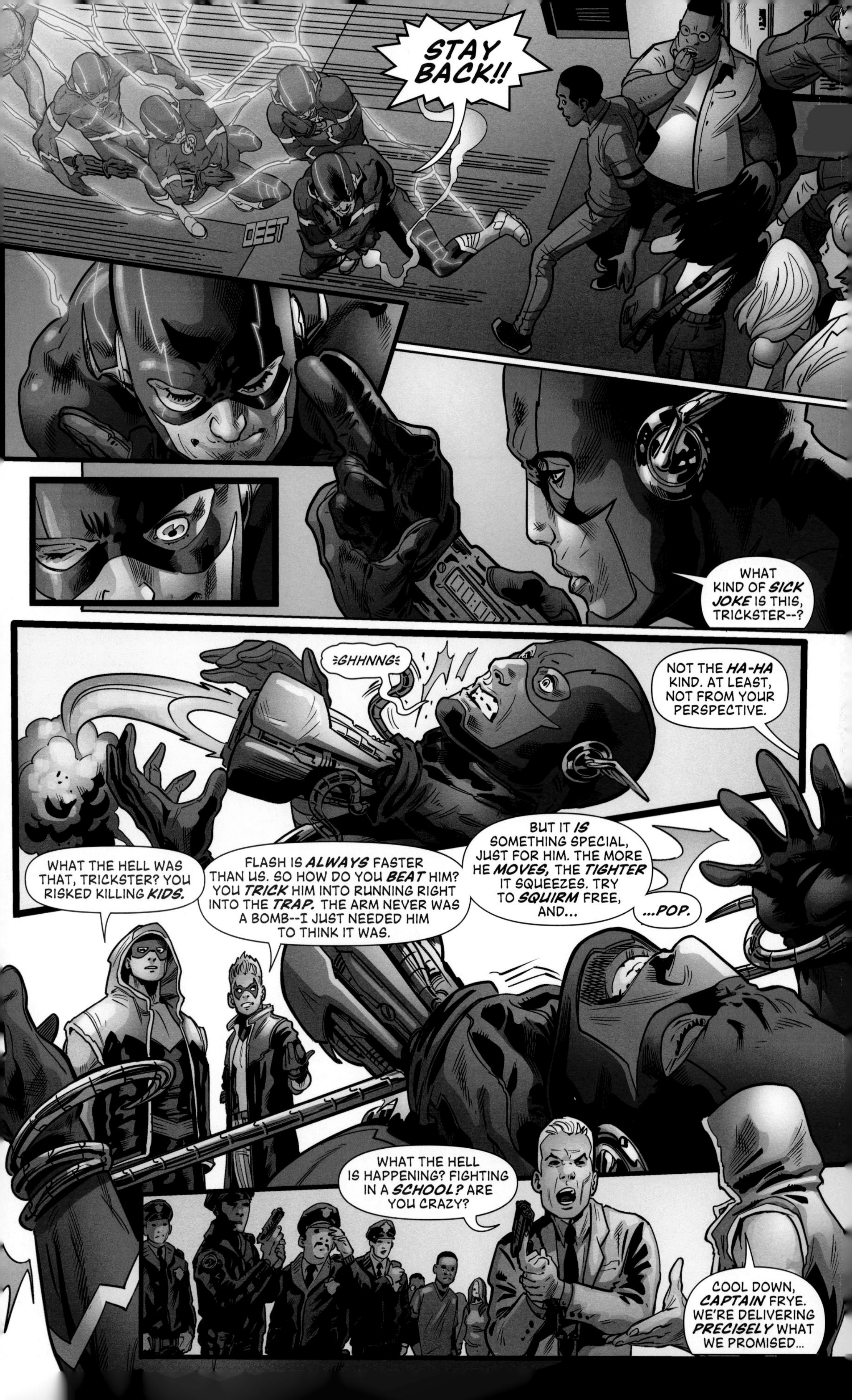
STAY BACK!!
BEEP
WHAT KIND OF SICK JOKE IS THIS, TRICKSTER--?
GHHNNG
NOT THE HA-HA KIND. AT LEAST, NOT FROM YOUR PERSPECTIVE.
WHAT THE HELL WAS THAT, TRICKSTER? YOU RISKED KILLING KIDS.
FLASH IS ALWAYS FASTER THAN US. SO HOW DO YOU BEAT HIM? YOU TRICK HIM INTO RUNNING RIGHT INTO THE TRAP. THE ARM NEVER WAS A BOMB--I JUST NEEDED HIM TO THINK IT WAS.
BUT IT IS SOMETHING SPECIAL, JUST FOR HIM. THE MORE HE MOVES, THE TIGHTER IT SQUEEZES. TRY TO SQUIRM FREE, AND...
...POP.
WHAT THE HELL IS HAPPENING? FIGHTING IN A SCHOOL? ARE YOU CRAZY?
COOL DOWN, CAPTAIN FRYE. WE'RE DELIVERING PRECISELY WHAT WE PROMISED...

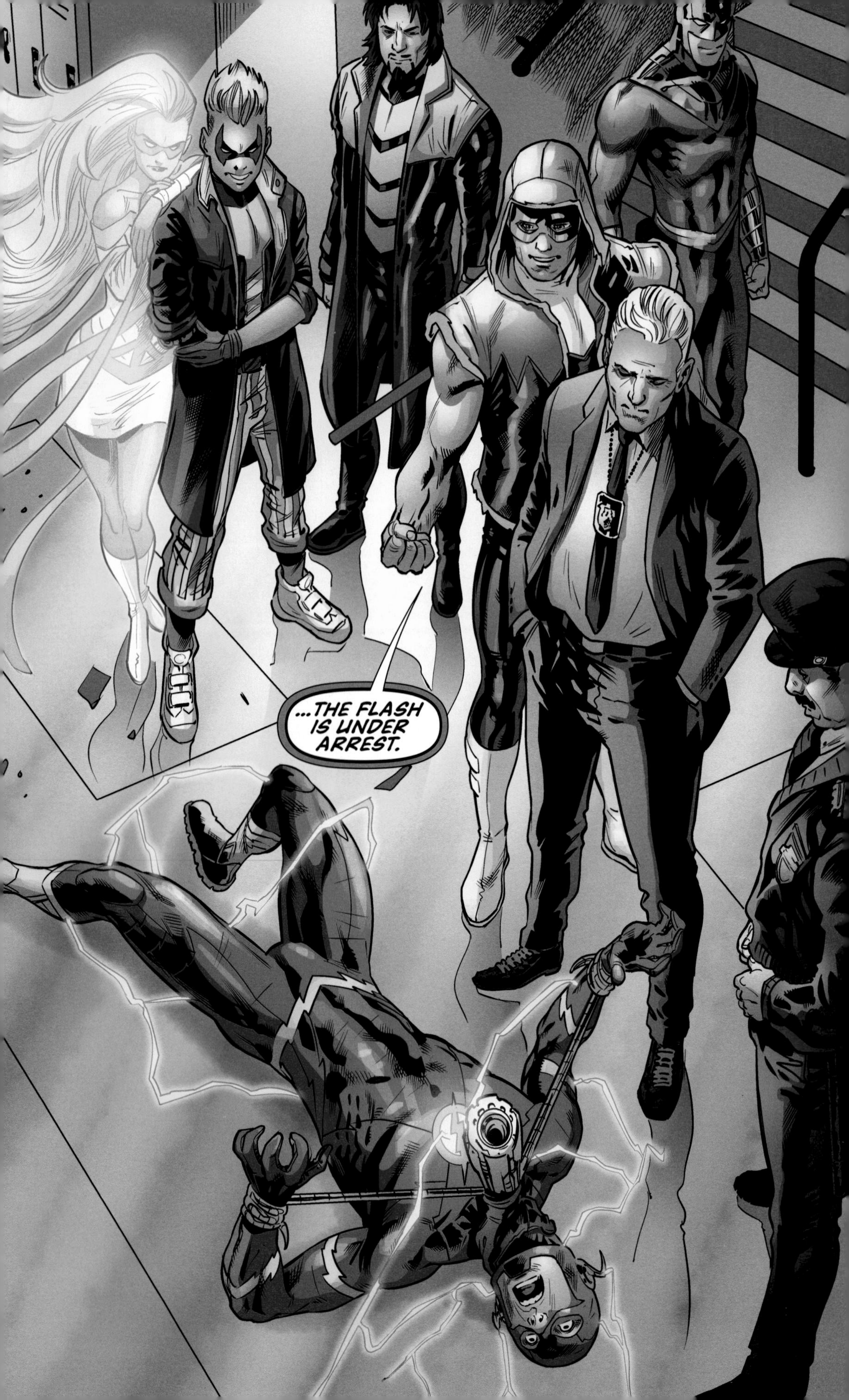
...THE FLASH IS UNDER ARREST.

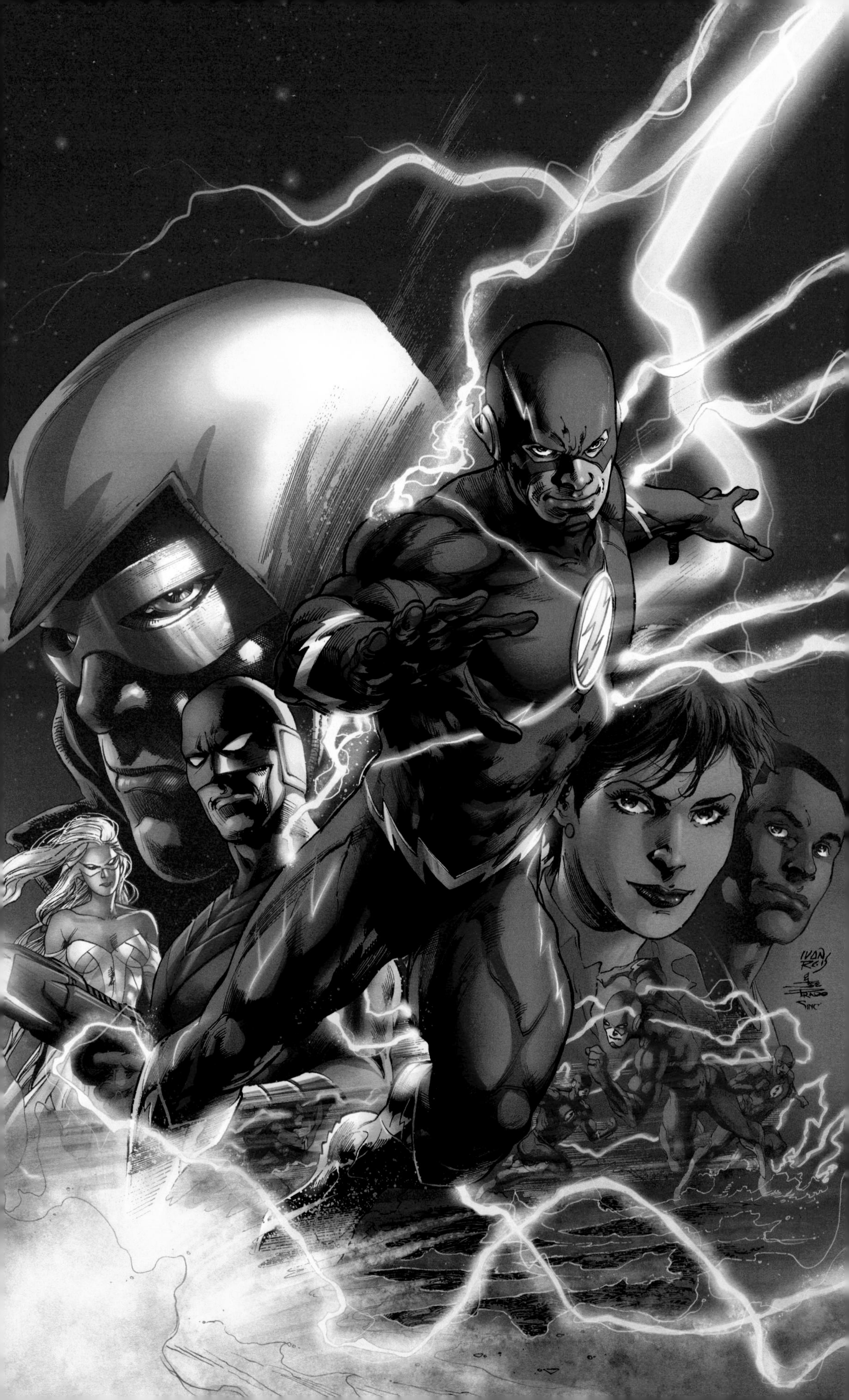

YOU'RE UNDER ARREST

VAN JENSEN writer **JESÚS MERINO PAUL PELLETIER** pencillers **JESÚS MERINO SCOTT HANNA TONY KORDOS WAYNE FAUCHER** inkers **GUY MAJOR PETE PANTAZIS** colorists **PAT BROSSEAU** letterer **IVAN REIS JOE PRADO ALEX SINCLAIR** cover

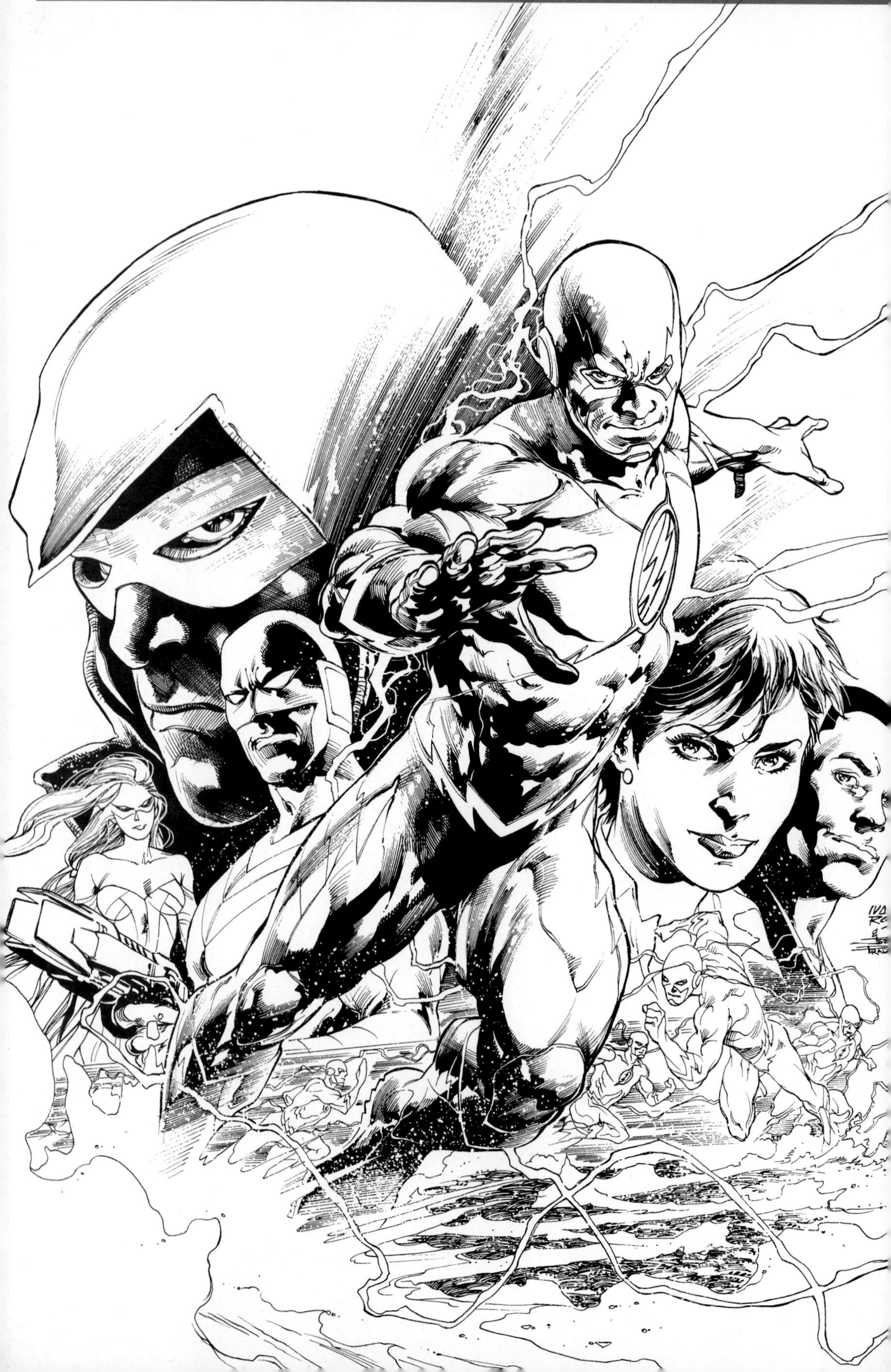

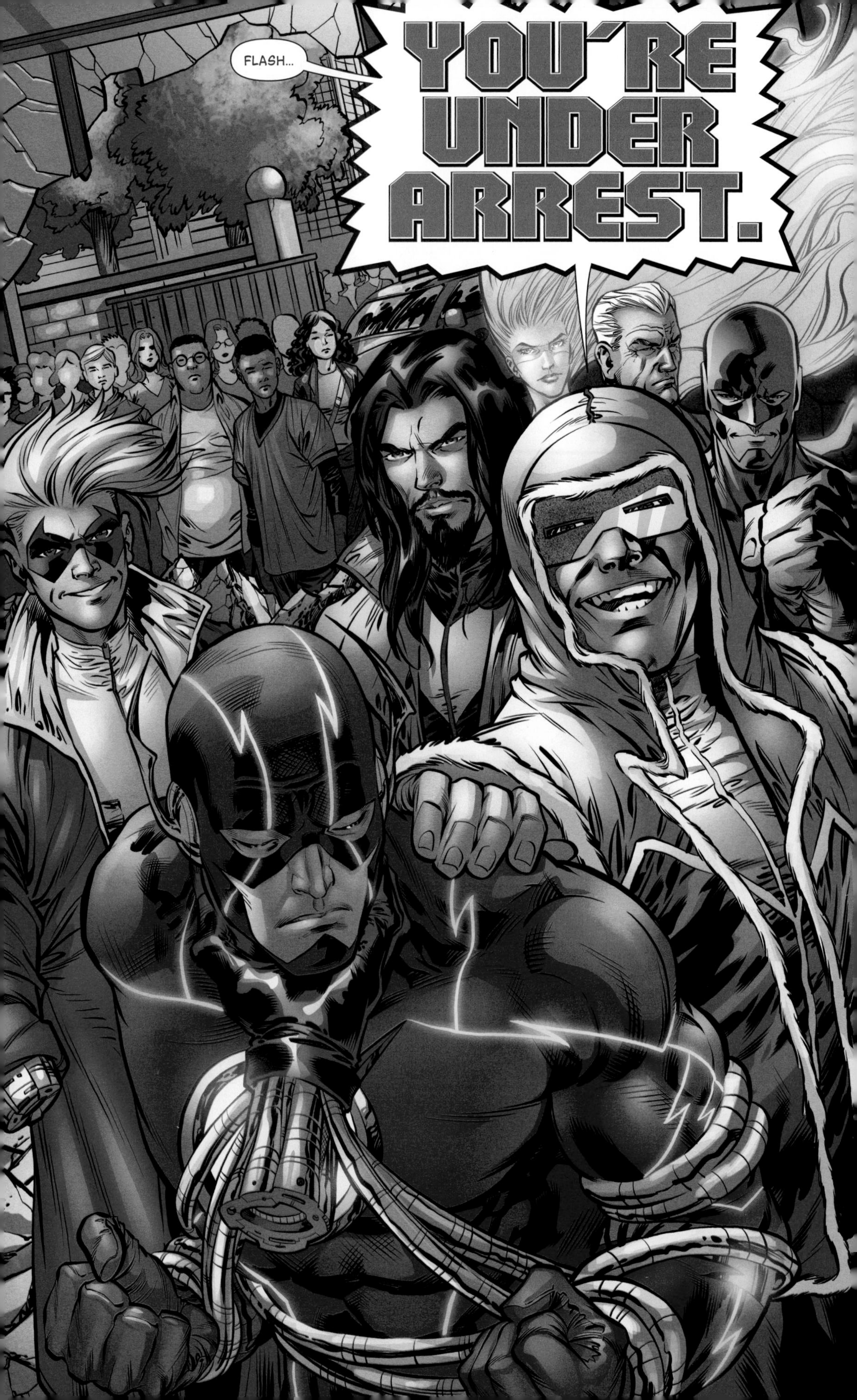
FLASH...
YOU'RE UNDER ARREST.

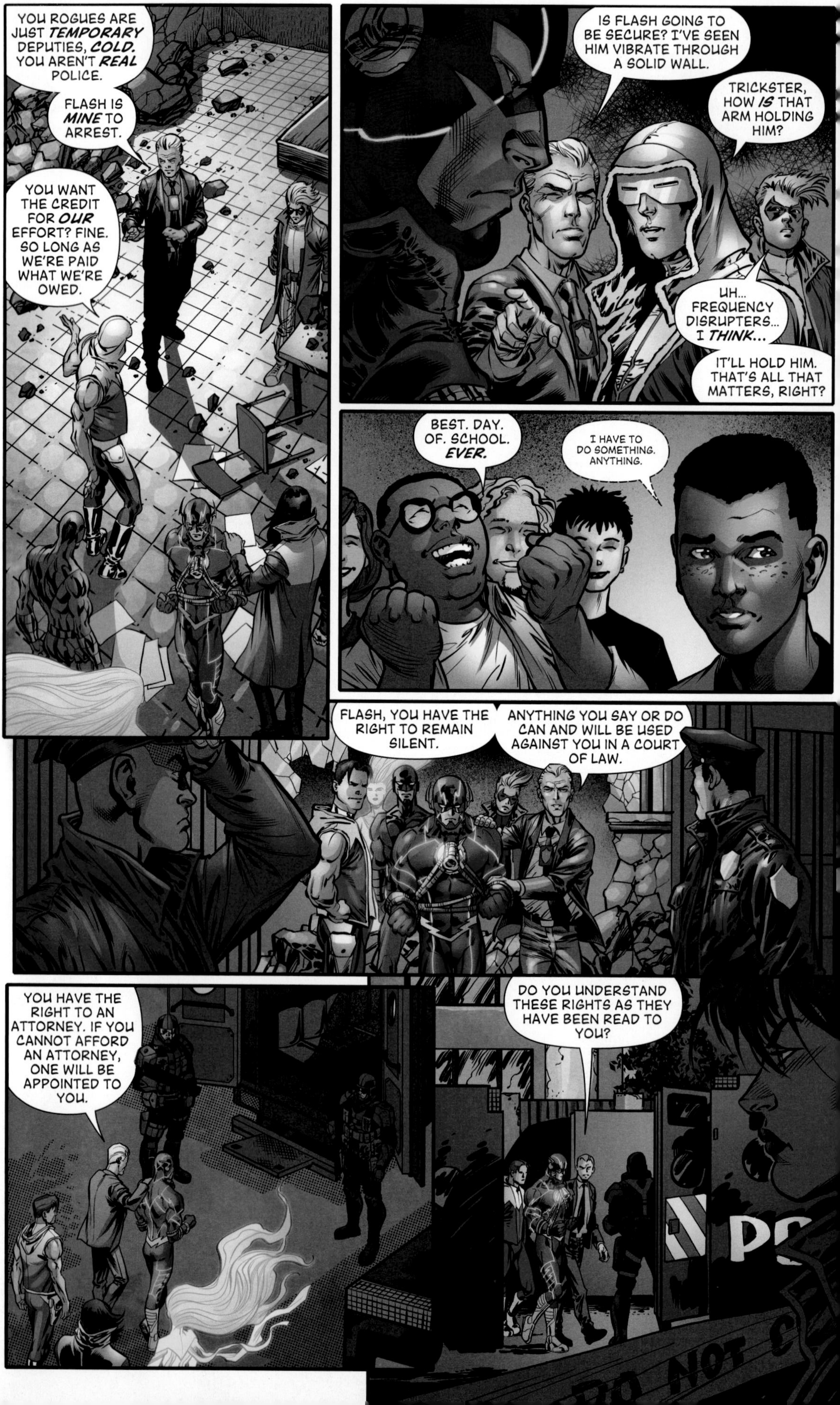
YOU ROGUES ARE JUST TEMPORARY DEPUTIES, COLD. YOU AREN'T REAL POLICE.
FLASH IS MINE TO ARREST.
YOU WANT THE CREDIT FOR OUR EFFORT? FINE. SO LONG AS WE'RE PAID WHAT WE'RE OWED.
IS FLASH GOING TO BE SECURE? I'VE SEEN HIM VIBRATE THROUGH A SOLID WALL.
TRICKSTER, HOW IS THAT ARM HOLDING HIM?
UH... FREQUENCY DISRUPTERS... I THINK...
IT'LL HOLD HIM. THAT'S ALL THAT MATTERS, RIGHT?
BEST. DAY. OF. SCHOOL. EVER.
I HAVE TO DO SOMETHING. ANYTHING.
FLASH, YOU HAVE THE RIGHT TO REMAIN SILENT.
ANYTHING YOU SAY OR DO CAN AND WILL BE USED AGAINST YOU IN A COURT OF LAW.
YOU HAVE THE RIGHT TO AN ATTORNEY. IF YOU CANNOT AFFORD AN ATTORNEY, ONE WILL BE APPOINTED TO YOU.
DO YOU UNDERSTAND THESE RIGHTS AS THEY HAVE BEEN READ TO YOU?

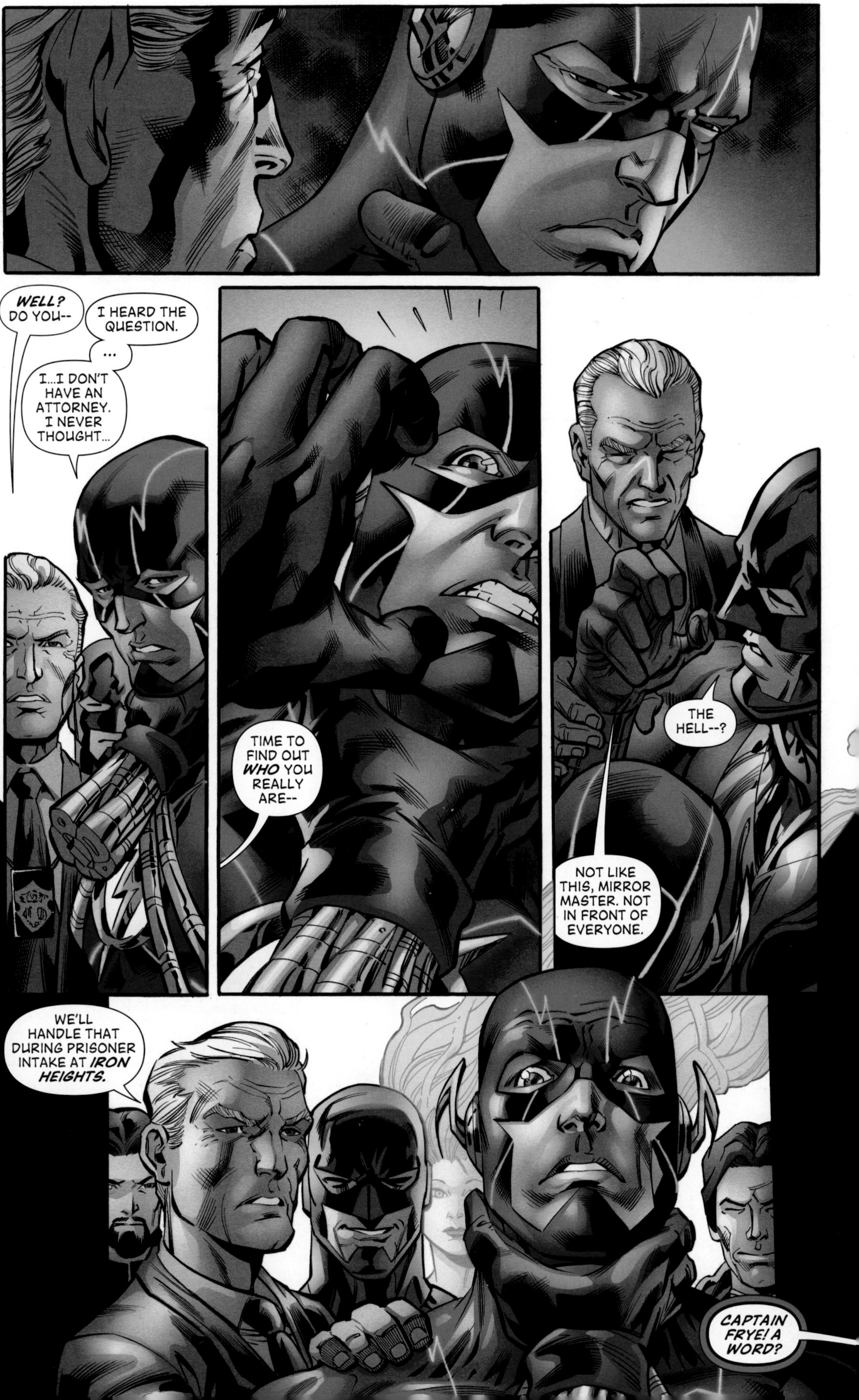
WELL? DO YOU--
I HEARD THE QUESTION.
...
I...I DON'T HAVE AN ATTORNEY. I NEVER THOUGHT...
TIME TO FIND OUT WHO YOU REALLY ARE--
THE HELL--?
NOT LIKE THIS, MIRROR MASTER. NOT IN FRONT OF EVERYONE.
WE'LL HANDLE THAT DURING PRISONER INTAKE AT IRON HEIGHTS.
CAPTAIN FRYE! A WORD?

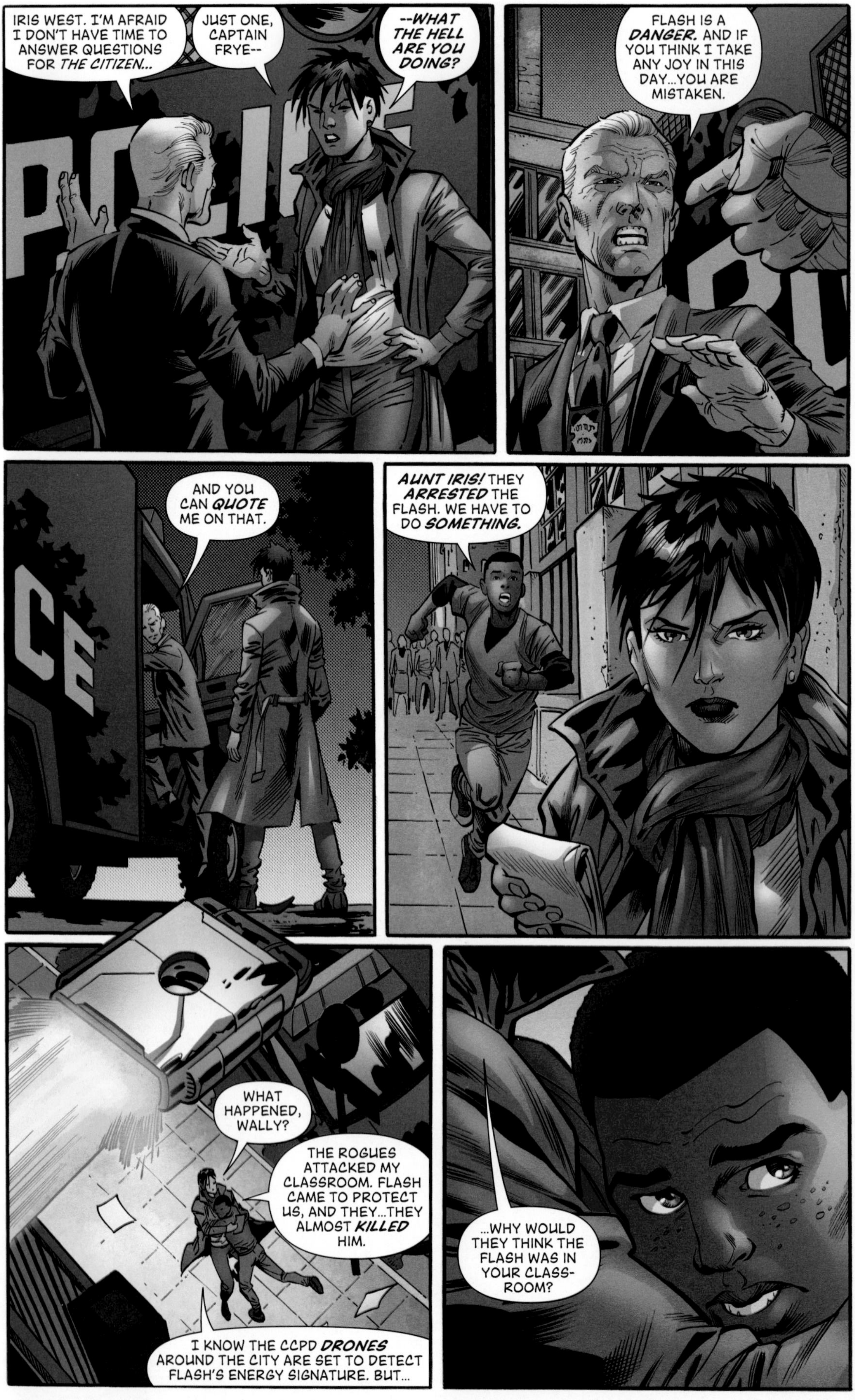
IRIS WEST. I'M AFRAID I DON'T HAVE TIME TO ANSWER QUESTIONS FOR THE CITIZEN...
JUST ONE, CAPTAIN FRYE--
--WHAT THE HELL ARE YOU DOING?
FLASH IS A DANGER. AND IF YOU THINK I TAKE ANY JOY IN THIS DAY...YOU ARE MISTAKEN.
AND YOU CAN QUOTE ME ON THAT.
AUNT IRIS! THEY ARRESTED THE FLASH. WE HAVE TO DO SOMETHING.
WHAT HAPPENED, WALLY?
THE ROGUES ATTACKED MY CLASSROOM. FLASH CAME TO PROTECT US, AND THEY...THEY ALMOST KILLED HIM.
I KNOW THE CCPD DRONES AROUND THE CITY ARE SET TO DETECT FLASH'S ENERGY SIGNATURE. BUT...
...WHY WOULD THEY THINK THE FLASH WAS IN YOUR CLASS-ROOM?

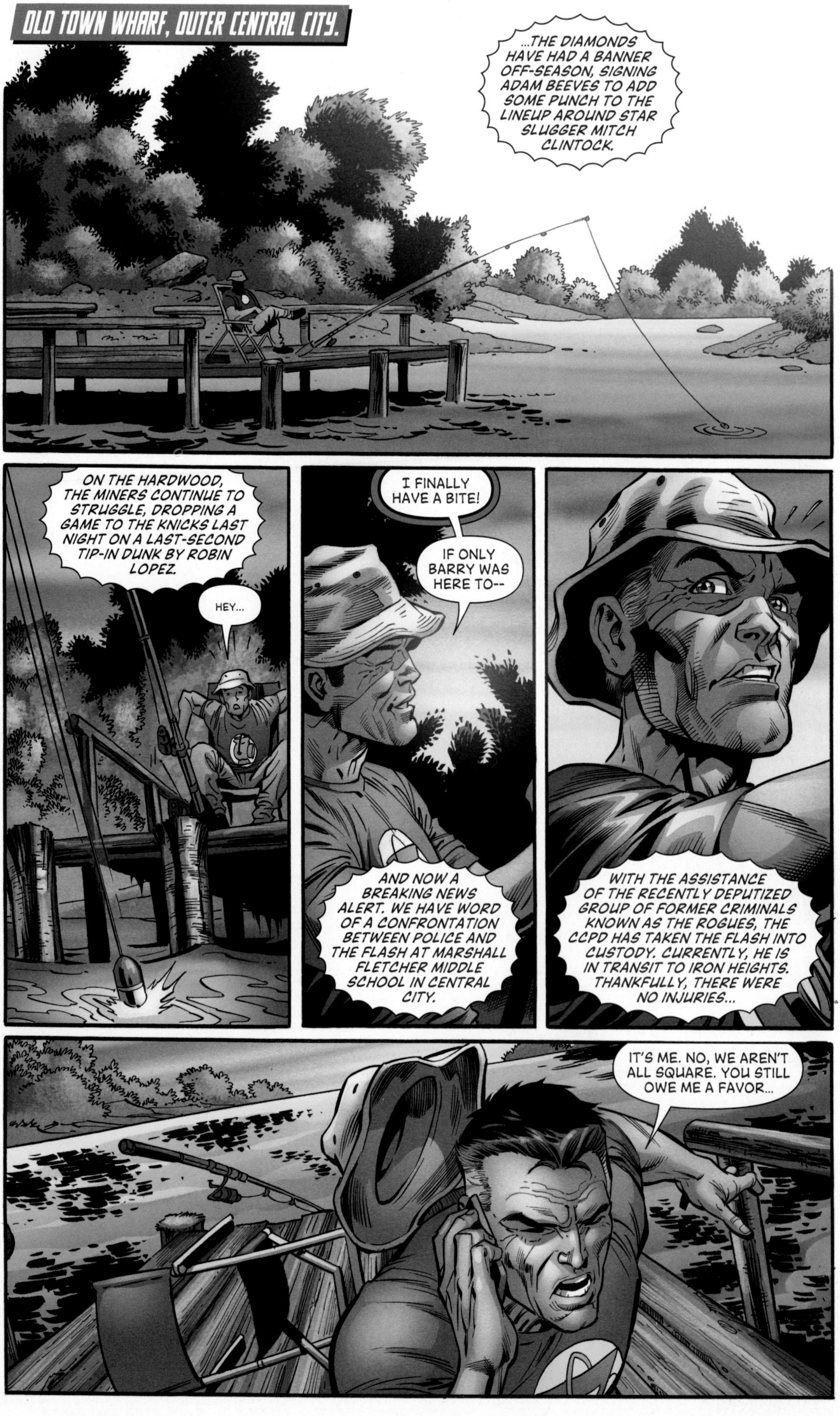

OLD TOWN WHARF, OUTER CENTRAL CITY.
...THE DIAMONDS HAVE HAD A BANNER OFF-SEASON, SIGNING ADAM BEEVES TO ADD SOME PUNCH TO THE LINEUP AROUND STAR SLUGGER MITCH CLINTOCK.
ON THE HARDWOOD, THE MINERS CONTINUE TO STRUGGLE, DROPPING A GAME TO THE KNICKS LAST NIGHT ON A LAST-SECOND TIP-IN DUNK BY ROBIN LOPEZ.
HEY...
I FINALLY HAVE A BITE!
IF ONLY BARRY WAS HERE TO--
AND NOW A BREAKING NEWS ALERT. WE HAVE WORD OF A CONFRONTATION BETWEEN POLICE AND THE FLASH AT MARSHALL FLETCHER MIDDLE SCHOOL IN CENTRAL CITY.
WITH THE ASSISTANCE OF THE RECENTLY DEPUTIZED GROUP OF FORMER CRIMINALS KNOWN AS THE ROGUES, THE CCPD HAS TAKEN THE FLASH INTO CUSTODY. CURRENTLY, HE IS IN TRANSIT TO IRON HEIGHTS. THANKFULLY, THERE WERE NO INJURIES...
IT'S ME. NO, WE AREN'T ALL SQUARE. YOU STILL OWE ME A FAVOR...

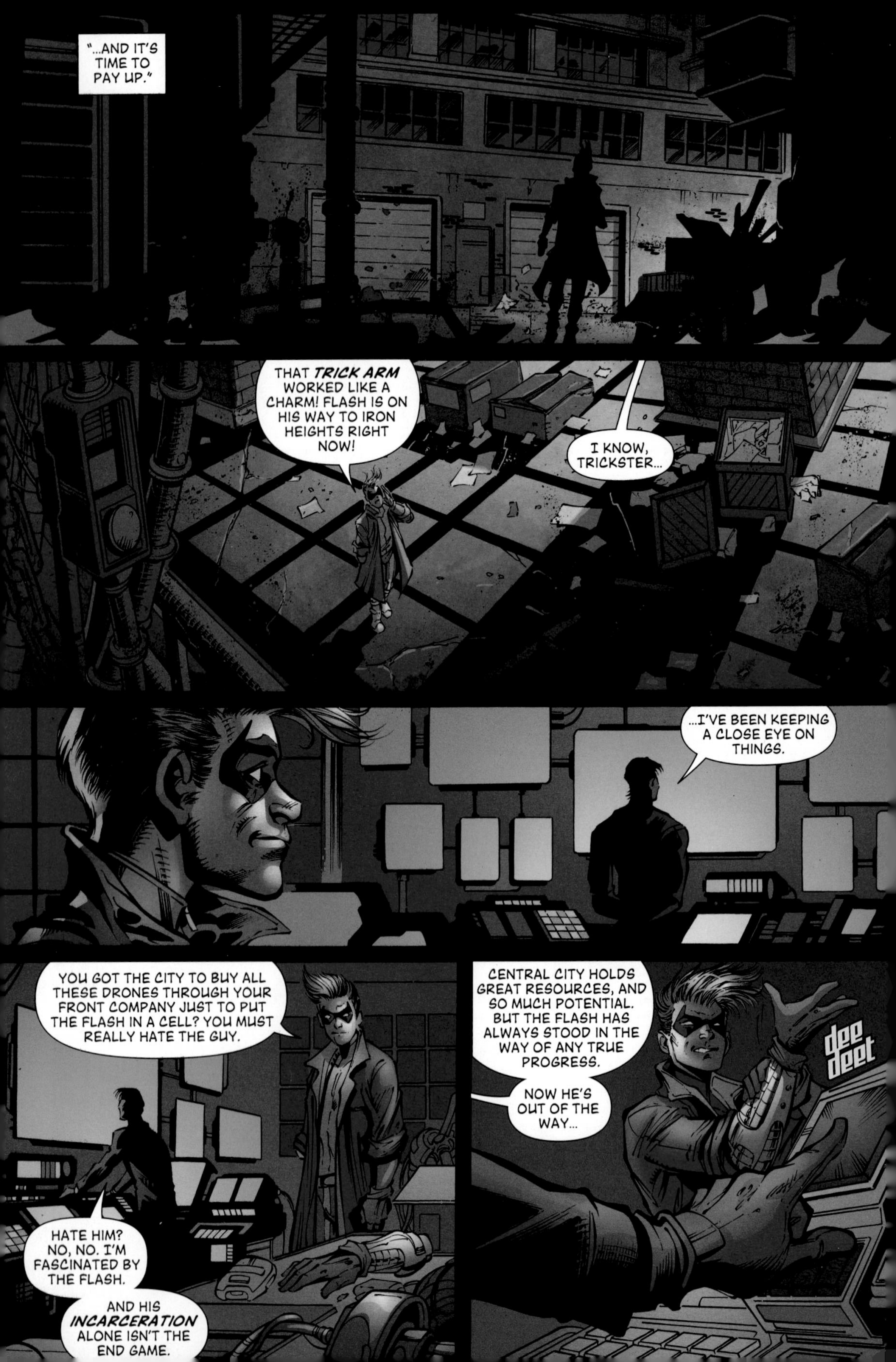
"...AND IT'S TIME TO PAY UP."
THAT TRICK ARM WORKED LIKE A CHARM! FLASH IS ON HIS WAY TO IRON HEIGHTS RIGHT NOW!
I KNOW, TRICKSTER...
...I'VE BEEN KEEPING A CLOSE EYE ON THINGS.
YOU GOT THE CITY TO BUY ALL THESE DRONES THROUGH YOUR FRONT COMPANY JUST TO PUT THE FLASH IN A CELL? YOU MUST REALLY HATE THE GUY.
HATE HIM? NO, NO. I'M FASCINATED BY THE FLASH.
AND HIS INCARCERATION ALONE ISN'T THE END GAME.
CENTRAL CITY HOLDS GREAT RESOURCES, AND SO MUCH POTENTIAL. BUT THE FLASH HAS ALWAYS STOOD IN THE WAY OF ANY TRUE PROGRESS.
NOW HE'S OUT OF THE WAY...
dee deet

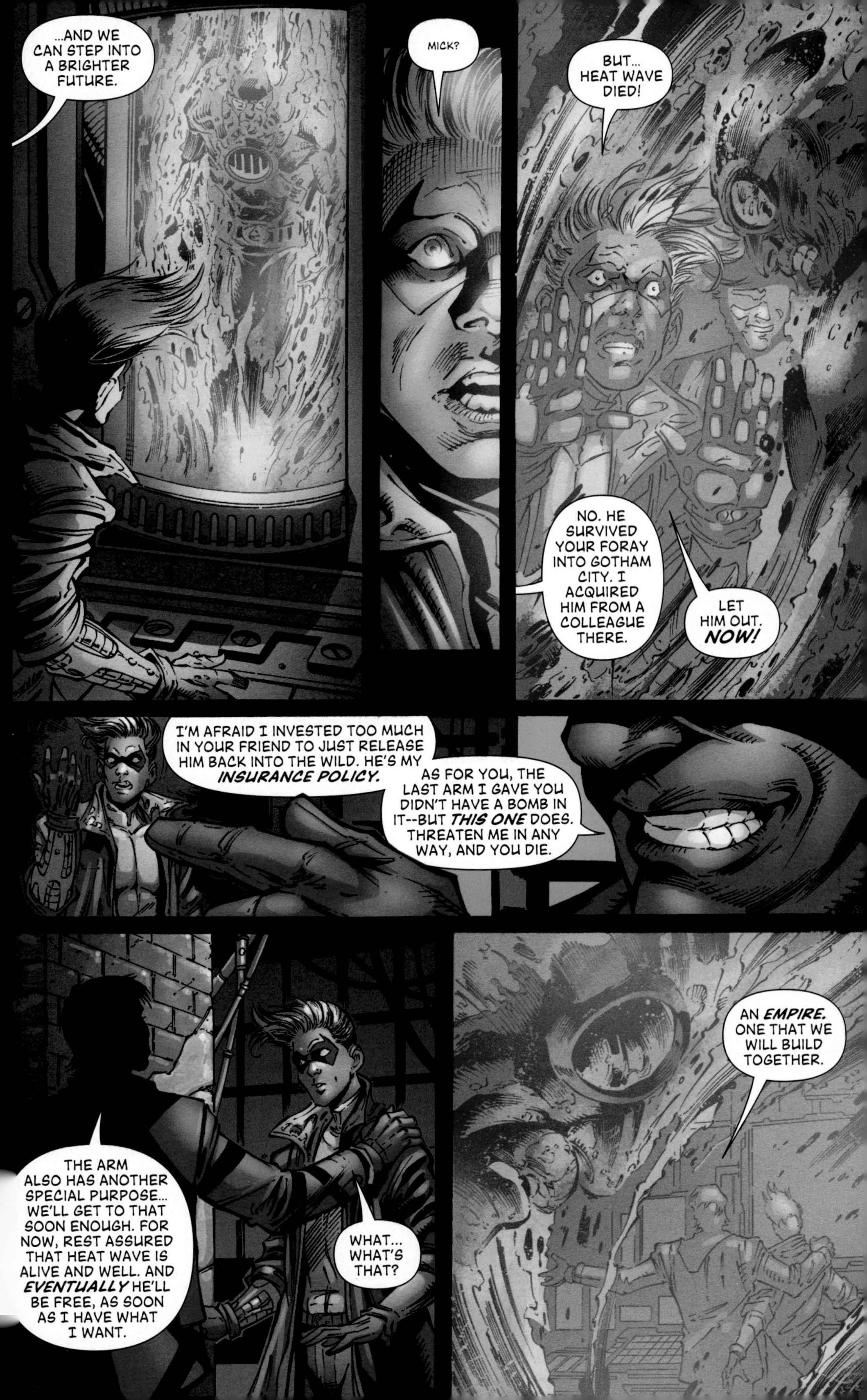
...AND WE CAN STEP INTO A BRIGHTER FUTURE.
MICK?
BUT... HEAT WAVE DIED!
NO. HE SURVIVED YOUR FORAY INTO GOTHAM CITY. I ACQUIRED HIM FROM A COLLEAGUE THERE.
LET HIM OUT. NOW!
I'M AFRAID I INVESTED TOO MUCH IN YOUR FRIEND TO JUST RELEASE HIM BACK INTO THE WILD. HE'S MY INSURANCE POLICY.
AS FOR YOU, THE LAST ARM I GAVE YOU DIDN'T HAVE A BOMB IN IT--BUT THIS ONE DOES. THREATEN ME IN ANY WAY, AND YOU DIE.
THE ARM ALSO HAS ANOTHER SPECIAL PURPOSE... WE'LL GET TO THAT SOON ENOUGH. FOR NOW, REST ASSURED THAT HEAT WAVE IS ALIVE AND WELL. AND EVENTUALLY HE'LL BE FREE, AS SOON AS I HAVE WHAT I WANT.
WHAT... WHAT'S THAT?
AN EMPIRE. ONE THAT WE WILL BUILD TOGETHER.

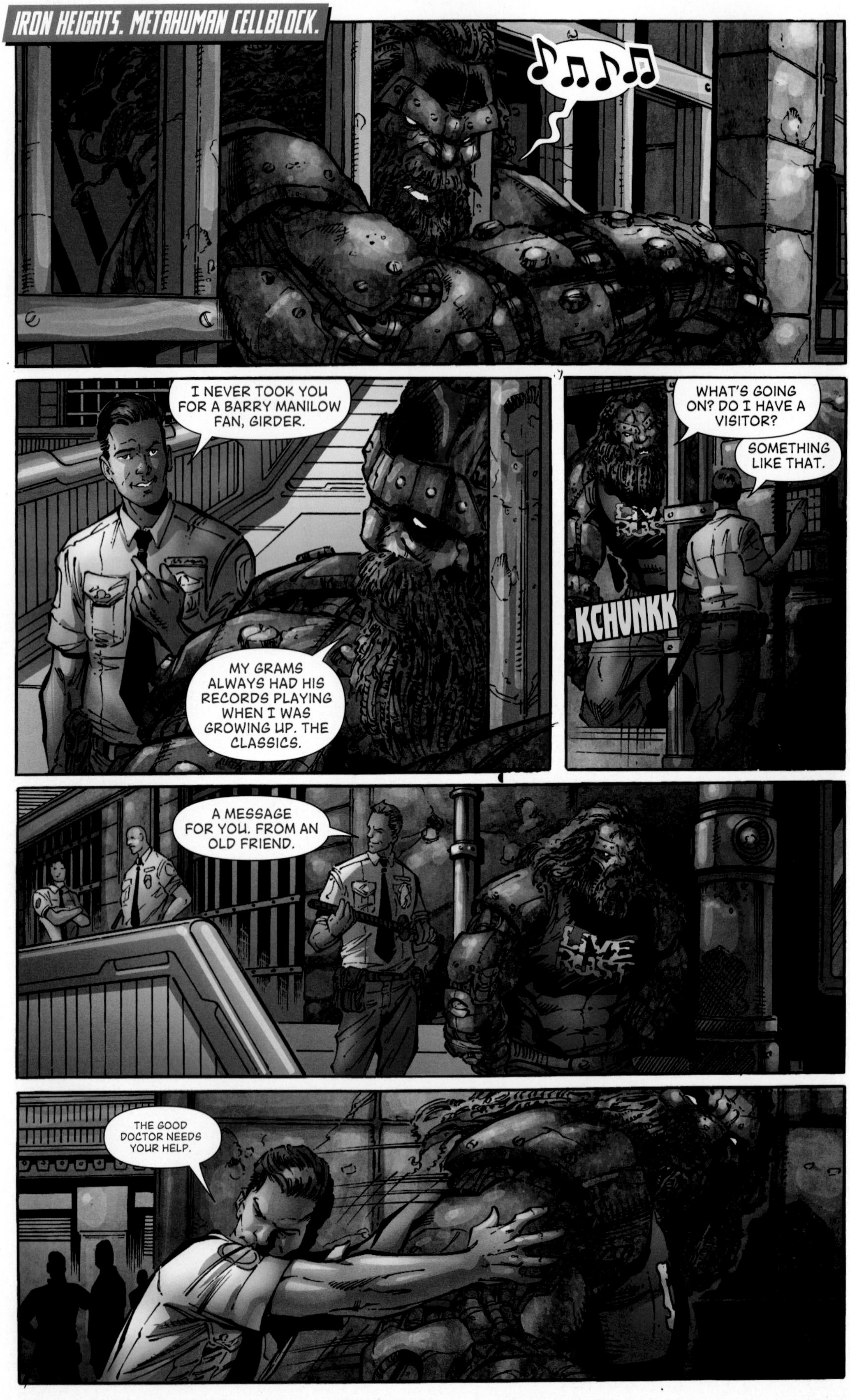
IRON HEIGHTS. METAHUMAN CELLBLOCK.
I NEVER TOOK YOU FOR A BARRY MANILOW FAN, GIRDER.
MY GRAMS ALWAYS HAD HIS RECORDS PLAYING WHEN I WAS GROWING UP. THE CLASSICS.
WHAT'S GOING ON? DO I HAVE A VISITOR?
SOMETHING LIKE THAT.
KCHUNKK
A MESSAGE FOR YOU. FROM AN OLD FRIEND.
THE GOOD DOCTOR NEEDS YOUR HELP.

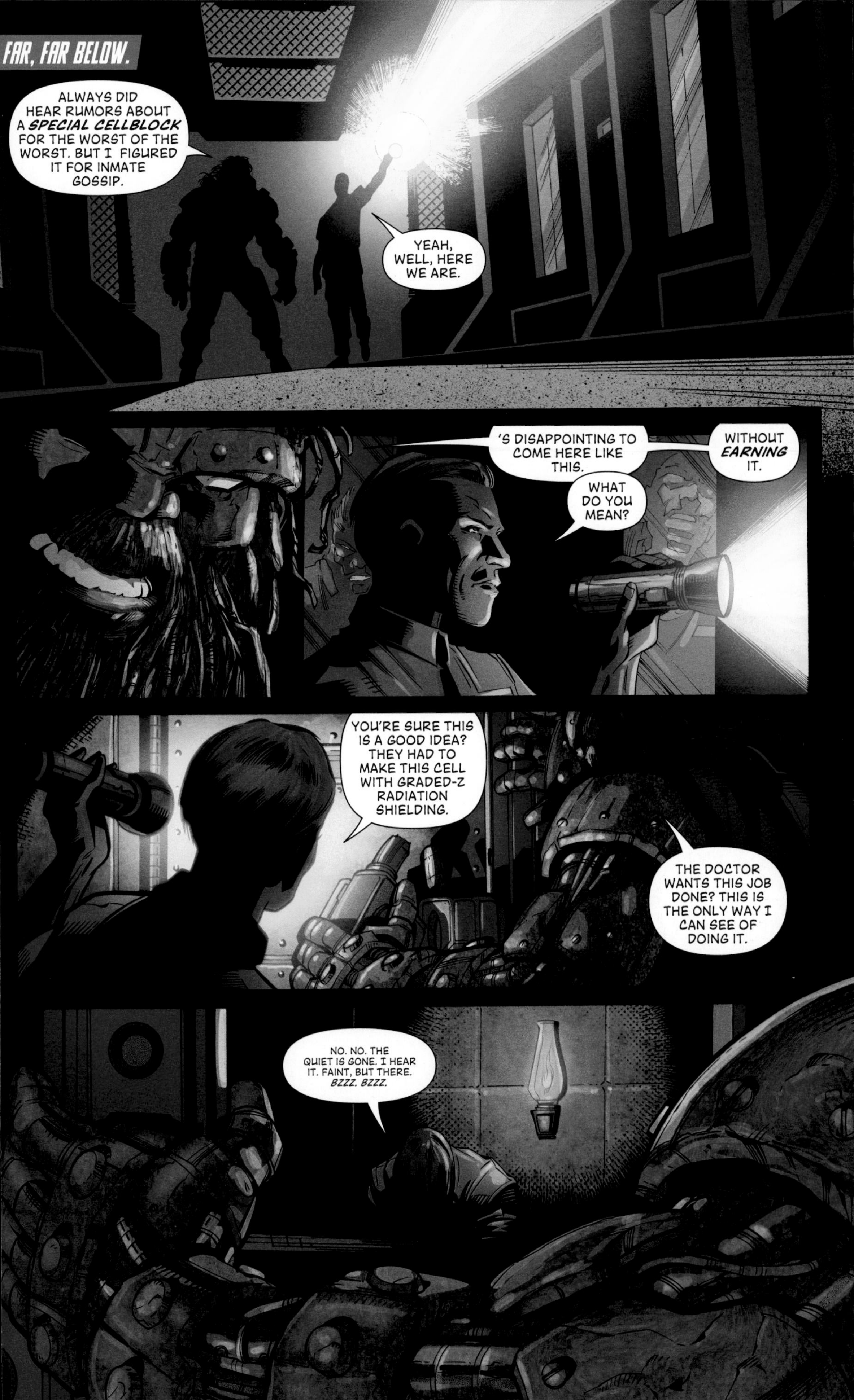
FAR, FAR BELOW.
ALWAYS DID HEAR RUMORS ABOUT A SPECIAL CELLBLOCK FOR THE WORST OF THE WORST. BUT I FIGURED IT FOR INMATE GOSSIP.
YEAH, WELL, HERE WE ARE.
'S DISAPPOINTING TO COME HERE LIKE THIS.
WITHOUT EARNING IT.
WHAT DO YOU MEAN?
YOU'RE SURE THIS IS A GOOD IDEA? THEY HAD TO MAKE THIS CELL WITH GRADED-Z RADIATION SHIELDING.
THE DOCTOR WANTS THIS JOB DONE? THIS IS THE ONLY WAY I CAN SEE OF DOING IT.
NO. NO. THE QUIET IS GONE. I HEAR IT. FAINT, BUT THERE. BZZZ. BZZZ.

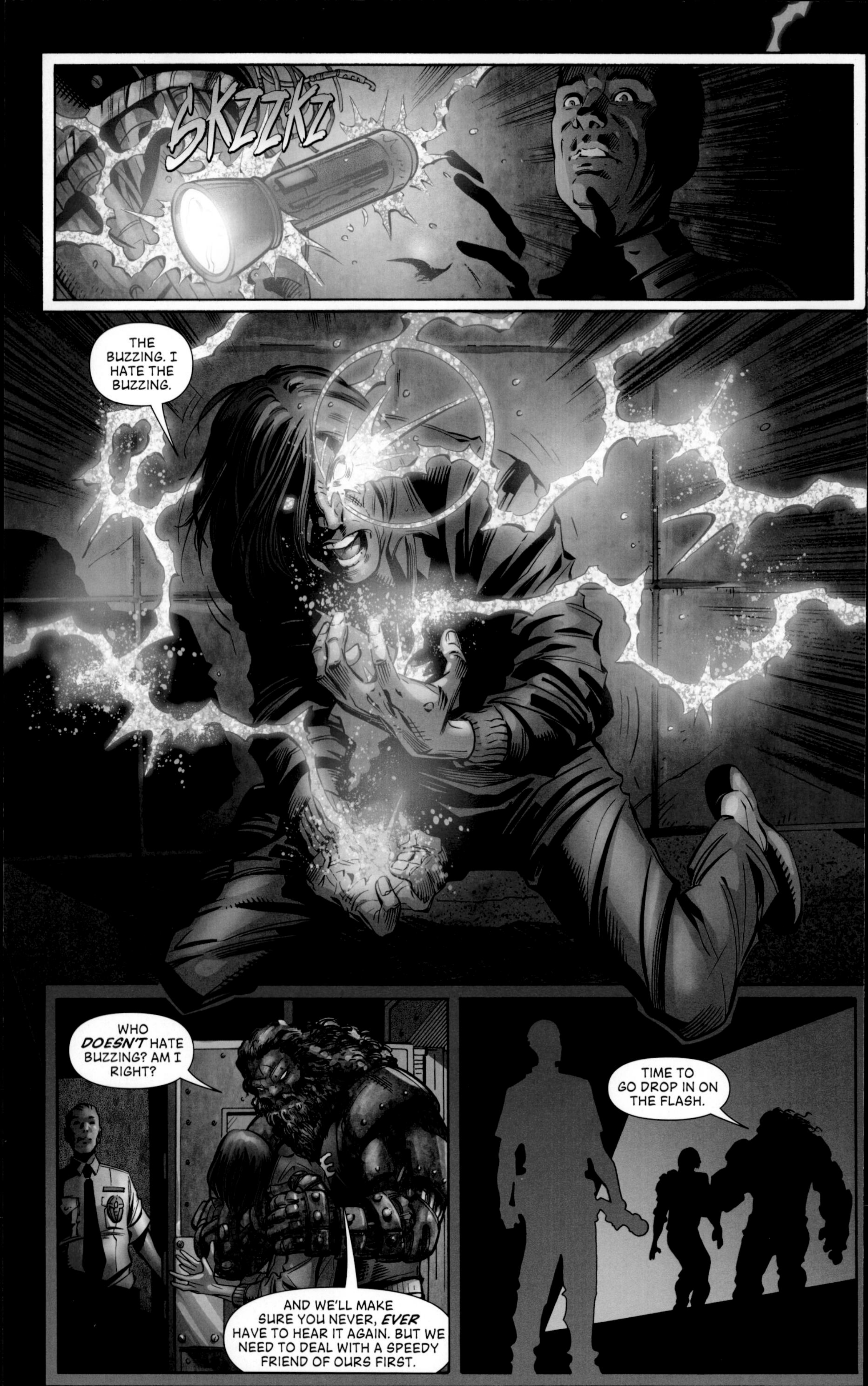
SKZZKZ
THE BUZZING. I HATE THE BUZZING.
WHO DOESN'T HATE BUZZING? AM I RIGHT?
AND WE'LL MAKE SURE YOU NEVER, EVER HAVE TO HEAR IT AGAIN. BUT WE NEED TO DEAL WITH A SPEEDY FRIEND OF OURS FIRST.
TIME TO GO DROP IN ON THE FLASH.

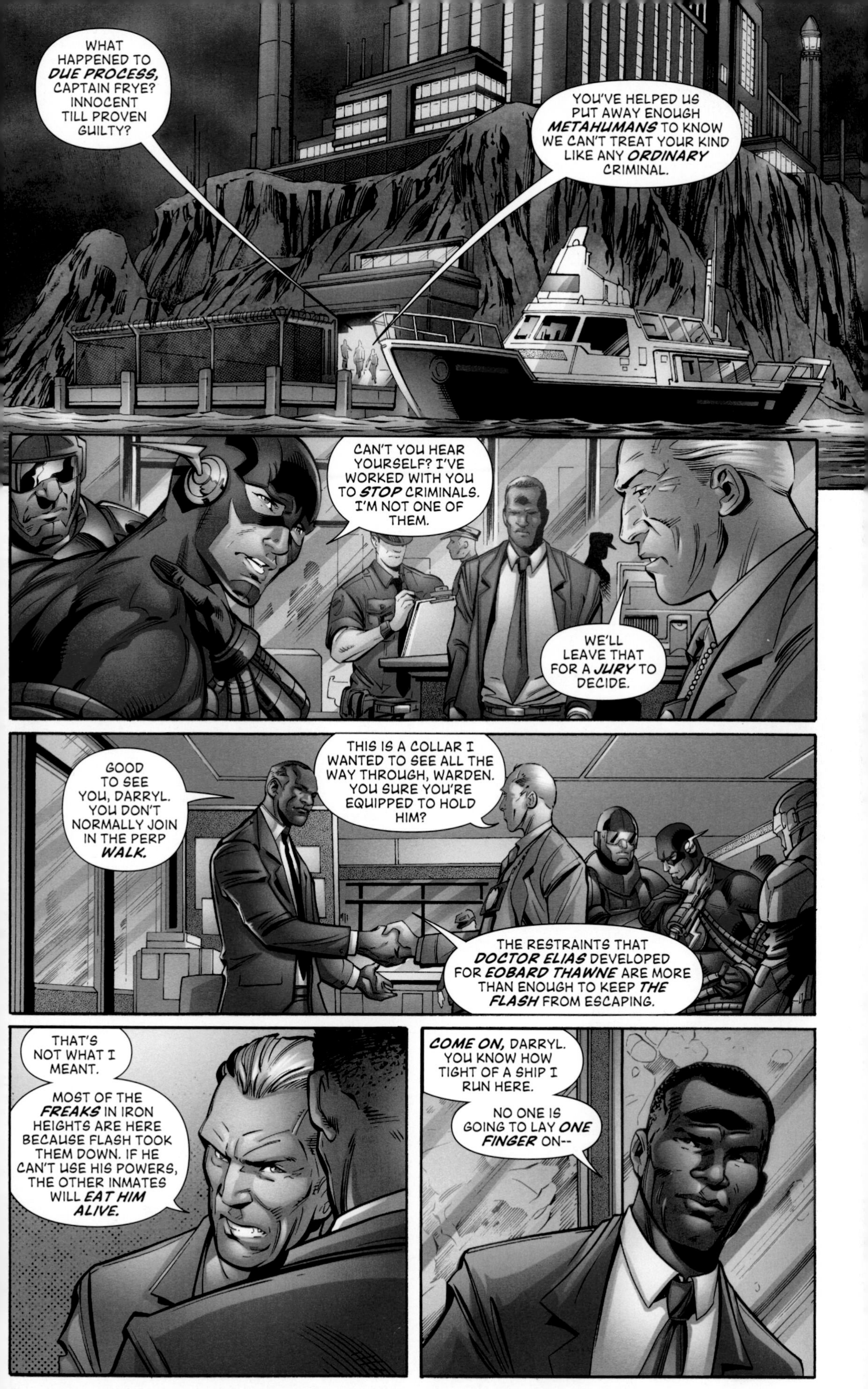

WHAT HAPPENED TO DUE PROCESS, CAPTAIN FRYE? INNOCENT TILL PROVEN GUILTY?
YOU'VE HELPED US PUT AWAY ENOUGH METAHUMANS TO KNOW WE CAN'T TREAT YOUR KIND LIKE ANY ORDINARY CRIMINAL.
CAN'T YOU HEAR YOURSELF? I'VE WORKED WITH YOU TO STOP CRIMINALS. I'M NOT ONE OF THEM.
WE'LL LEAVE THAT FOR A JURY TO DECIDE.
GOOD TO SEE YOU, DARRYL. YOU DON'T NORMALLY JOIN IN THE PERP WALK.
THIS IS A COLLAR I WANTED TO SEE ALL THE WAY THROUGH, WARDEN. YOU SURE YOU'RE EQUIPPED TO HOLD HIM?
THE RESTRAINTS THAT DOCTOR ELIAS DEVELOPED FOR EOBARD THAWNE ARE MORE THAN ENOUGH TO KEEP THE FLASH FROM ESCAPING.
THAT'S NOT WHAT I MEANT.
MOST OF THE FREAKS IN IRON HEIGHTS ARE HERE BECAUSE FLASH TOOK THEM DOWN. IF HE CAN'T USE HIS POWERS, THE OTHER INMATES WILL EAT HIM ALIVE.
COME ON, DARRYL. YOU KNOW HOW TIGHT OF A SHIP I RUN HERE.
NO ONE IS GOING TO LAY ONE FINGER ON--

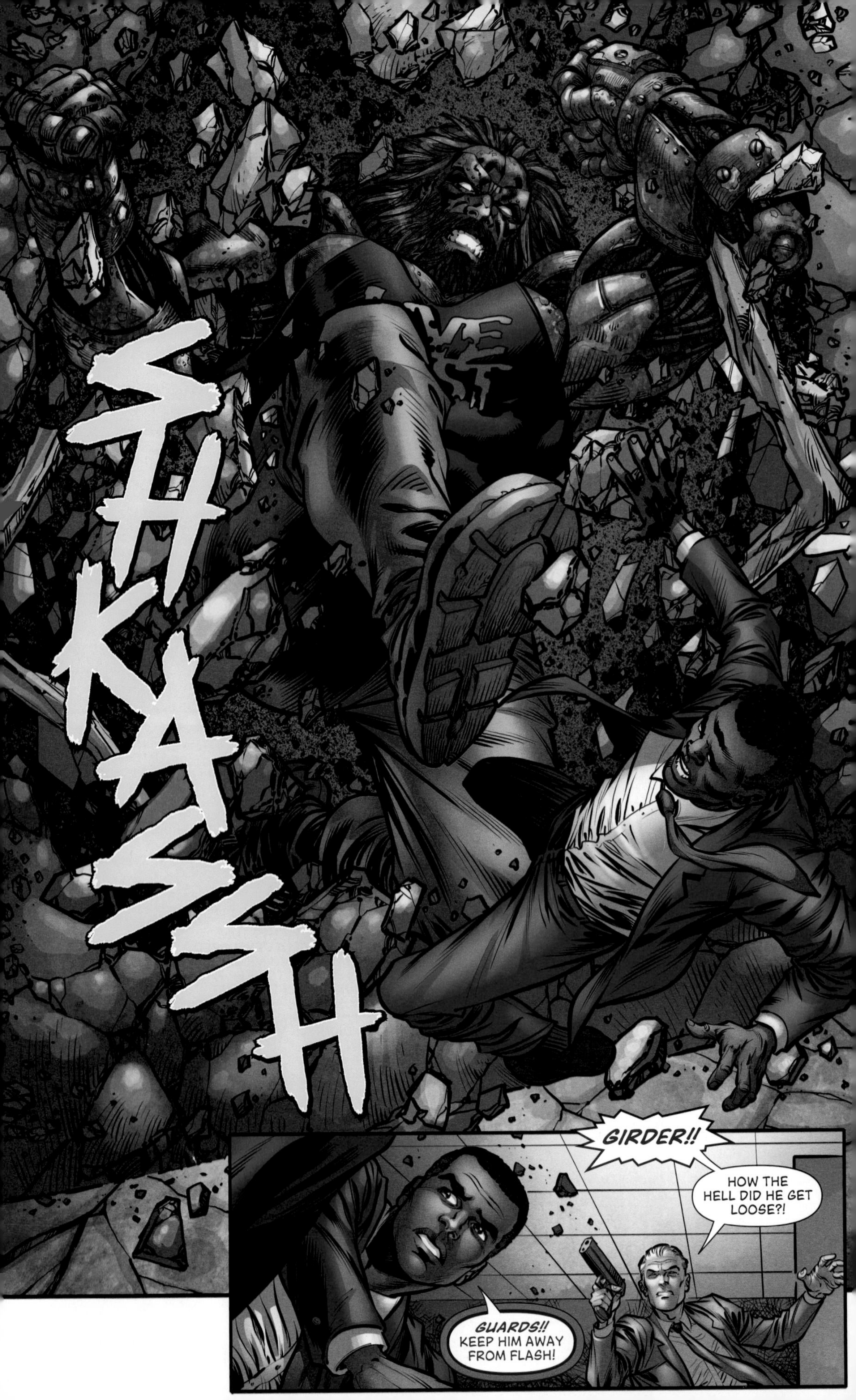
SHKASSH
GIRDER!!
HOW THE HELL DID HE GET LOOSE?!
GUARDS!! KEEP HIM AWAY FROM FLASH!

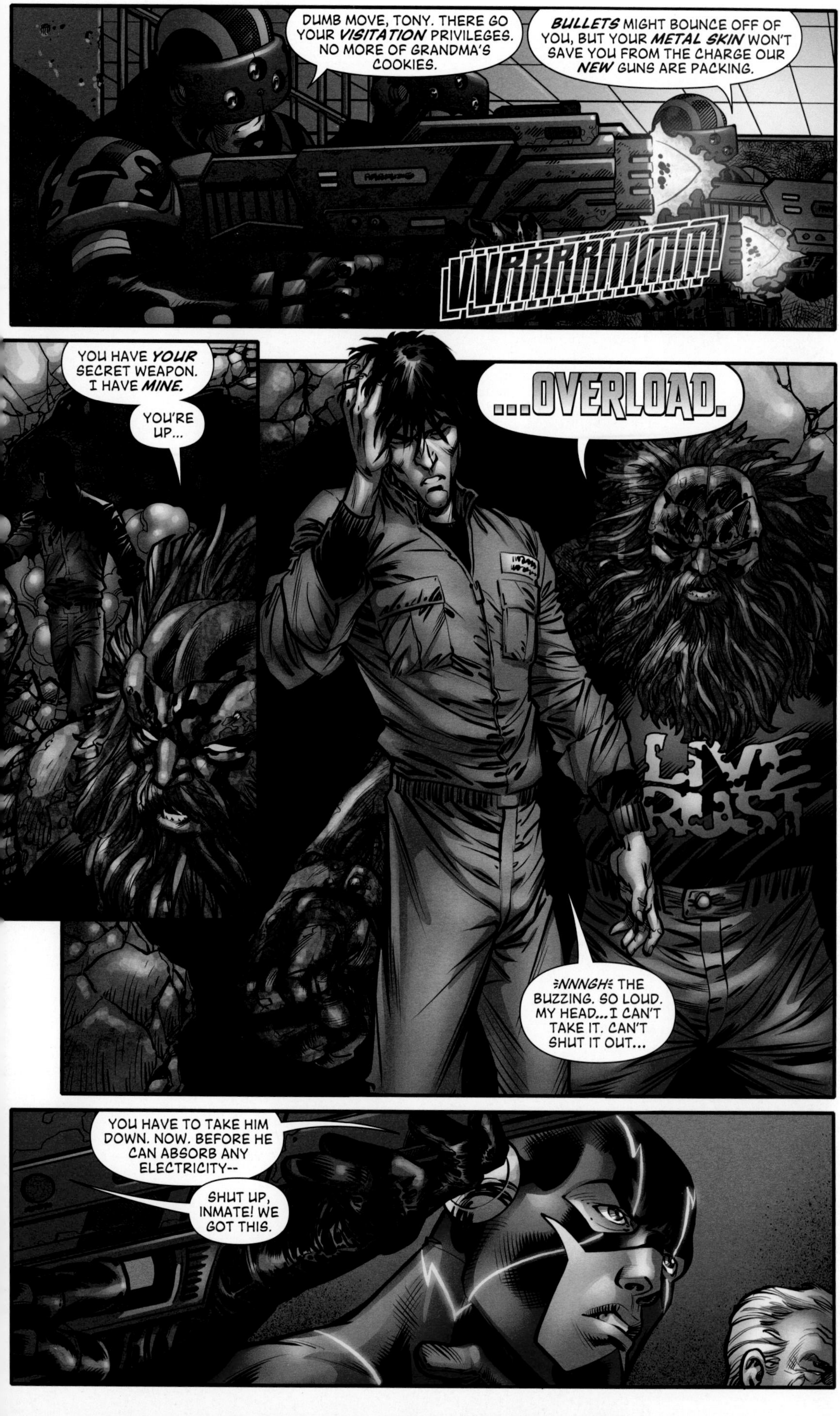
DUMB MOVE, TONY. THERE GO YOUR VISITATION PRIVILEGES. NO MORE OF GRANDMA'S COOKIES.
BULLETS MIGHT BOUNCE OFF OF YOU, BUT YOUR METAL SKIN WON'T SAVE YOU FROM THE CHARGE OUR NEW GUNS ARE PACKING.
VVRRRRMMMM
YOU HAVE YOUR SECRET WEAPON. I HAVE MINE.
YOU'RE UP...
...OVERLOAD.
LIVE RUST
NNNGH THE BUZZING. SO LOUD. MY HEAD...I CAN'T TAKE IT. CAN'T SHUT IT OUT...
YOU HAVE TO TAKE HIM DOWN. NOW. BEFORE HE CAN ABSORB ANY ELECTRICITY--
SHUT UP, INMATE! WE GOT THIS.

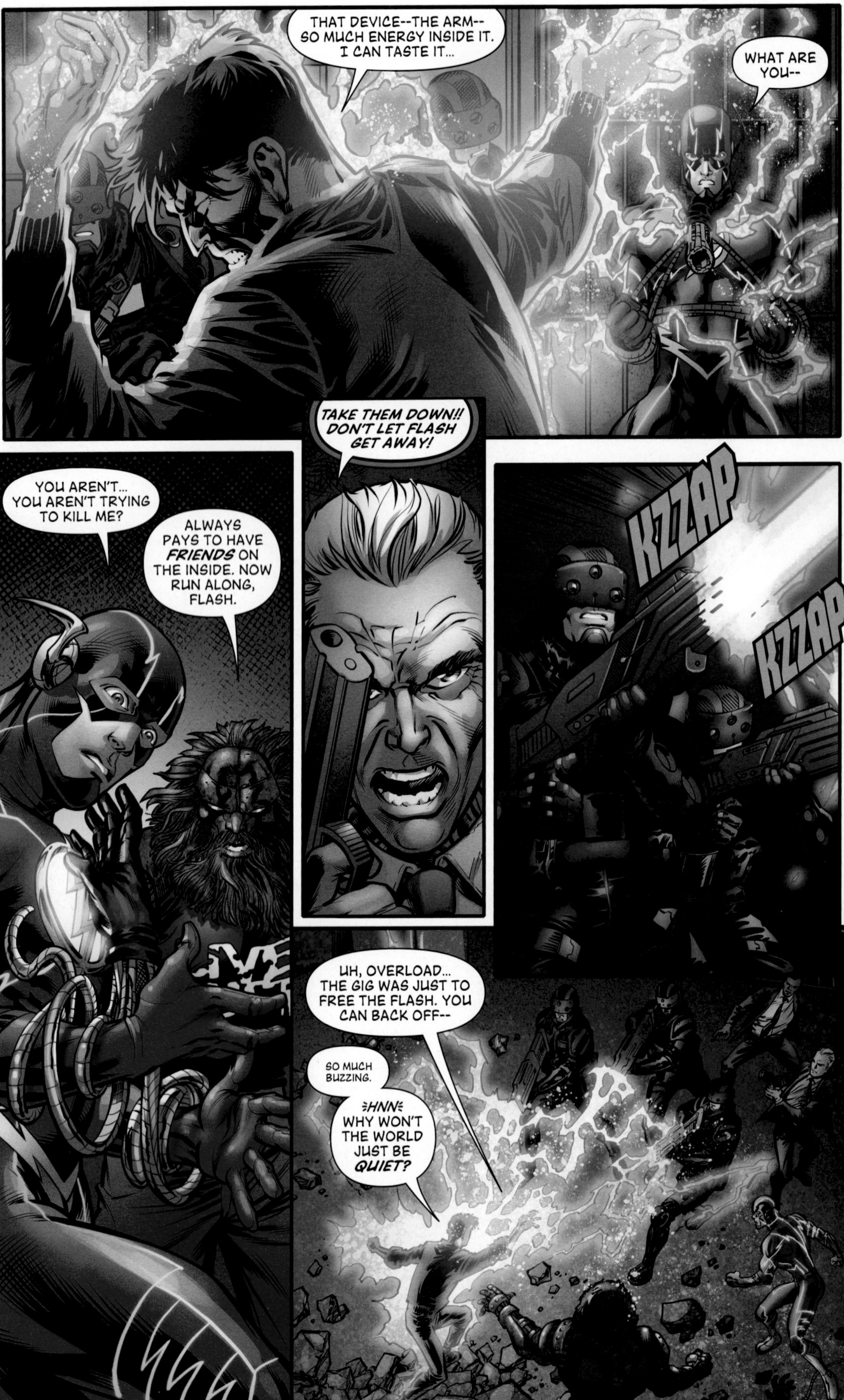
THAT DEVICE--THE ARM--
SO MUCH ENERGY INSIDE IT.
I CAN TASTE IT...
WHAT ARE YOU--
YOU AREN'T... YOU AREN'T TRYING TO KILL ME?
ALWAYS PAYS TO HAVE FRIENDS ON THE INSIDE. NOW RUN ALONG, FLASH.
TAKE THEM DOWN!! DON'T LET FLASH GET AWAY!
KZZAP
KZZAP
UH, OVERLOAD... THE GIG WAS JUST TO FREE THE FLASH. YOU CAN BACK OFF--
SO MUCH BUZZING.
HNN
WHY WON'T THE WORLD JUST BE QUIET?

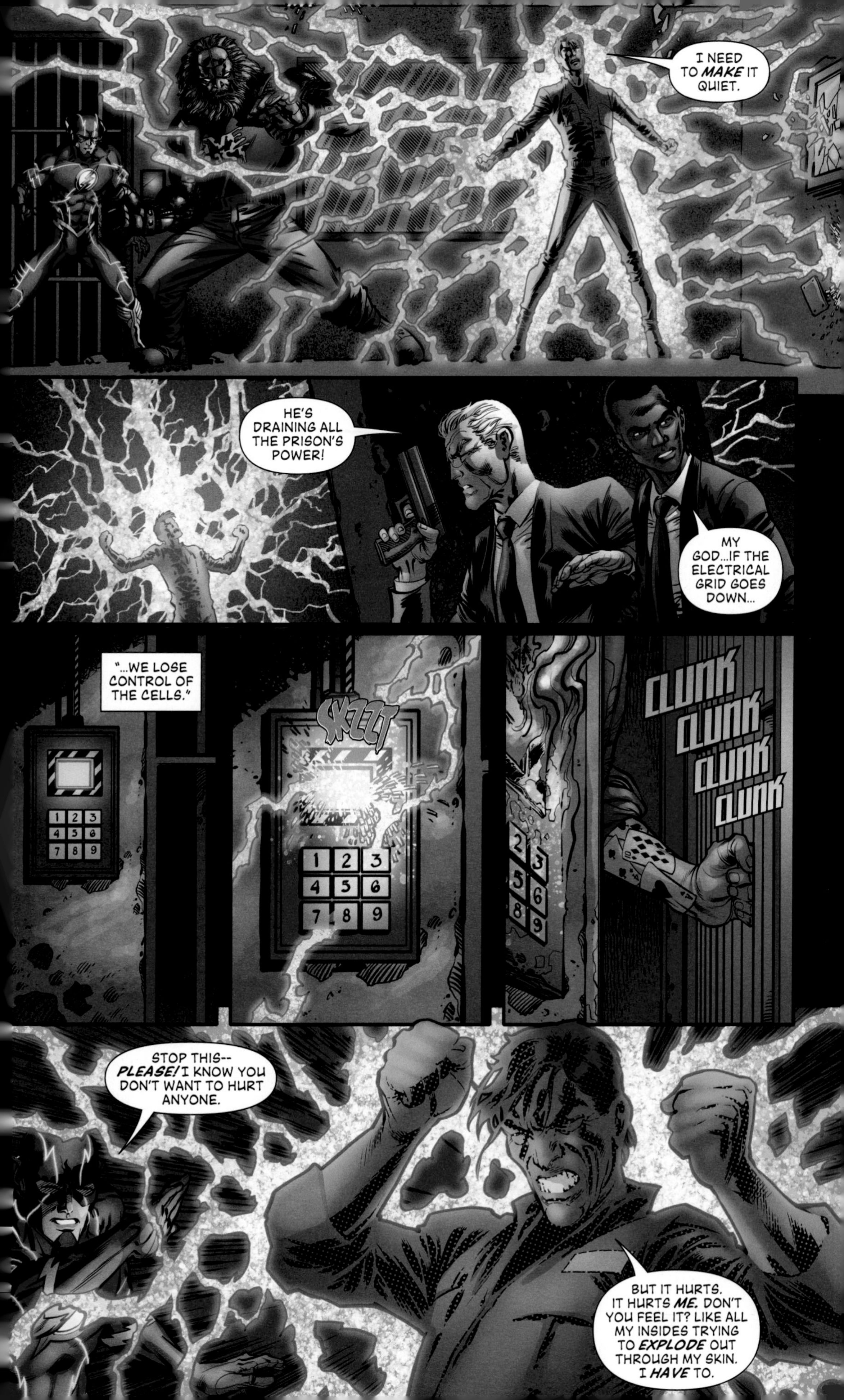
I NEED TO MAKE IT QUIET.
HE'S DRAINING ALL THE PRISON'S POWER!
MY GOD...IF THE ELECTRICAL GRID GOES DOWN...
"...WE LOSE CONTROL OF THE CELLS."
SKZZZT
CLUNK CLUNK CLUNK CLUNK
STOP THIS-- PLEASE! I KNOW YOU DON'T WANT TO HURT ANYONE.
BUT IT HURTS. IT HURTS ME. DON'T YOU FEEL IT? LIKE ALL MY INSIDES TRYING TO EXPLODE OUT THROUGH MY SKIN. I HAVE TO.

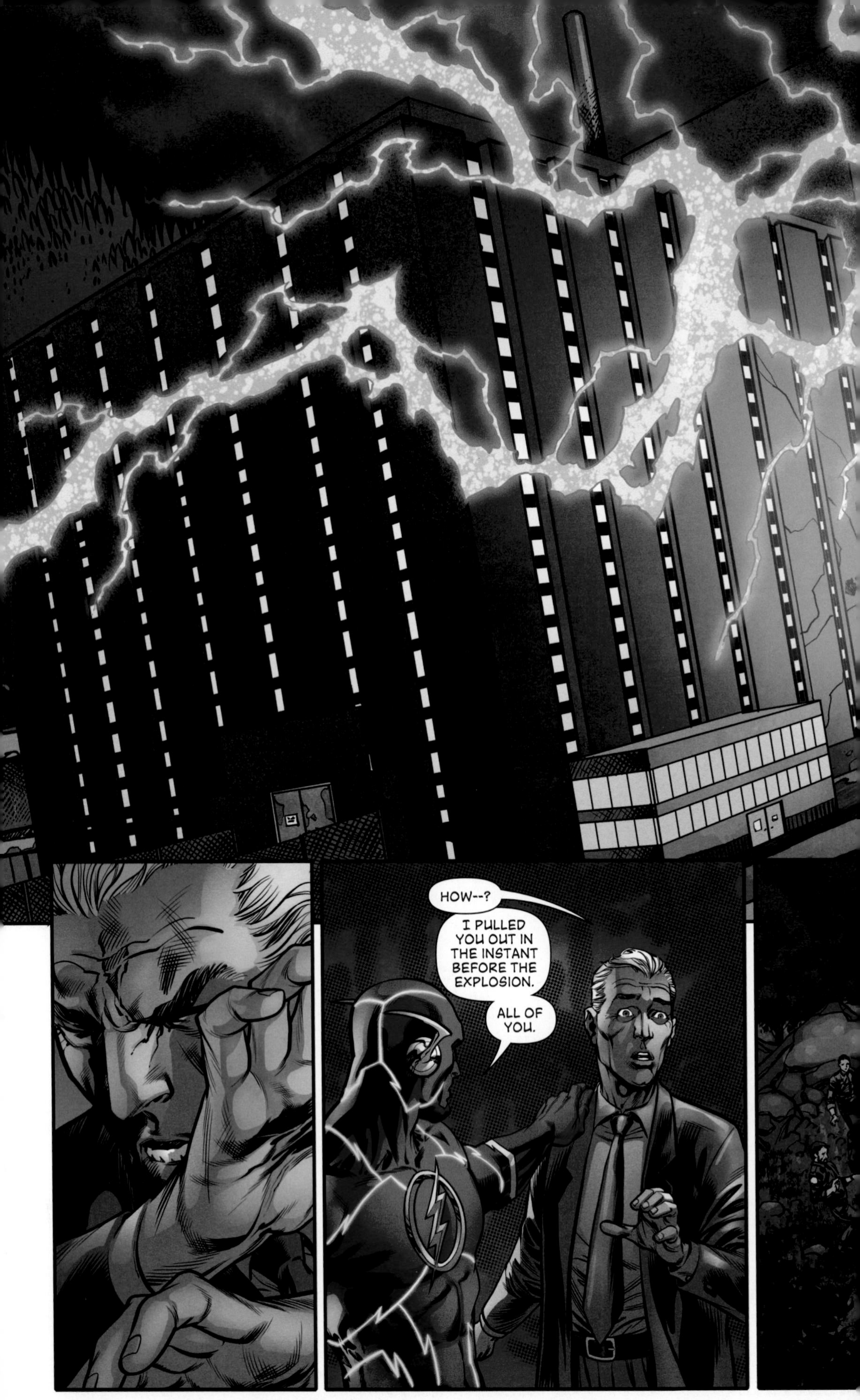
HOW--?
I PULLED YOU OUT IN THE INSTANT BEFORE THE EXPLOSION.
ALL OF YOU.

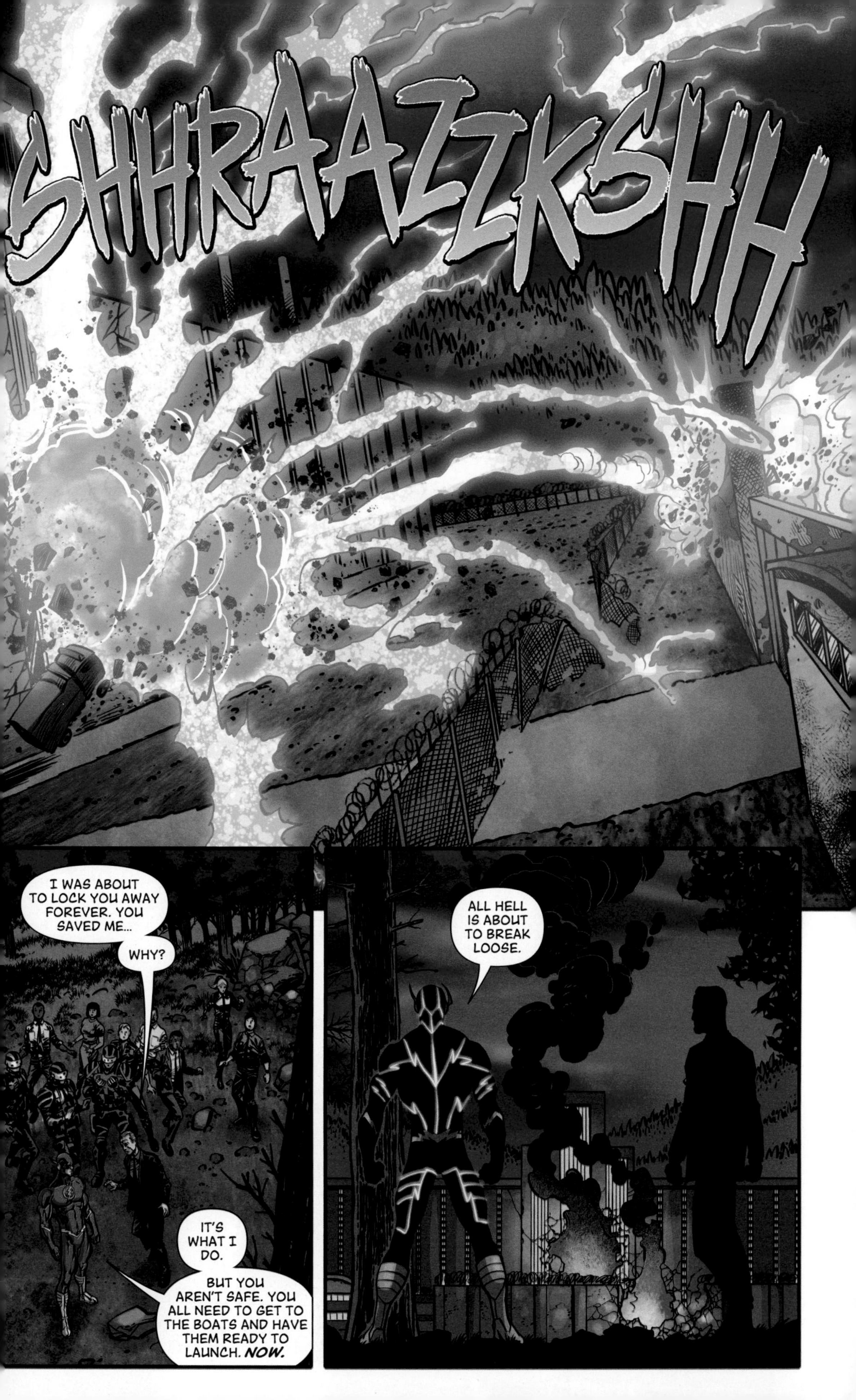
SHHRAAZZKSHH
I WAS ABOUT TO LOCK YOU AWAY FOREVER. YOU SAVED ME...
WHY?
IT'S WHAT I DO.
BUT YOU AREN'T SAFE. YOU ALL NEED TO GET TO THE BOATS AND HAVE THEM READY TO LAUNCH. *NOW.*
ALL HELL IS ABOUT TO BREAK LOOSE.

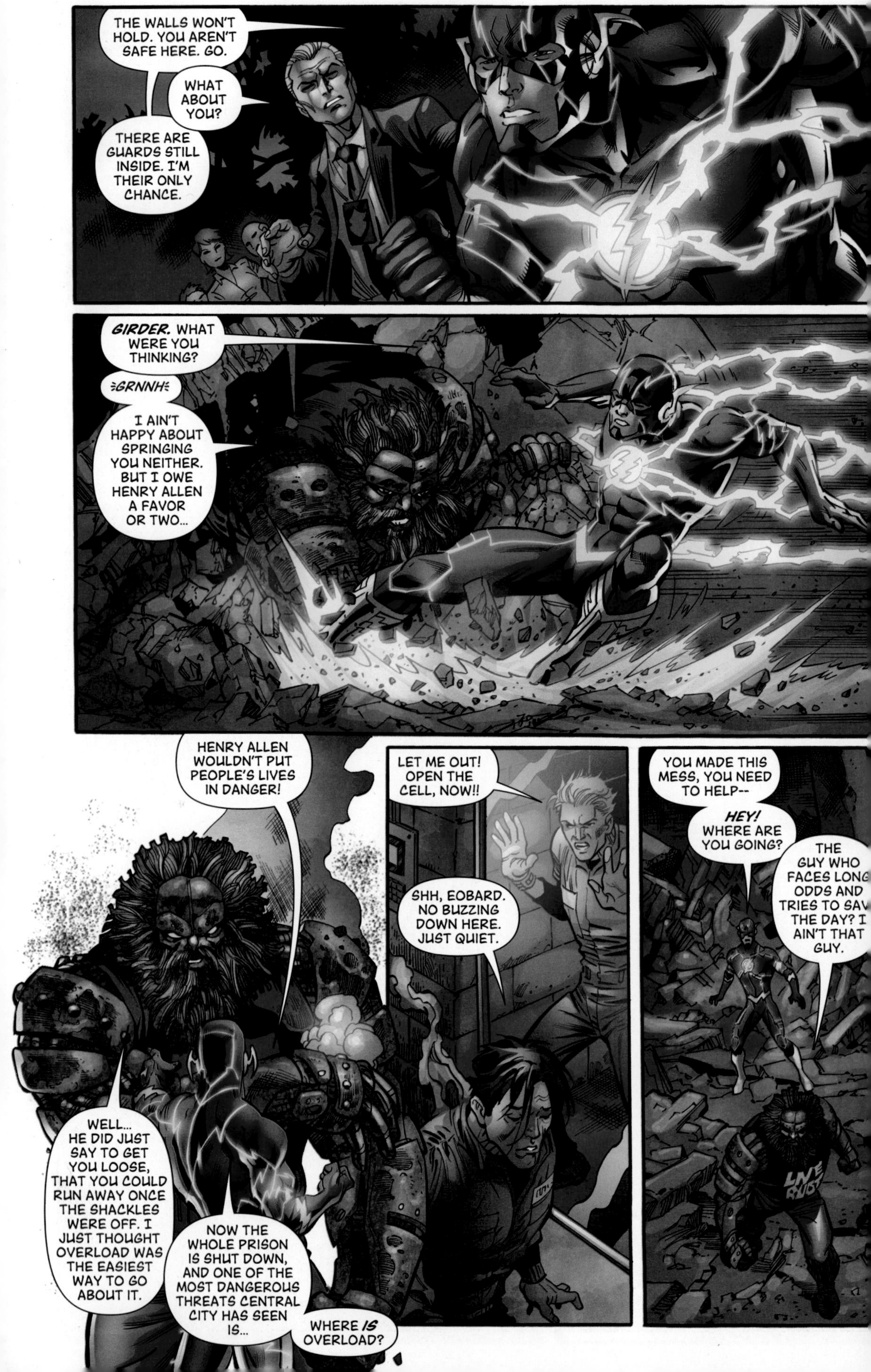
THE WALLS WON'T HOLD. YOU AREN'T SAFE HERE. GO.
WHAT ABOUT YOU?
THERE ARE GUARDS STILL INSIDE. I'M THEIR ONLY CHANCE.
GIRDER. WHAT WERE YOU THINKING?
GRNNH
I AIN'T HAPPY ABOUT SPRINGING YOU NEITHER. BUT I OWE HENRY ALLEN A FAVOR OR TWO...
HENRY ALLEN WOULDN'T PUT PEOPLE'S LIVES IN DANGER!
WELL... HE DID JUST SAY TO GET YOU LOOSE, THAT YOU COULD RUN AWAY ONCE THE SHACKLES WERE OFF. I JUST THOUGHT OVERLOAD WAS THE EASIEST WAY TO GO ABOUT IT.
NOW THE WHOLE PRISON IS SHUT DOWN, AND ONE OF THE MOST DANGEROUS THREATS CENTRAL CITY HAS SEEN IS...
WHERE IS OVERLOAD?
LET ME OUT! OPEN THE CELL, NOW!!
SHH, EOBARD. NO BUZZING DOWN HERE. JUST QUIET.
YOU MADE THIS MESS, YOU NEED TO HELP--
HEY! WHERE ARE YOU GOING?
THE GUY WHO FACES LONG ODDS AND TRIES TO SAV THE DAY? I AIN'T THAT GUY.

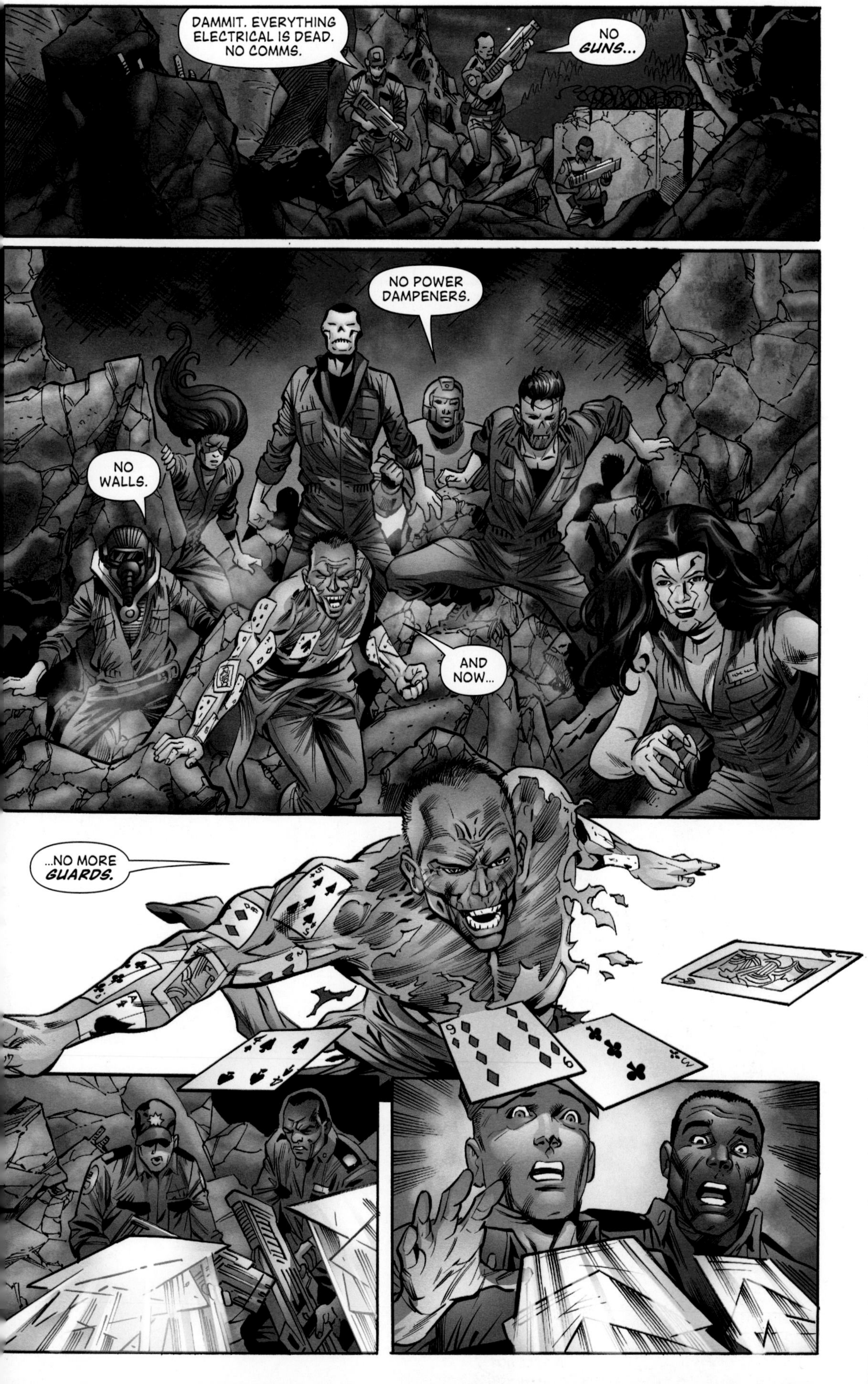
DAMMIT. EVERYTHING ELECTRICAL IS DEAD. NO COMMS.
NO *GUNS...*
NO POWER DAMPENERS.
NO WALLS.
AND NOW...
...NO MORE *GUARDS.*

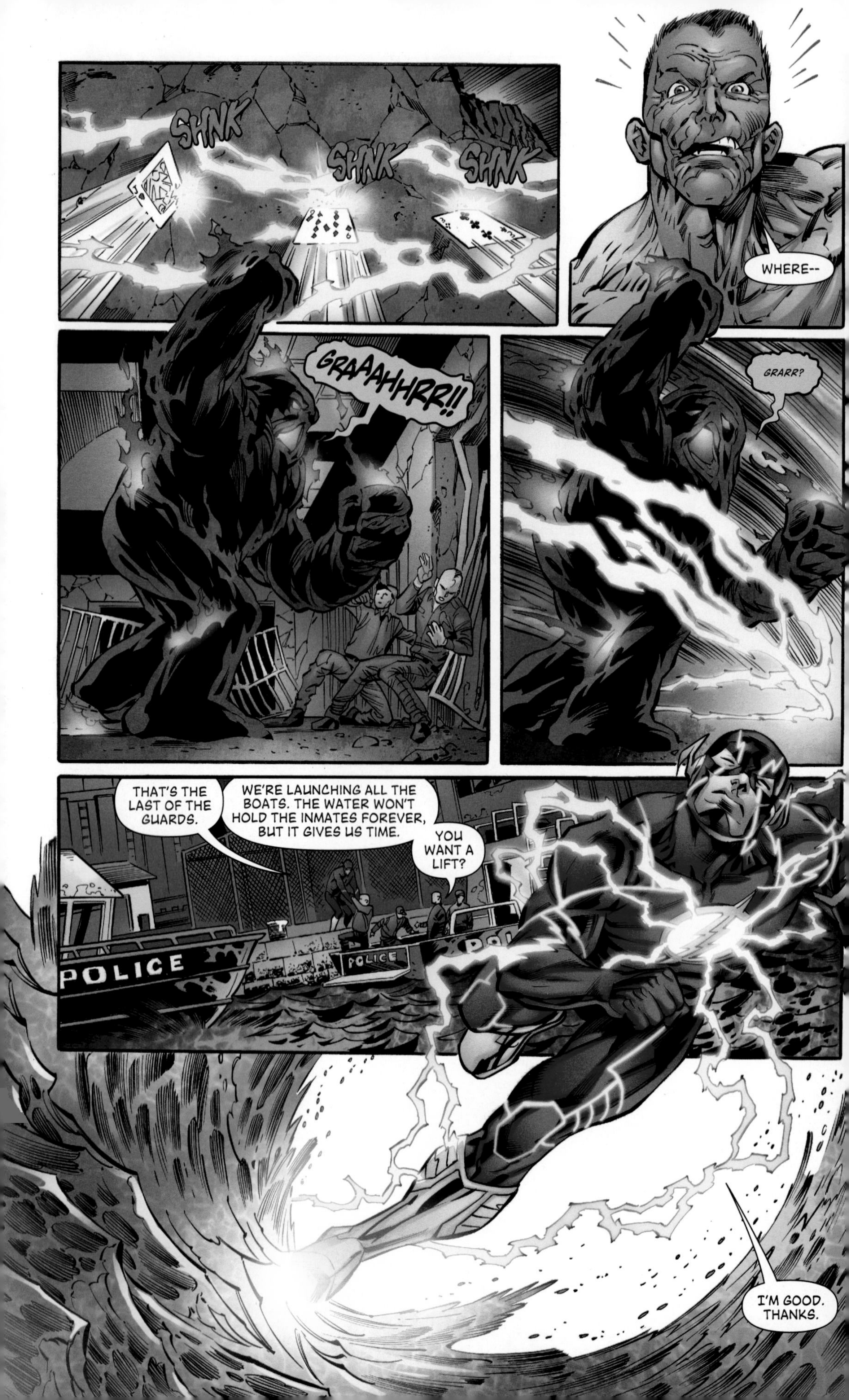
SHNK
SHNK
SHNK
WHERE--
GRAAAHHRR!!
GRARR?
THAT'S THE LAST OF THE GUARDS.
WE'RE LAUNCHING ALL THE BOATS. THE WATER WON'T HOLD THE INMATES FOREVER, BUT IT GIVES US TIME.
YOU WANT A LIFT?
POLICE
POLICE
I'M GOOD. THANKS.

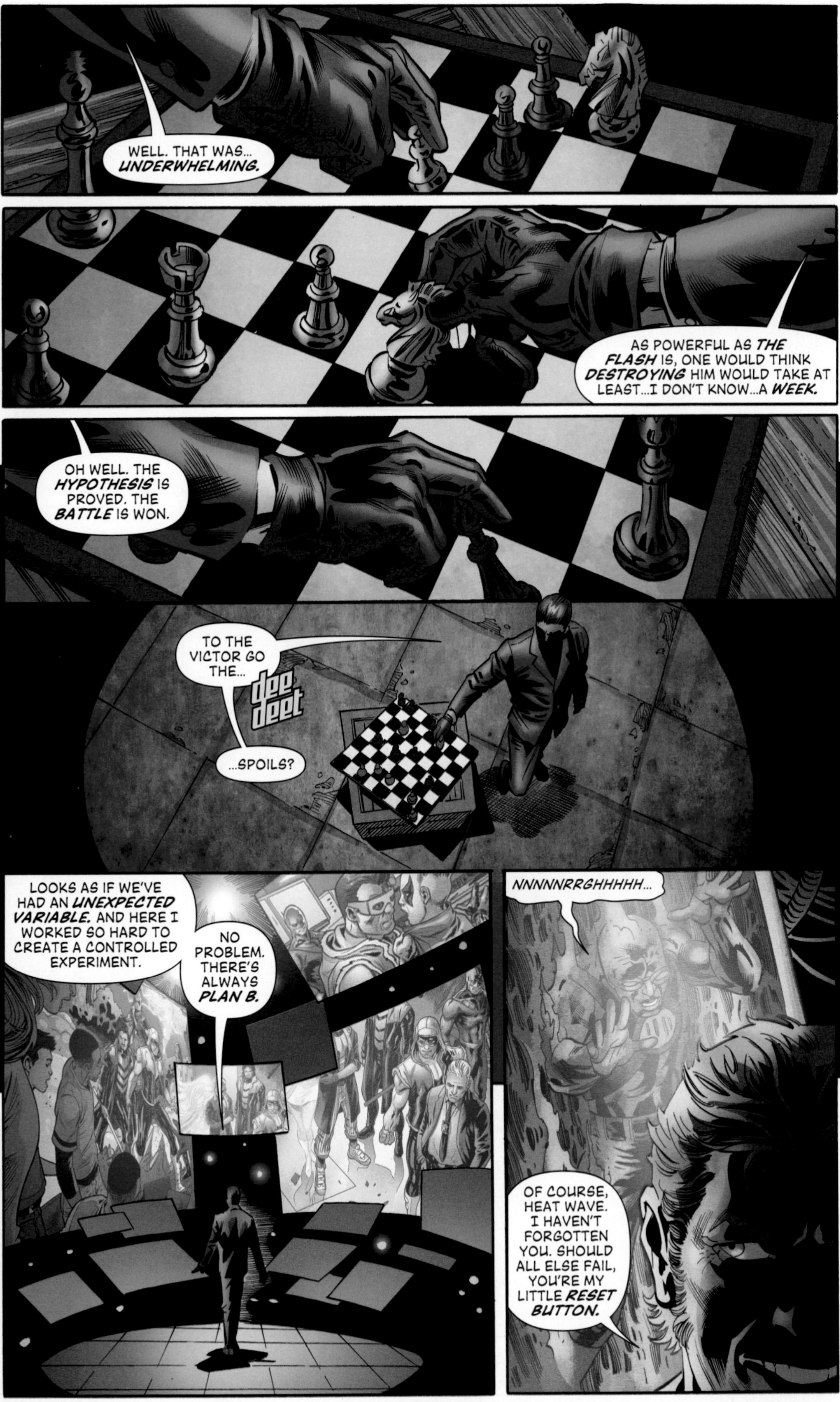
WELL. THAT WAS... UNDERWHELMING.
AS POWERFUL AS THE FLASH IS, ONE WOULD THINK DESTROYING HIM WOULD TAKE AT LEAST...I DON'T KNOW...A WEEK.
OH WELL. THE HYPOTHESIS IS PROVED. THE BATTLE IS WON.
TO THE VICTOR GO THE...
dee deet
...SPOILS?
LOOKS AS IF WE'VE HAD AN UNEXPECTED VARIABLE. AND HERE I WORKED SO HARD TO CREATE A CONTROLLED EXPERIMENT.
NO PROBLEM. THERE'S ALWAYS PLAN B.
NNNNNRRGHHHHH...
OF COURSE, HEAT WAVE. I HAVEN'T FORGOTTEN YOU. SHOULD ALL ELSE FAIL, YOU'RE MY LITTLE RESET BUTTON.

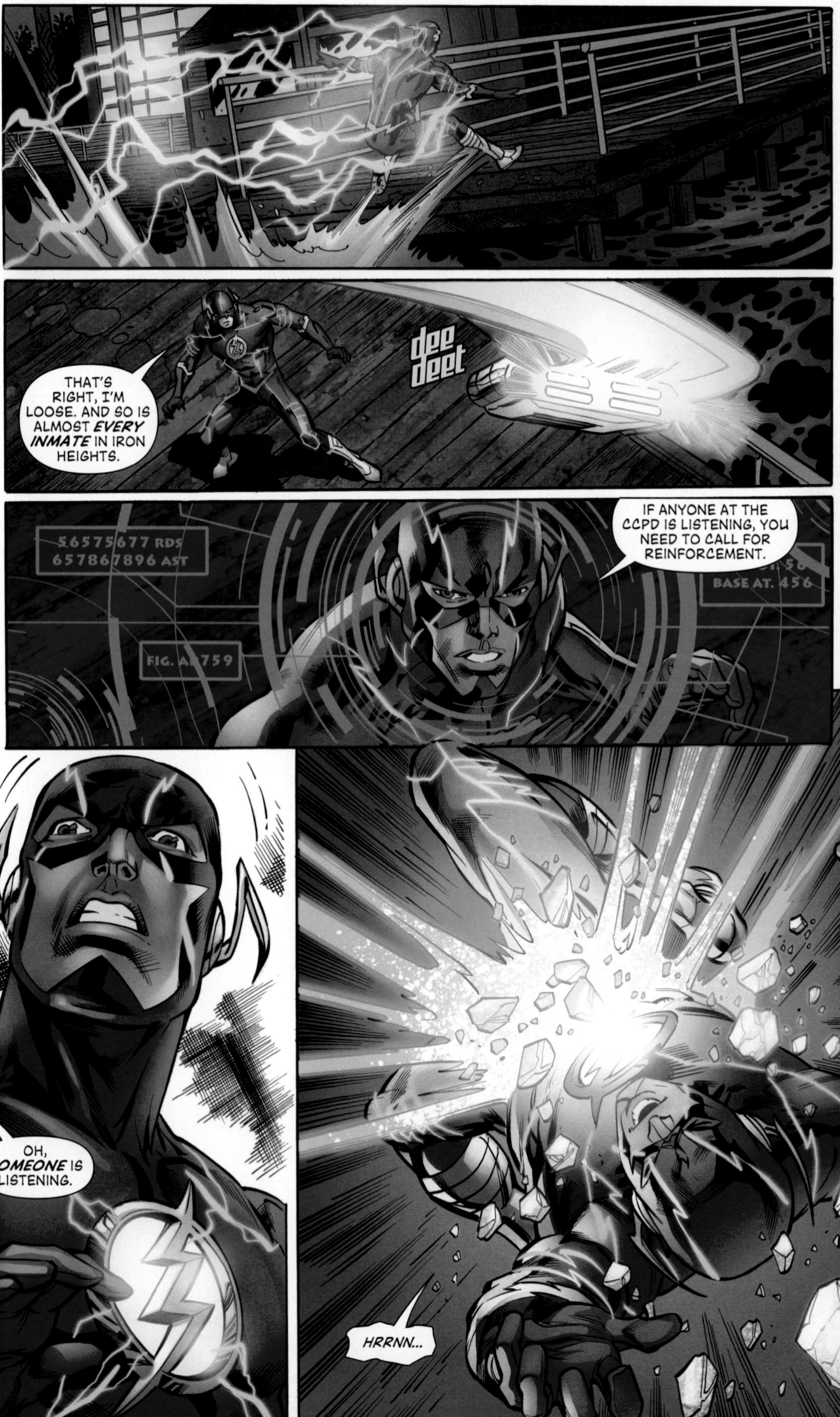

THAT'S RIGHT, I'M LOOSE. AND SO IS ALMOST *EVERY INMATE* IN IRON HEIGHTS.
dee deet
56575677 RDS
657867896 AST
BASE AT. 456
IF ANYONE AT THE CCPD IS LISTENING, YOU NEED TO CALL FOR REINFORCEMENT.
OH, *SOMEONE* IS LISTENING.
HRRNN...

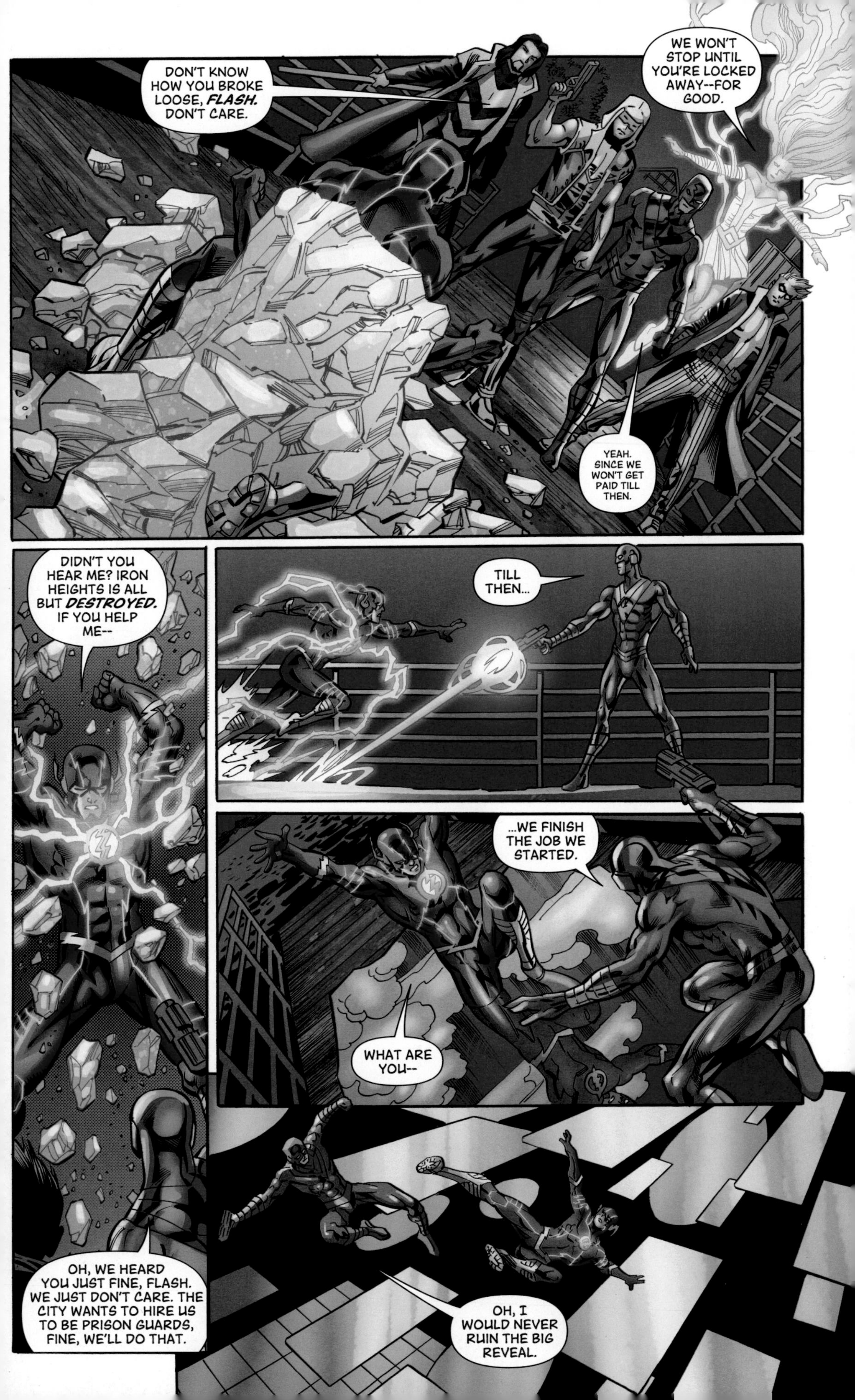
DON'T KNOW HOW YOU BROKE LOOSE, ***FLASH.*** DON'T CARE.
WE WON'T STOP UNTIL YOU'RE LOCKED AWAY--FOR GOOD.
YEAH. SINCE WE WON'T GET PAID TILL THEN.
DIDN'T YOU HEAR ME? IRON HEIGHTS IS ALL BUT ***DESTROYED.*** IF YOU HELP ME--
TILL THEN...
...WE FINISH THE JOB WE STARTED.
WHAT ARE YOU--
OH, WE HEARD YOU JUST FINE, FLASH. WE JUST DON'T CARE. THE CITY WANTS TO HIRE US TO BE PRISON GUARDS, FINE, WE'LL DO THAT.
OH, I WOULD NEVER RUIN THE BIG REVEAL.

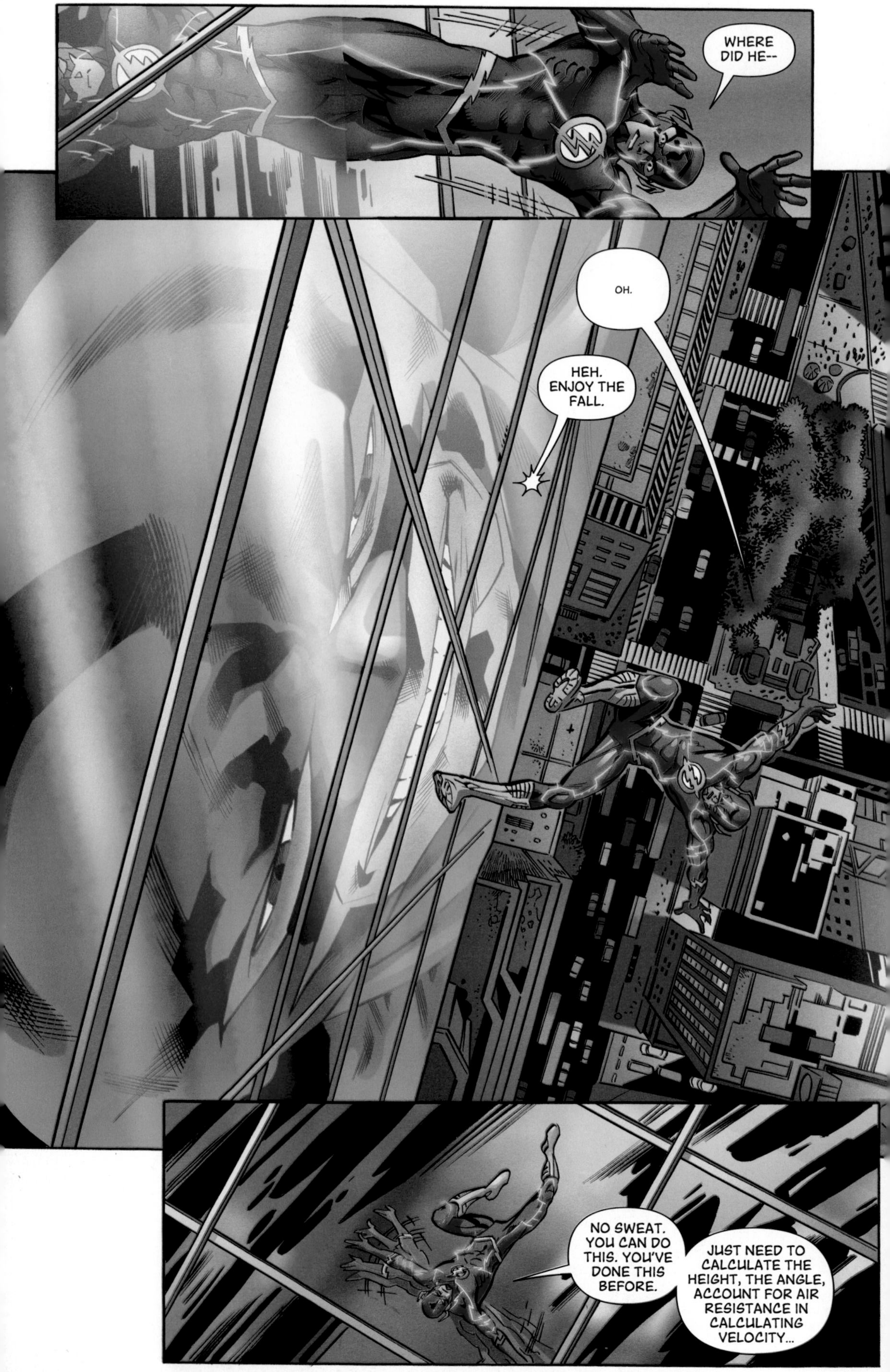
WHERE DID HE--
OH.
HEH. ENJOY THE FALL.
NO SWEAT. YOU CAN DO THIS. YOU'VE DONE THIS BEFORE.
JUST NEED TO CALCULATE THE HEIGHT, THE ANGLE, ACCOUNT FOR AIR RESISTANCE IN CALCULATING VELOCITY...

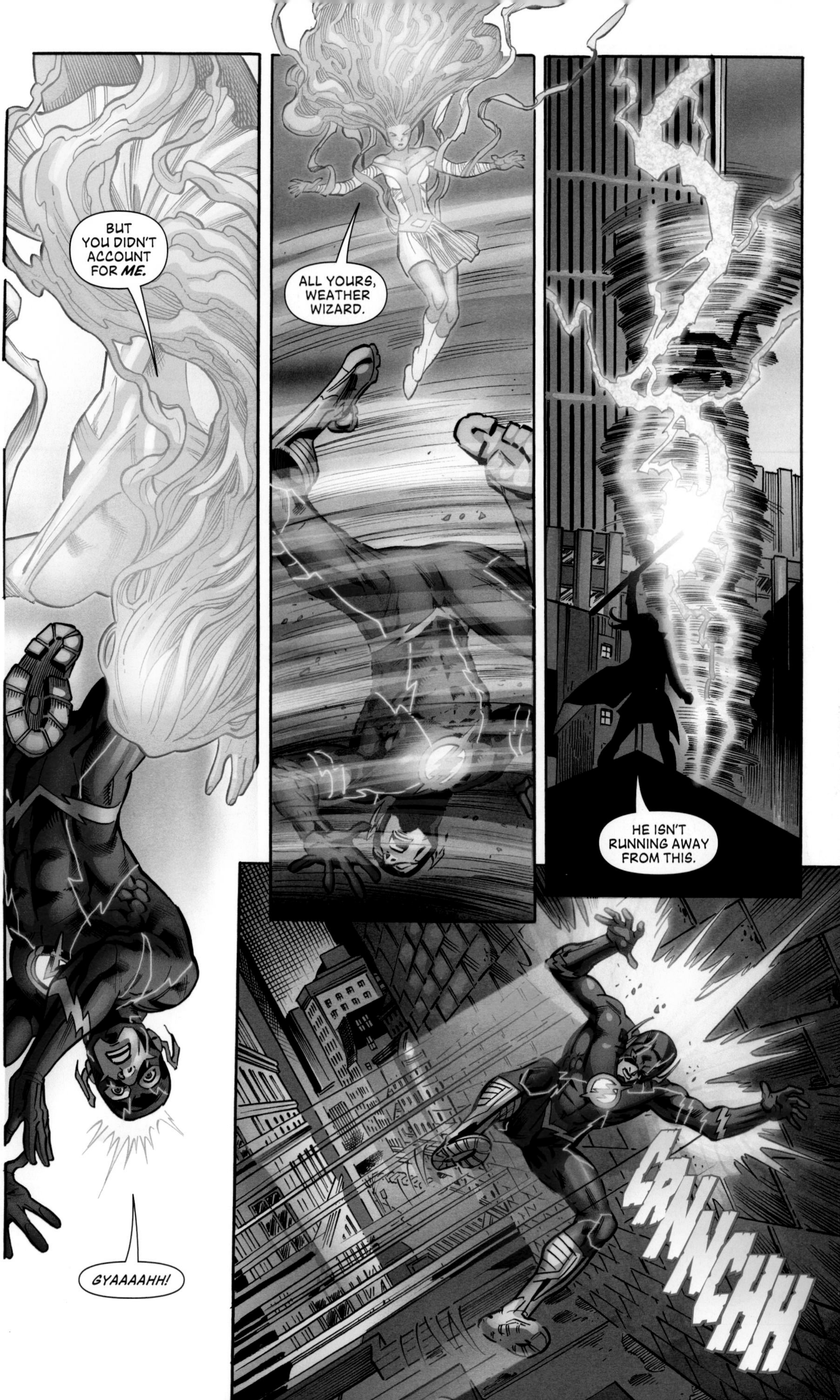
BUT YOU DIDN'T ACCOUNT FOR *ME.*
GYAAAAHH!
ALL YOURS, WEATHER WIZARD.
HE ISN'T RUNNING AWAY FROM THIS.
CRNNCHH

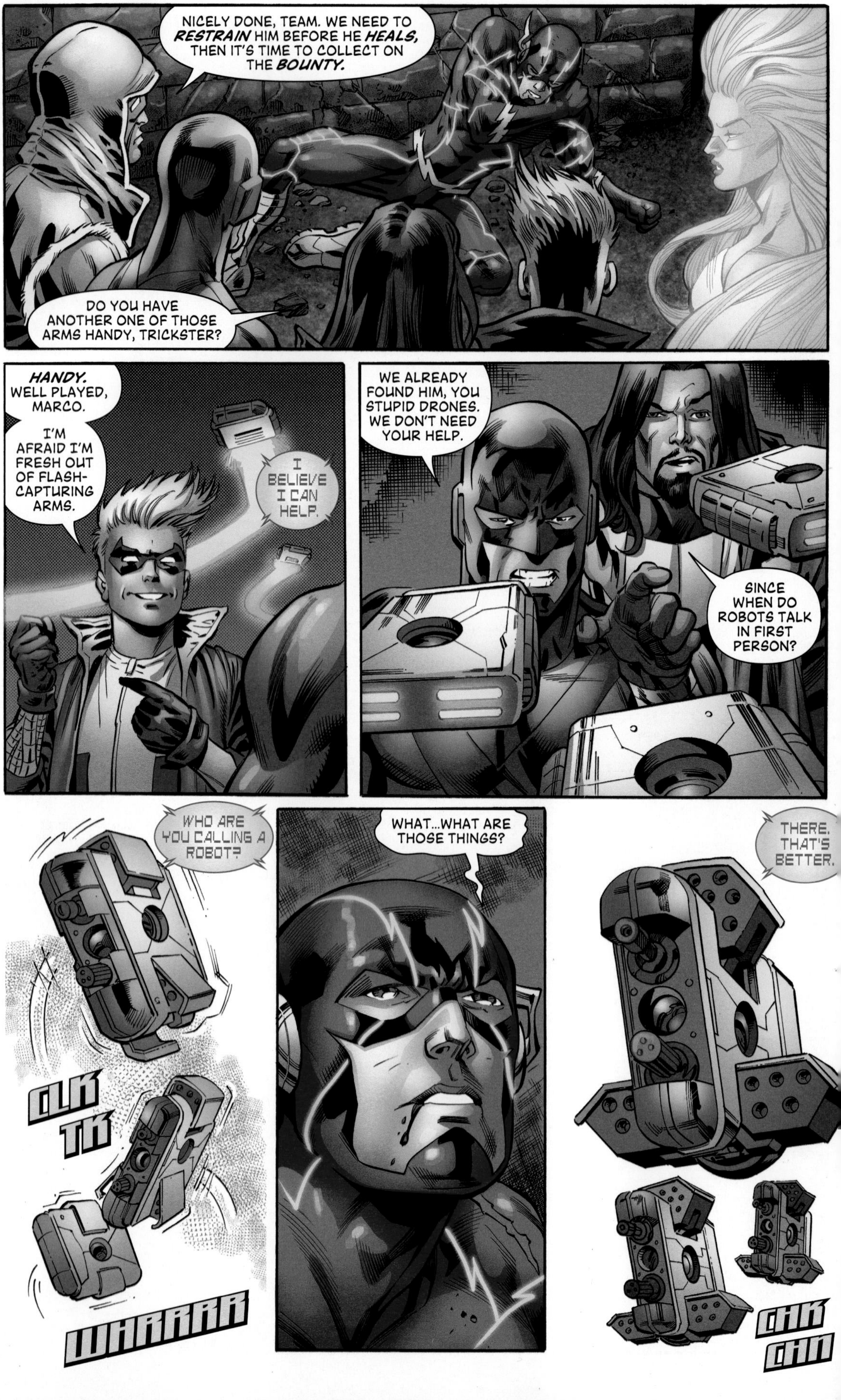
NICELY DONE, TEAM. WE NEED TO RESTRAIN HIM BEFORE HE HEALS, THEN IT'S TIME TO COLLECT ON THE BOUNTY.
DO YOU HAVE ANOTHER ONE OF THOSE ARMS HANDY, TRICKSTER?
HANDY. WELL PLAYED, MARCO.
I'M AFRAID I'M FRESH OUT OF FLASH-CAPTURING ARMS.
I BELIEVE I CAN HELP.
WE ALREADY FOUND HIM, YOU STUPID DRONES. WE DON'T NEED YOUR HELP.
SINCE WHEN DO ROBOTS TALK IN FIRST PERSON?
WHO ARE YOU CALLING A ROBOT?
CLK
TK
WHRRRR
WHAT...WHAT ARE THOSE THINGS?
THERE. THAT'S BETTER.
CHK
CHN

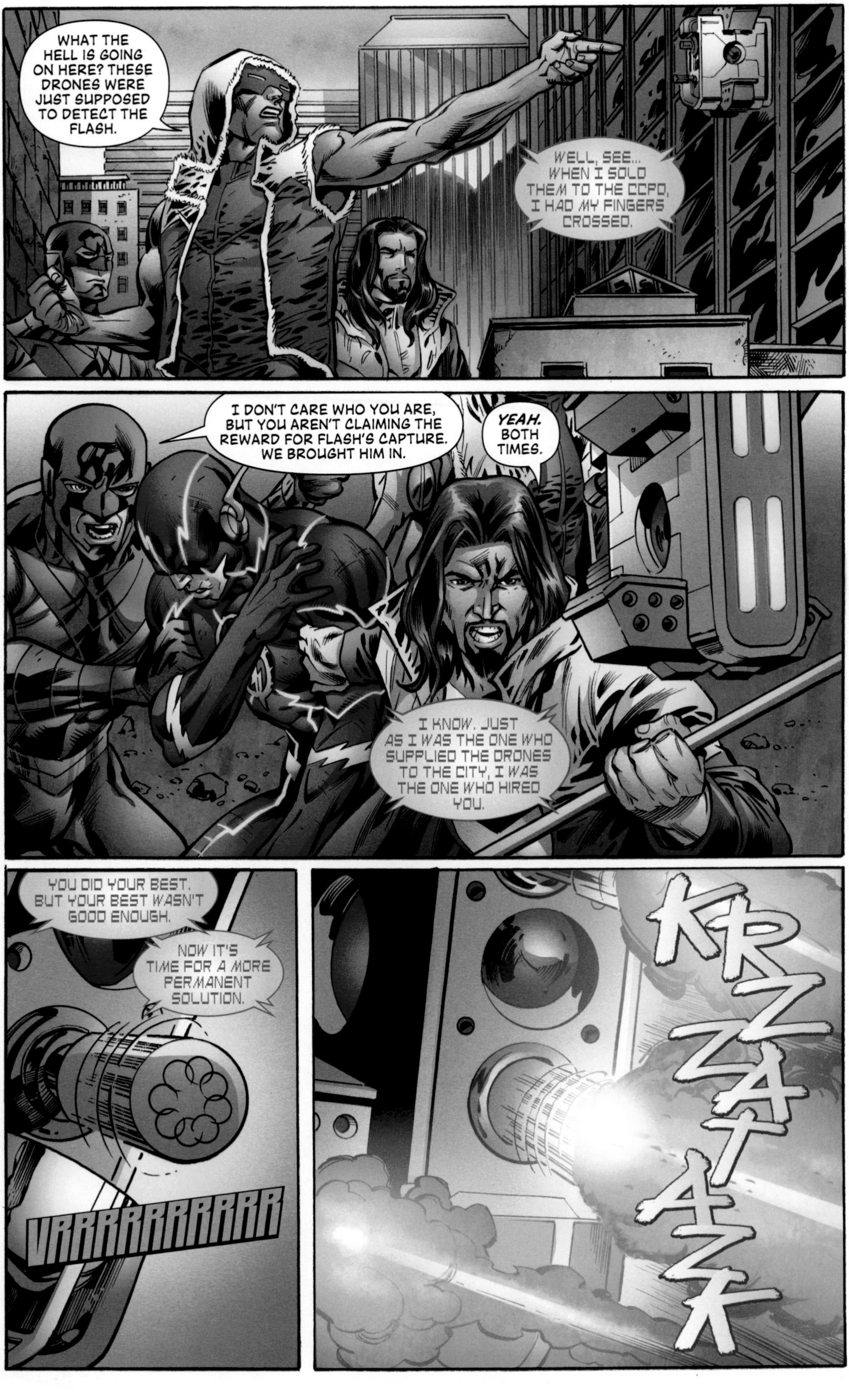

WHAT THE HELL IS GOING ON HERE? THESE DRONES WERE JUST SUPPOSED TO DETECT THE FLASH.
WELL, SEE... WHEN I SOLD THEM TO THE CCPD, I HAD MY FINGERS CROSSED.
I DON'T CARE WHO YOU ARE, BUT YOU AREN'T CLAIMING THE REWARD FOR FLASH'S CAPTURE. WE BROUGHT HIM IN.
YEAH. BOTH TIMES.
I KNOW. JUST AS I WAS THE ONE WHO SUPPLIED THE DRONES TO THE CITY, I WAS THE ONE WHO HIRED YOU.
YOU DID YOUR BEST. BUT YOUR BEST WASN'T GOOD ENOUGH.
NOW IT'S TIME FOR A MORE PERMANENT SOLUTION.
VRRRRRRRRRR
KRZZATAZK

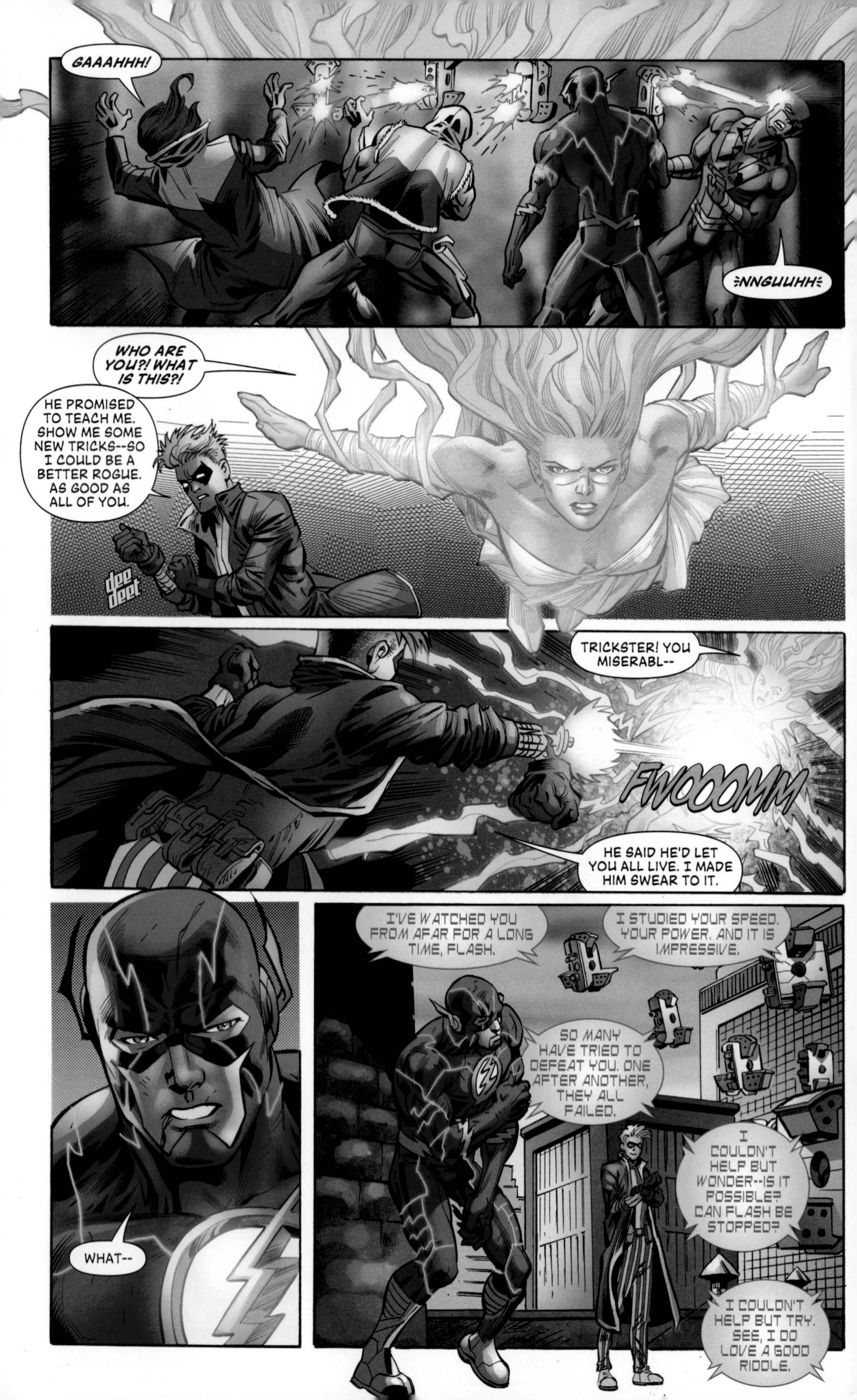
GAAAHHH!
NNGUUHH
WHO ARE YOU?! WHAT IS THIS?!
HE PROMISED TO TEACH ME. SHOW ME SOME NEW TRICKS--SO I COULD BE A BETTER ROGUE. AS GOOD AS ALL OF YOU.
TRICKSTER! YOU MISERABL--
FWOOOMM
HE SAID HE'D LET YOU ALL LIVE. I MADE HIM SWEAR TO IT.
WHAT--
I'VE WATCHED YOU FROM AFAR FOR A LONG TIME, FLASH.
I STUDIED YOUR SPEED. YOUR POWER. AND IT IS IMPRESSIVE.
SO MANY HAVE TRIED TO DEFEAT YOU. ONE AFTER ANOTHER, THEY ALL FAILED.
I COULDN'T HELP BUT WONDER--IS IT POSSIBLE? CAN FLASH BE STOPPED?
I COULDN'T HELP BUT TRY. SEE, I DO LOVE A GOOD RIDDLE.

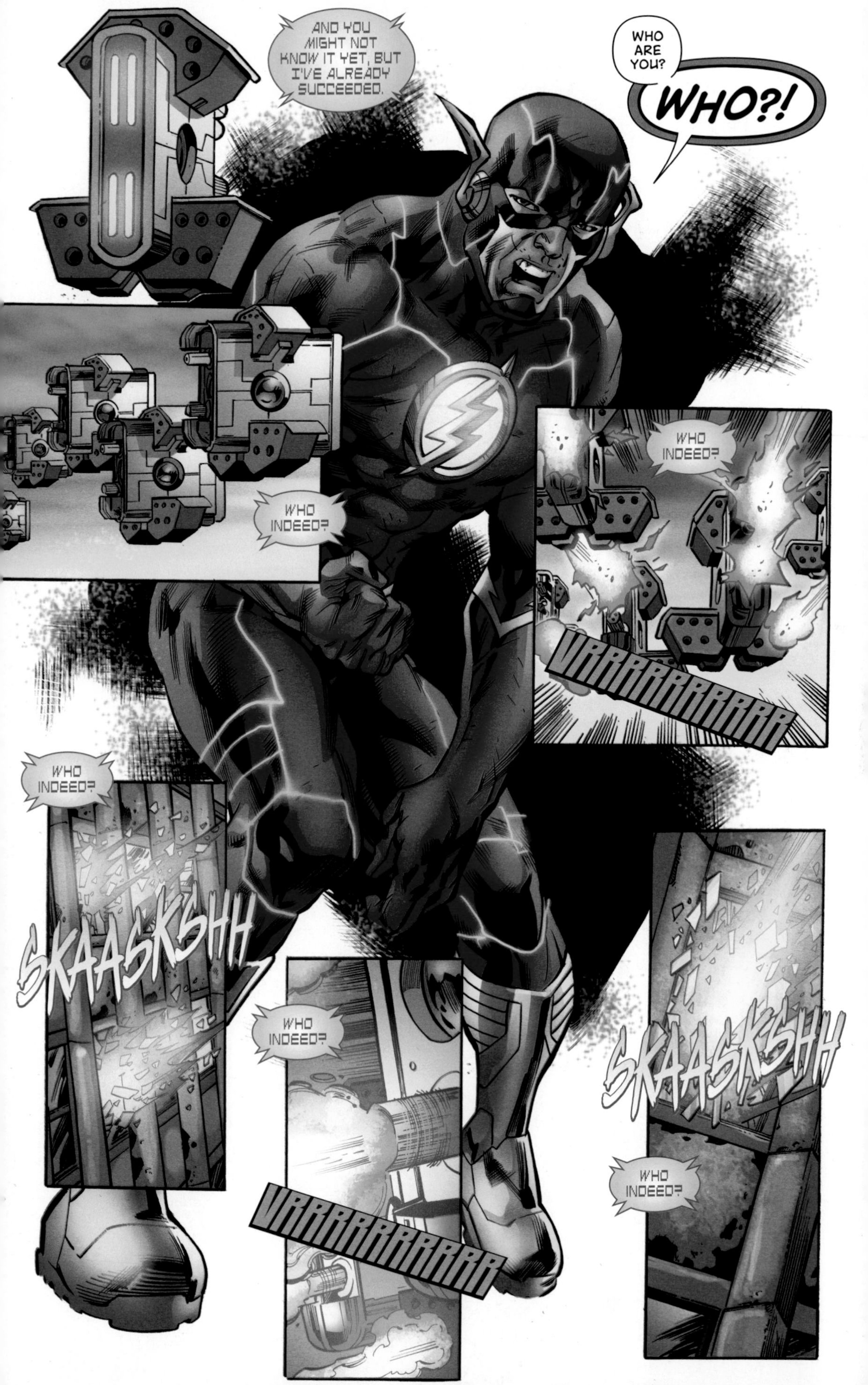
AND YOU MIGHT NOT KNOW IT YET, BUT I'VE ALREADY SUCCEEDED.
WHO ARE YOU?
WHO?!
WHO INDEED?
WHO INDEED?
VRRRRRRRRRRR
WHO INDEED?
SKAASKSHH
WHO INDEED?
VRRRRRRRRRRR
SKAASKSHH
WHO INDEED?

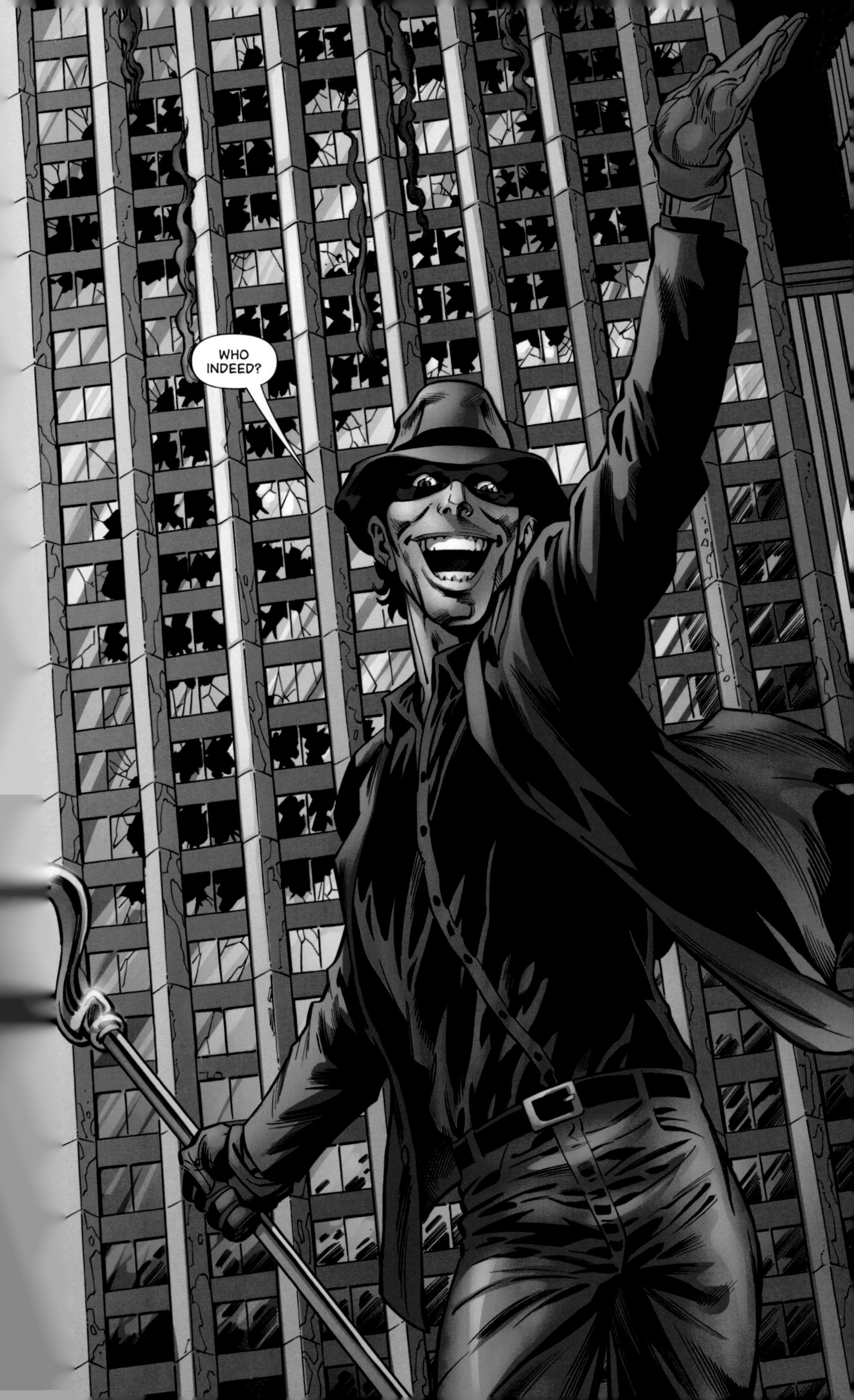
WHO INDEED?

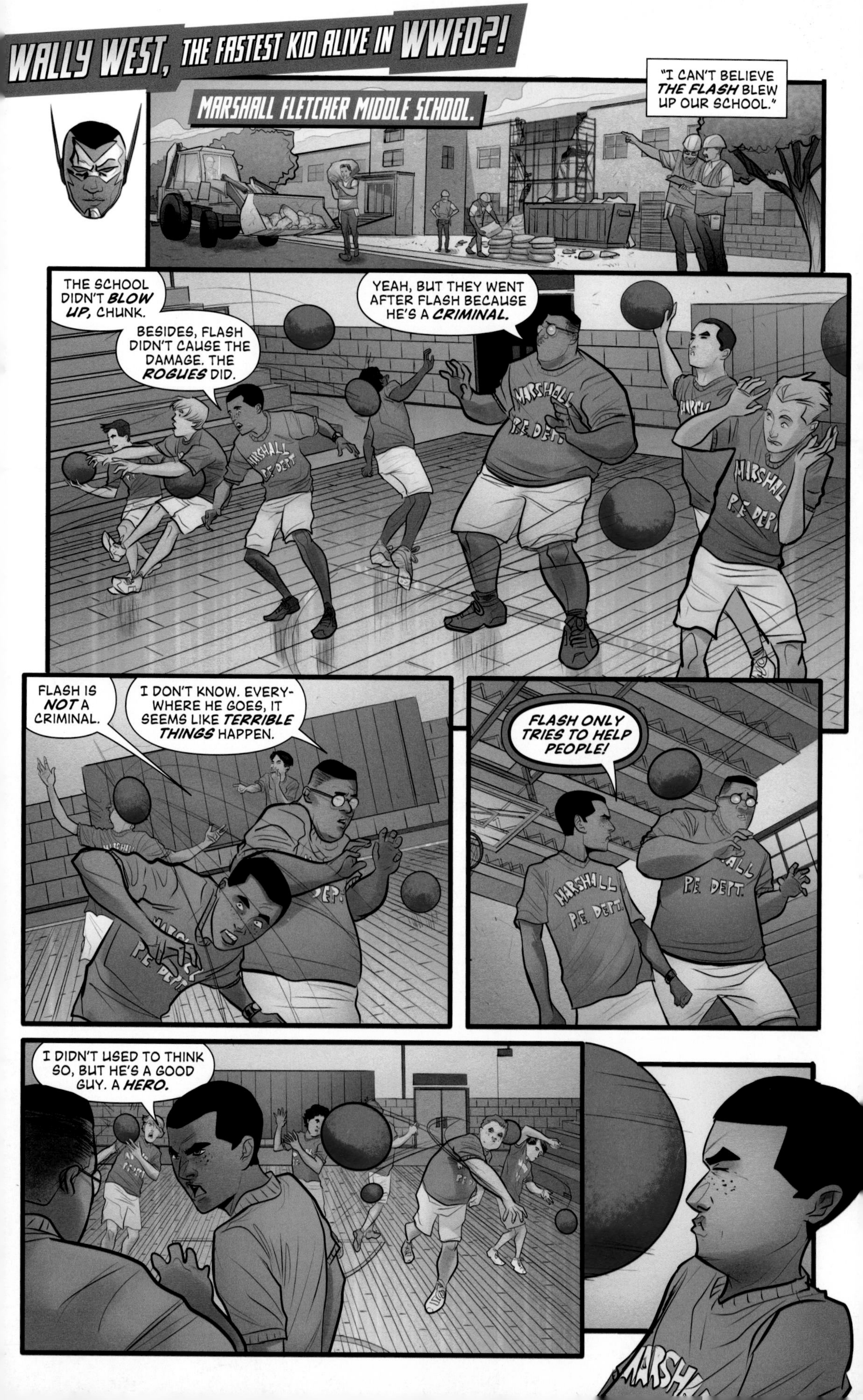

WALLY WEST, THE FASTEST KID ALIVE IN WWFD?!
MARSHALL FLETCHER MIDDLE SCHOOL.
"I CAN'T BELIEVE THE FLASH BLEW UP OUR SCHOOL."
THE SCHOOL DIDN'T BLOW UP, CHUNK.
BESIDES, FLASH DIDN'T CAUSE THE DAMAGE. THE ROGUES DID.
YEAH, BUT THEY WENT AFTER FLASH BECAUSE HE'S A CRIMINAL.
MARSHALL P.E. DEPT.
FLASH IS NOT A CRIMINAL.
I DON'T KNOW. EVERY-WHERE HE GOES, IT SEEMS LIKE TERRIBLE THINGS HAPPEN.
FLASH ONLY TRIES TO HELP PEOPLE!
I DIDN'T USED TO THINK SO, BUT HE'S A GOOD GUY. A HERO.

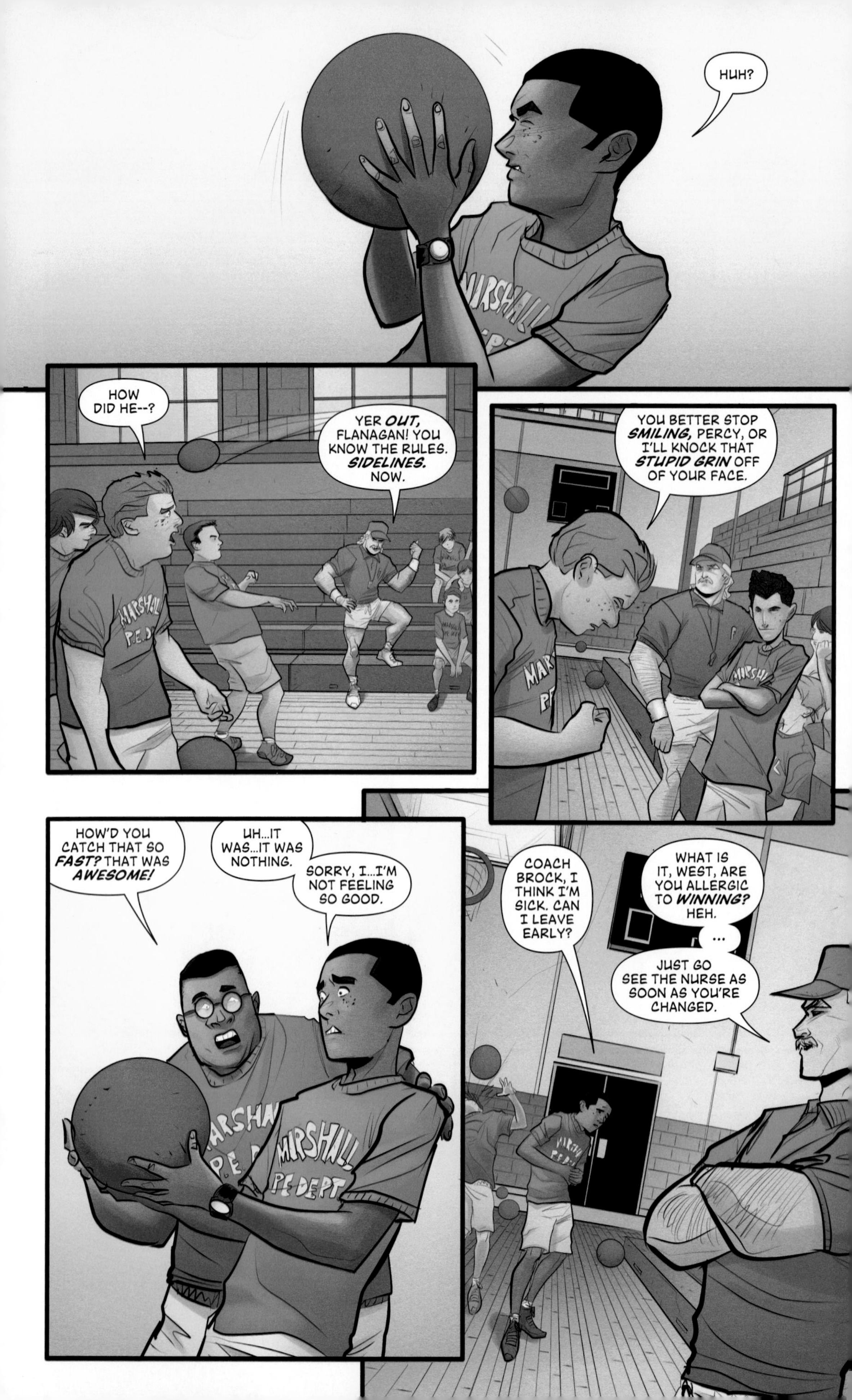

HUH?
HOW DID HE--?
YER *OUT,* FLANAGAN! YOU KNOW THE RULES. *SIDELINES.* NOW.
YOU BETTER STOP *SMILING,* PERCY, OR I'LL KNOCK THAT *STUPID GRIN* OFF OF YOUR FACE.
HOW'D YOU CATCH THAT SO *FAST?* THAT WAS *AWESOME!*
UH...IT WAS...IT WAS NOTHING.
SORRY, I...I'M NOT FEELING SO GOOD.
COACH BROCK, I THINK I'M SICK. CAN I LEAVE EARLY?
WHAT IS IT, WEST, ARE YOU ALLERGIC TO *WINNING?* HEH.
...
JUST GO SEE THE NURSE AS SOON AS YOU'RE CHANGED.

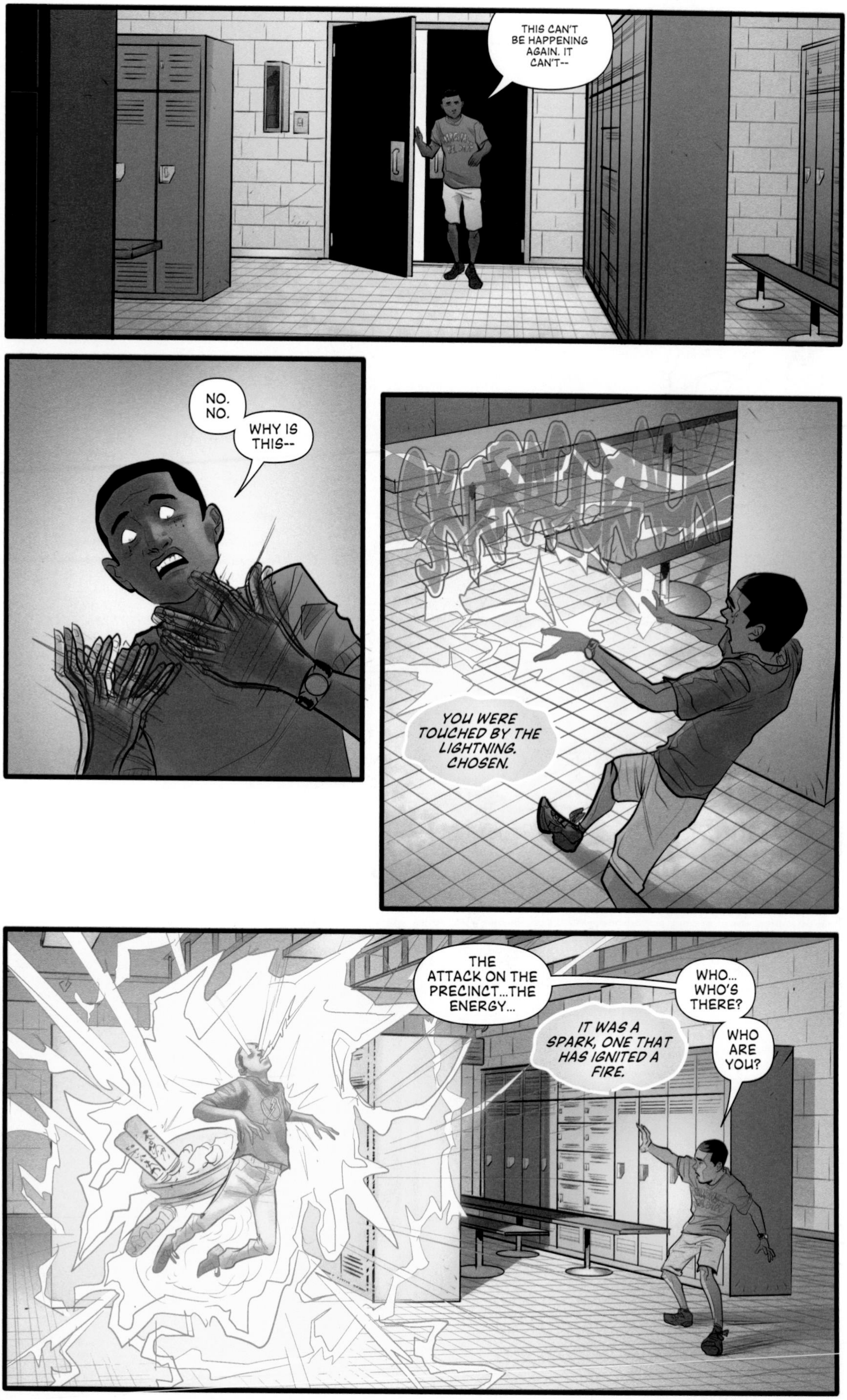
THIS CAN'T BE HAPPENING AGAIN. IT CAN'T--
NO. NO.
WHY IS THIS--
YOU WERE TOUCHED BY THE LIGHTNING. CHOSEN.
THE ATTACK ON THE PRECINCT...THE ENERGY...
WHO... WHO'S THERE?
IT WAS A SPARK, ONE THAT HAS IGNITED A FIRE.
WHO ARE YOU?

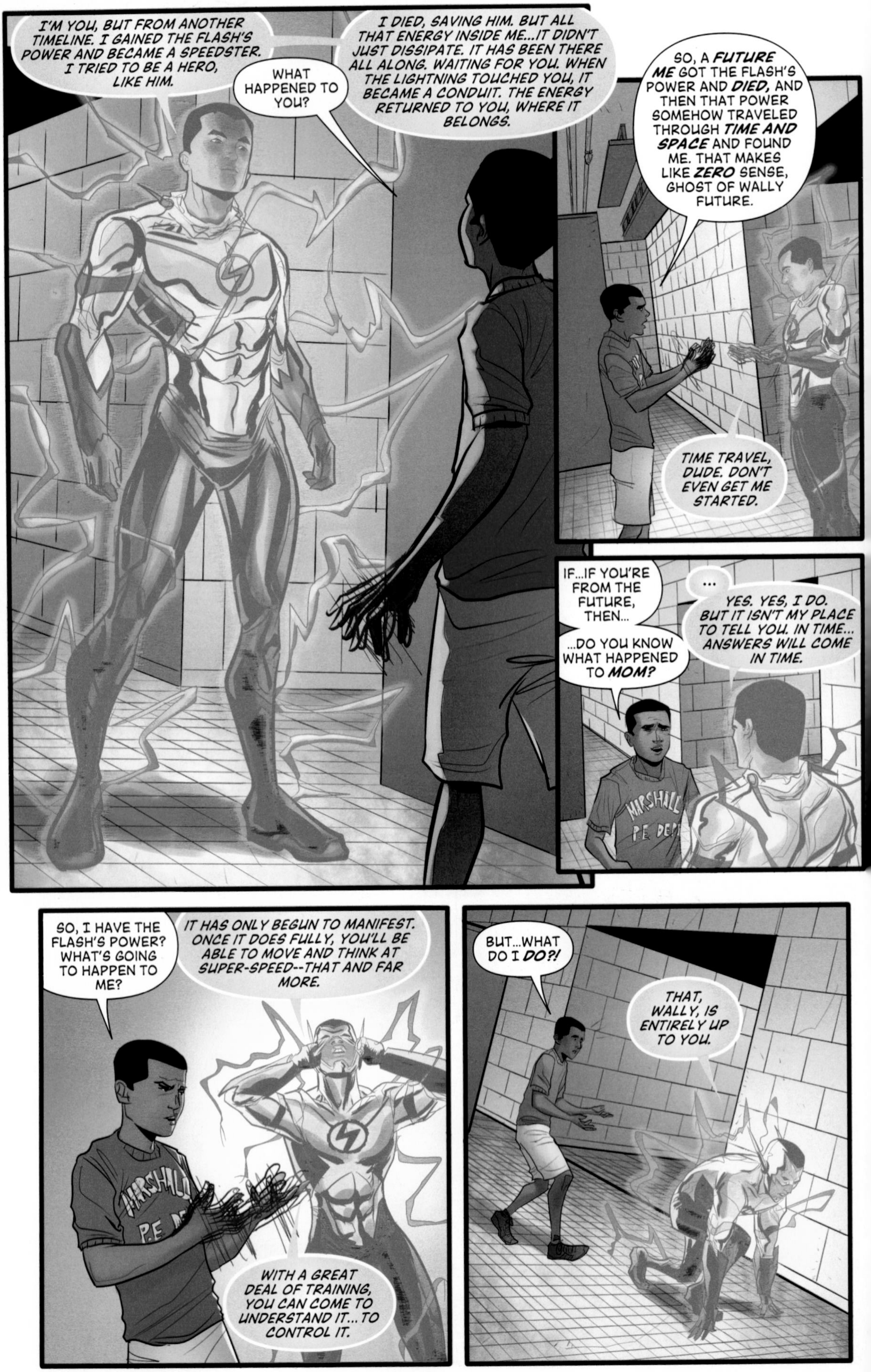
I'M YOU, BUT FROM ANOTHER TIMELINE. I GAINED THE FLASH'S POWER AND BECAME A SPEEDSTER. I TRIED TO BE A HERO, LIKE HIM.
WHAT HAPPENED TO YOU?
I DIED, SAVING HIM. BUT ALL THAT ENERGY INSIDE ME...IT DIDN'T JUST DISSIPATE. IT HAS BEEN THERE ALL ALONG. WAITING FOR YOU. WHEN THE LIGHTNING TOUCHED YOU, IT BECAME A CONDUIT. THE ENERGY RETURNED TO YOU, WHERE IT BELONGS.
SO, A FUTURE ME GOT THE FLASH'S POWER AND DIED, AND THEN THAT POWER SOMEHOW TRAVELED THROUGH TIME AND SPACE AND FOUND ME. THAT MAKES LIKE ZERO SENSE, GHOST OF WALLY FUTURE.
TIME TRAVEL, DUDE. DON'T EVEN GET ME STARTED.
IF...IF YOU'RE FROM THE FUTURE, THEN...
...DO YOU KNOW WHAT HAPPENED TO MOM?
...
YES. YES, I DO. BUT IT ISN'T MY PLACE TO TELL YOU. IN TIME... ANSWERS WILL COME IN TIME.
MARSHALL P.E. DEPT
SO, I HAVE THE FLASH'S POWER? WHAT'S GOING TO HAPPEN TO ME?
IT HAS ONLY BEGUN TO MANIFEST. ONCE IT DOES FULLY, YOU'LL BE ABLE TO MOVE AND THINK AT SUPER-SPEED--THAT AND FAR MORE.
WITH A GREAT DEAL OF TRAINING, YOU CAN COME TO UNDERSTAND IT... TO CONTROL IT.
BUT...WHAT DO I DO?!
THAT, WALLY, IS ENTIRELY UP TO YOU.

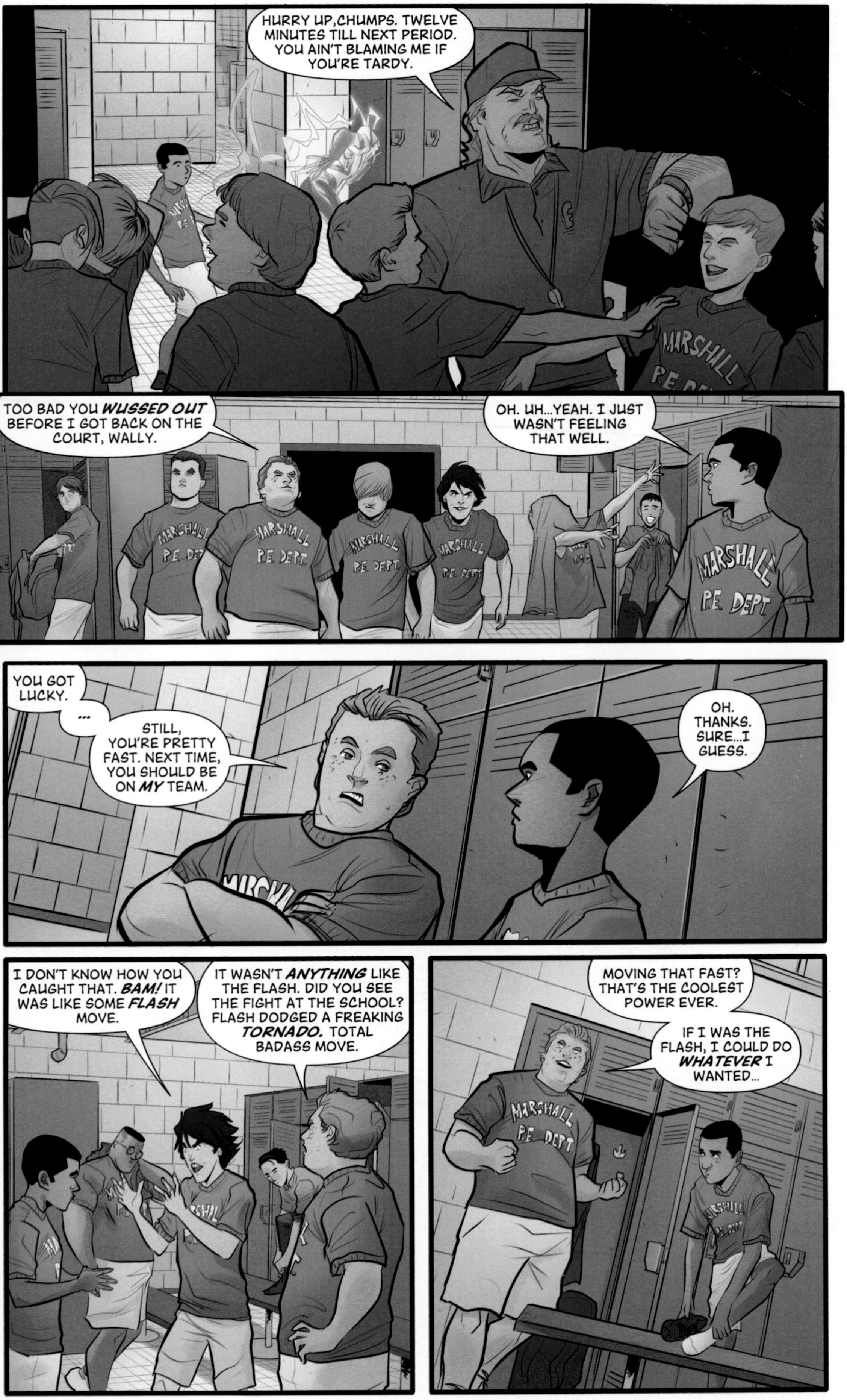
HURRY UP, CHUMPS. TWELVE MINUTES TILL NEXT PERIOD. YOU AIN'T BLAMING ME IF YOU'RE TARDY.
TOO BAD YOU WUSSED OUT BEFORE I GOT BACK ON THE COURT, WALLY.
OH. UH...YEAH. I JUST WASN'T FEELING THAT WELL.
MARSHALL P.E. DEPT.
YOU GOT LUCKY.
...
STILL, YOU'RE PRETTY FAST. NEXT TIME, YOU SHOULD BE ON MY TEAM.
OH. THANKS. SURE...I GUESS.
I DON'T KNOW HOW YOU CAUGHT THAT. BAM! IT WAS LIKE SOME FLASH MOVE.
IT WASN'T ANYTHING LIKE THE FLASH. DID YOU SEE THE FIGHT AT THE SCHOOL? FLASH DODGED A FREAKING TORNADO. TOTAL BADASS MOVE.
MOVING THAT FAST? THAT'S THE COOLEST POWER EVER.
IF I WAS THE FLASH, I COULD DO WHATEVER I WANTED...

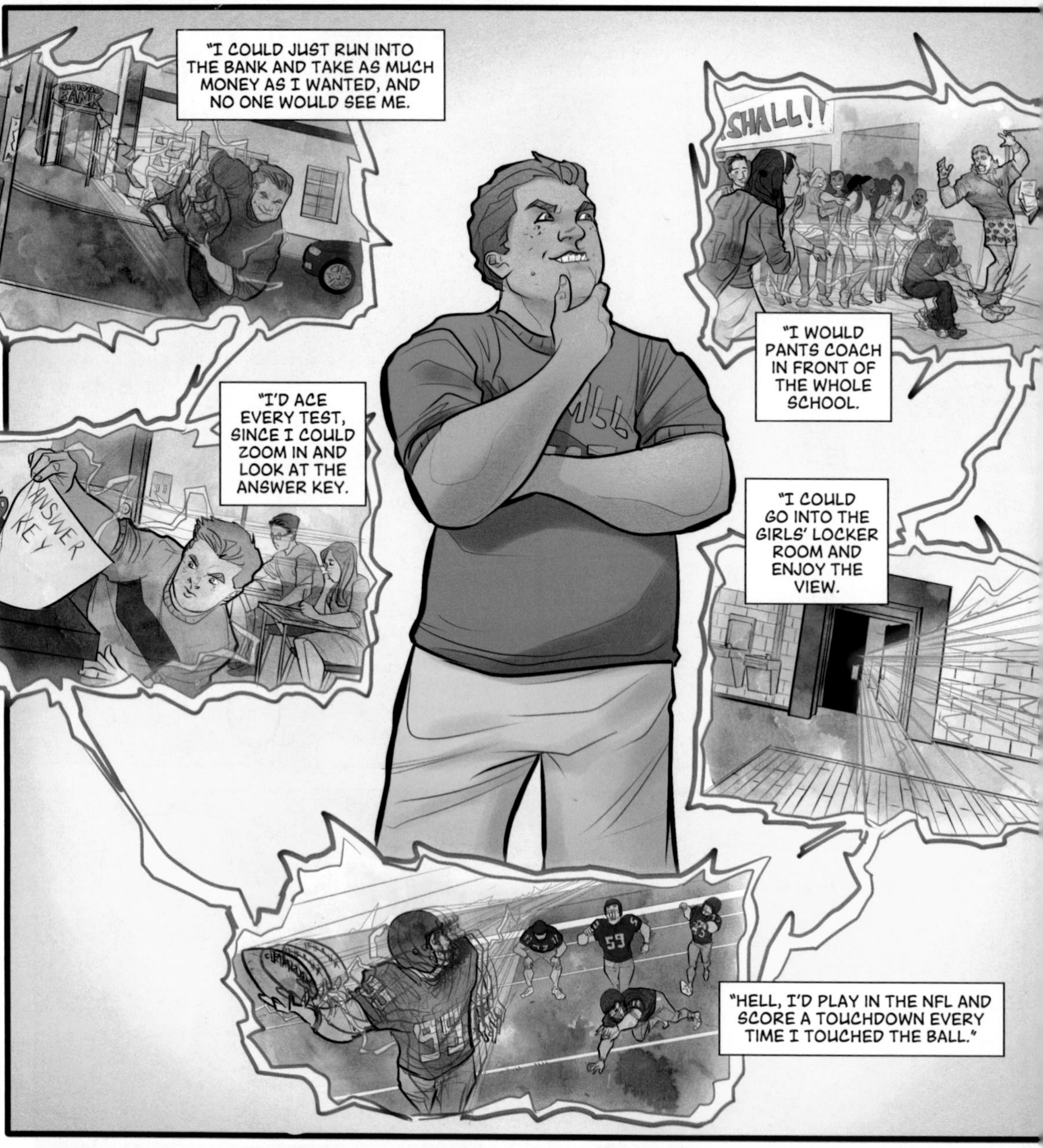
"I COULD JUST RUN INTO THE BANK AND TAKE AS MUCH MONEY AS I WANTED, AND NO ONE WOULD SEE ME.
BANK
SHALL!!
"I WOULD PANTS COACH IN FRONT OF THE WHOLE SCHOOL.
"I'D ACE EVERY TEST, SINCE I COULD ZOOM IN AND LOOK AT THE ANSWER KEY.
ANSWER KEY
"I COULD GO INTO THE GIRLS' LOCKER ROOM AND ENJOY THE VIEW.
"HELL, I'D PLAY IN THE NFL AND SCORE A TOUCHDOWN EVERY TIME I TOUCHED THE BALL."

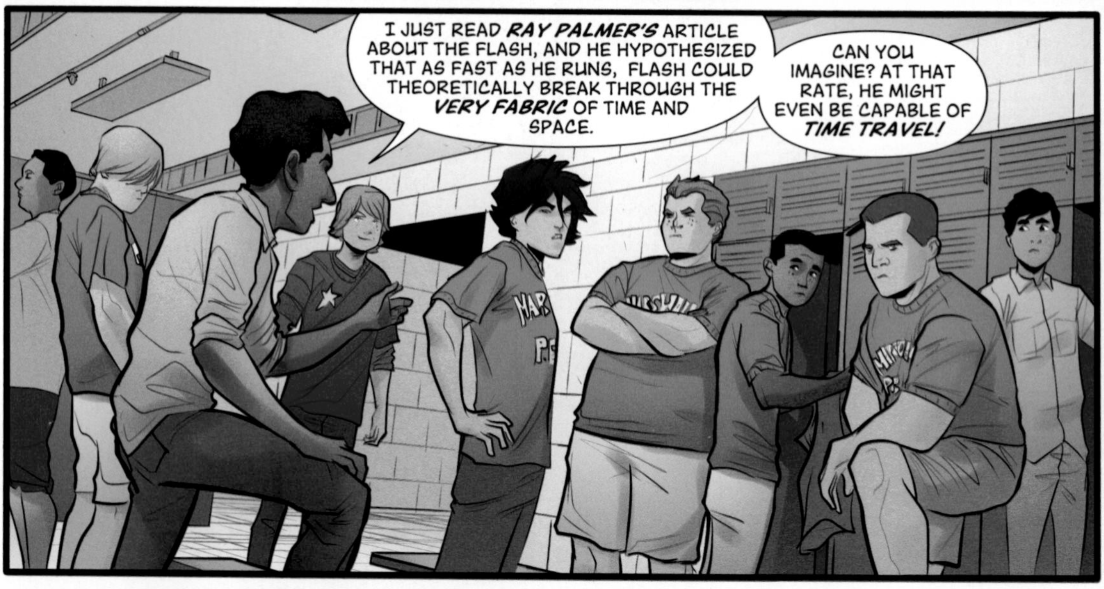
I JUST READ ***RAY PALMER'S*** ARTICLE ABOUT THE FLASH, AND HE HYPOTHESIZED THAT AS FAST AS HE RUNS, FLASH COULD THEORETICALLY BREAK THROUGH THE ***VERY FABRIC*** OF TIME AND SPACE.
CAN YOU IMAGINE? AT THAT RATE, HE MIGHT EVEN BE CAPABLE OF ***TIME TRAVEL!***

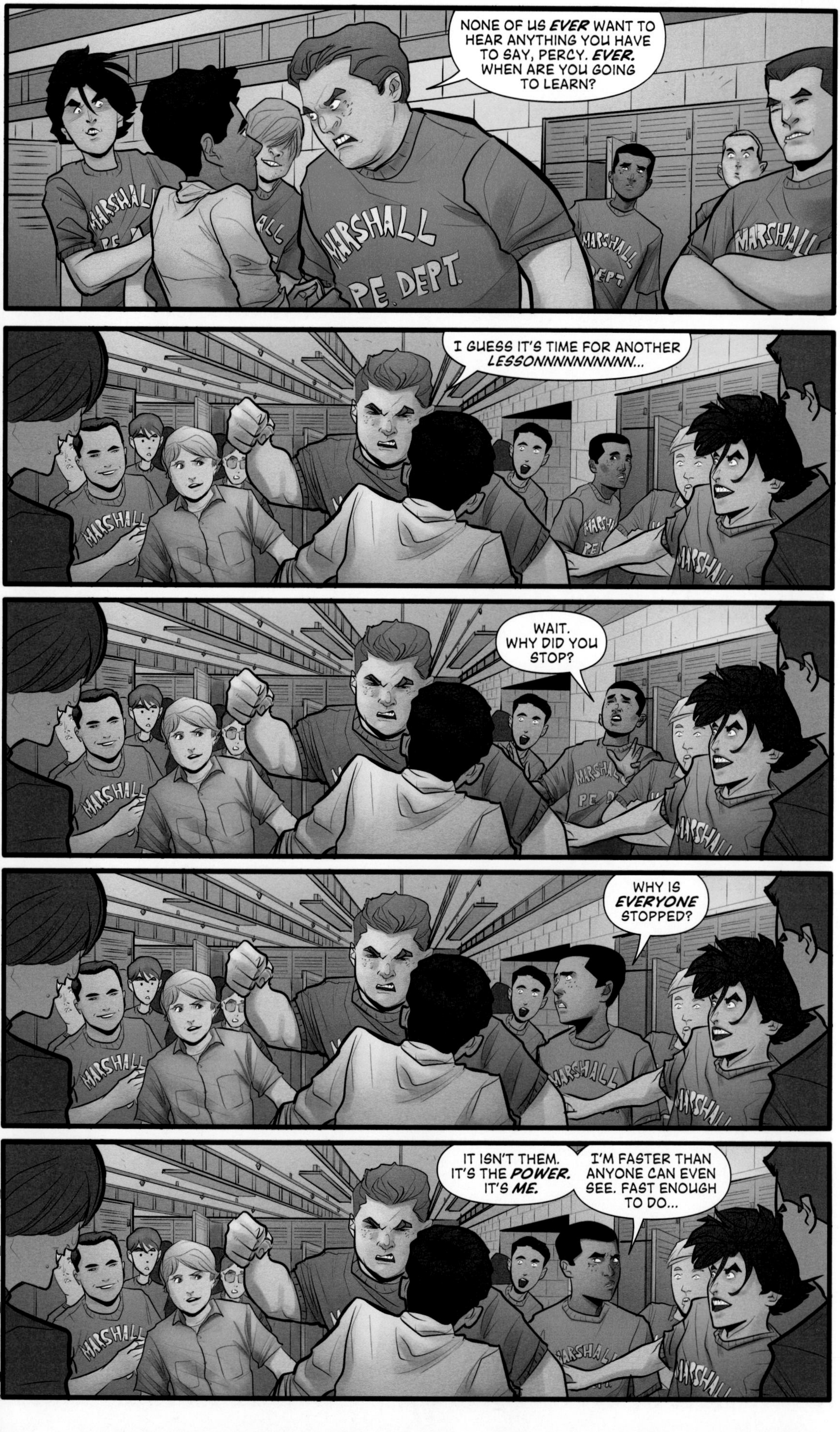
NONE OF US *EVER* WANT TO HEAR ANYTHING YOU HAVE TO SAY, PERCY. *EVER.* WHEN ARE YOU GOING TO LEARN?
MARSHALL P.E. DEPT.
I GUESS IT'S TIME FOR ANOTHER *LESSONNNNNNNNNN...*
MARSHALL
WAIT. WHY DID YOU STOP?
WHY IS *EVERYONE* STOPPED?
IT ISN'T THEM. IT'S THE *POWER.* IT'S *ME.*
I'M FASTER THAN ANYONE CAN EVEN SEE. FAST ENOUGH TO DO...

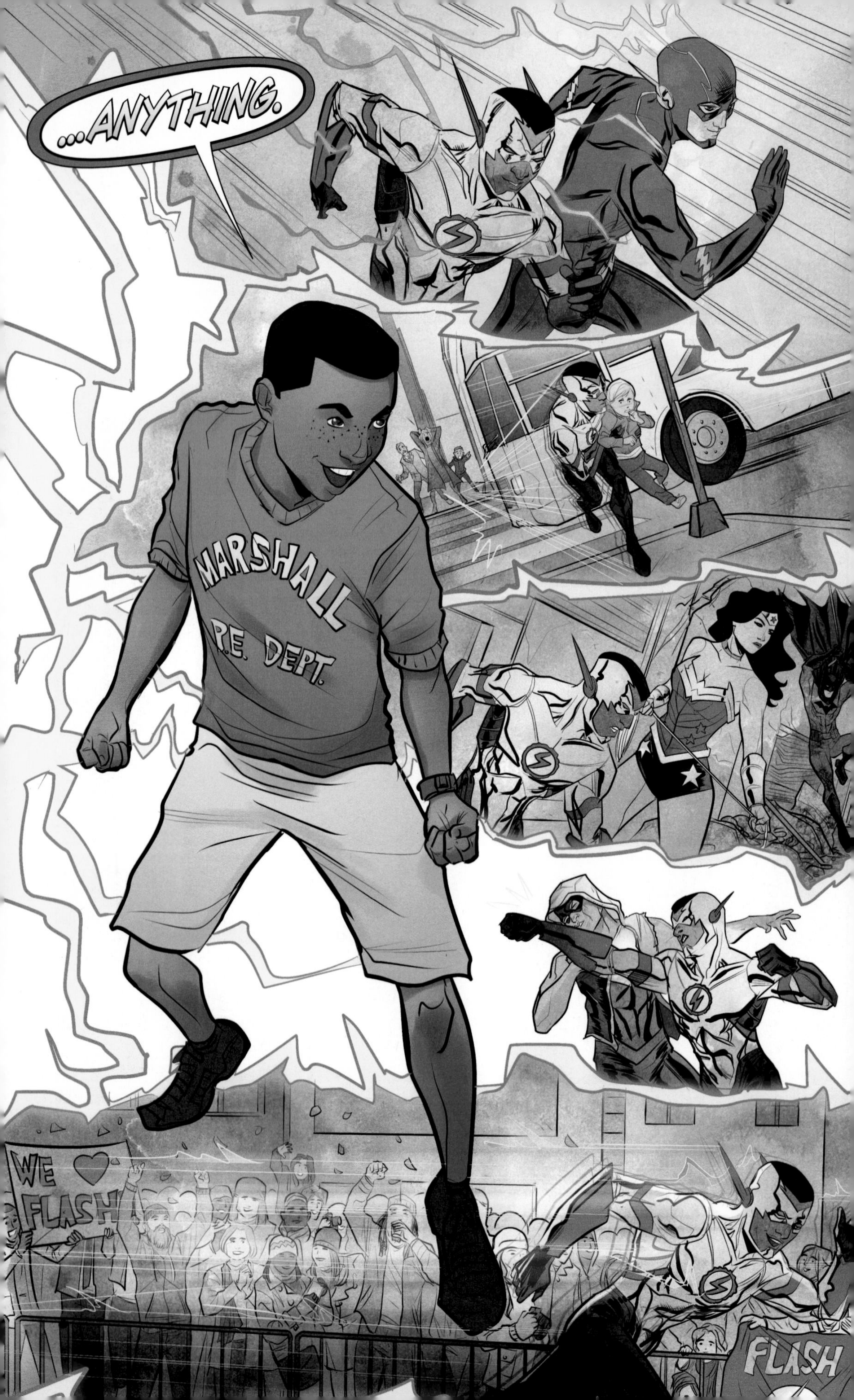

...ANYTHING.
MARSHALL P.E. DEPT.
WE ♥ FLASH
FLASH

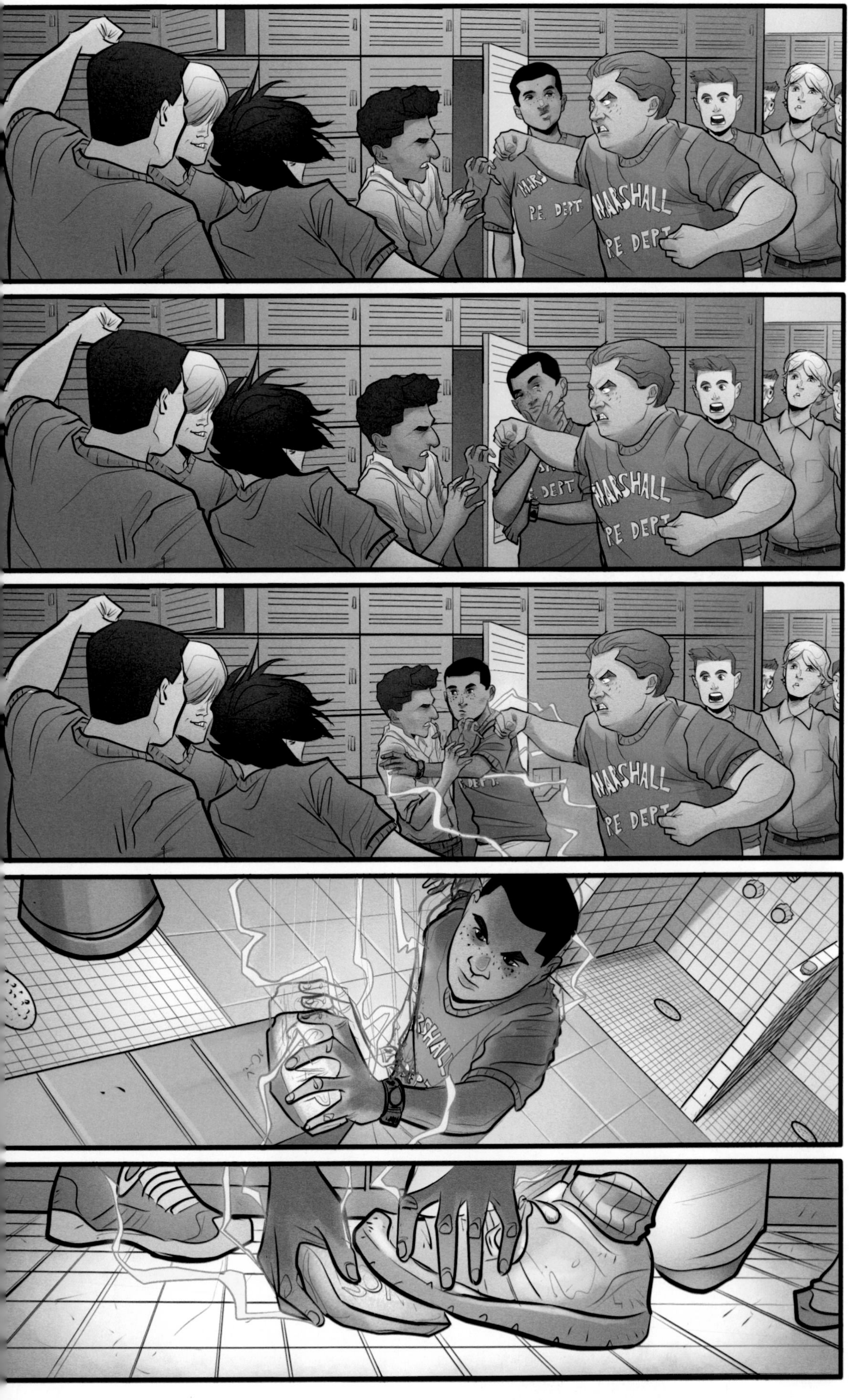
MARSHALL
P.E. DEPT

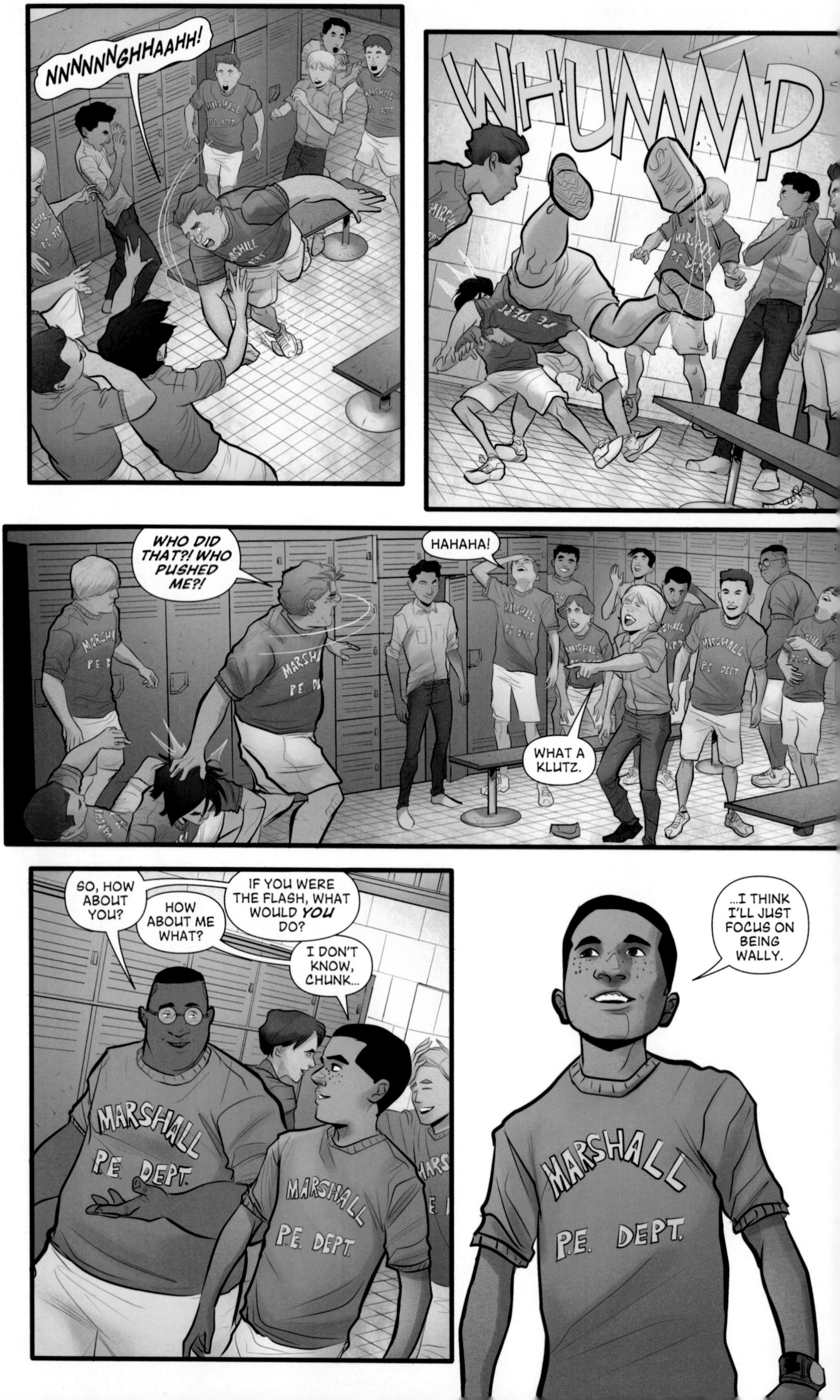
NNNNNNGHHAAHH!
WHUMMP
WHO DID THAT?! WHO PUSHED ME?!
HAHAHA!
WHAT A KLUTZ.
SO, HOW ABOUT YOU?
HOW ABOUT ME WHAT?
IF YOU WERE THE FLASH, WHAT WOULD *YOU* DO?
I DON'T KNOW, CHUNK...
...I THINK I'LL JUST FOCUS ON BEING WALLY.

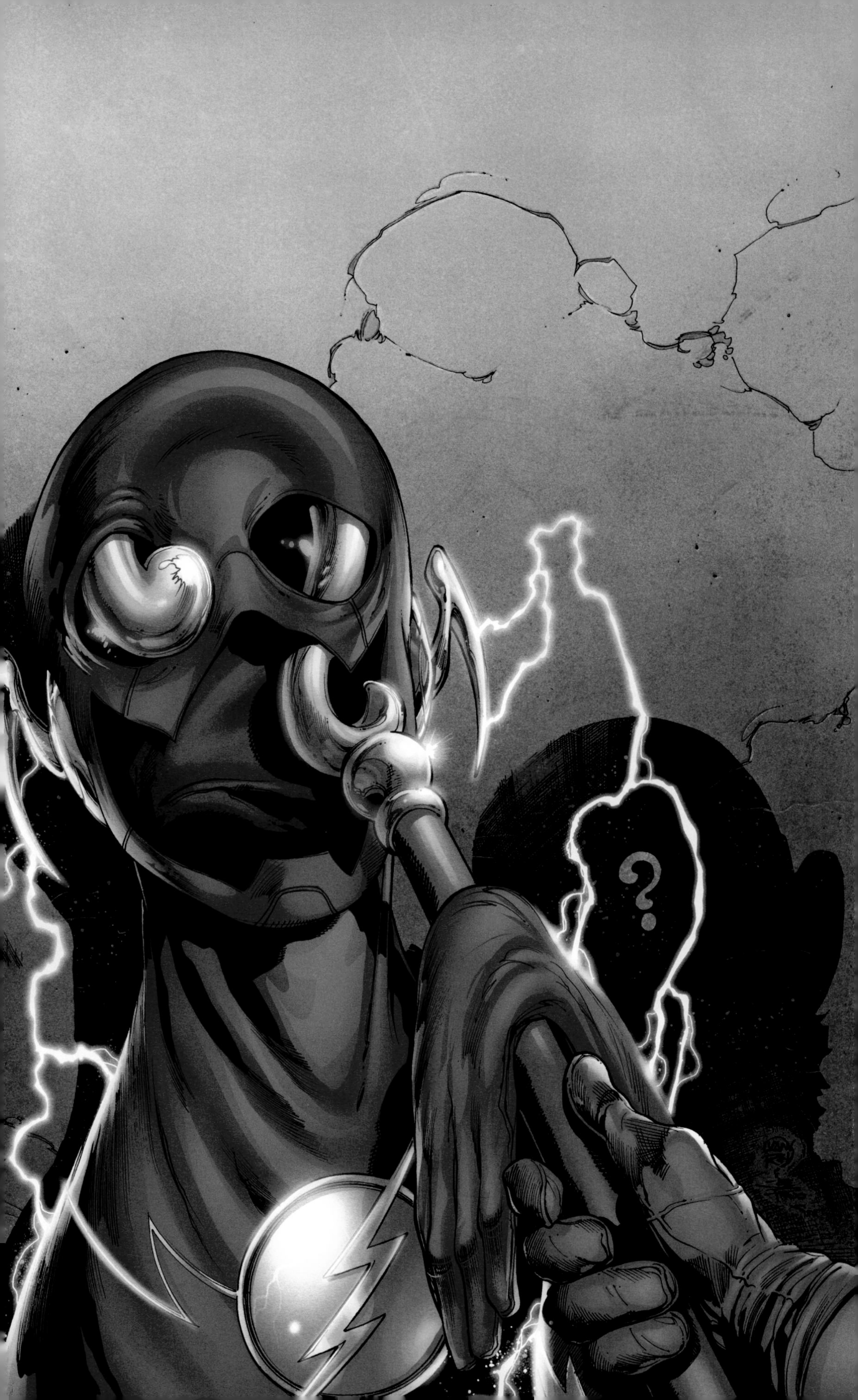

UNDER THE GUN

VAN JENSEN writer **GUS VAZQUEZ JOE EISMA** artists **GUY MAJOR** colorist **PAT BROSSEAU** letterer **IVAN REIS JOE PRADO ALEX SINCLAIR** cover

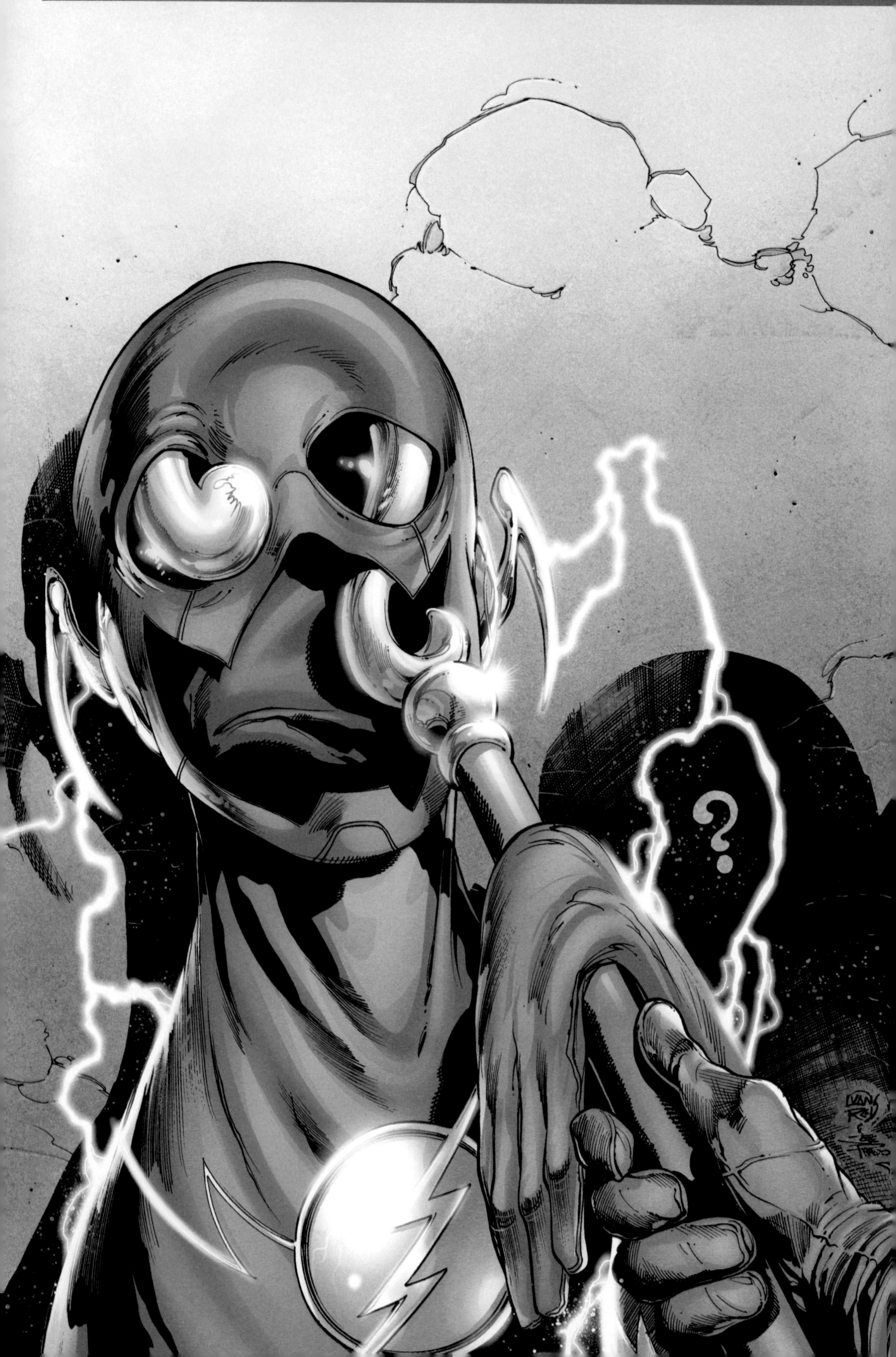

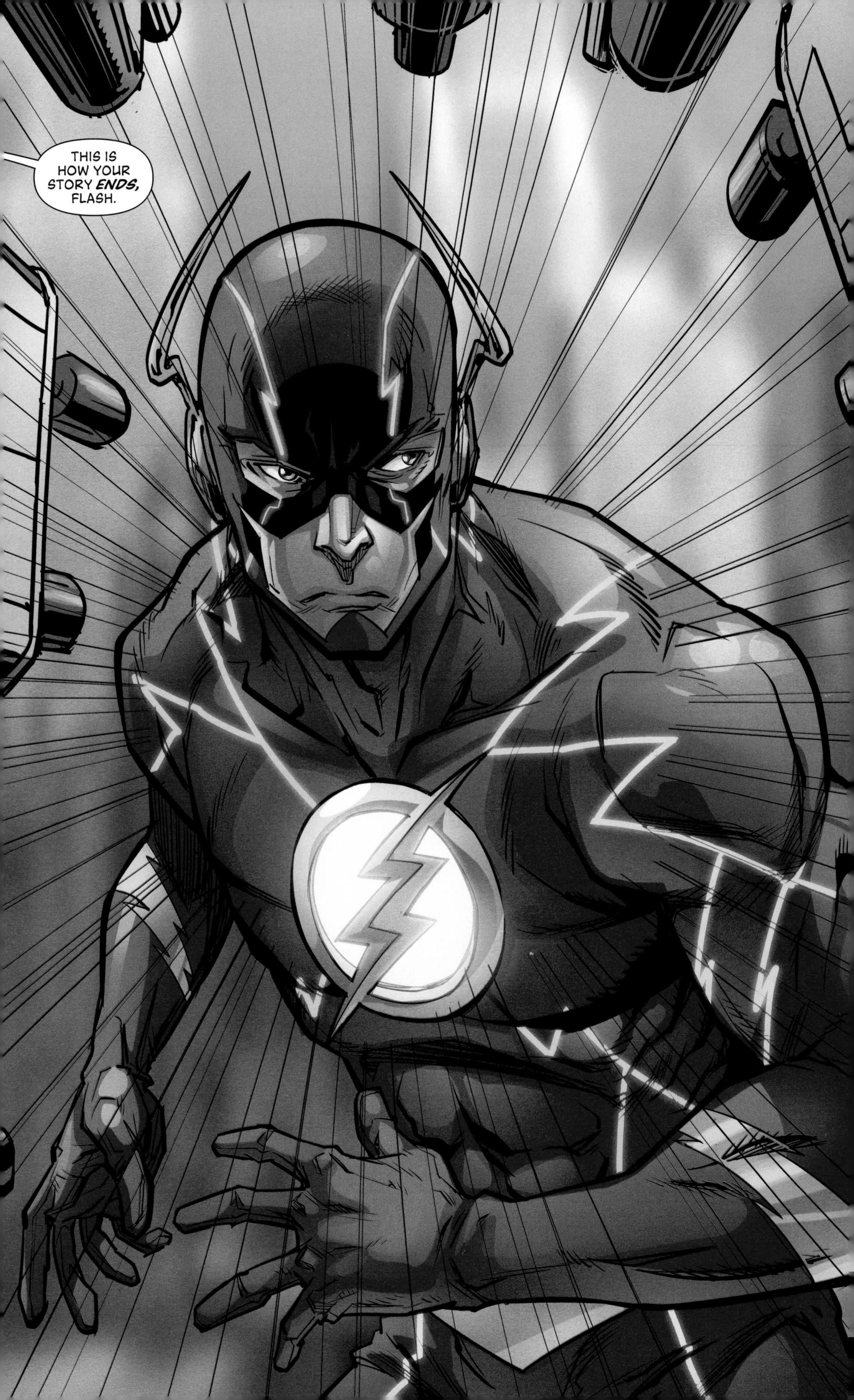
THIS IS HOW YOUR STORY ENDS, FLASH.

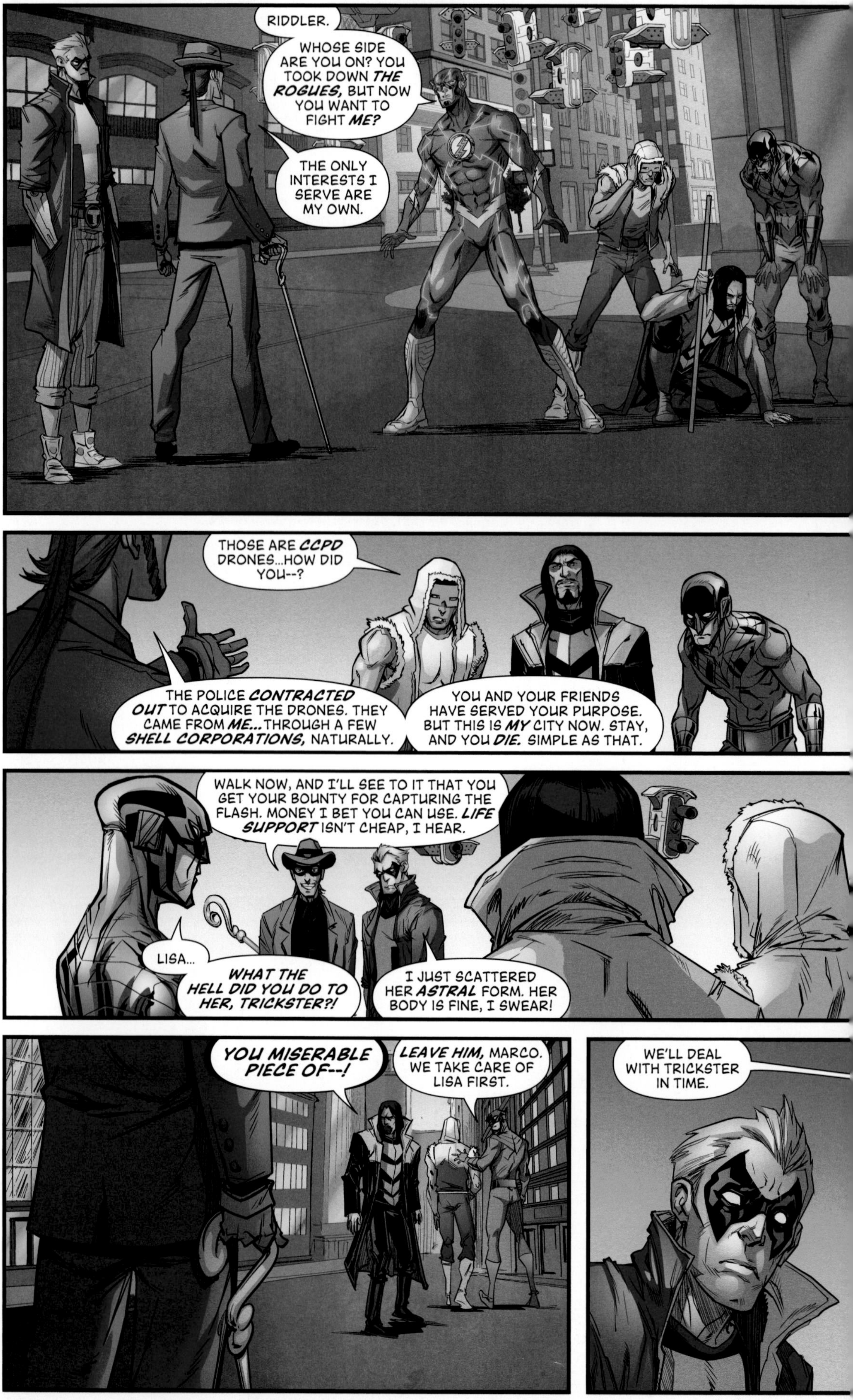
RIDDLER.
WHOSE SIDE ARE YOU ON? YOU TOOK DOWN THE ROGUES, BUT NOW YOU WANT TO FIGHT ME?
THE ONLY INTERESTS I SERVE ARE MY OWN.
THOSE ARE CCPD DRONES...HOW DID YOU--?
THE POLICE CONTRACTED OUT TO ACQUIRE THE DRONES. THEY CAME FROM ME...THROUGH A FEW SHELL CORPORATIONS, NATURALLY.
YOU AND YOUR FRIENDS HAVE SERVED YOUR PURPOSE. BUT THIS IS MY CITY NOW. STAY, AND YOU DIE. SIMPLE AS THAT.
WALK NOW, AND I'LL SEE TO IT THAT YOU GET YOUR BOUNTY FOR CAPTURING THE FLASH. MONEY I BET YOU CAN USE. LIFE SUPPORT ISN'T CHEAP, I HEAR.
LISA...
WHAT THE HELL DID YOU DO TO HER, TRICKSTER?!
I JUST SCATTERED HER ASTRAL FORM. HER BODY IS FINE, I SWEAR!
YOU MISERABLE PIECE OF--!
LEAVE HIM, MARCO. WE TAKE CARE OF LISA FIRST.
WE'LL DEAL WITH TRICKSTER IN TIME.

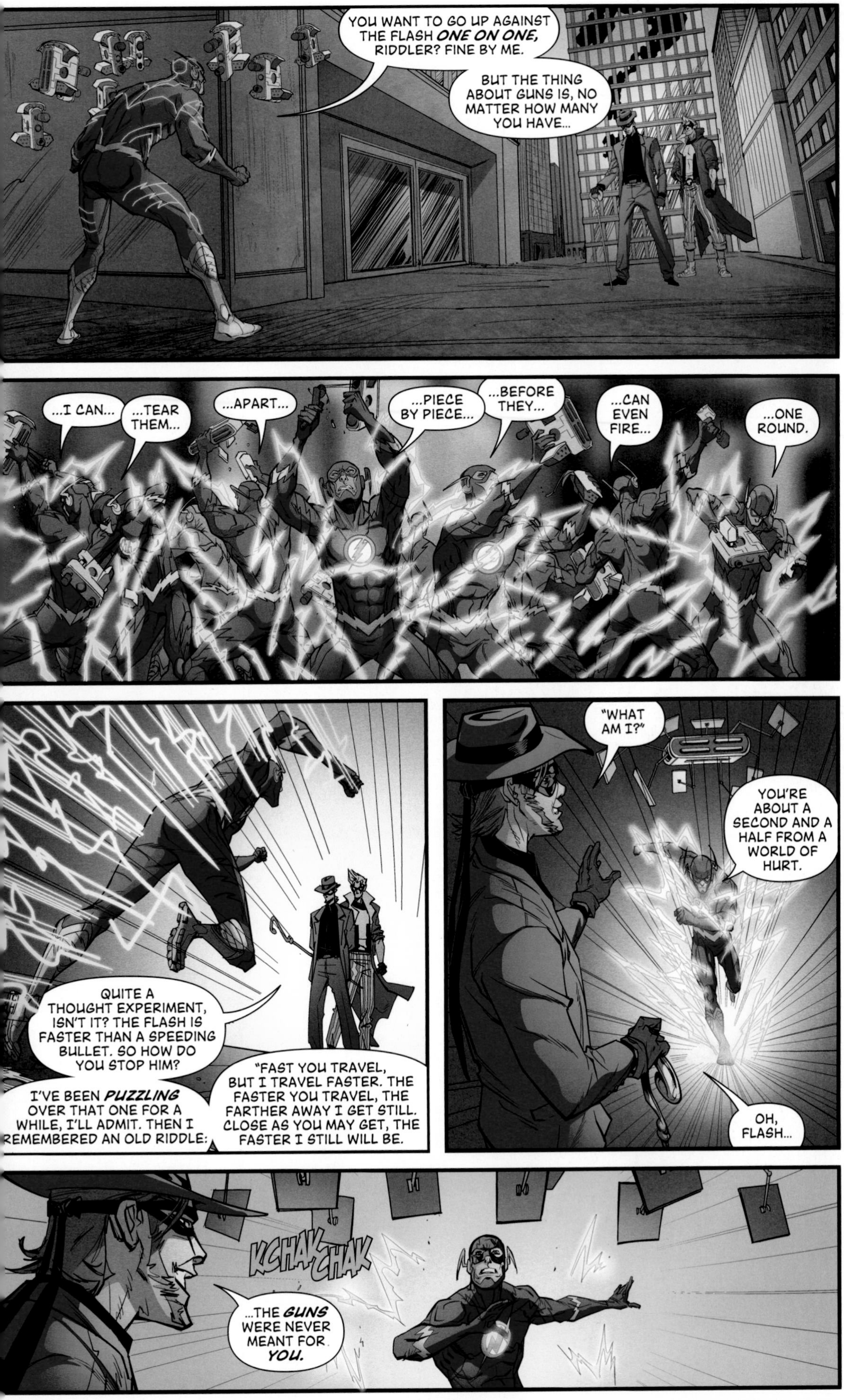
YOU WANT TO GO UP AGAINST THE FLASH ONE ON ONE, RIDDLER? FINE BY ME.
BUT THE THING ABOUT GUNS IS, NO MATTER HOW MANY YOU HAVE...
...I CAN...
...TEAR THEM...
...APART...
...PIECE BY PIECE...
...BEFORE THEY...
...CAN EVEN FIRE...
...ONE ROUND.
QUITE A THOUGHT EXPERIMENT, ISN'T IT? THE FLASH IS FASTER THAN A SPEEDING BULLET. SO HOW DO YOU STOP HIM?
I'VE BEEN PUZZLING OVER THAT ONE FOR A WHILE, I'LL ADMIT. THEN I REMEMBERED AN OLD RIDDLE:
"FAST YOU TRAVEL, BUT I TRAVEL FASTER. THE FASTER YOU TRAVEL, THE FARTHER AWAY I GET STILL. CLOSE AS YOU MAY GET, THE FASTER I STILL WILL BE.
"WHAT AM I?"
YOU'RE ABOUT A SECOND AND A HALF FROM A WORLD OF HURT.
OH, FLASH...
KCHAK CHAK
...THE GUNS WERE NEVER MEANT FOR YOU.

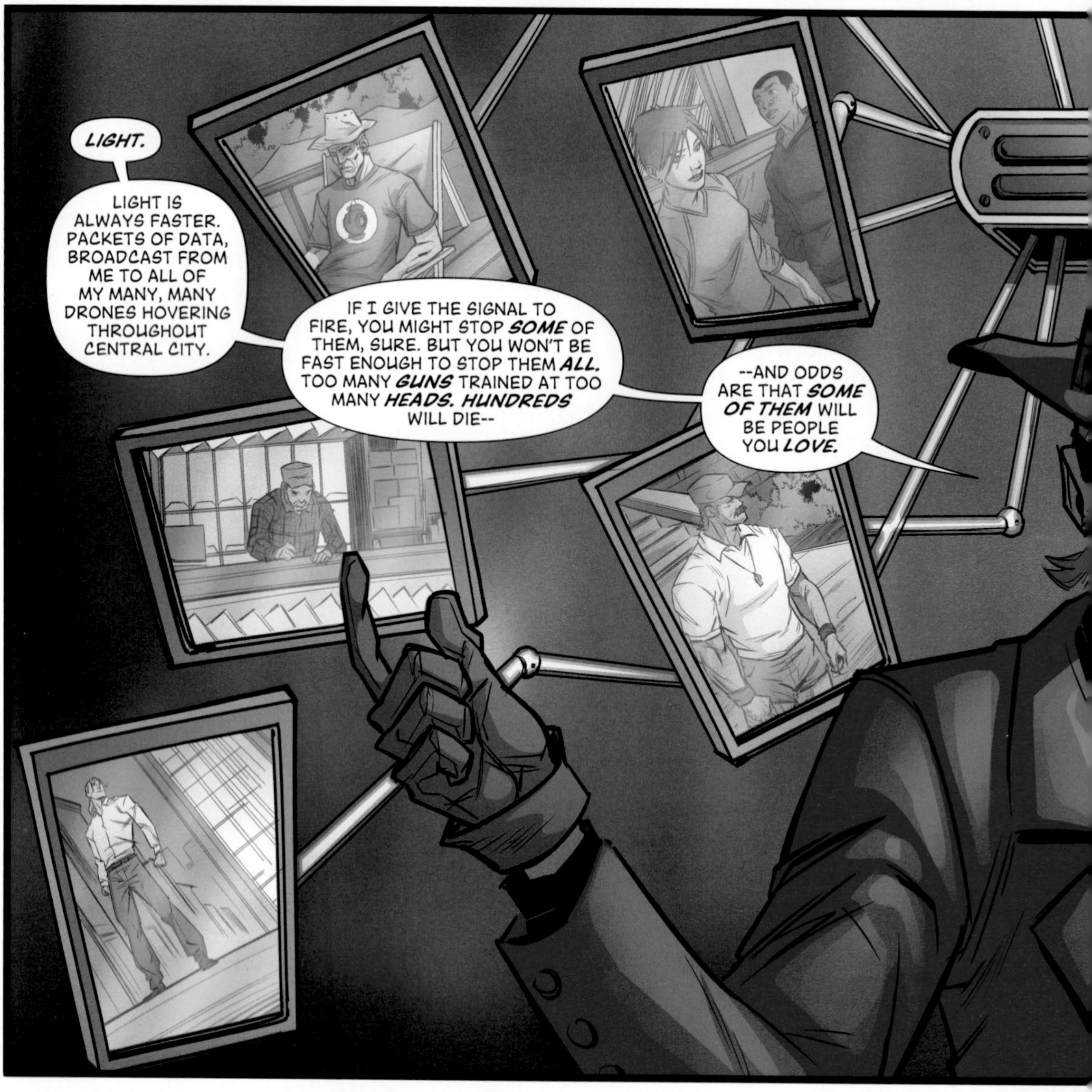
LIGHT.
LIGHT IS ALWAYS FASTER. PACKETS OF DATA, BROADCAST FROM ME TO ALL OF MY MANY, MANY DRONES HOVERING THROUGHOUT CENTRAL CITY.
IF I GIVE THE SIGNAL TO FIRE, YOU MIGHT STOP SOME OF THEM, SURE. BUT YOU WON'T BE FAST ENOUGH TO STOP THEM ALL. TOO MANY GUNS TRAINED AT TOO MANY HEADS. HUNDREDS WILL DIE--
--AND ODDS ARE THAT SOME OF THEM WILL BE PEOPLE YOU LOVE.

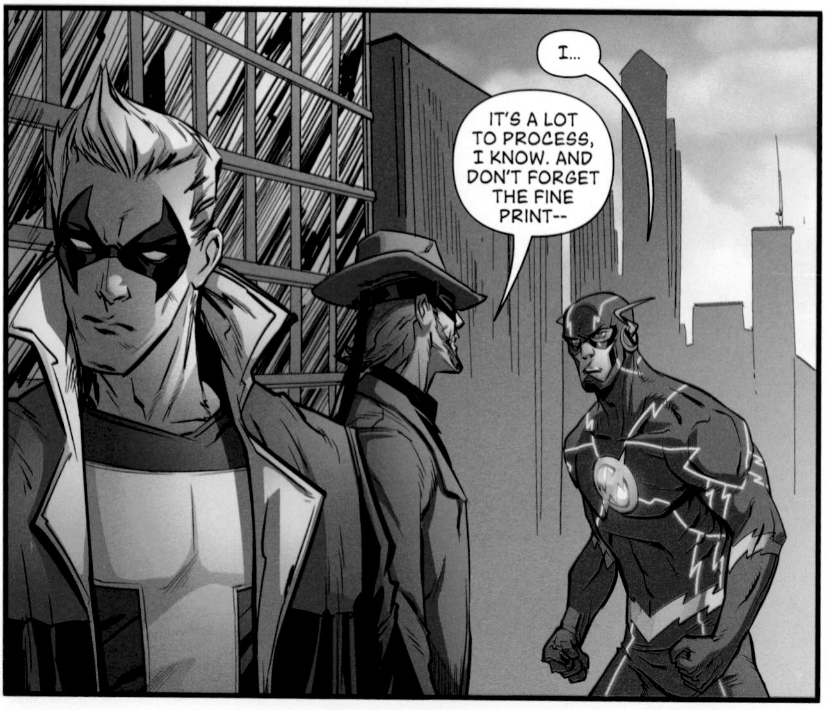
I...
IT'S A LOT TO PROCESS, I KNOW. AND DON'T FORGET THE FINE PRINT--

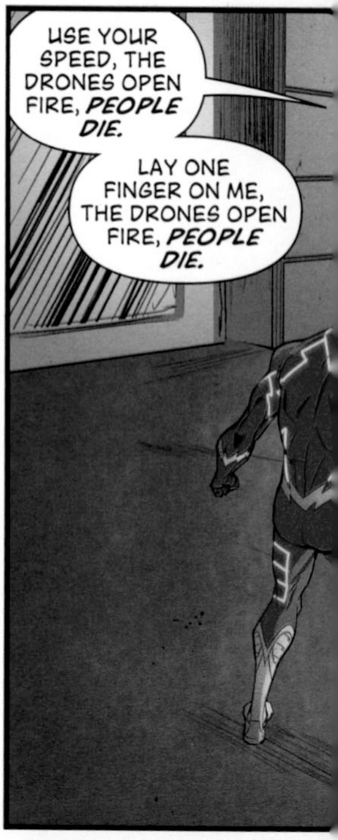
USE YOUR SPEED, THE DRONES OPEN FIRE, PEOPLE DIE.
LAY ONE FINGER ON ME, THE DRONES OPEN FIRE, PEOPLE DIE.

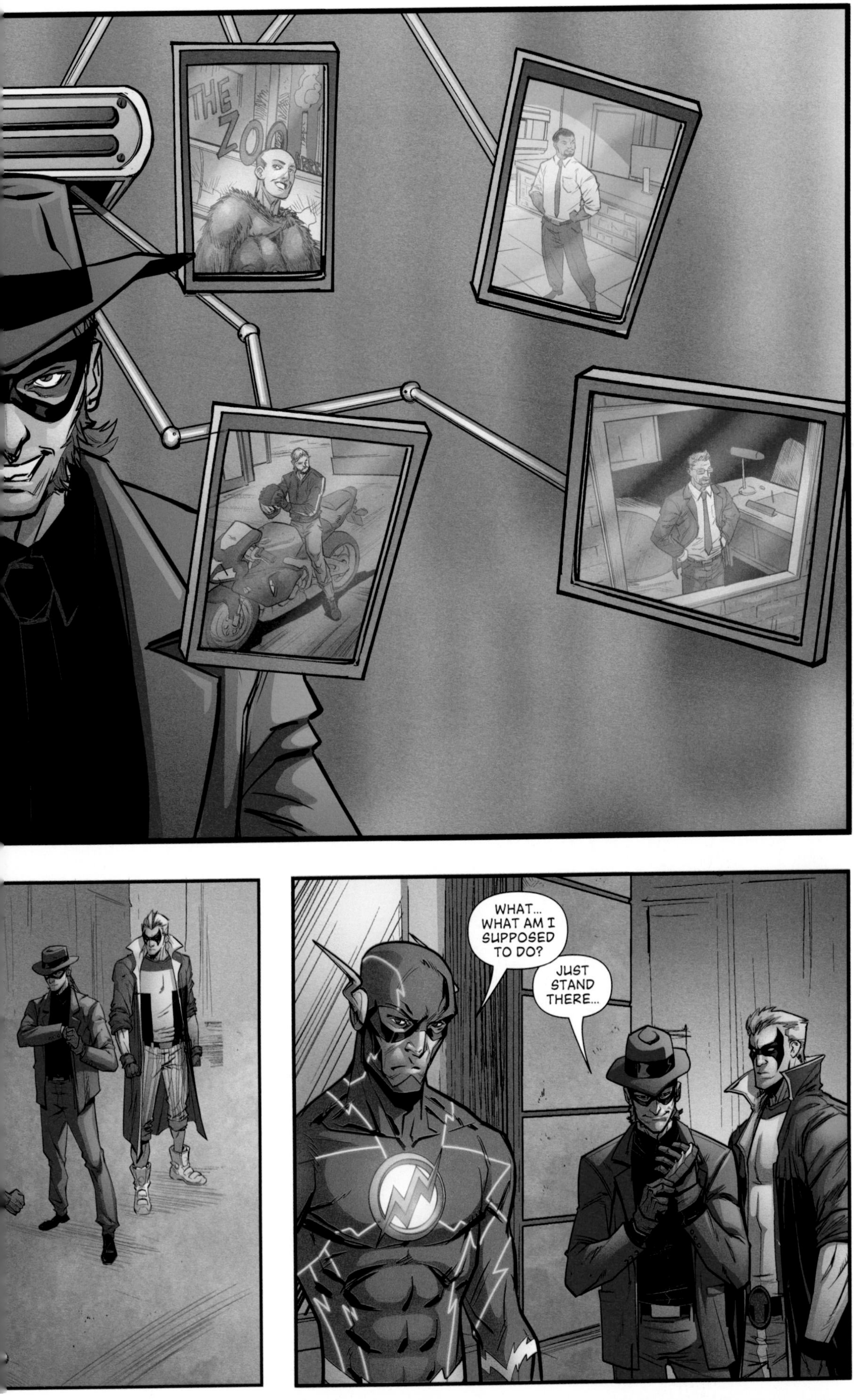
THE ZOO
WHAT... WHAT AM I SUPPOSED TO DO?
JUST STAND THERE...

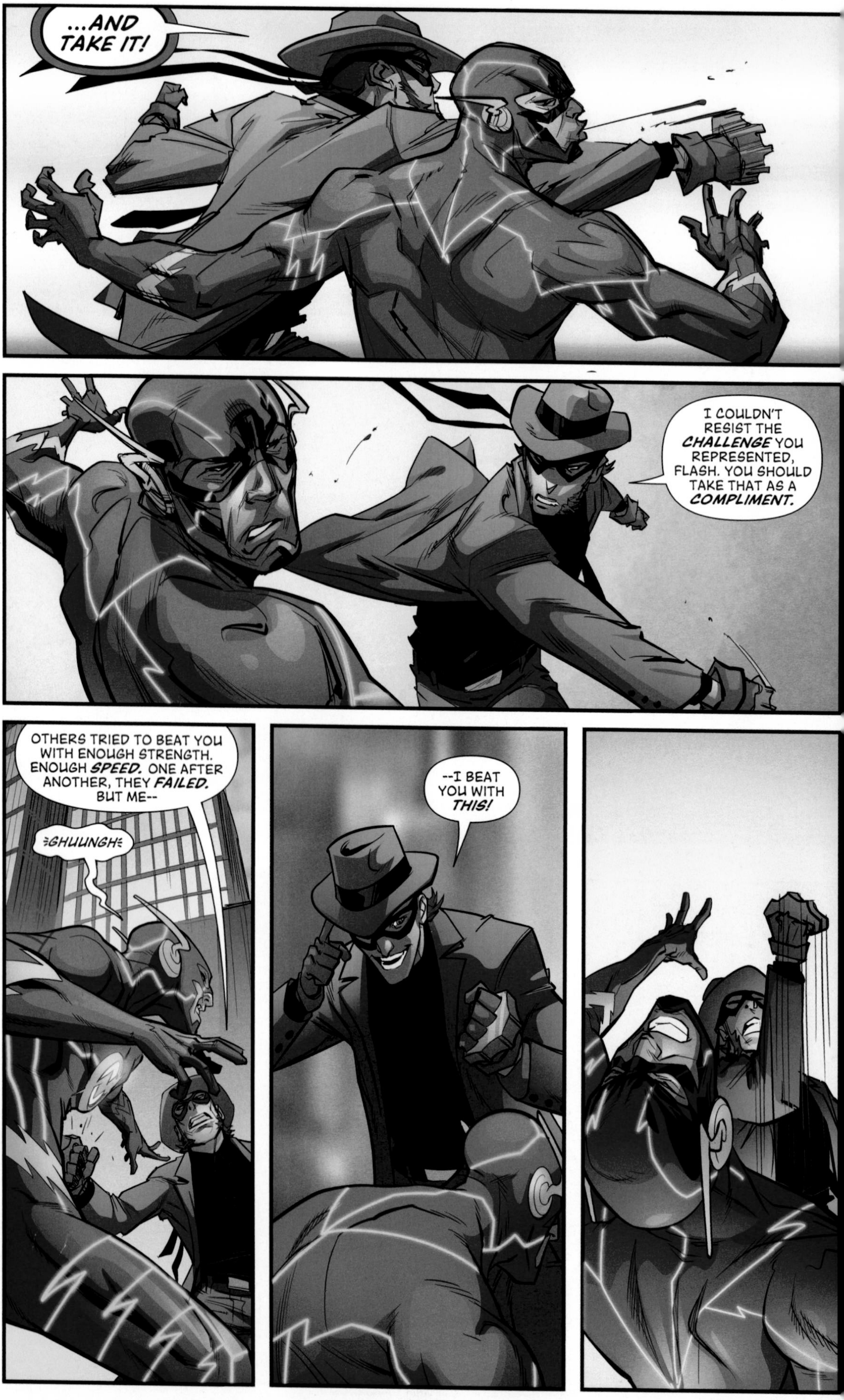
...AND TAKE IT!
I COULDN'T RESIST THE CHALLENGE YOU REPRESENTED, FLASH. YOU SHOULD TAKE THAT AS A COMPLIMENT.
OTHERS TRIED TO BEAT YOU WITH ENOUGH STRENGTH. ENOUGH SPEED. ONE AFTER ANOTHER, THEY FAILED. BUT ME--
GHUUNGH
--I BEAT YOU WITH THIS!

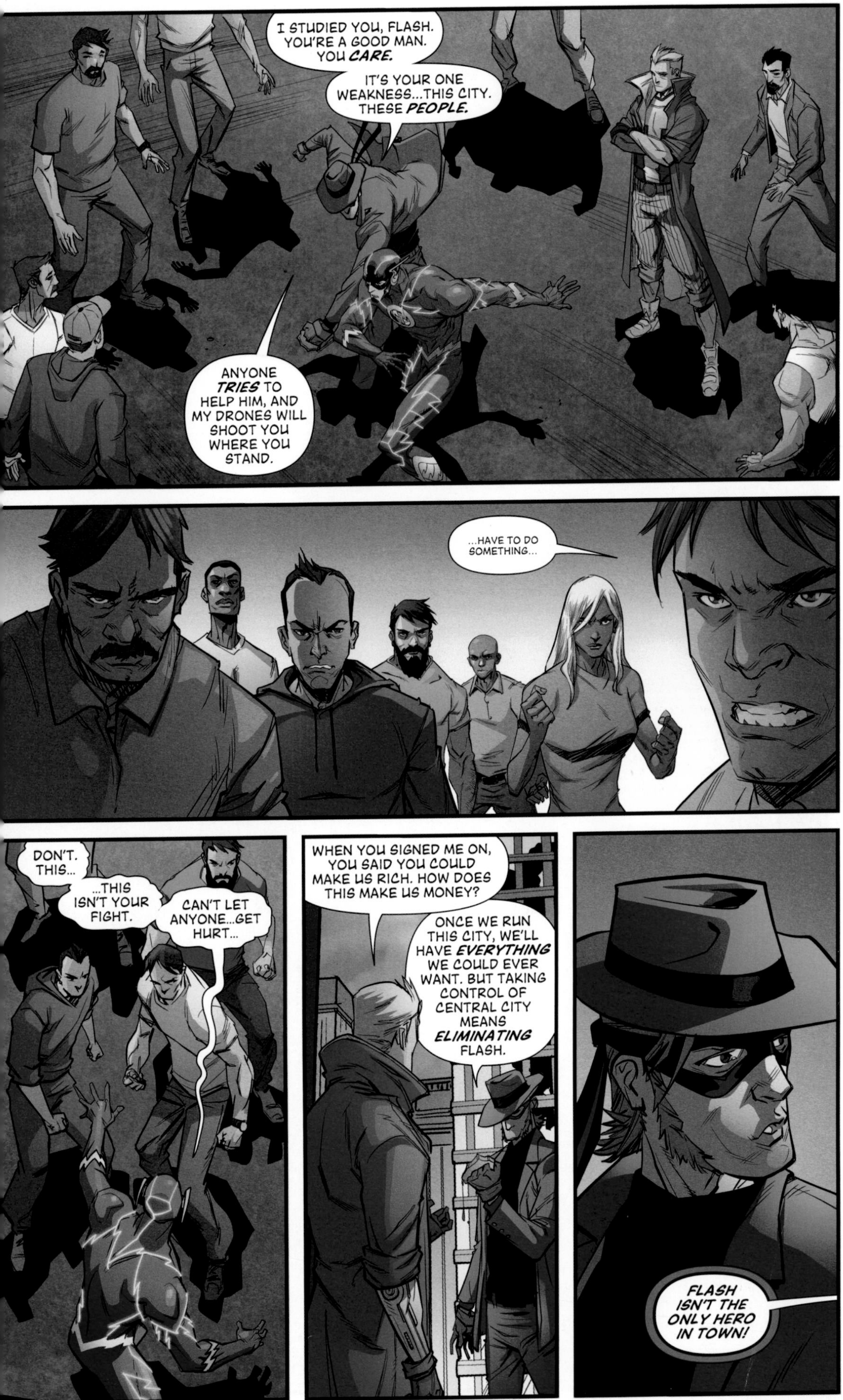

I STUDIED YOU, FLASH. YOU'RE A GOOD MAN. YOU *CARE.*
IT'S YOUR ONE WEAKNESS...THIS CITY. THESE *PEOPLE.*
ANYONE *TRIES* TO HELP HIM, AND MY DRONES WILL SHOOT YOU WHERE YOU STAND.
...HAVE TO DO SOMETHING...
DON'T. THIS...
...THIS ISN'T YOUR FIGHT.
CAN'T LET ANYONE...GET HURT...
WHEN YOU SIGNED ME ON, YOU SAID YOU COULD MAKE US RICH. HOW DOES THIS MAKE US MONEY?
ONCE WE RUN THIS CITY, WE'LL HAVE *EVERYTHING* WE COULD EVER WANT. BUT TAKING CONTROL OF CENTRAL CITY MEANS *ELIMINATING* FLASH.
FLASH ISN'T THE ONLY HERO IN TOWN!

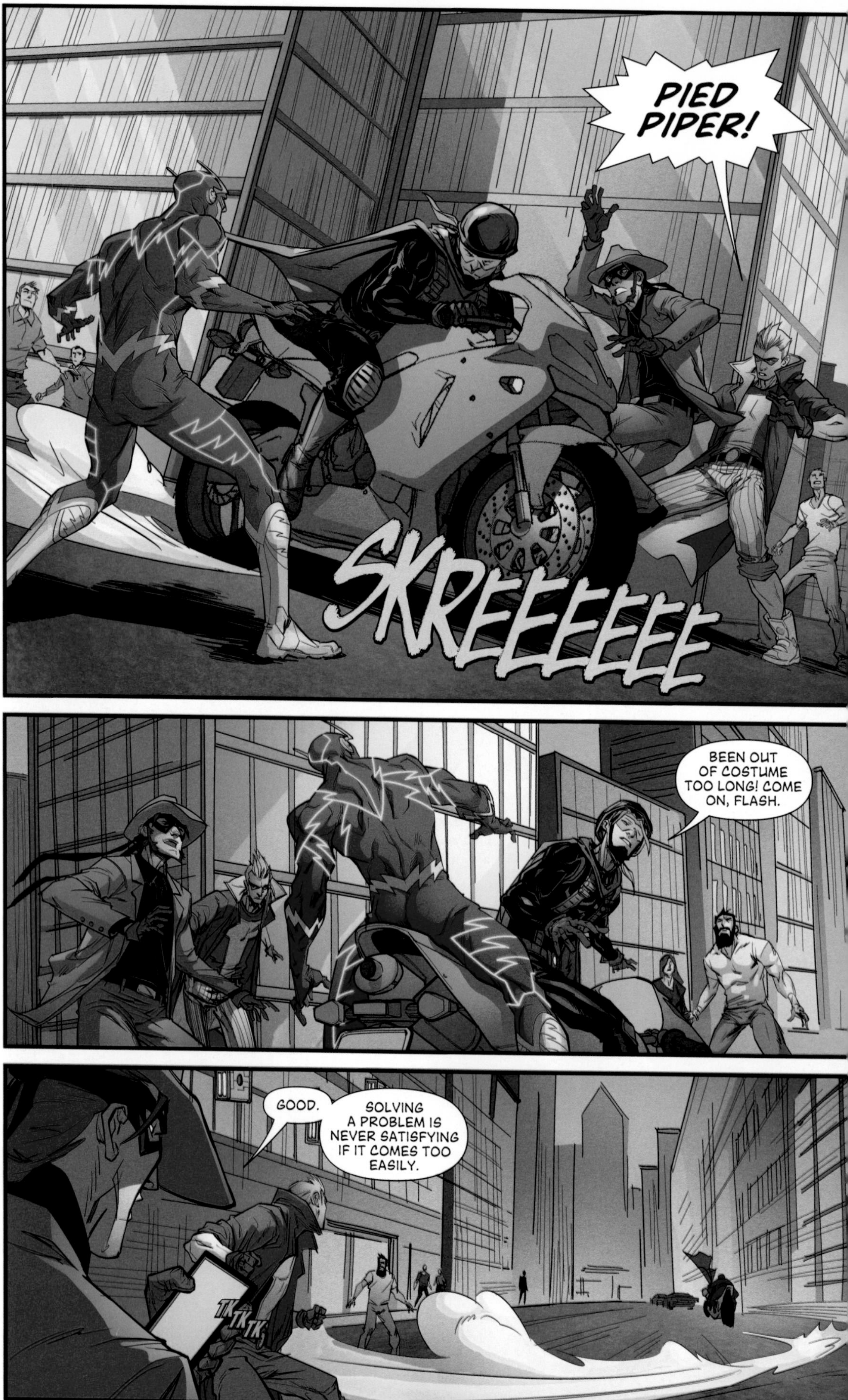
PIED PIPER!
SKREEEEEEE
BEEN OUT OF COSTUME TOO LONG! COME ON, FLASH.
GOOD.
SOLVING A PROBLEM IS NEVER SATISFYING IF IT COMES TOO EASILY.
TK TK TK

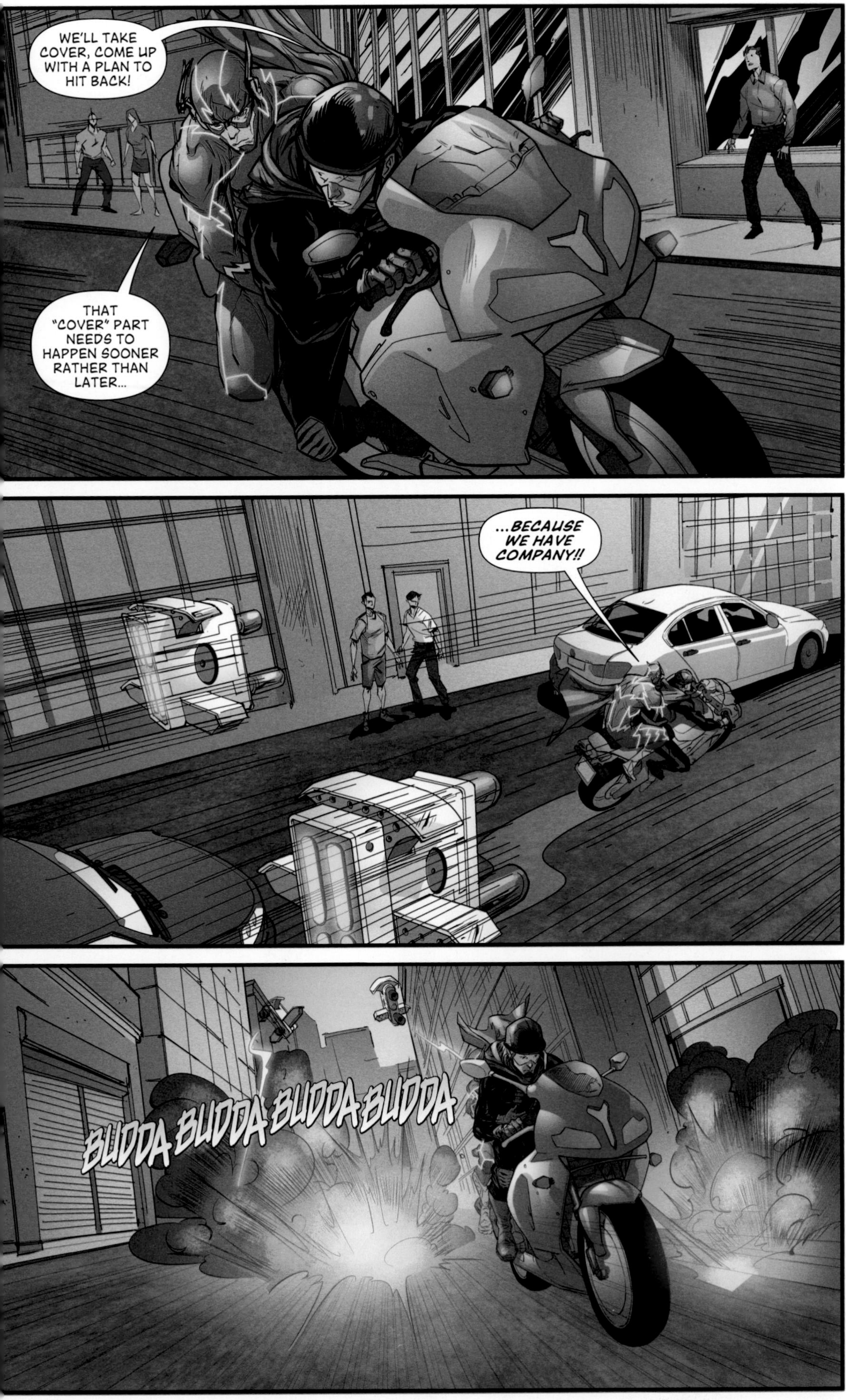
WE'LL TAKE COVER, COME UP WITH A PLAN TO HIT BACK!
THAT "COVER" PART NEEDS TO HAPPEN SOONER RATHER THAN LATER...
...BECAUSE WE HAVE COMPANY!!
BUDDA BUDDA BUDDA BUDDA

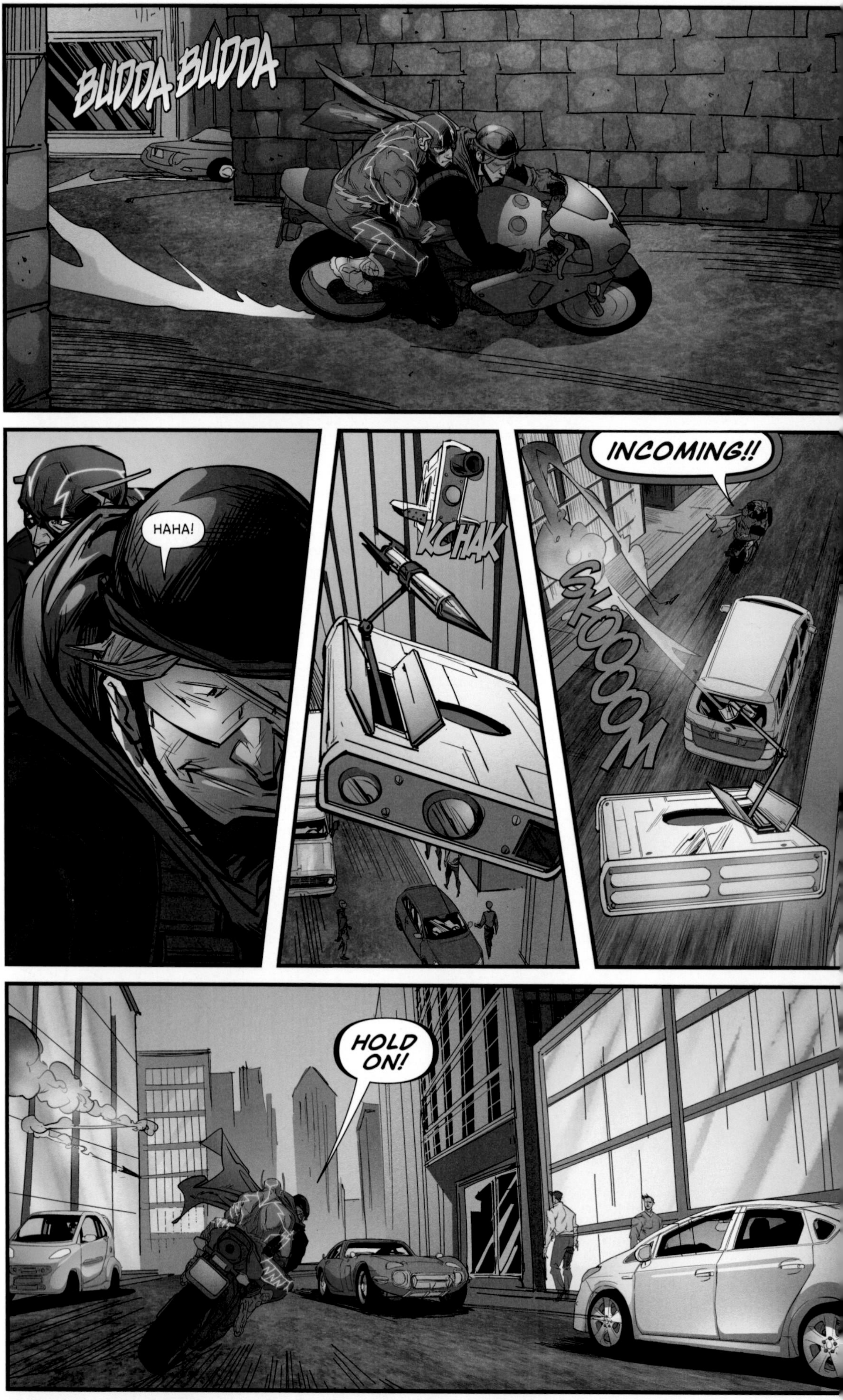
BUDDA BUDDA
HAHA!
KCHAK
INCOMING!!
SKOOOOM
HOLD ON!

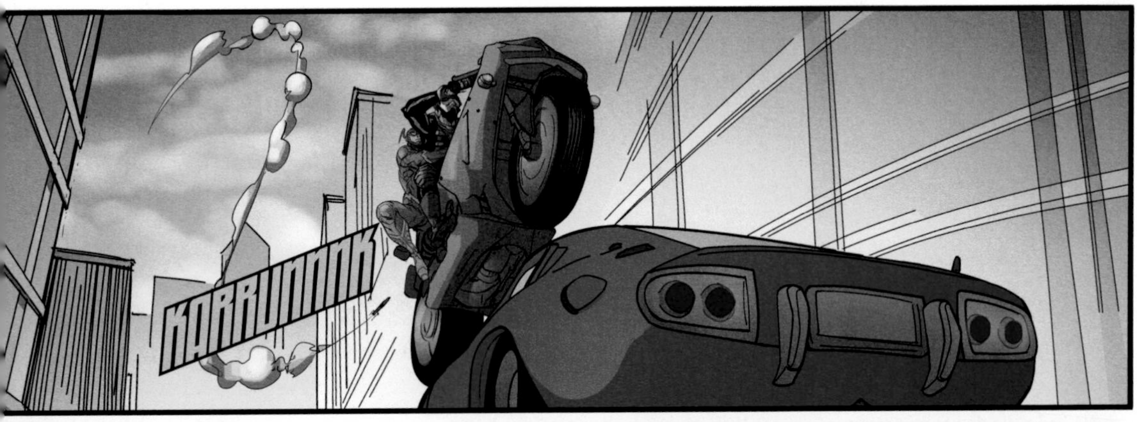
KORRUNNNK

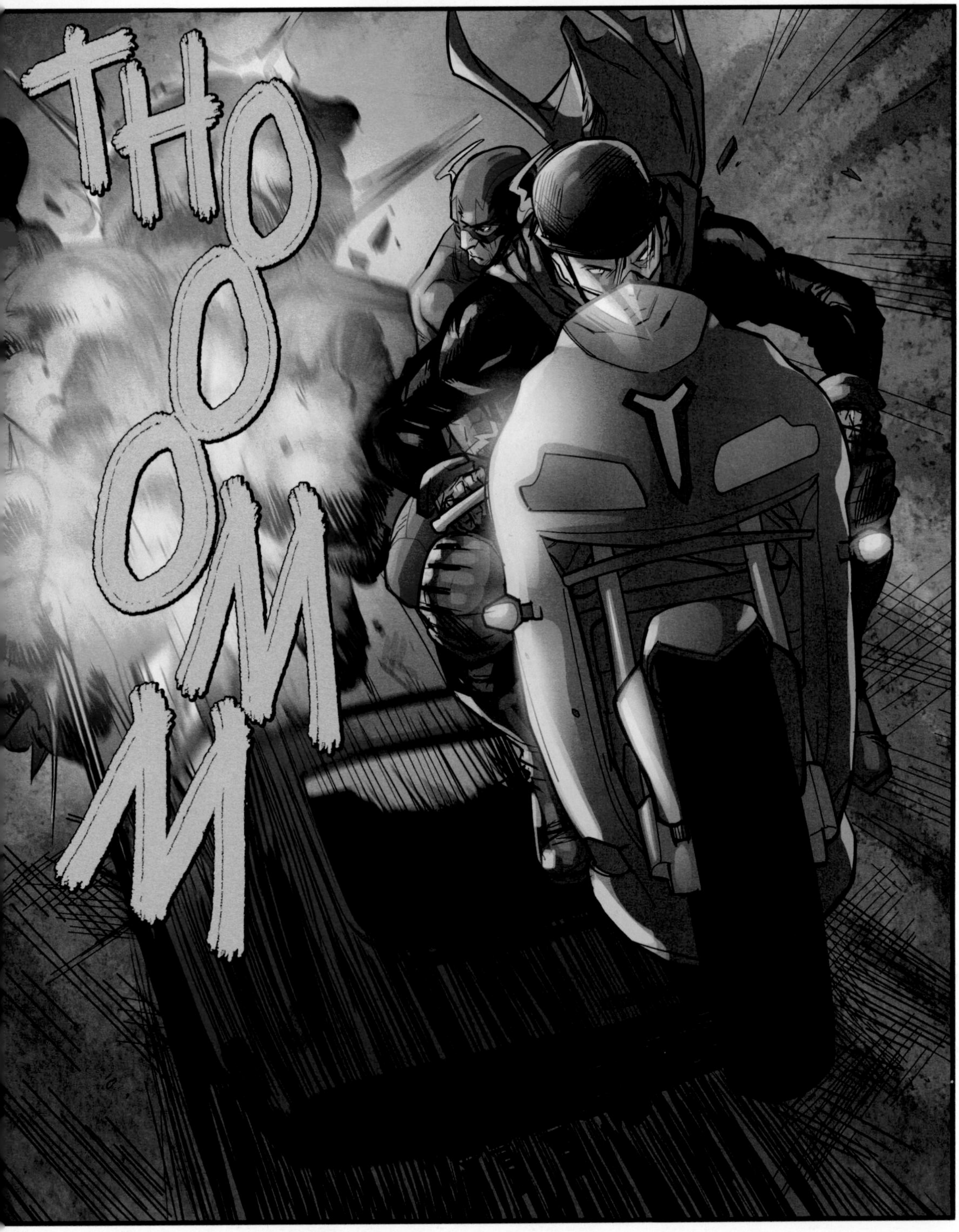
THOOOMM

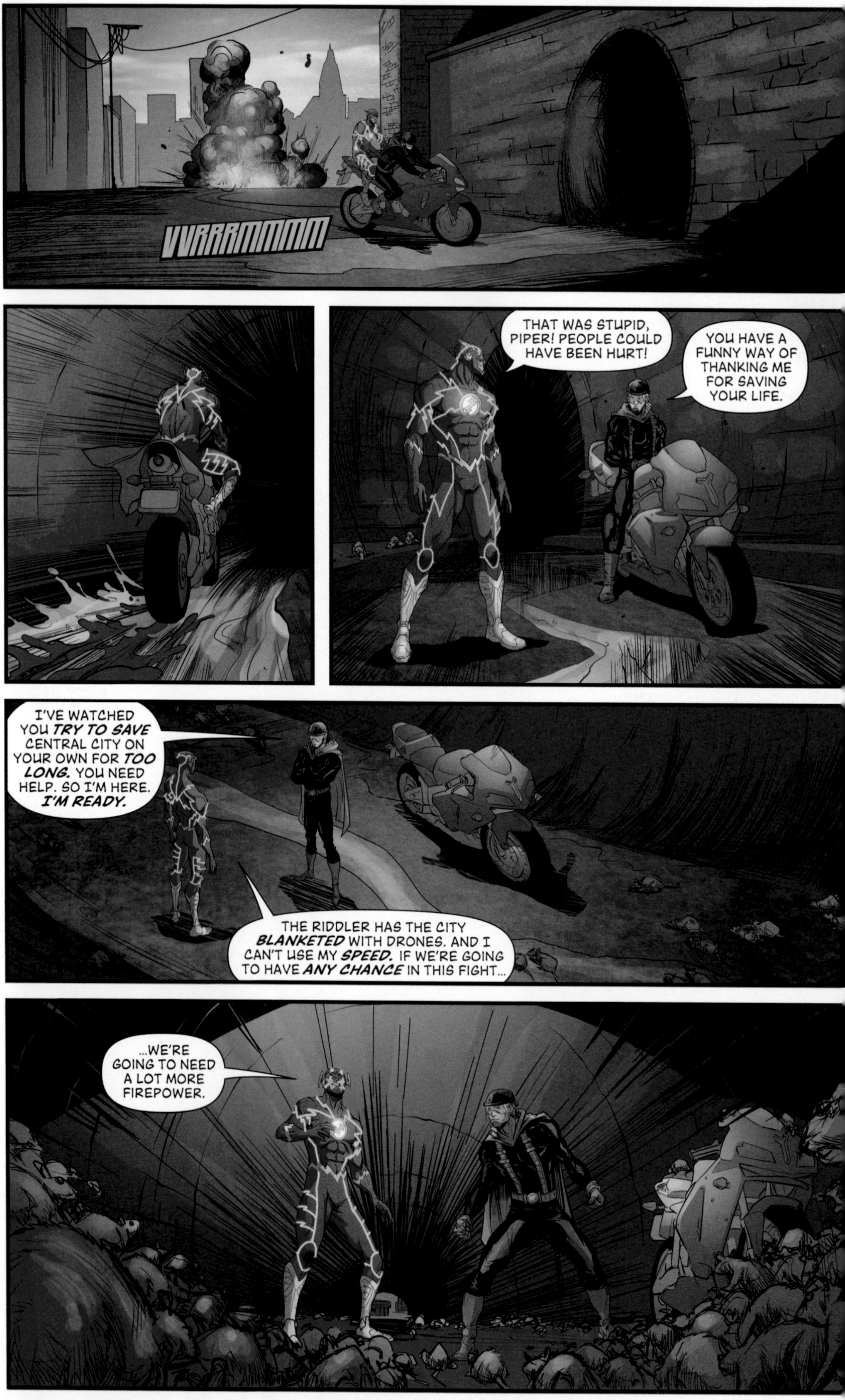
VVRRRMMMM
THAT WAS STUPID, PIPER! PEOPLE COULD HAVE BEEN HURT!
YOU HAVE A FUNNY WAY OF THANKING ME FOR SAVING YOUR LIFE.
I'VE WATCHED YOU TRY TO SAVE CENTRAL CITY ON YOUR OWN FOR TOO LONG. YOU NEED HELP. SO I'M HERE. I'M READY.
THE RIDDLER HAS THE CITY BLANKETED WITH DRONES. AND I CAN'T USE MY SPEED. IF WE'RE GOING TO HAVE ANY CHANCE IN THIS FIGHT...
...WE'RE GOING TO NEED A LOT MORE FIREPOWER.

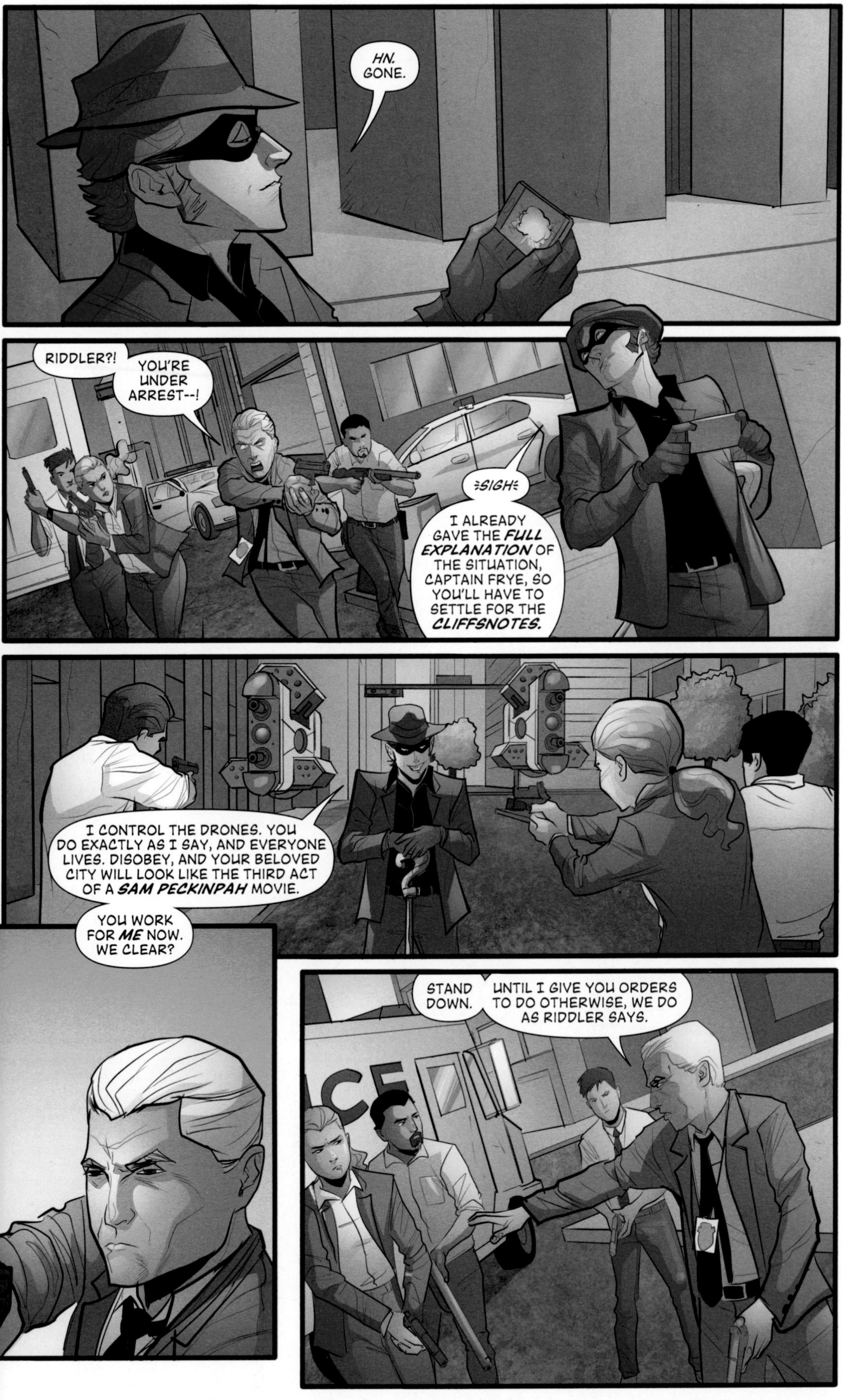
HN. GONE.
RIDDLER?!
YOU'RE UNDER ARREST--!
SIGH
I ALREADY GAVE THE FULL EXPLANATION OF THE SITUATION, CAPTAIN FRYE, SO YOU'LL HAVE TO SETTLE FOR THE CLIFFSNOTES.
I CONTROL THE DRONES. YOU DO EXACTLY AS I SAY, AND EVERYONE LIVES. DISOBEY, AND YOUR BELOVED CITY WILL LOOK LIKE THE THIRD ACT OF A SAM PECKINPAH MOVIE.
YOU WORK FOR ME NOW. WE CLEAR?
STAND DOWN.
UNTIL I GIVE YOU ORDERS TO DO OTHERWISE, WE DO AS RIDDLER SAYS.

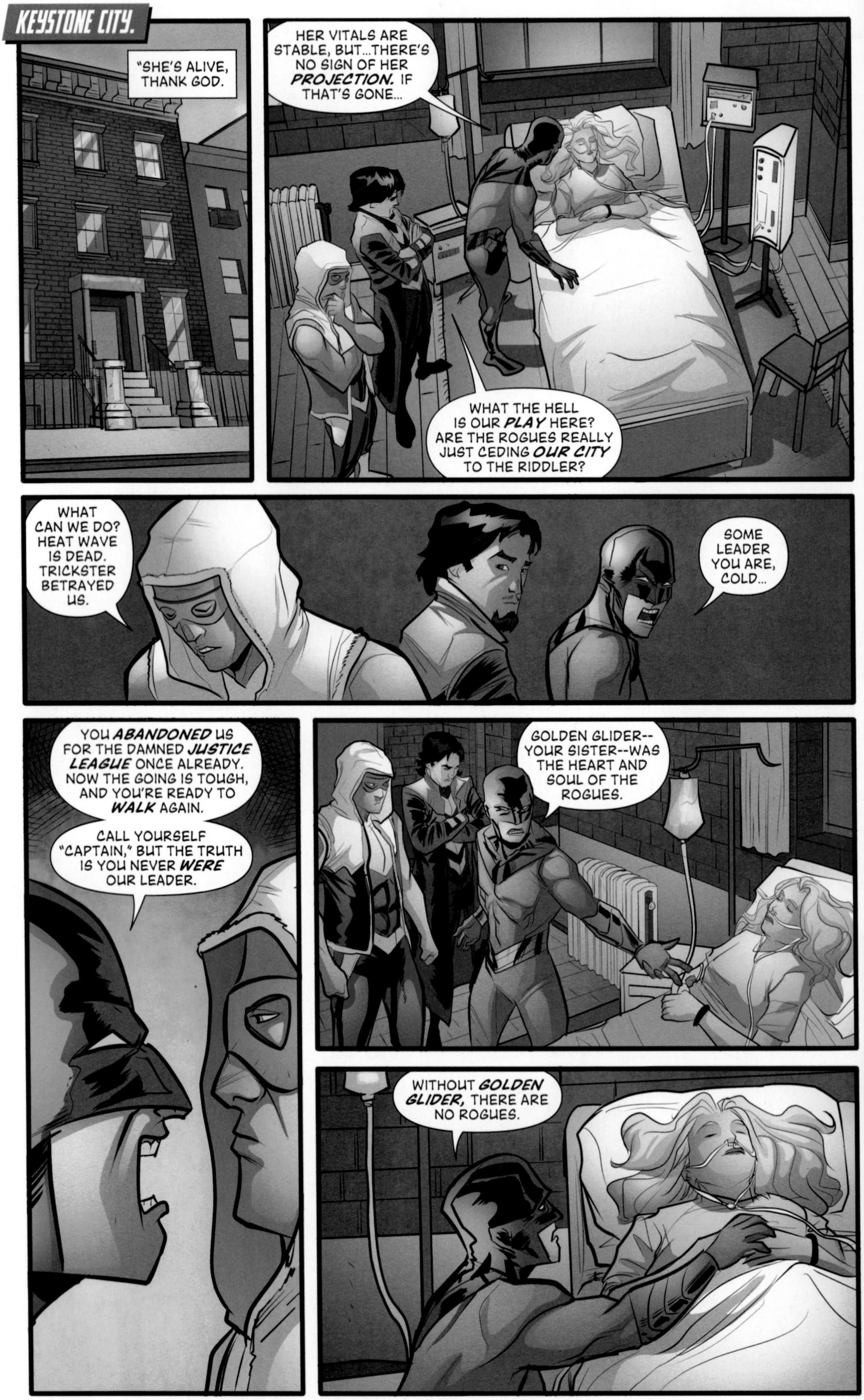
KEYSTONE CITY.
"SHE'S ALIVE, THANK GOD.
HER VITALS ARE STABLE, BUT...THERE'S NO SIGN OF HER PROJECTION. IF THAT'S GONE...
WHAT THE HELL IS OUR PLAY HERE? ARE THE ROGUES REALLY JUST CEDING OUR CITY TO THE RIDDLER?
WHAT CAN WE DO? HEAT WAVE IS DEAD. TRICKSTER BETRAYED US.
SOME LEADER YOU ARE, COLD...
YOU ABANDONED US FOR THE DAMNED JUSTICE LEAGUE ONCE ALREADY. NOW THE GOING IS TOUGH, AND YOU'RE READY TO WALK AGAIN.
CALL YOURSELF "CAPTAIN," BUT THE TRUTH IS YOU NEVER WERE OUR LEADER.
GOLDEN GLIDER--YOUR SISTER--WAS THE HEART AND SOUL OF THE ROGUES.
WITHOUT GOLDEN GLIDER, THERE ARE NO ROGUES.

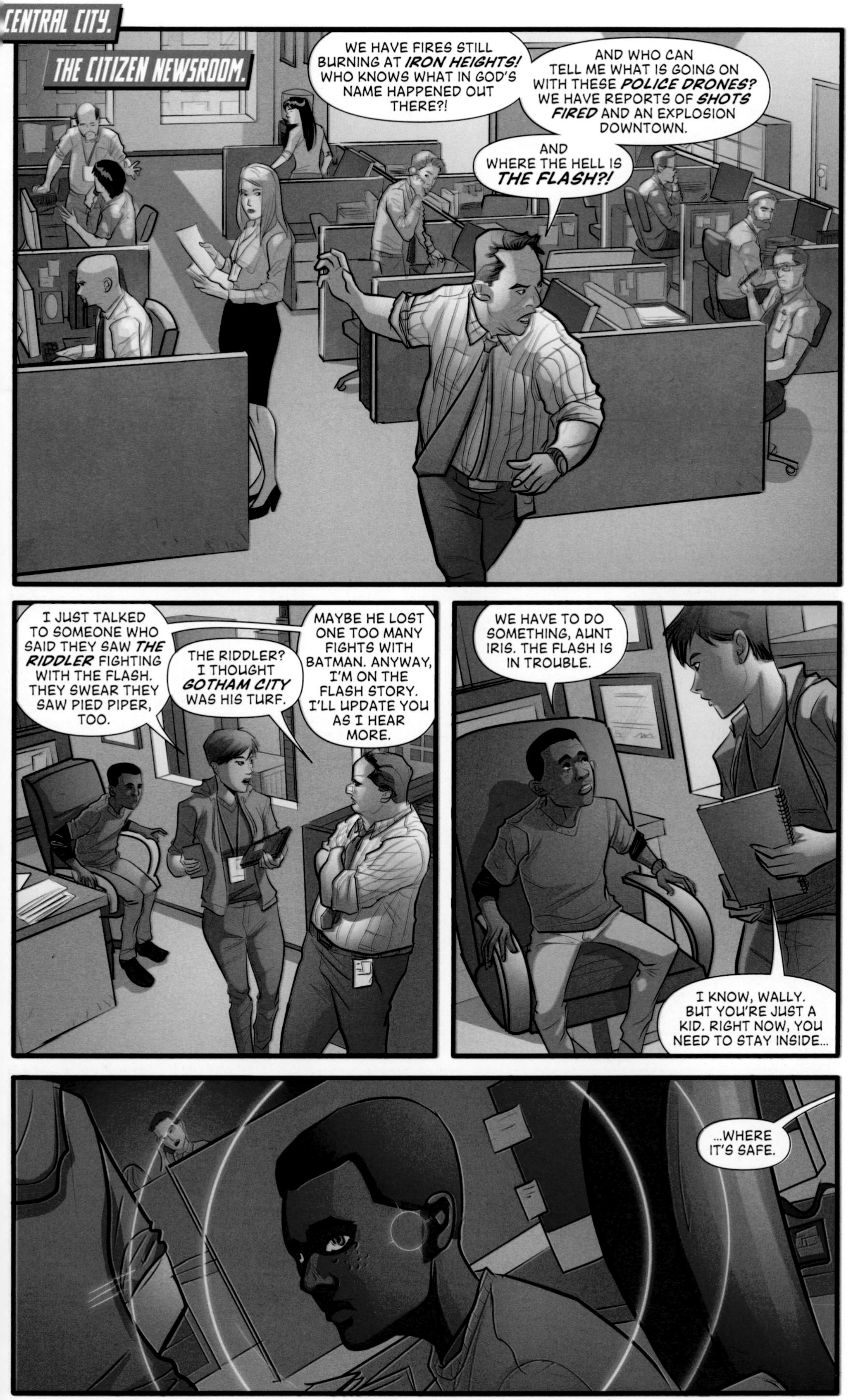
CENTRAL CITY.
THE CITIZEN NEWSROOM.
WE HAVE FIRES STILL BURNING AT IRON HEIGHTS! WHO KNOWS WHAT IN GOD'S NAME HAPPENED OUT THERE?!
AND WHO CAN TELL ME WHAT IS GOING ON WITH THESE POLICE DRONES? WE HAVE REPORTS OF SHOTS FIRED AND AN EXPLOSION DOWNTOWN.
AND WHERE THE HELL IS THE FLASH?!
I JUST TALKED TO SOMEONE WHO SAID THEY SAW THE RIDDLER FIGHTING WITH THE FLASH. THEY SWEAR THEY SAW PIED PIPER, TOO.
THE RIDDLER? I THOUGHT GOTHAM CITY WAS HIS TURF.
MAYBE HE LOST ONE TOO MANY FIGHTS WITH BATMAN. ANYWAY, I'M ON THE FLASH STORY. I'LL UPDATE YOU AS I HEAR MORE.
WE HAVE TO DO SOMETHING, AUNT IRIS. THE FLASH IS IN TROUBLE.
I KNOW, WALLY. BUT YOU'RE JUST A KID. RIGHT NOW, YOU NEED TO STAY INSIDE...
...WHERE IT'S SAFE.

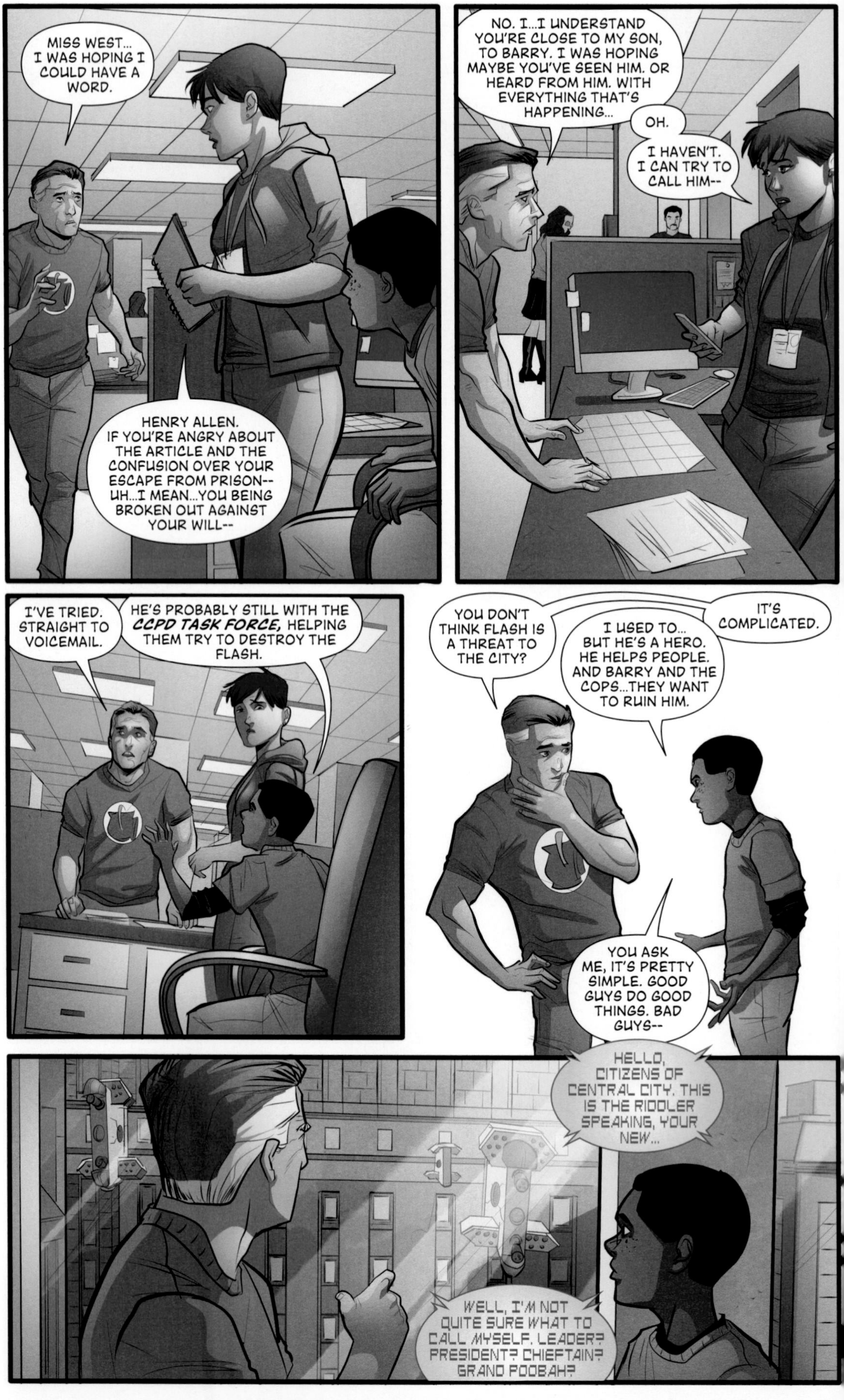
MISS WEST... I WAS HOPING I COULD HAVE A WORD.
HENRY ALLEN. IF YOU'RE ANGRY ABOUT THE ARTICLE AND THE CONFUSION OVER YOUR ESCAPE FROM PRISON-- UH...I MEAN...YOU BEING BROKEN OUT AGAINST YOUR WILL--
NO. I...I UNDERSTAND YOU'RE CLOSE TO MY SON, TO BARRY. I WAS HOPING MAYBE YOU'VE SEEN HIM. OR HEARD FROM HIM. WITH EVERYTHING THAT'S HAPPENING...
OH.
I HAVEN'T. I CAN TRY TO CALL HIM--
I'VE TRIED. STRAIGHT TO VOICEMAIL.
HE'S PROBABLY STILL WITH THE *CCPD TASK FORCE,* HELPING THEM TRY TO DESTROY THE FLASH.
YOU DON'T THINK FLASH IS A THREAT TO THE CITY?
I USED TO... BUT HE'S A HERO. HE HELPS PEOPLE. AND BARRY AND THE COPS...THEY WANT TO RUIN HIM.
IT'S COMPLICATED.
YOU ASK ME, IT'S PRETTY SIMPLE. GOOD GUYS DO GOOD THINGS. BAD GUYS--
HELLO, CITIZENS OF CENTRAL CITY. THIS IS THE RIDDLER SPEAKING, YOUR NEW...
WELL, I'M NOT QUITE SURE WHAT TO CALL MYSELF. LEADER? PRESIDENT? CHIEFTAIN? GRAND POOBAH?

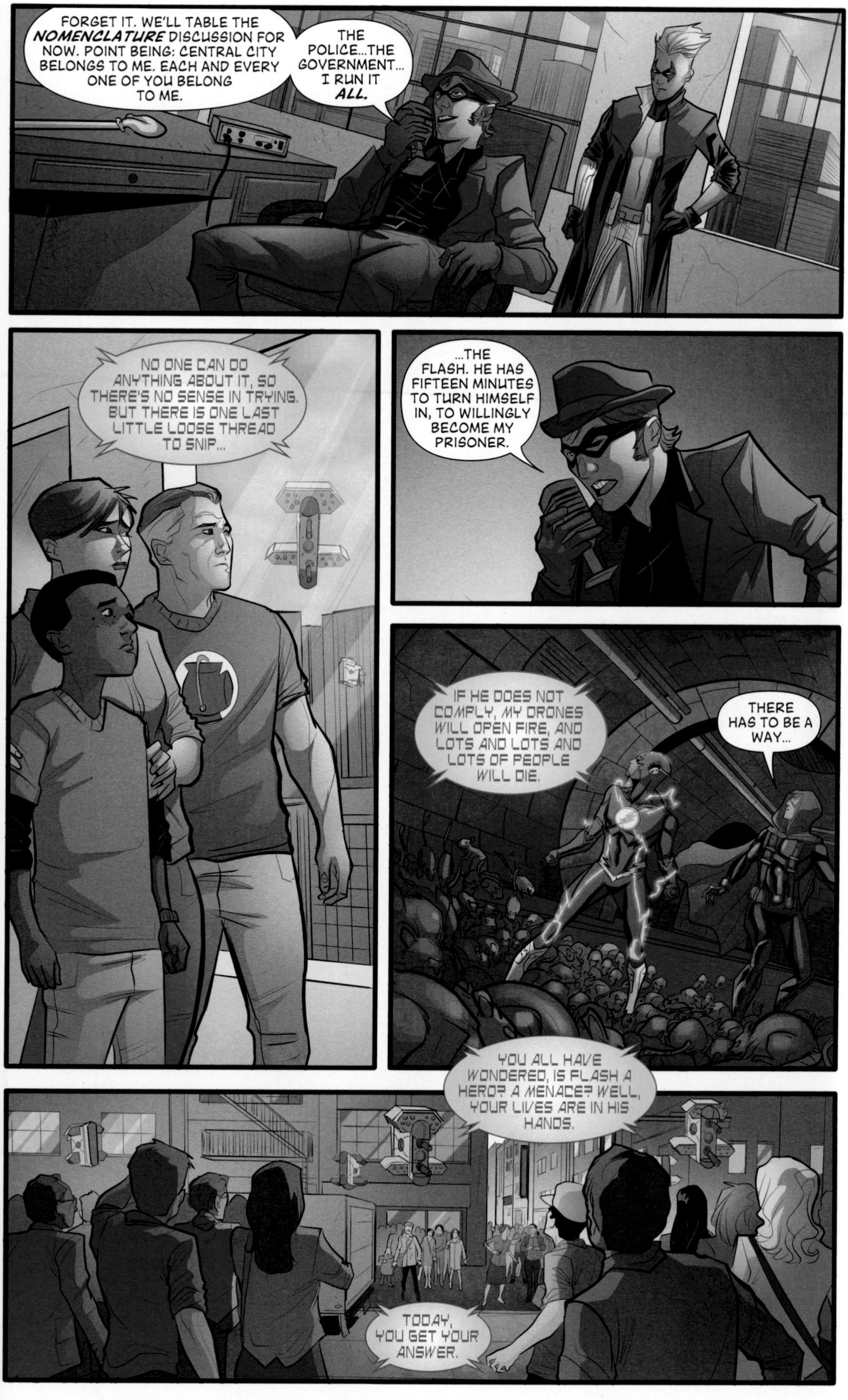
FORGET IT. WE'LL TABLE THE *NOMENCLATURE* DISCUSSION FOR NOW. POINT BEING: CENTRAL CITY BELONGS TO ME. EACH AND EVERY ONE OF YOU BELONG TO ME.
THE POLICE...THE GOVERNMENT... I RUN IT *ALL.*
NO ONE CAN DO ANYTHING ABOUT IT, SO THERE'S NO SENSE IN TRYING. BUT THERE IS ONE LAST LITTLE LOOSE THREAD TO SNIP...
...THE FLASH. HE HAS FIFTEEN MINUTES TO TURN HIMSELF IN, TO WILLINGLY BECOME MY PRISONER.
IF HE DOES NOT COMPLY, MY DRONES WILL OPEN FIRE, AND LOTS AND LOTS AND LOTS OF PEOPLE WILL DIE.
THERE HAS TO BE A WAY...
YOU ALL HAVE WONDERED, IS FLASH A HERO? A MENACE? WELL, YOUR LIVES ARE IN HIS HANDS.
TODAY, YOU GET YOUR ANSWER.

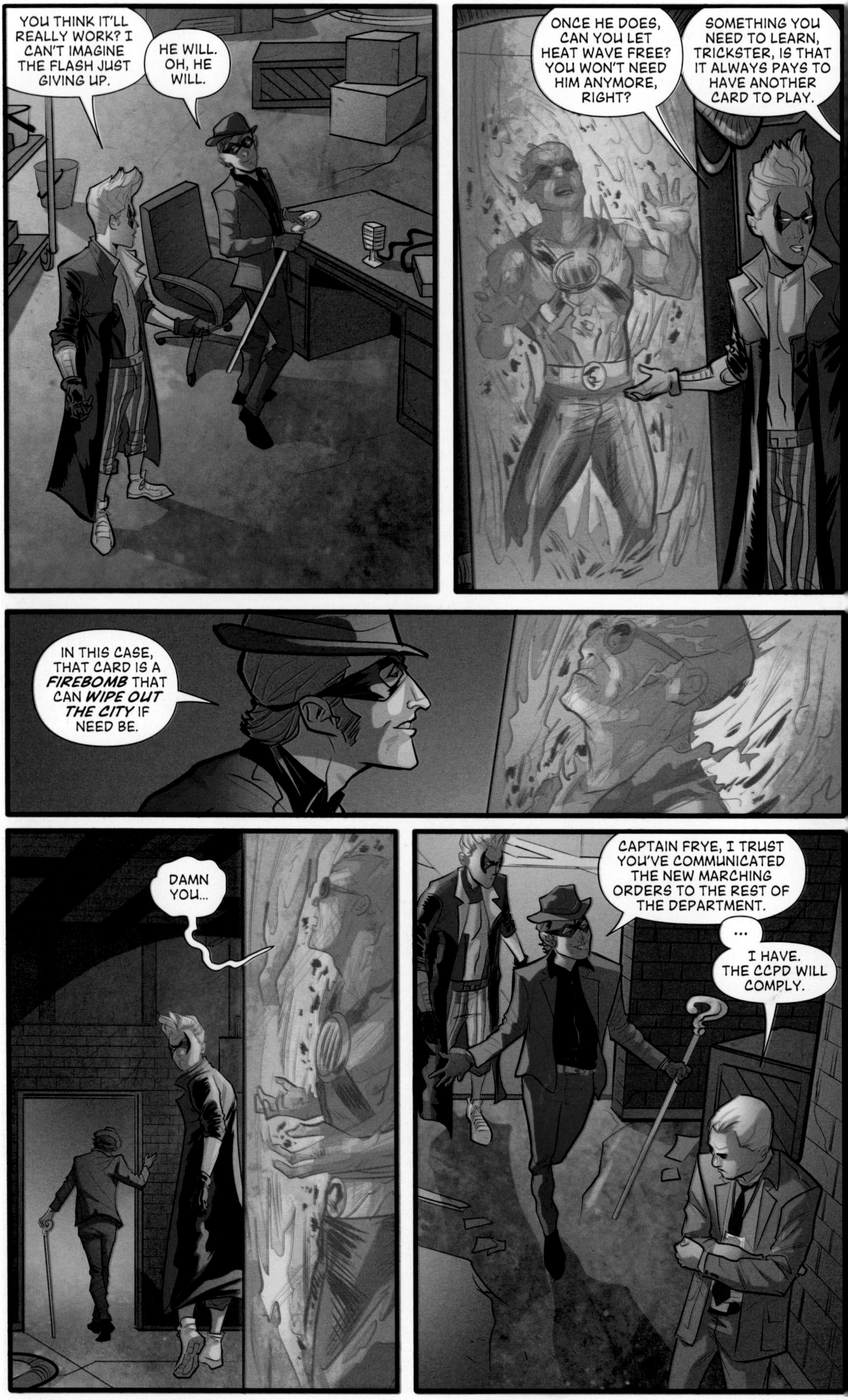

YOU THINK IT'LL REALLY WORK? I CAN'T IMAGINE THE FLASH JUST GIVING UP.
HE WILL. OH, HE WILL.
ONCE HE DOES, CAN YOU LET HEAT WAVE FREE? YOU WON'T NEED HIM ANYMORE, RIGHT?
SOMETHING YOU NEED TO LEARN, TRICKSTER, IS THAT IT ALWAYS PAYS TO HAVE ANOTHER CARD TO PLAY.
IN THIS CASE, THAT CARD IS A ***FIREBOMB*** THAT CAN ***WIPE OUT THE CITY*** IF NEED BE.
DAMN YOU...
CAPTAIN FRYE, I TRUST YOU'VE COMMUNICATED THE NEW MARCHING ORDERS TO THE REST OF THE DEPARTMENT.
...
I HAVE. THE CCPD WILL COMPLY.

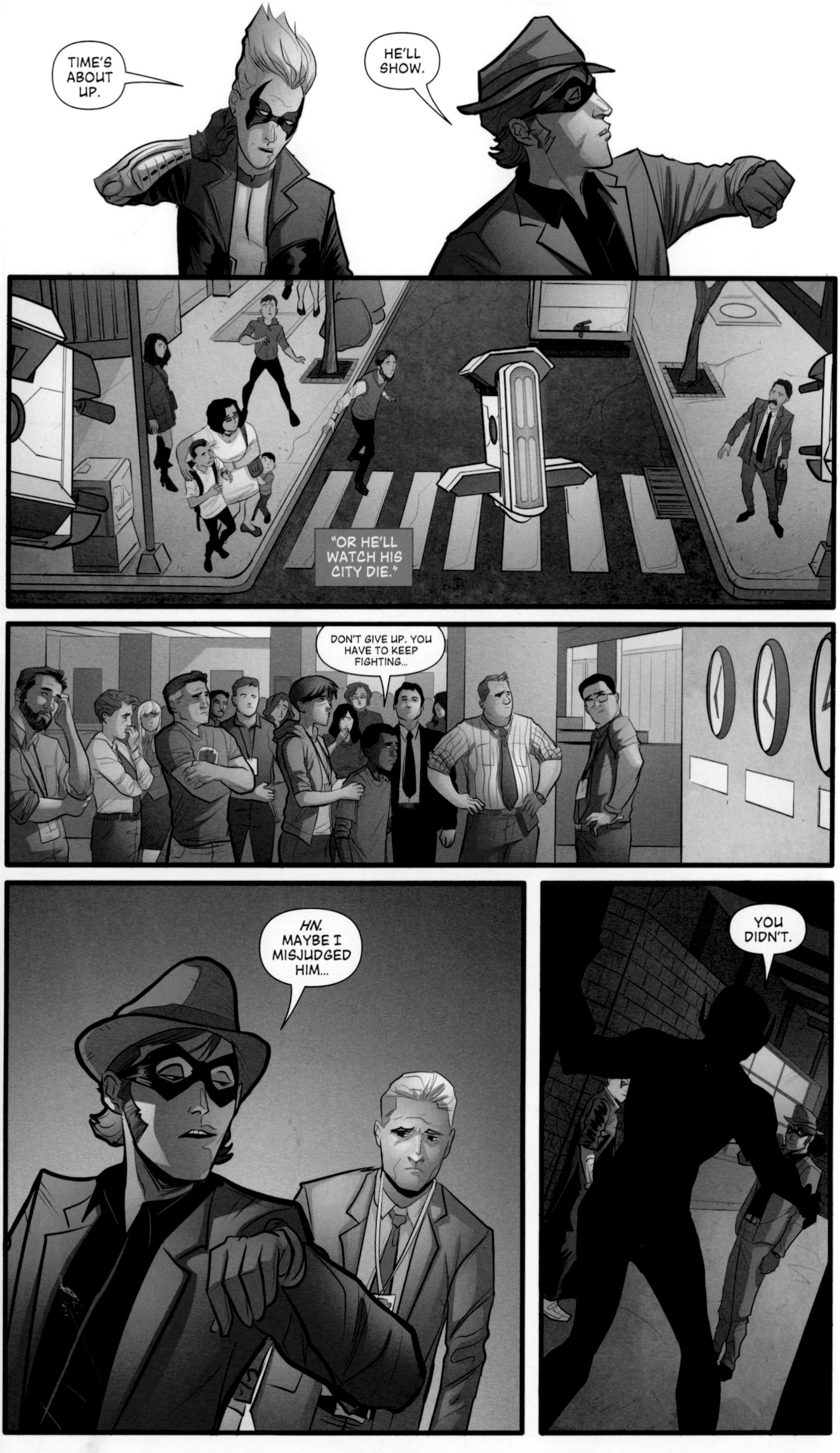
TIME'S ABOUT UP.
HE'LL SHOW.
"OR HE'LL WATCH HIS CITY DIE."
DON'T GIVE UP. YOU HAVE TO KEEP FIGHTING...
HN. MAYBE I MISJUDGED HIM...
YOU DIDN'T.

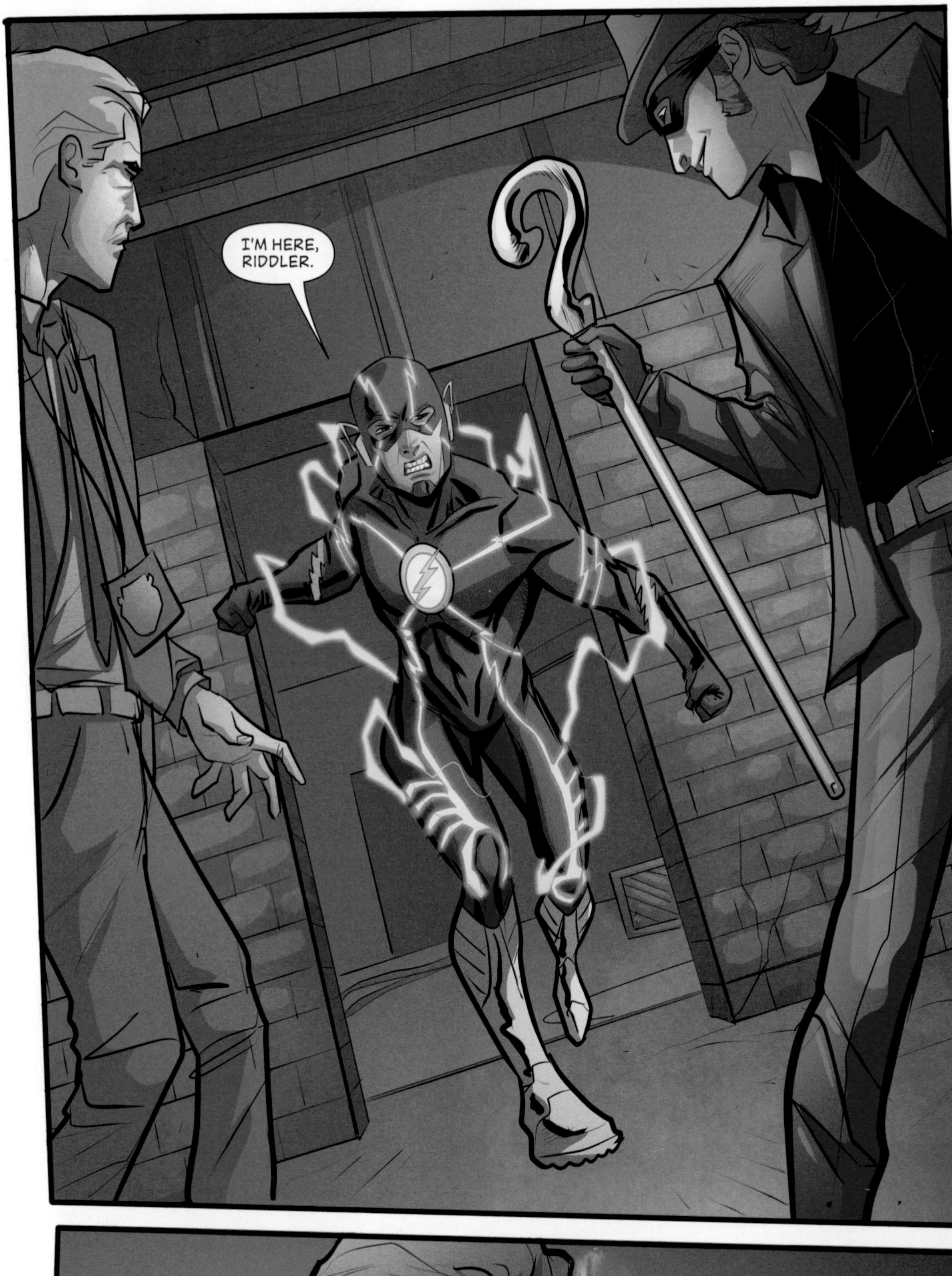
I'M HERE, RIDDLER.

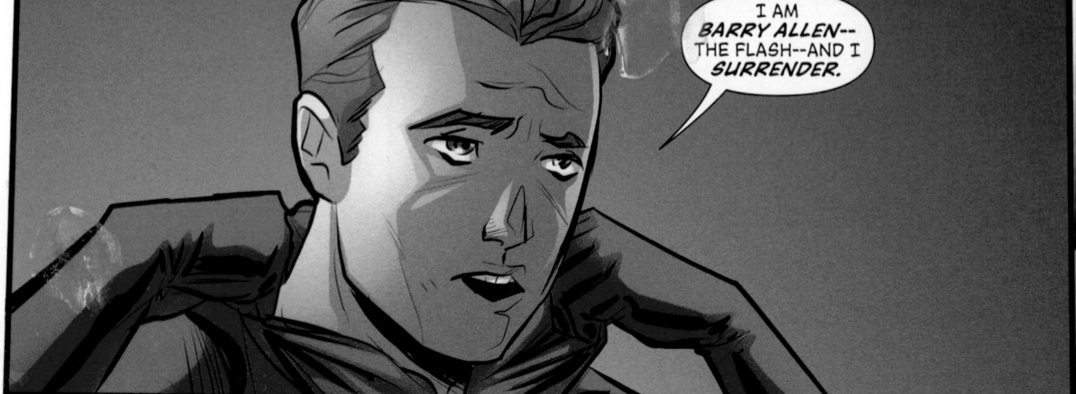
I AM BARRY ALLEN-- THE FLASH--AND I SURRENDER.

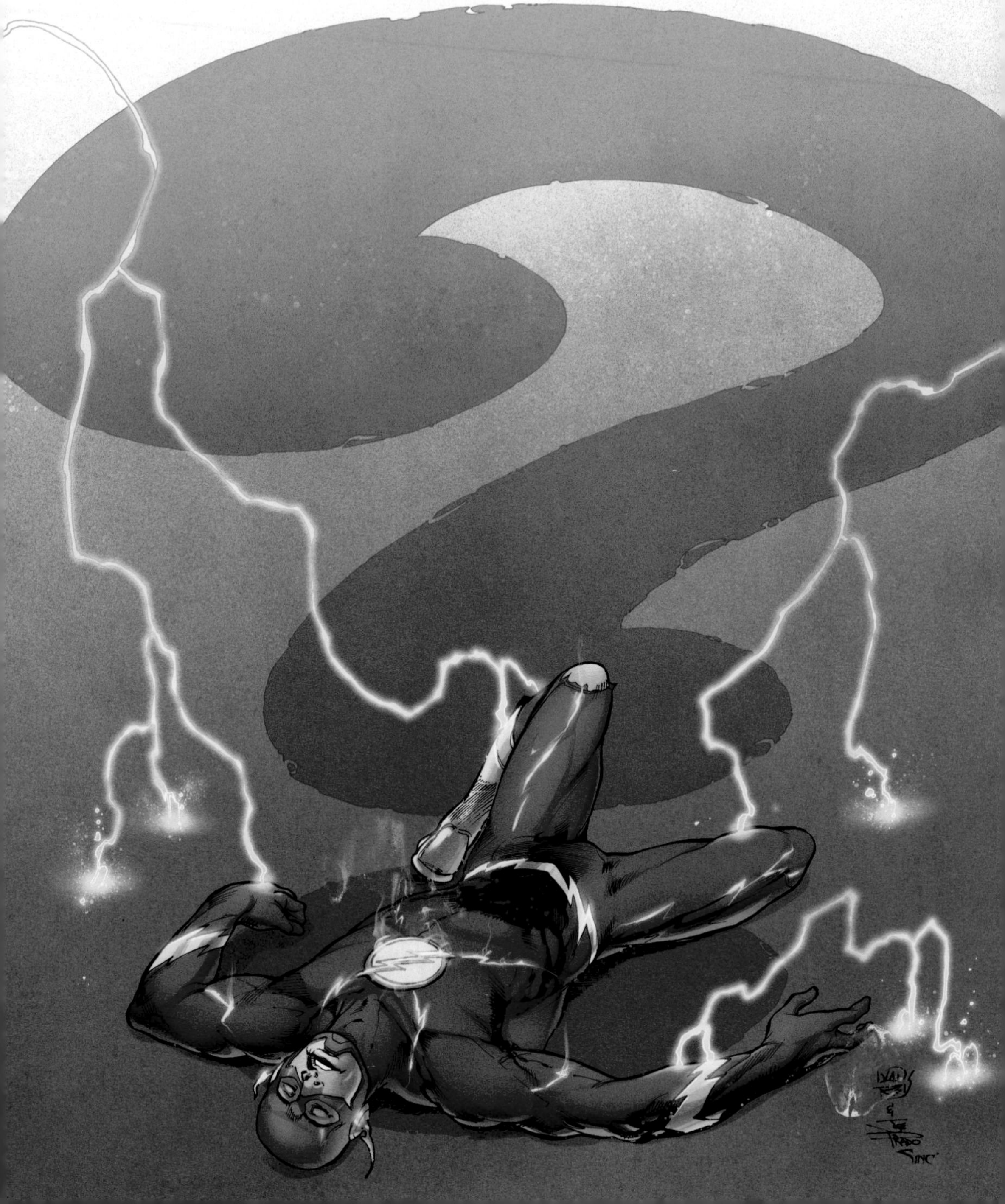

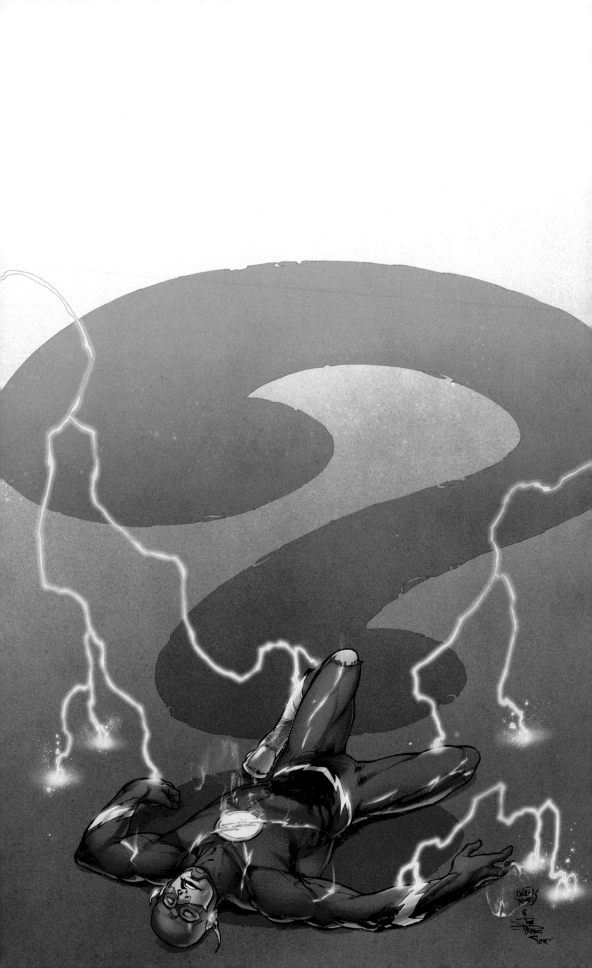

FULL STOP

VAN JENSEN writer JESÚS MERINO artist GUY MAJOR colorist PAT BROSSEAU letterer IVAN REIS JOE PRADO ALEX SINCLAIR cover

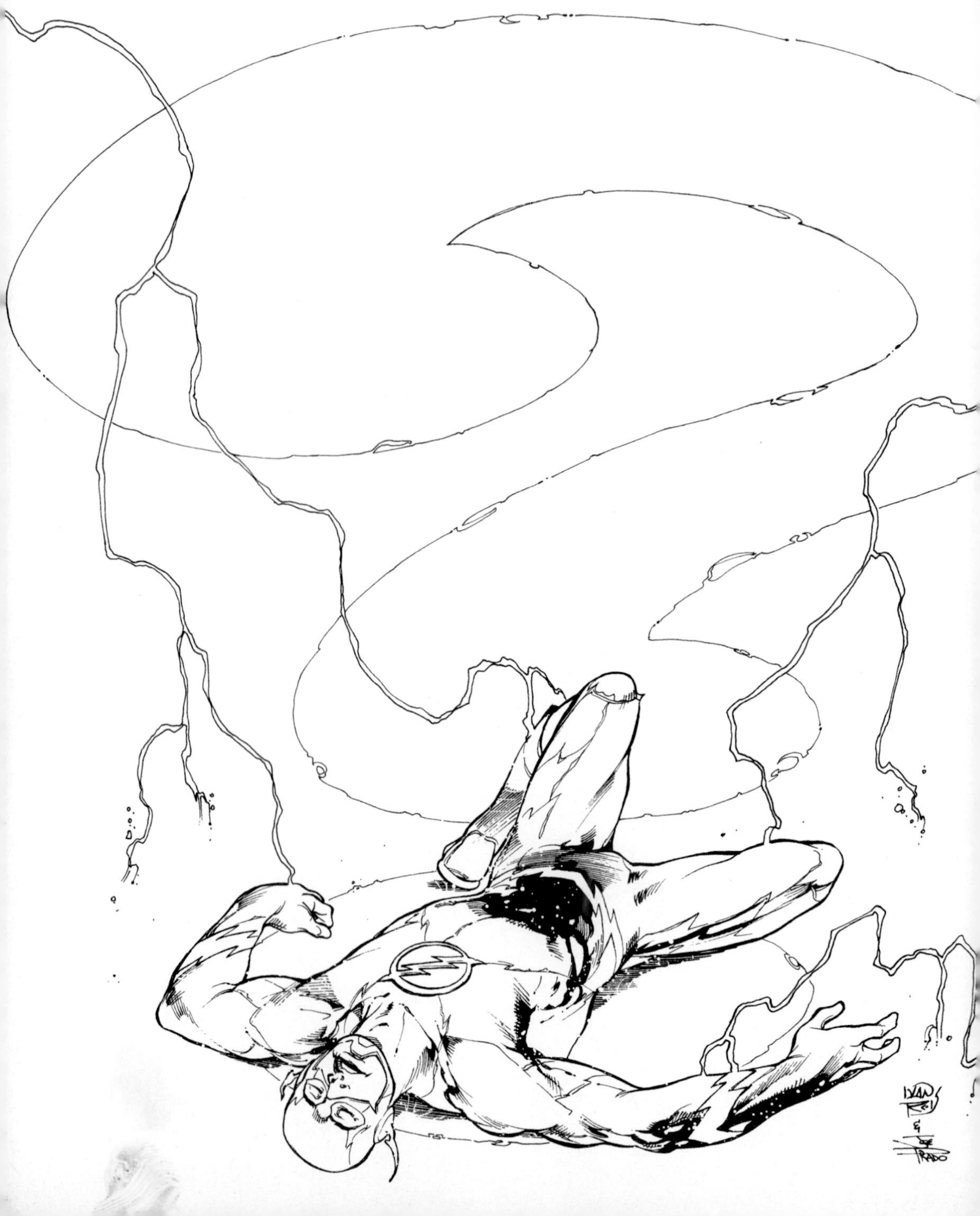

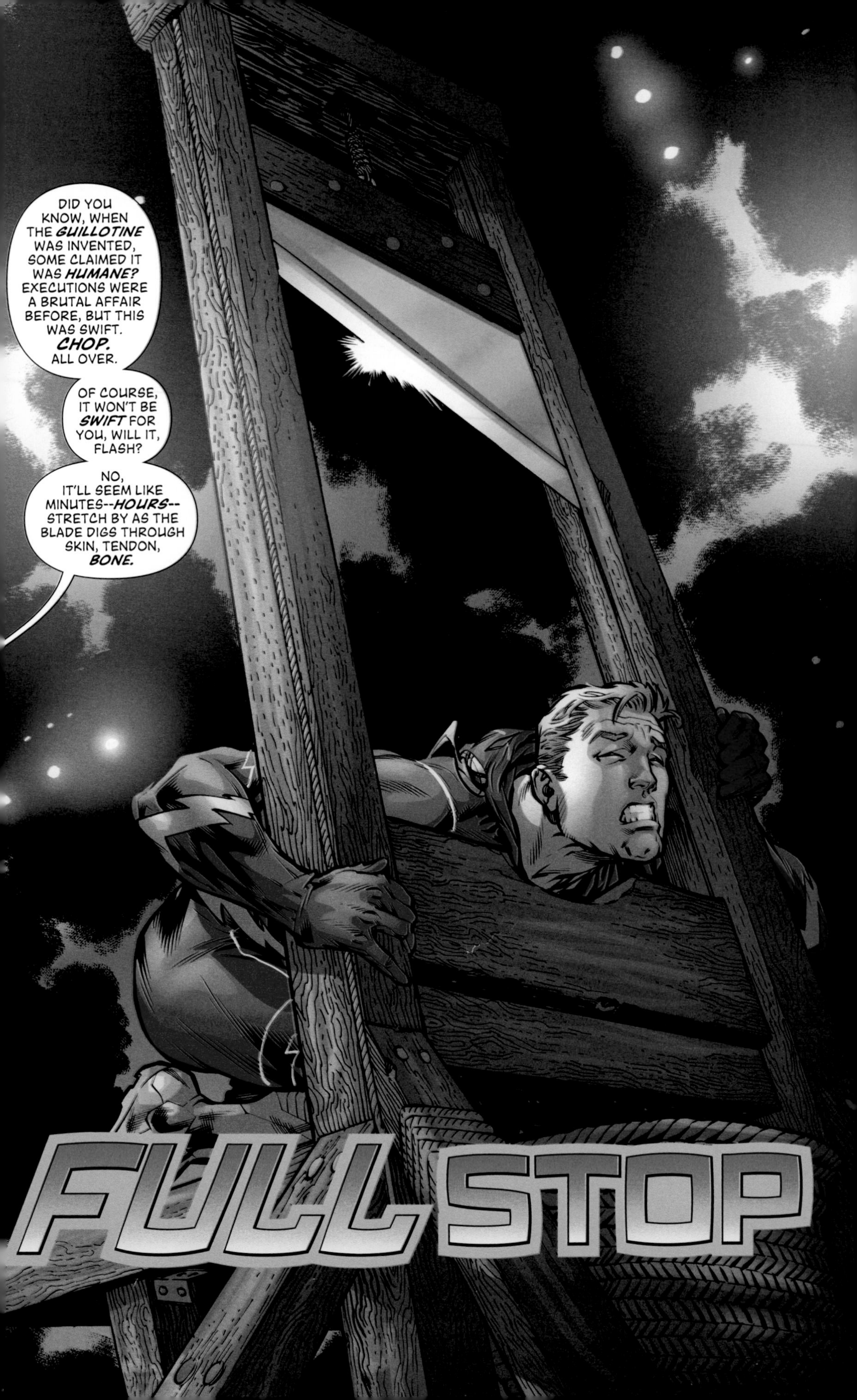
DID YOU KNOW, WHEN THE GUILLOTINE WAS INVENTED, SOME CLAIMED IT WAS HUMANE? EXECUTIONS WERE A BRUTAL AFFAIR BEFORE, BUT THIS WAS SWIFT. CHOP. ALL OVER.
OF COURSE, IT WON'T BE SWIFT FOR YOU, WILL IT, FLASH?
NO, IT'LL SEEM LIKE MINUTES--HOURS--STRETCH BY AS THE BLADE DIGS THROUGH SKIN, TENDON, BONE.
FULL STOP

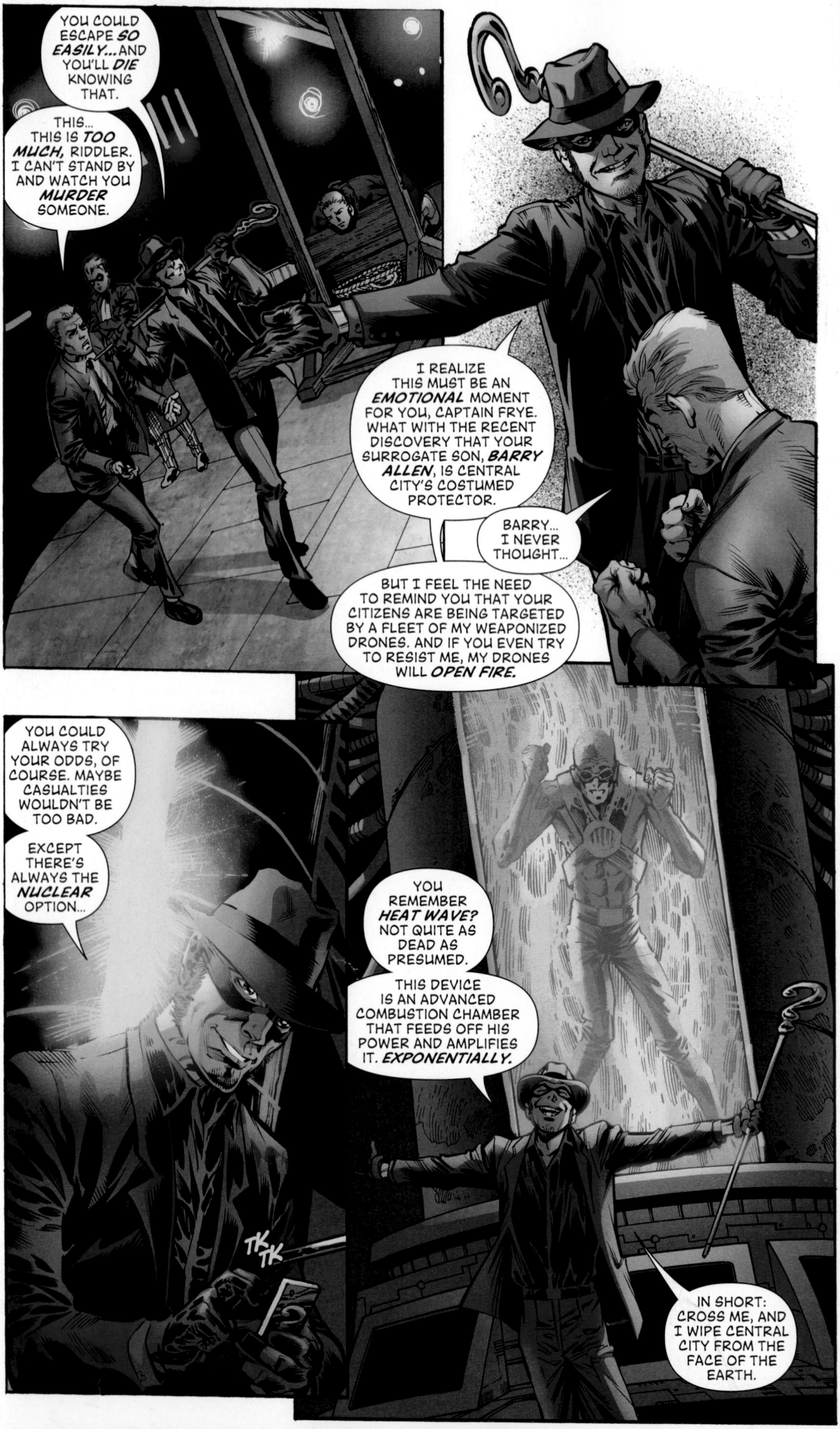
YOU COULD ESCAPE SO EASILY... AND YOU'LL DIE KNOWING THAT.
THIS... THIS IS TOO MUCH, RIDDLER. I CAN'T STAND BY AND WATCH YOU MURDER SOMEONE.
I REALIZE THIS MUST BE AN EMOTIONAL MOMENT FOR YOU, CAPTAIN FRYE. WHAT WITH THE RECENT DISCOVERY THAT YOUR SURROGATE SON, BARRY ALLEN, IS CENTRAL CITY'S COSTUMED PROTECTOR.
BARRY... I NEVER THOUGHT...
BUT I FEEL THE NEED TO REMIND YOU THAT YOUR CITIZENS ARE BEING TARGETED BY A FLEET OF MY WEAPONIZED DRONES. AND IF YOU EVEN TRY TO RESIST ME, MY DRONES WILL OPEN FIRE.
YOU COULD ALWAYS TRY YOUR ODDS, OF COURSE. MAYBE CASUALTIES WOULDN'T BE TOO BAD.
EXCEPT THERE'S ALWAYS THE NUCLEAR OPTION...
TK TK
YOU REMEMBER HEAT WAVE? NOT QUITE AS DEAD AS PRESUMED.
THIS DEVICE IS AN ADVANCED COMBUSTION CHAMBER THAT FEEDS OFF HIS POWER AND AMPLIFIES IT. EXPONENTIALLY.
IN SHORT: CROSS ME, AND I WIPE CENTRAL CITY FROM THE FACE OF THE EARTH.

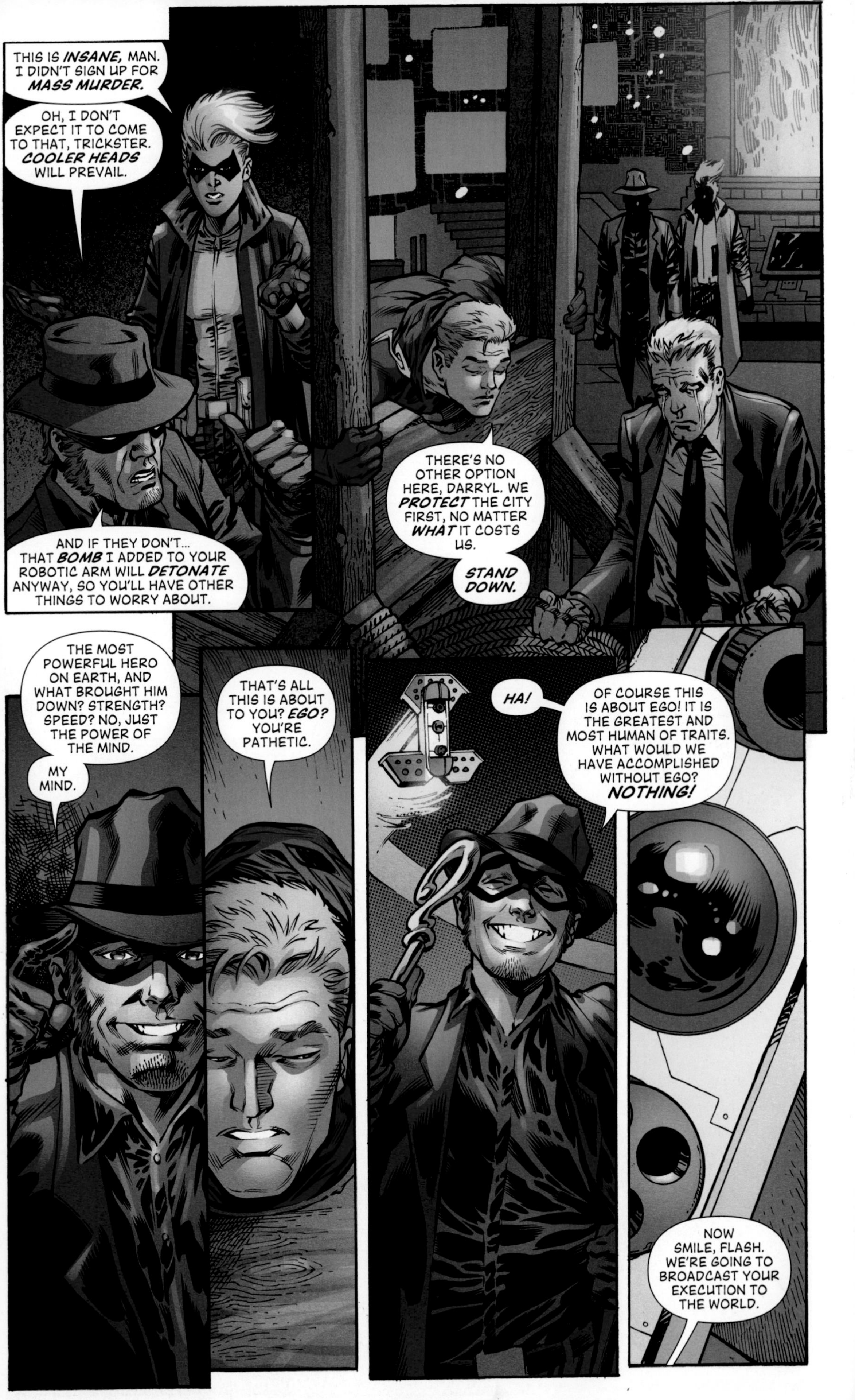

THIS IS *INSANE,* MAN. I DIDN'T SIGN UP FOR *MASS MURDER.*
OH, I DON'T EXPECT IT TO COME TO THAT, TRICKSTER. *COOLER HEADS* WILL PREVAIL.
AND IF THEY DON'T... THAT *BOMB* I ADDED TO YOUR ROBOTIC ARM WILL *DETONATE* ANYWAY, SO YOU'LL HAVE OTHER THINGS TO WORRY ABOUT.
THERE'S NO OTHER OPTION HERE, DARRYL. WE *PROTECT* THE CITY FIRST, NO MATTER *WHAT* IT COSTS US.
STAND DOWN.
THE MOST POWERFUL HERO ON EARTH, AND WHAT BROUGHT HIM DOWN? STRENGTH? SPEED? NO, JUST THE POWER OF THE MIND.
MY MIND.
THAT'S ALL THIS IS ABOUT TO YOU? *EGO?* YOU'RE PATHETIC.
HA!
OF COURSE THIS IS ABOUT EGO! IT IS THE GREATEST AND MOST HUMAN OF TRAITS. WHAT WOULD WE HAVE ACCOMPLISHED WITHOUT EGO? *NOTHING!*
NOW SMILE, FLASH. WE'RE GOING TO BROADCAST YOUR EXECUTION TO THE WORLD.

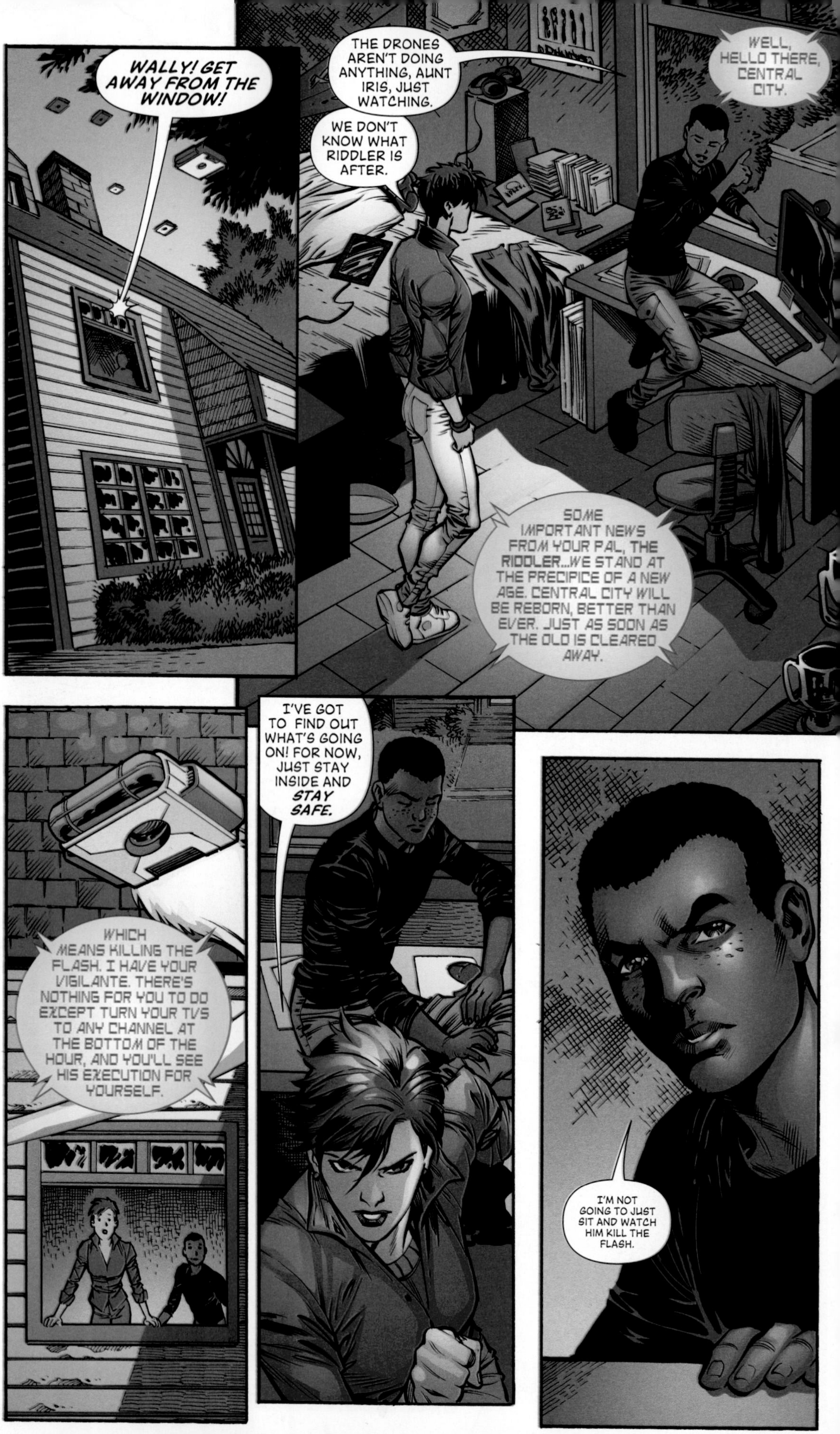
WALLY! GET AWAY FROM THE WINDOW!
THE DRONES AREN'T DOING ANYTHING, AUNT IRIS, JUST WATCHING.
WE DON'T KNOW WHAT RIDDLER IS AFTER.
WELL, HELLO THERE, CENTRAL CITY.
SOME IMPORTANT NEWS FROM YOUR PAL, THE RIDDLER...WE STAND AT THE PRECIPICE OF A NEW AGE. CENTRAL CITY WILL BE REBORN, BETTER THAN EVER. JUST AS SOON AS THE OLD IS CLEARED AWAY.
WHICH MEANS KILLING THE FLASH. I HAVE YOUR VIGILANTE. THERE'S NOTHING FOR YOU TO DO EXCEPT TURN YOUR TVS TO ANY CHANNEL AT THE BOTTOM OF THE HOUR, AND YOU'LL SEE HIS EXECUTION FOR YOURSELF.
I'VE GOT TO FIND OUT WHAT'S GOING ON! FOR NOW, JUST STAY INSIDE AND STAY SAFE.
I'M NOT GOING TO JUST SIT AND WATCH HIM KILL THE FLASH.

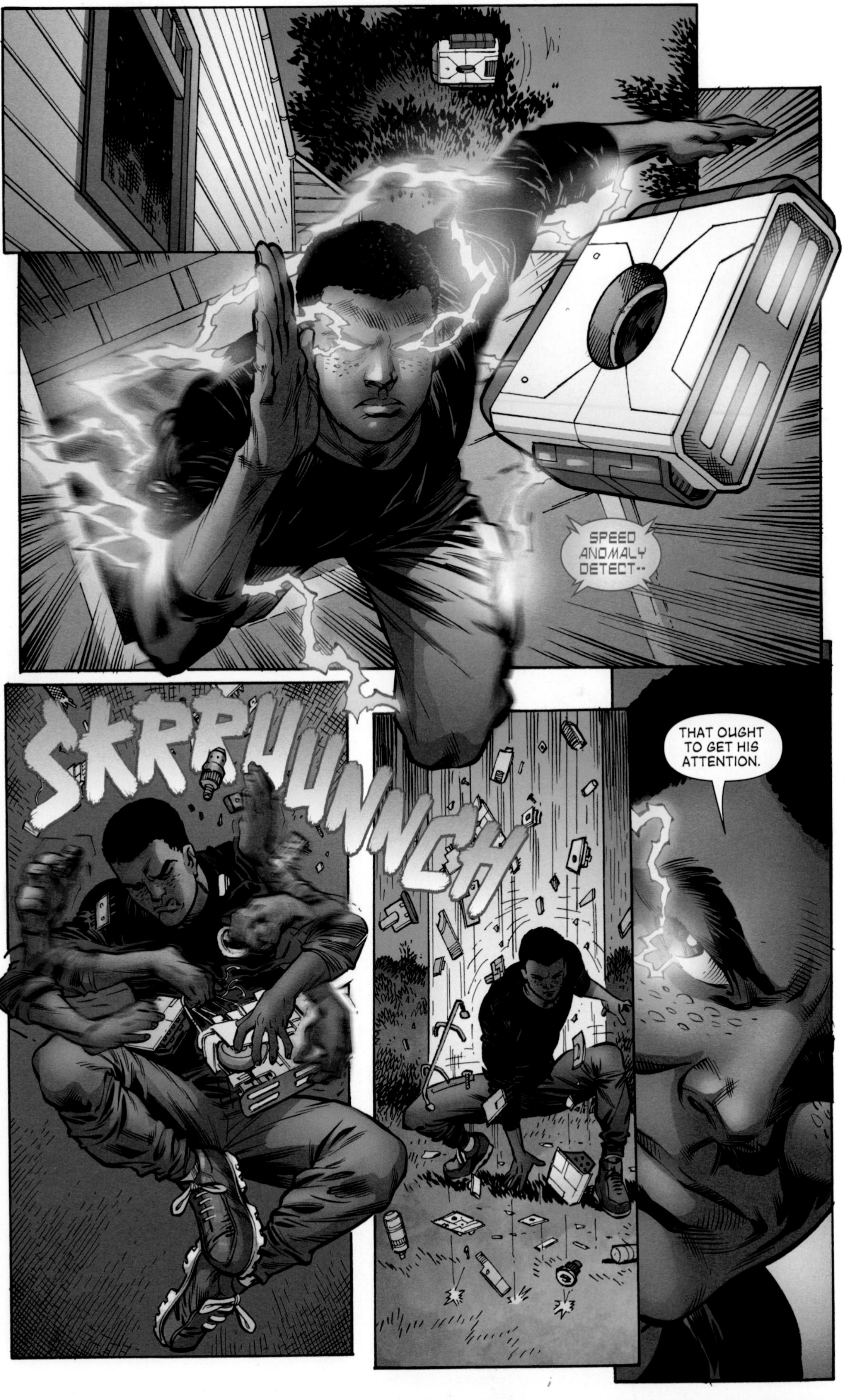
SPEED ANOMALY DETECT--
SKRRUUNNCH
THAT OUGHT TO GET HIS ATTENTION.

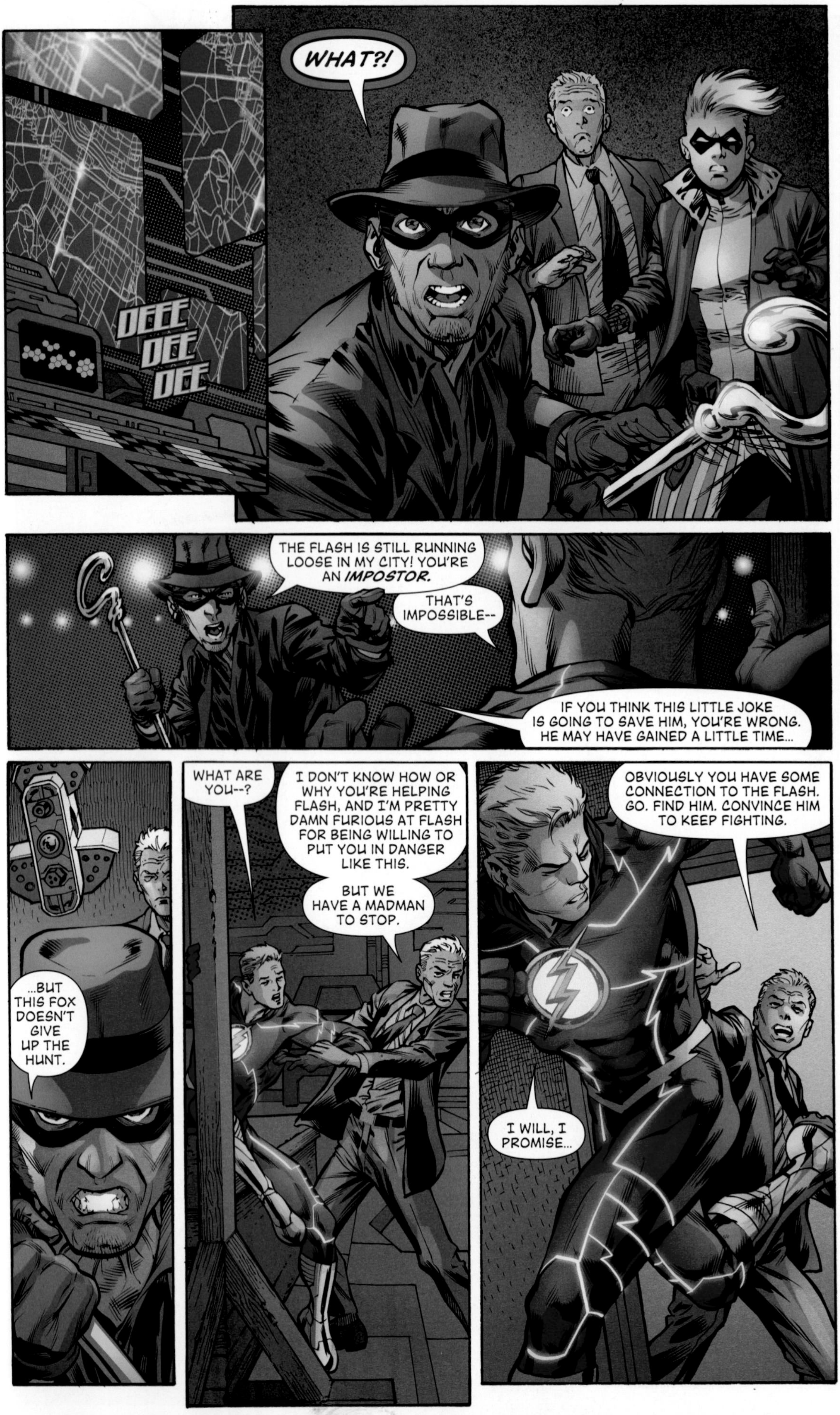
WHAT?!
DEEE DEE DEE
THE FLASH IS STILL RUNNING LOOSE IN MY CITY! YOU'RE AN *IMPOSTOR.*
THAT'S IMPOSSIBLE--
IF YOU THINK THIS LITTLE JOKE IS GOING TO SAVE HIM, YOU'RE WRONG. HE MAY HAVE GAINED A LITTLE TIME...
...BUT THIS FOX DOESN'T GIVE UP THE HUNT.
WHAT ARE YOU--?
I DON'T KNOW HOW OR WHY YOU'RE HELPING FLASH, AND I'M PRETTY DAMN FURIOUS AT FLASH FOR BEING WILLING TO PUT YOU IN DANGER LIKE THIS.
BUT WE HAVE A MADMAN TO STOP.
OBVIOUSLY YOU HAVE SOME CONNECTION TO THE FLASH. GO. FIND HIM. CONVINCE HIM TO KEEP FIGHTING.
I WILL, I PROMISE...

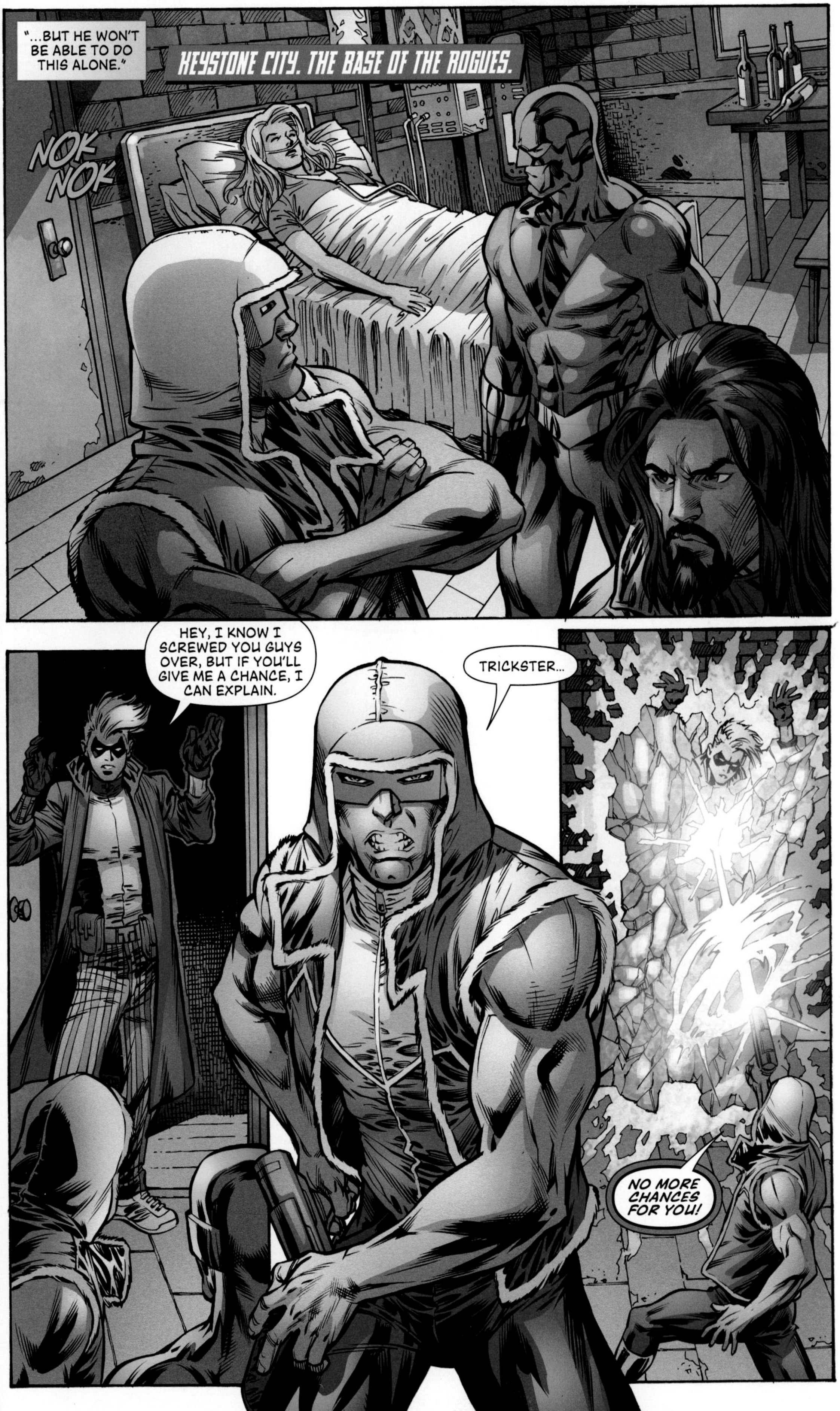
"...BUT HE WON'T BE ABLE TO DO THIS ALONE."
KEYSTONE CITY. THE BASE OF THE ROGUES.
NOK NOK
HEY, I KNOW I SCREWED YOU GUYS OVER, BUT IF YOU'LL GIVE ME A CHANCE, I CAN EXPLAIN.
TRICKSTER...
NO MORE CHANCES FOR YOU!

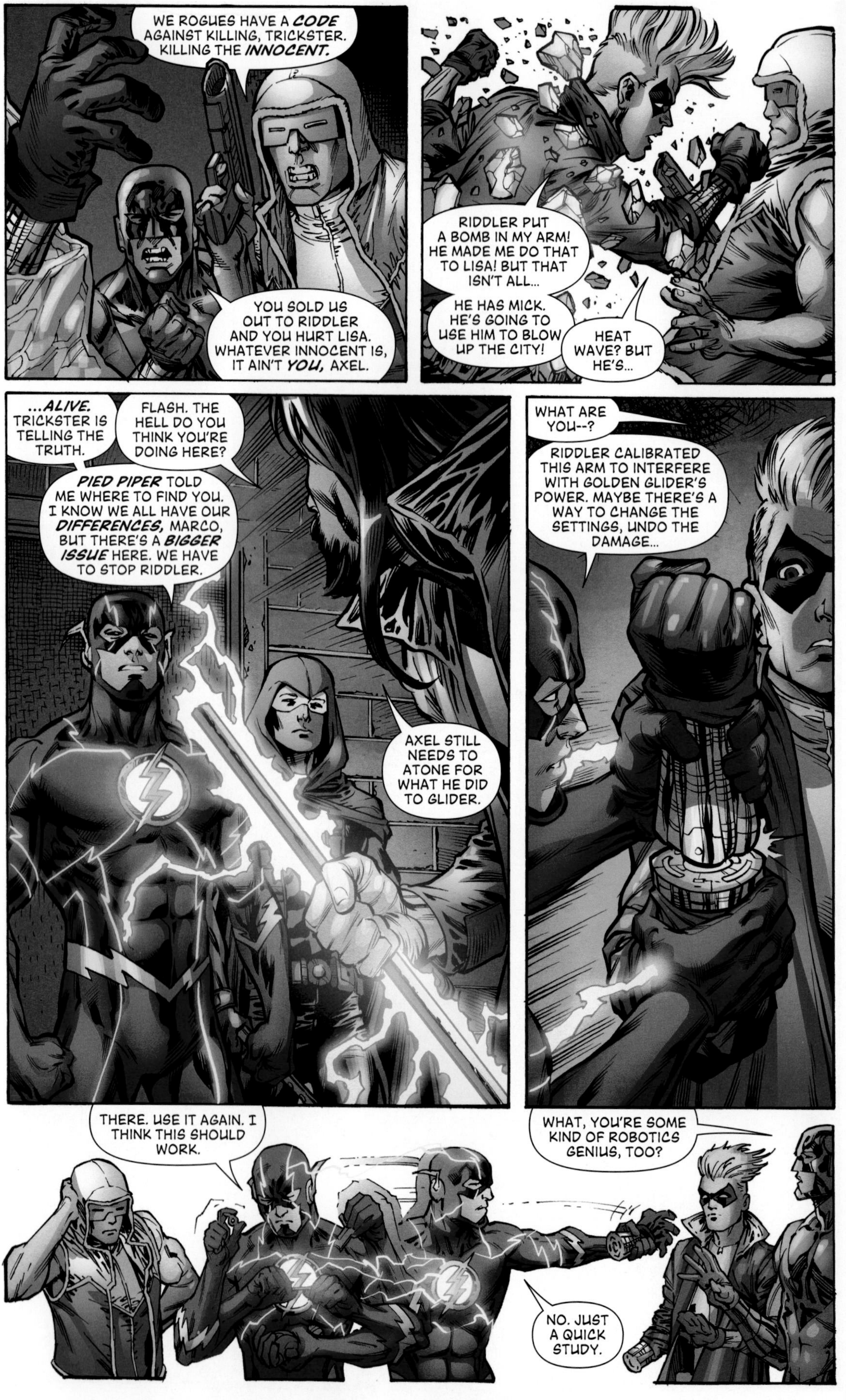
WE ROGUES HAVE A *CODE* AGAINST KILLING, TRICKSTER. KILLING THE *INNOCENT.*
YOU SOLD US OUT TO RIDDLER AND YOU HURT LISA. WHATEVER INNOCENT IS, IT AIN'T *YOU,* AXEL.
RIDDLER PUT A BOMB IN MY ARM! HE MADE ME DO THAT TO LISA! BUT THAT ISN'T ALL...
HE HAS MICK. HE'S GOING TO USE HIM TO BLOW UP THE CITY!
HEAT WAVE? BUT HE'S...
...ALIVE. TRICKSTER IS TELLING THE TRUTH.
FLASH. THE HELL DO YOU THINK YOU'RE DOING HERE?
PIED PIPER TOLD ME WHERE TO FIND YOU. I KNOW WE ALL HAVE OUR *DIFFERENCES,* MARCO, BUT THERE'S A *BIGGER ISSUE* HERE. WE HAVE TO STOP RIDDLER.
AXEL STILL NEEDS TO ATONE FOR WHAT HE DID TO GLIDER.
WHAT ARE YOU--?
RIDDLER CALIBRATED THIS ARM TO INTERFERE WITH GOLDEN GLIDER'S POWER. MAYBE THERE'S A WAY TO CHANGE THE SETTINGS, UNDO THE DAMAGE...
THERE. USE IT AGAIN. I THINK THIS SHOULD WORK.
WHAT, YOU'RE SOME KIND OF ROBOTICS GENIUS, TOO?
NO. JUST A QUICK STUDY.

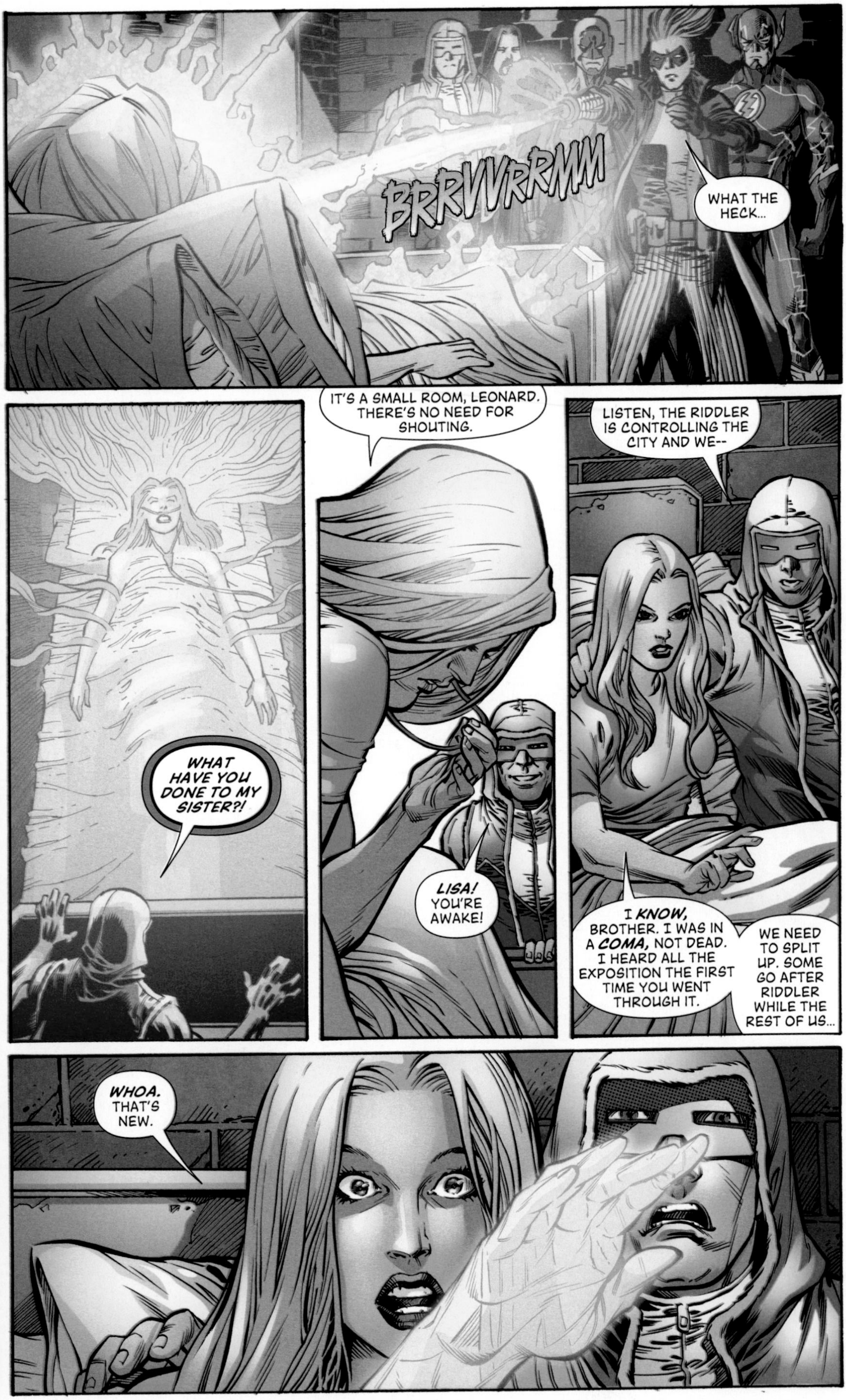

BRRVVRRMM
WHAT THE HECK...
WHAT HAVE YOU DONE TO MY SISTER?!
IT'S A SMALL ROOM, LEONARD. THERE'S NO NEED FOR SHOUTING.
LISA! YOU'RE AWAKE!
LISTEN, THE RIDDLER IS CONTROLLING THE CITY AND WE--
I KNOW, BROTHER. I WAS IN A COMA, NOT DEAD. I HEARD ALL THE EXPOSITION THE FIRST TIME YOU WENT THROUGH IT.
WE NEED TO SPLIT UP. SOME GO AFTER RIDDLER WHILE THE REST OF US...
WHOA. THAT'S NEW.

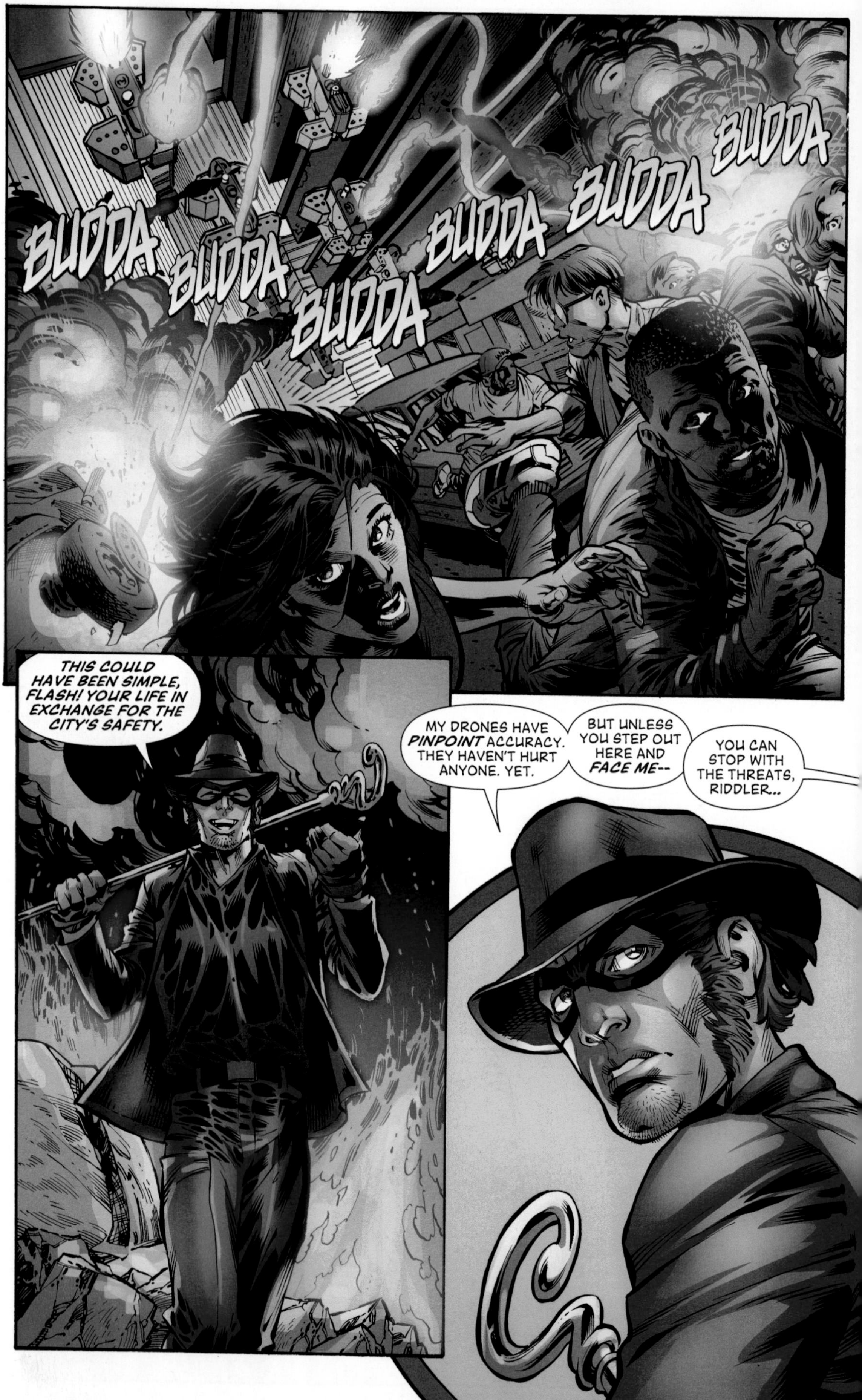
BUDDA
BUDDA
BUDDA
BUDDA
BUDDA
BUDDA
THIS COULD HAVE BEEN SIMPLE, FLASH! YOUR LIFE IN EXCHANGE FOR THE CITY'S SAFETY.
MY DRONES HAVE PINPOINT ACCURACY. THEY HAVEN'T HURT ANYONE. YET.
BUT UNLESS YOU STEP OUT HERE AND FACE ME--
YOU CAN STOP WITH THE THREATS, RIDDLER...

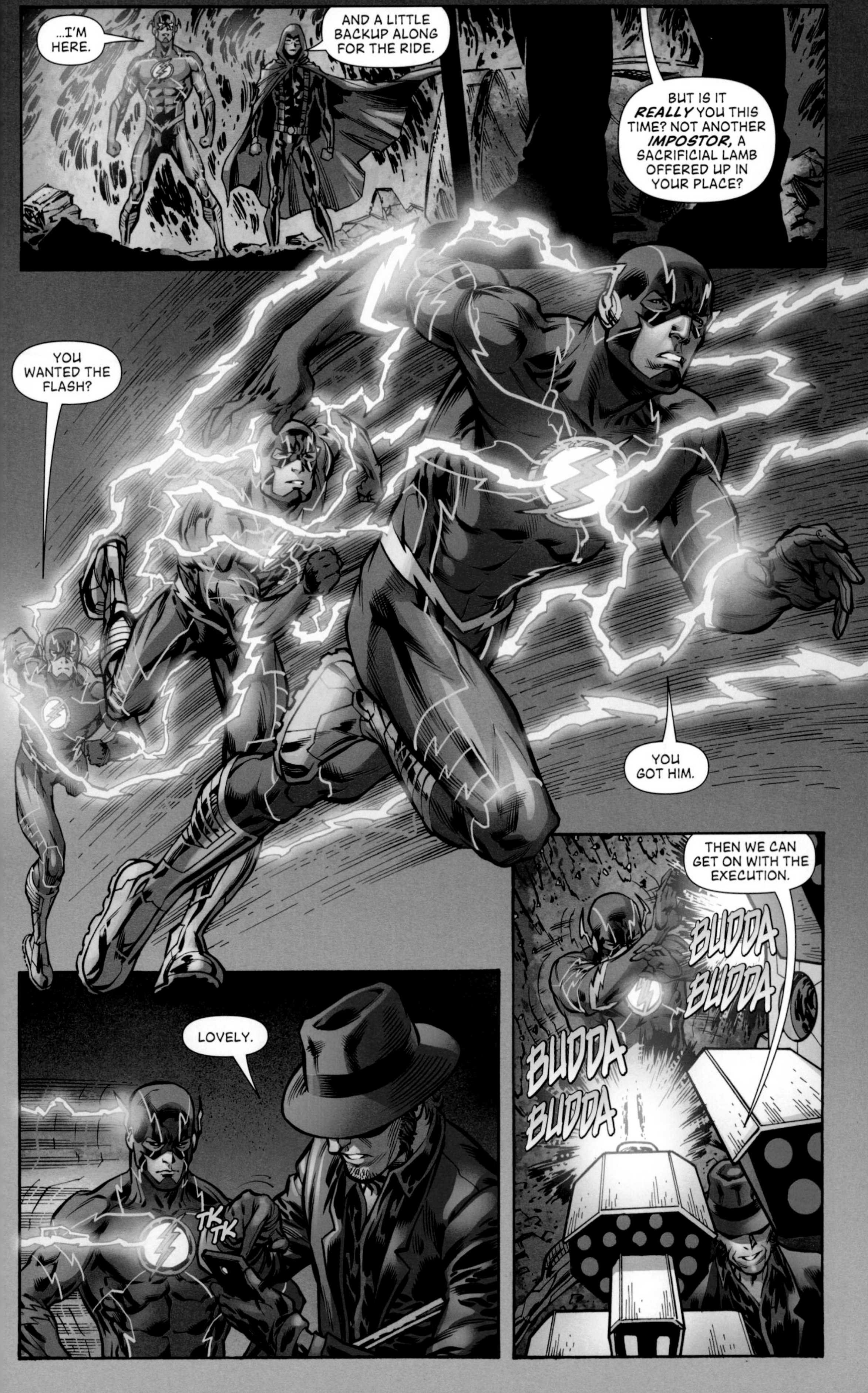
...I'M HERE.
AND A LITTLE BACKUP ALONG FOR THE RIDE.
BUT IS IT *REALLY* YOU THIS TIME? NOT ANOTHER *IMPOSTOR*, A SACRIFICIAL LAMB OFFERED UP IN YOUR PLACE?
YOU WANTED THE FLASH?
YOU GOT HIM.
THEN WE CAN GET ON WITH THE EXECUTION.
BUDDA BUDDA
BUDDA BUDDA
LOVELY.
TK TK

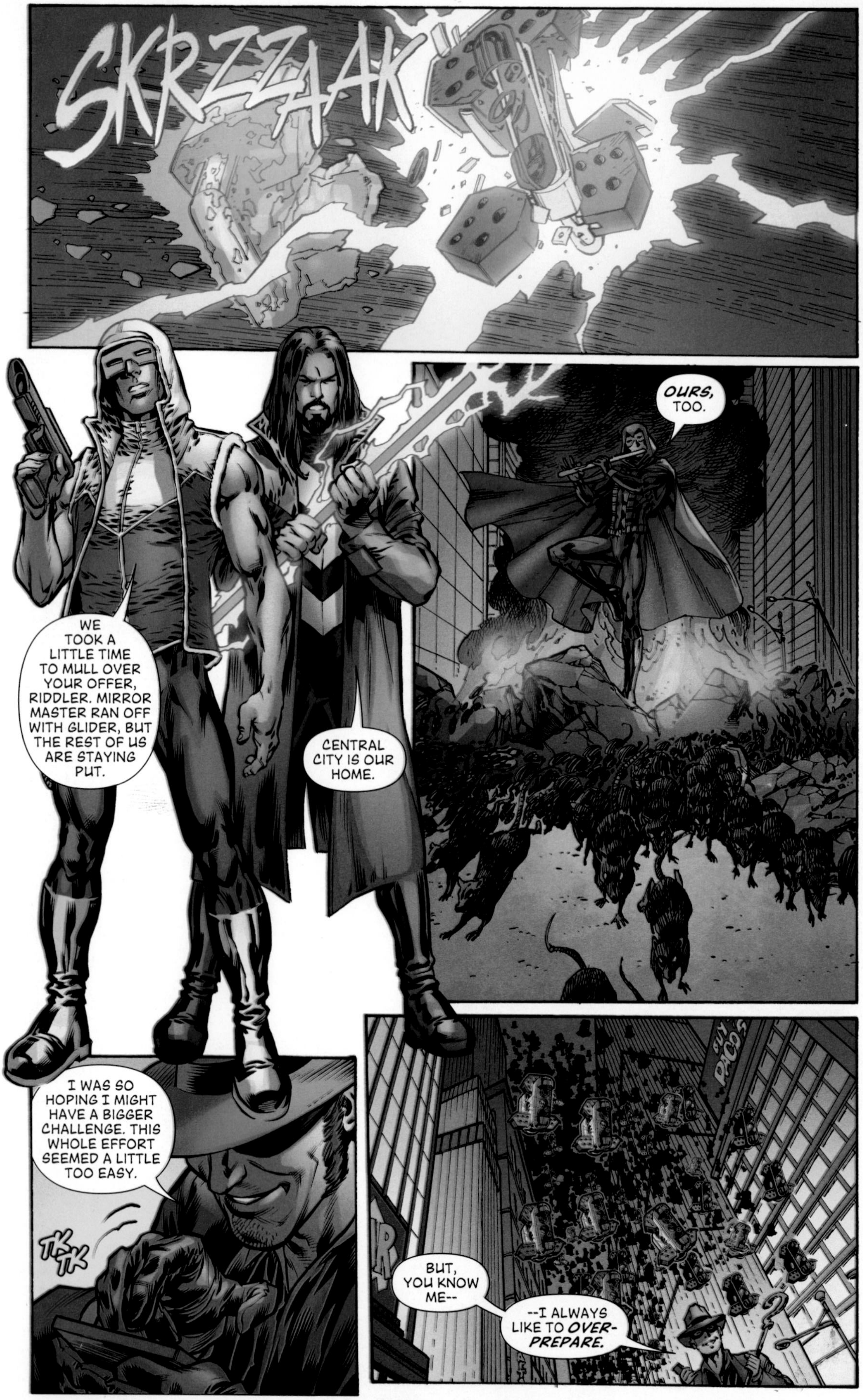
SKRZZAAK
WE TOOK A LITTLE TIME TO MULL OVER YOUR OFFER, RIDDLER. MIRROR MASTER RAN OFF WITH GLIDER, BUT THE REST OF US ARE STAYING PUT.
CENTRAL CITY IS OUR HOME.
OURS, TOO.
I WAS SO HOPING I MIGHT HAVE A BIGGER CHALLENGE. THIS WHOLE EFFORT SEEMED A LITTLE TOO EASY.
TK TK
BUT, YOU KNOW ME--
--I ALWAYS LIKE TO OVER-PREPARE.

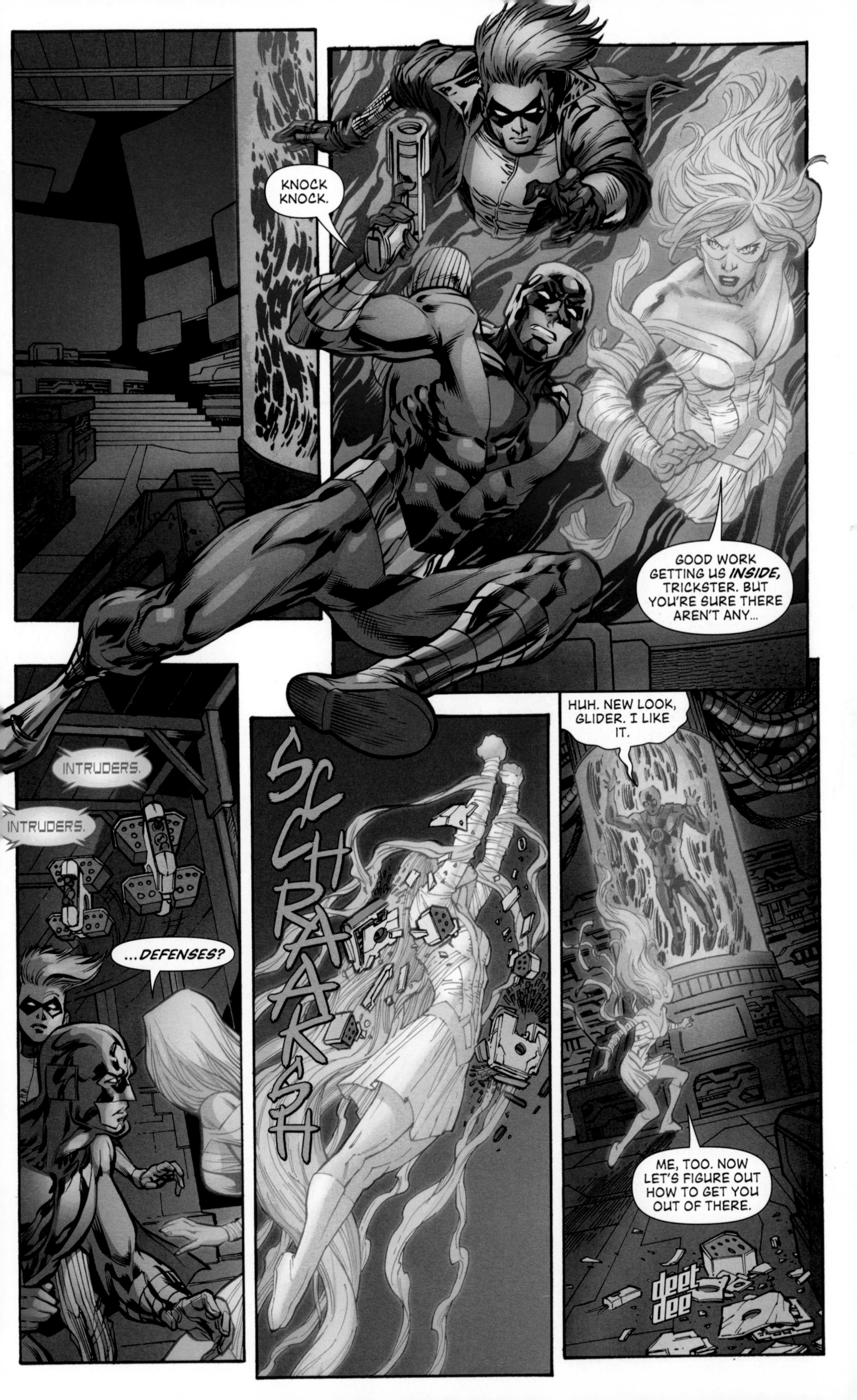
KNOCK KNOCK.
GOOD WORK GETTING US *INSIDE,* TRICKSTER. BUT YOU'RE SURE THERE AREN'T ANY...
INTRUDERS.
INTRUDERS.
...*DEFENSES?*
SCHRAAKSH
HUH. NEW LOOK, GLIDER. I LIKE IT.
ME, TOO. NOW LET'S FIGURE OUT HOW TO GET YOU OUT OF THERE.
deet dee

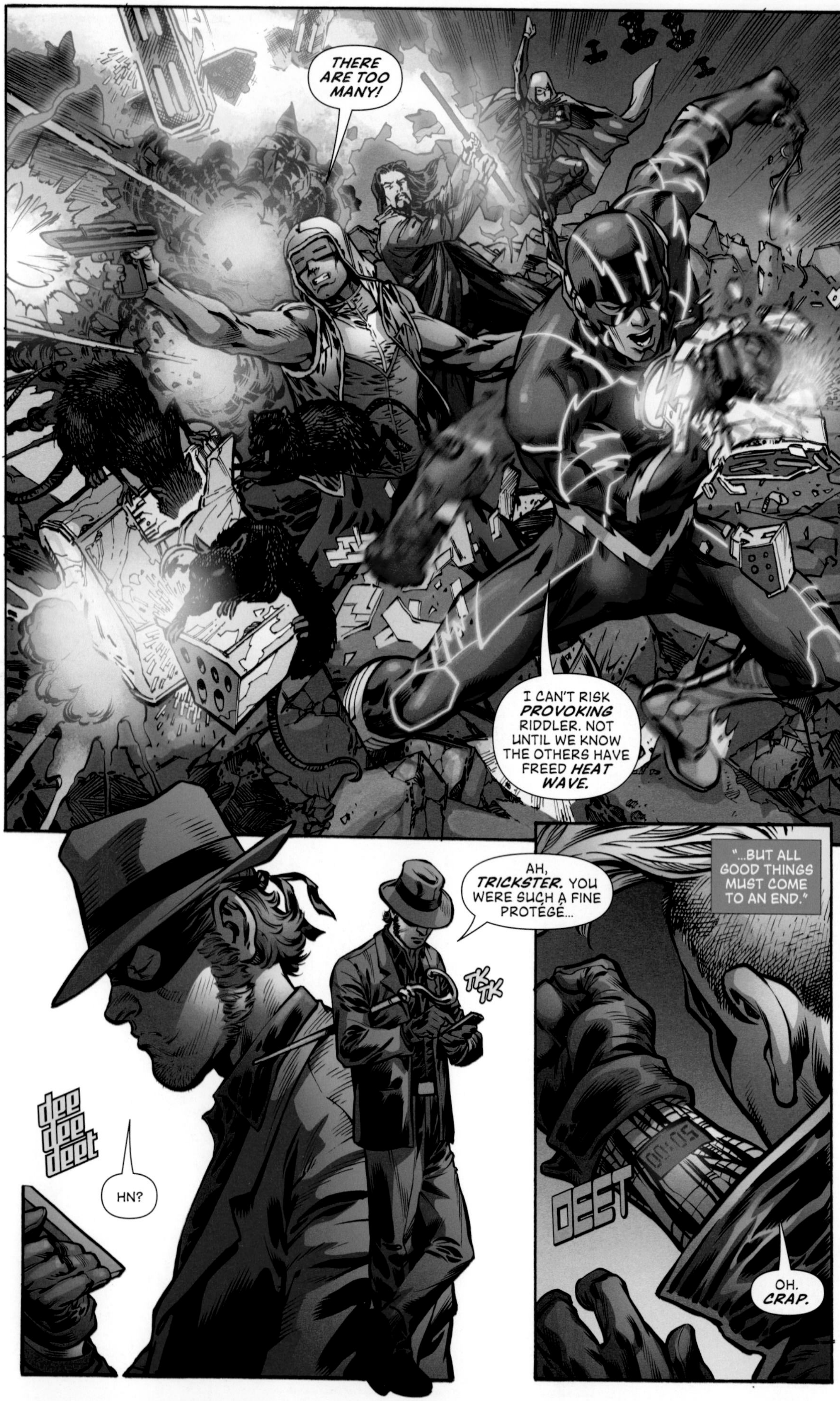
THERE ARE TOO MANY!
I CAN'T RISK PROVOKING RIDDLER. NOT UNTIL WE KNOW THE OTHERS HAVE FREED HEAT WAVE.
AH, TRICKSTER. YOU WERE SUCH A FINE PROTÉGÉ...
TK TK
dee dee deet
HN?
"...BUT ALL GOOD THINGS MUST COME TO AN END."
DEET
OH. CRAP.

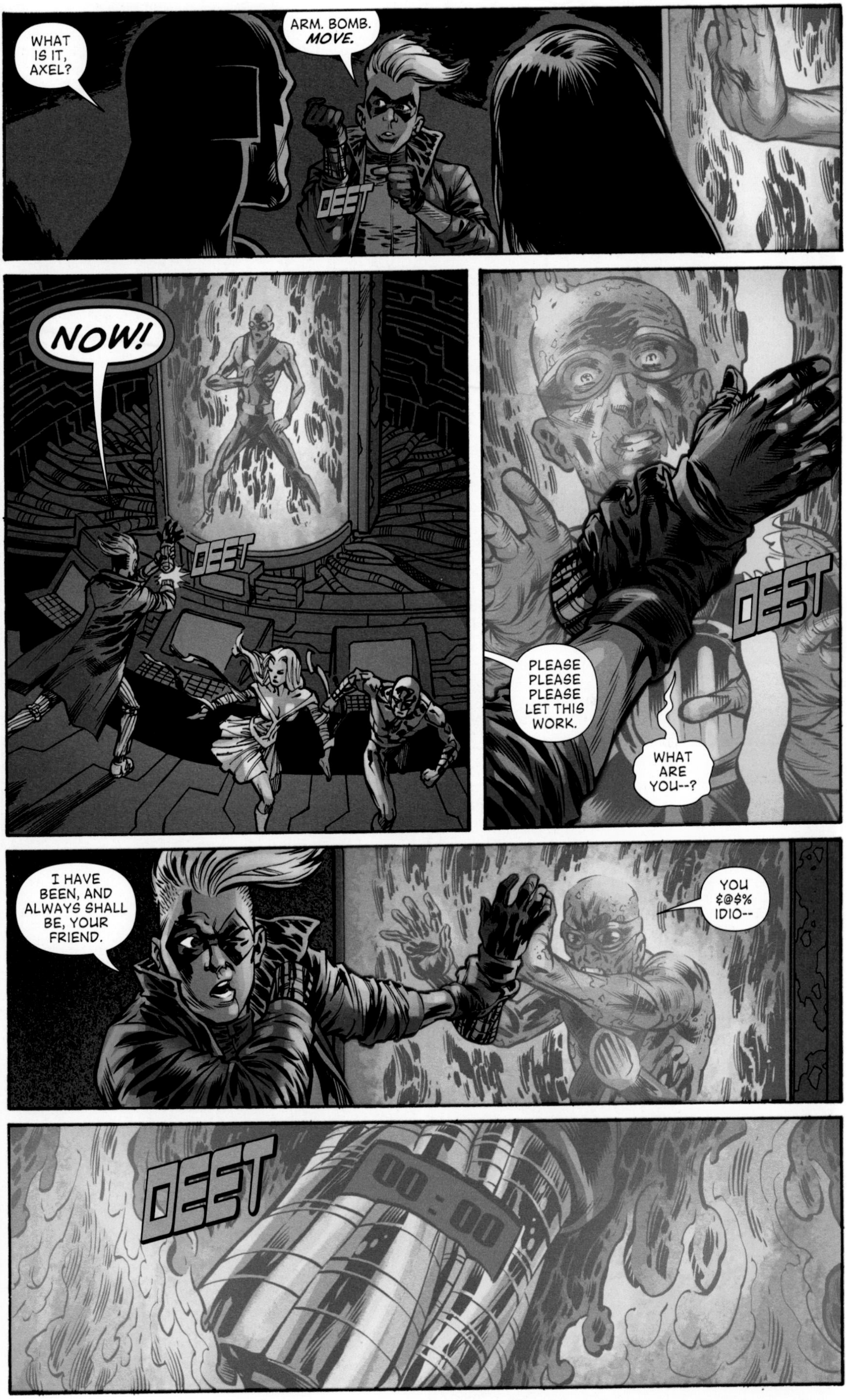
WHAT IS IT, AXEL?
ARM. BOMB. *MOVE.*
DEET
NOW!
DEET
DEET
PLEASE PLEASE PLEASE LET THIS WORK.
WHAT ARE YOU--?
I HAVE BEEN, AND ALWAYS SHALL BE, YOUR FRIEND.
YOU $@$% IDIO--
DEET
00:00

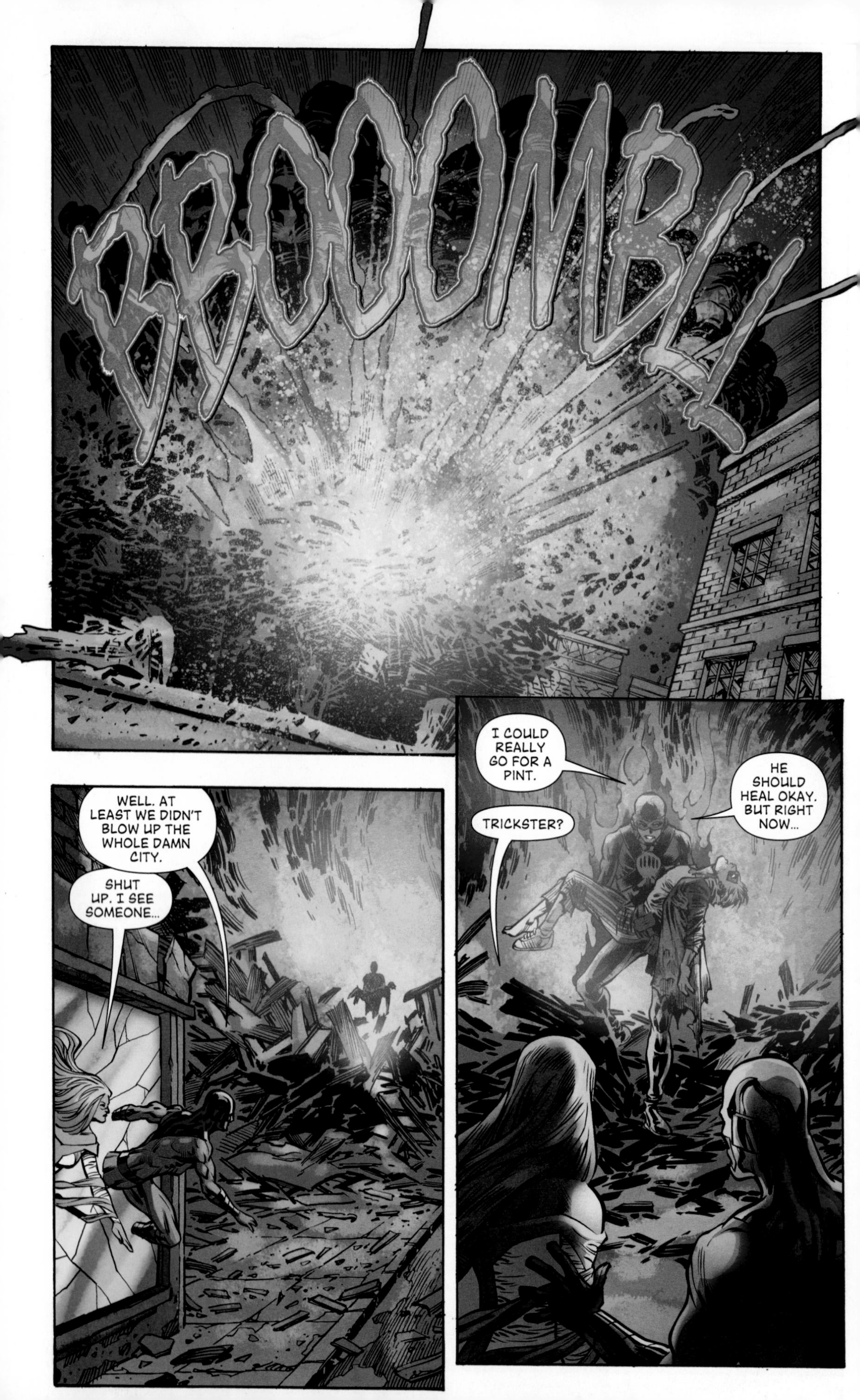
BBOOOMBL!
WELL. AT LEAST WE DIDN'T BLOW UP THE WHOLE DAMN CITY.
SHUT UP. I SEE SOMEONE...
I COULD REALLY GO FOR A PINT.
TRICKSTER?
HE SHOULD HEAL OKAY. BUT RIGHT NOW...

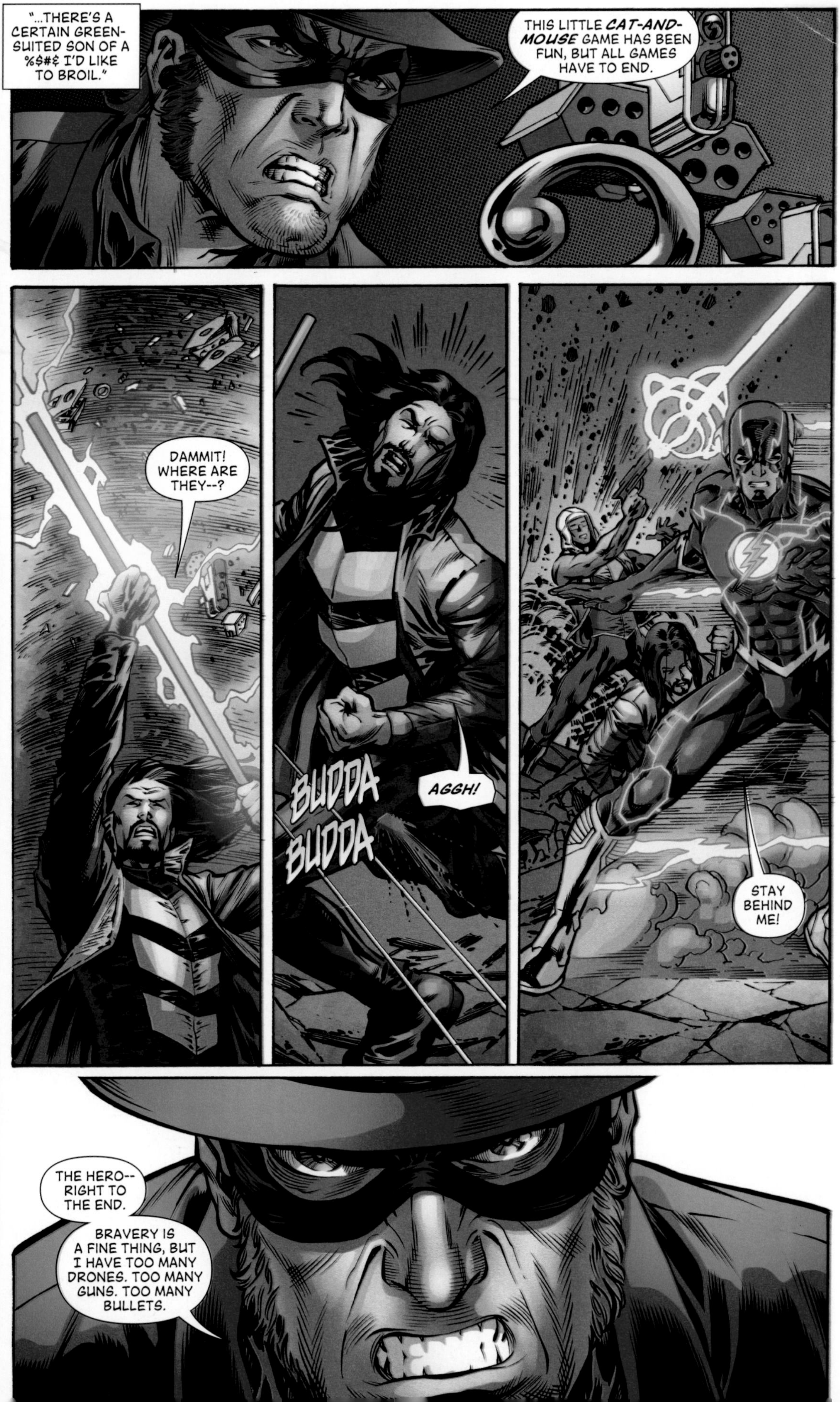
"...THERE'S A CERTAIN GREEN-SUITED SON OF A %$#& I'D LIKE TO BROIL."
THIS LITTLE CAT-AND-MOUSE GAME HAS BEEN FUN, BUT ALL GAMES HAVE TO END.
DAMMIT! WHERE ARE THEY--?
BUDDA BUDDA
AGGH!
STAY BEHIND ME!
THE HERO--RIGHT TO THE END.
BRAVERY IS A FINE THING, BUT I HAVE TOO MANY DRONES. TOO MANY GUNS. TOO MANY BULLETS.

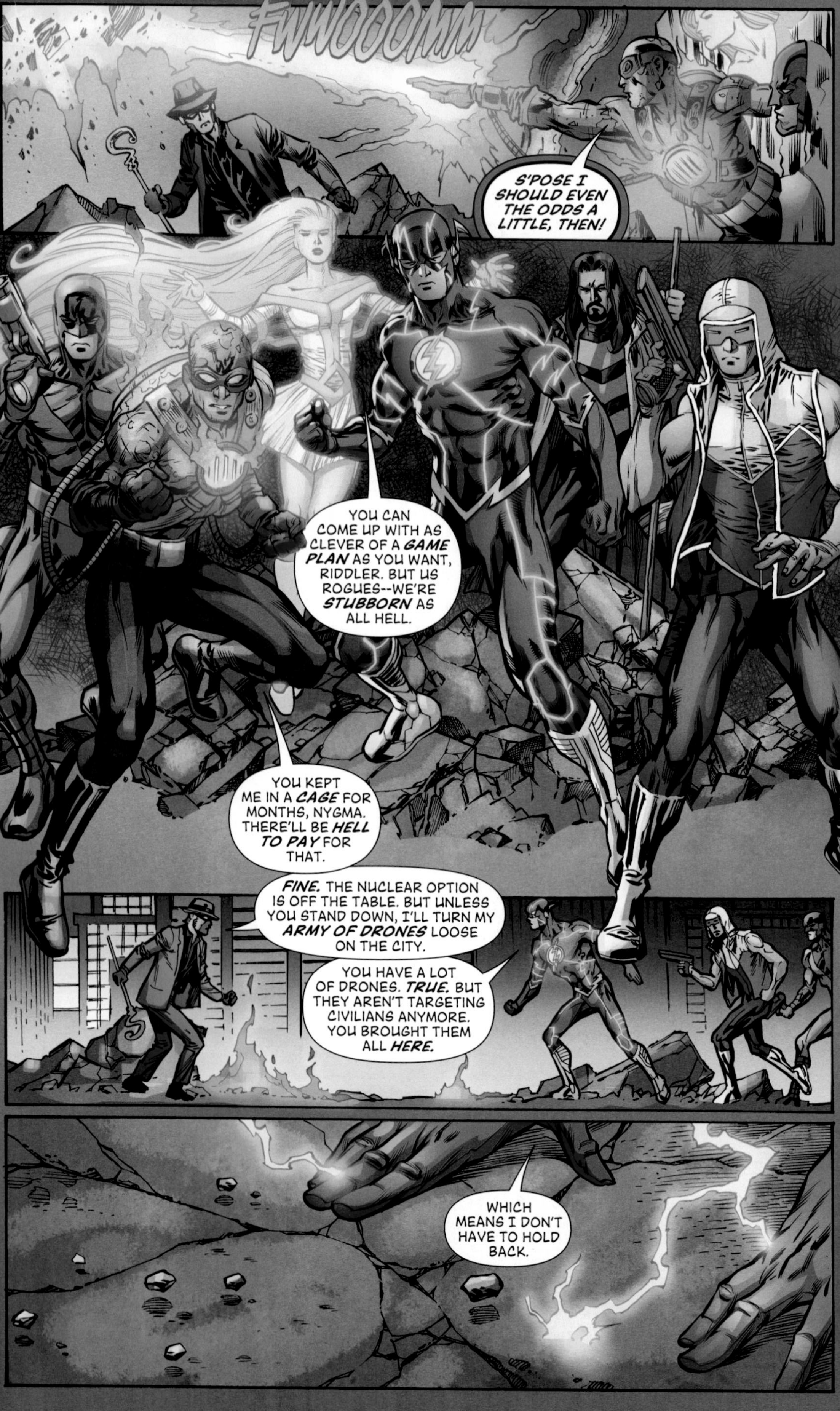
FWWOOOMM
S'POSE I SHOULD EVEN THE ODDS A LITTLE, THEN!
YOU CAN COME UP WITH AS CLEVER OF A GAME PLAN AS YOU WANT, RIDDLER. BUT US ROGUES--WE'RE STUBBORN AS ALL HELL.
YOU KEPT ME IN A CAGE FOR MONTHS, NYGMA. THERE'LL BE HELL TO PAY FOR THAT.
FINE. THE NUCLEAR OPTION IS OFF THE TABLE. BUT UNLESS YOU STAND DOWN, I'LL TURN MY ARMY OF DRONES LOOSE ON THE CITY.
YOU HAVE A LOT OF DRONES. TRUE. BUT THEY AREN'T TARGETING CIVILIANS ANYMORE. YOU BROUGHT THEM ALL HERE.
WHICH MEANS I DON'T HAVE TO HOLD BACK.

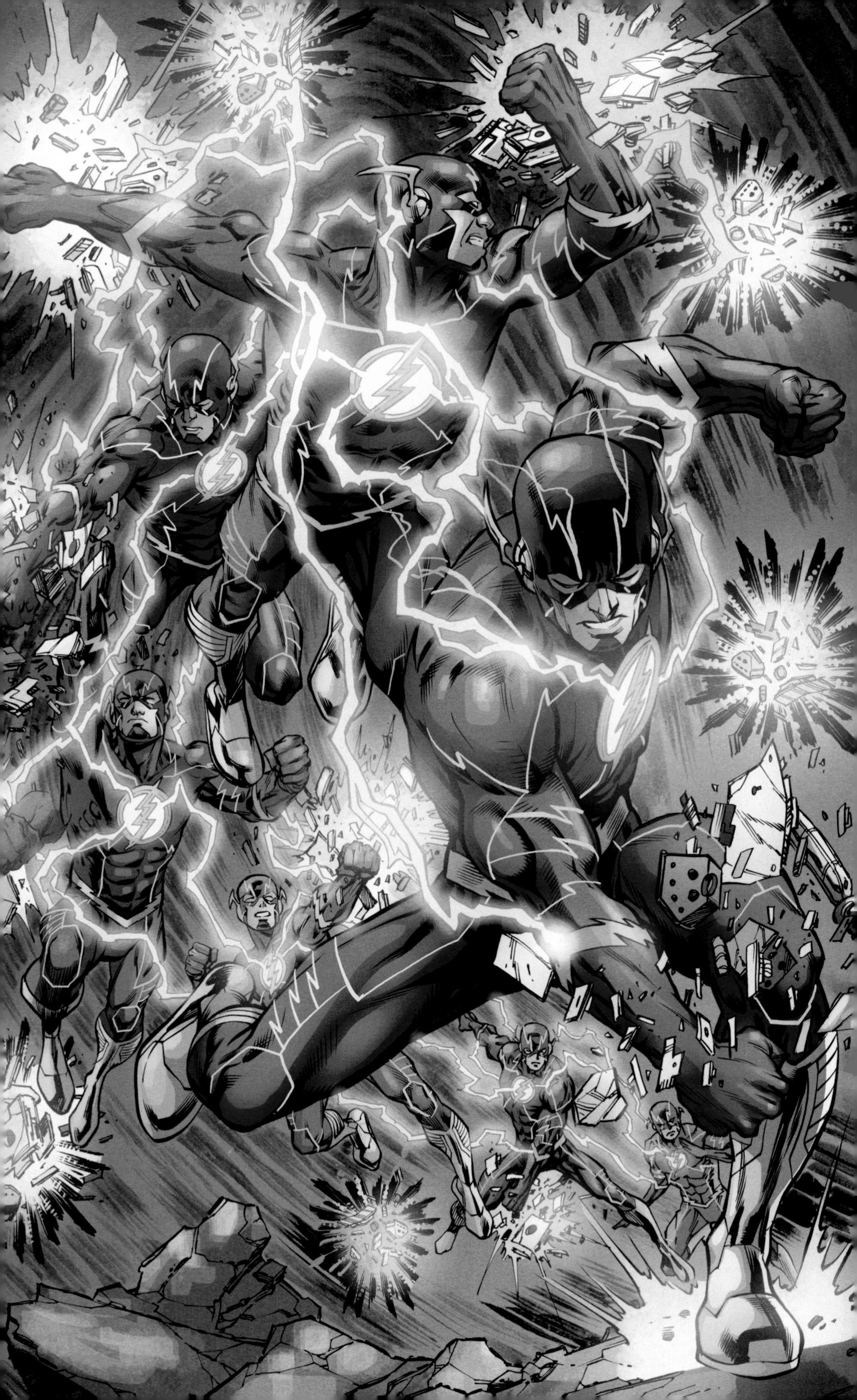

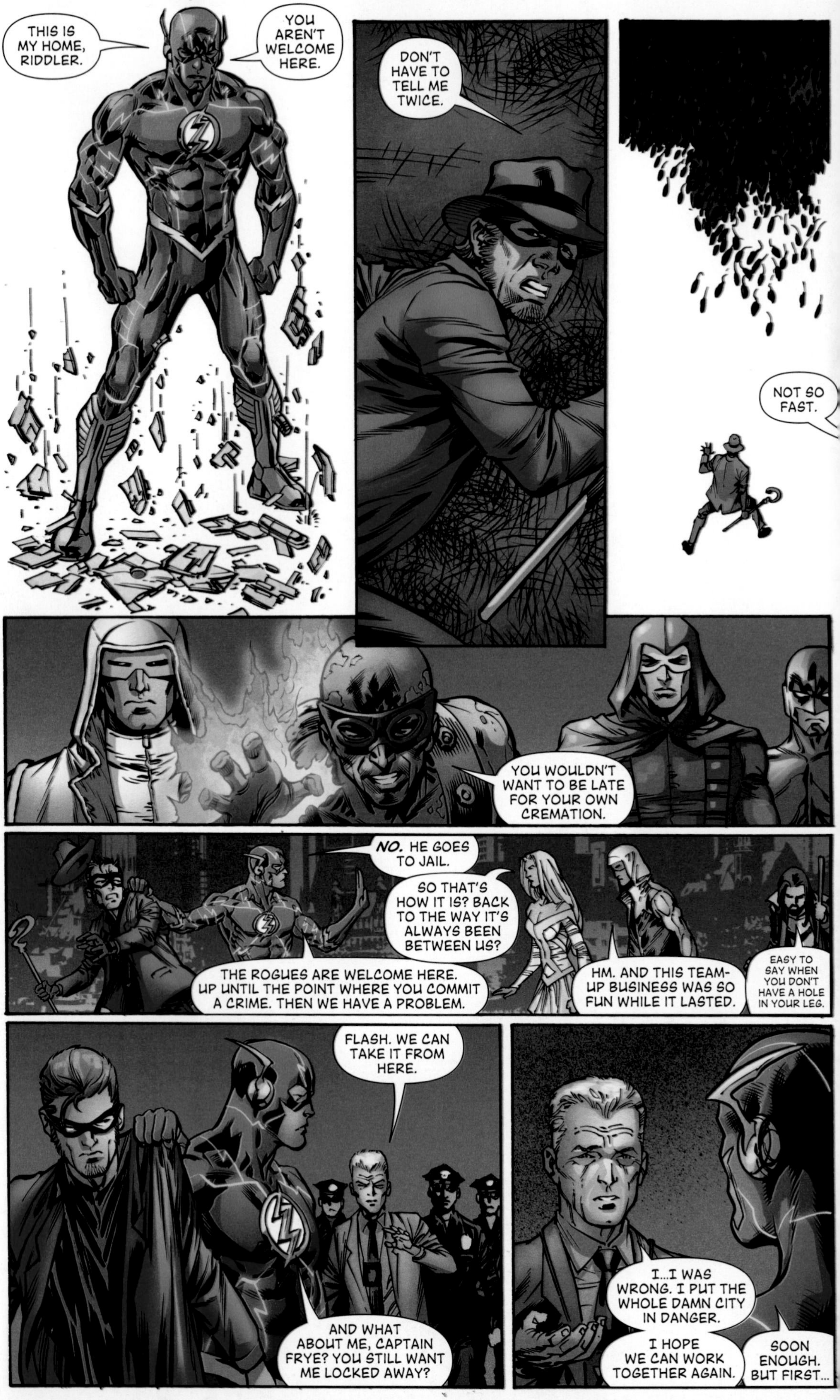
THIS IS MY HOME, RIDDLER.
YOU AREN'T WELCOME HERE.
DON'T HAVE TO TELL ME TWICE.
NOT SO FAST.
YOU WOULDN'T WANT TO BE LATE FOR YOUR OWN CREMATION.
NO. HE GOES TO JAIL.
SO THAT'S HOW IT IS? BACK TO THE WAY IT'S ALWAYS BEEN BETWEEN US?
THE ROGUES ARE WELCOME HERE. UP UNTIL THE POINT WHERE YOU COMMIT A CRIME. THEN WE HAVE A PROBLEM.
HM. AND THIS TEAM-UP BUSINESS WAS SO FUN WHILE IT LASTED.
EASY TO SAY WHEN YOU DON'T HAVE A HOLE IN YOUR LEG.
FLASH. WE CAN TAKE IT FROM HERE.
AND WHAT ABOUT ME, CAPTAIN FRYE? YOU STILL WANT ME LOCKED AWAY?
I...I WAS WRONG. I PUT THE WHOLE DAMN CITY IN DANGER.
I HOPE WE CAN WORK TOGETHER AGAIN.
SOON ENOUGH. BUT FIRST...

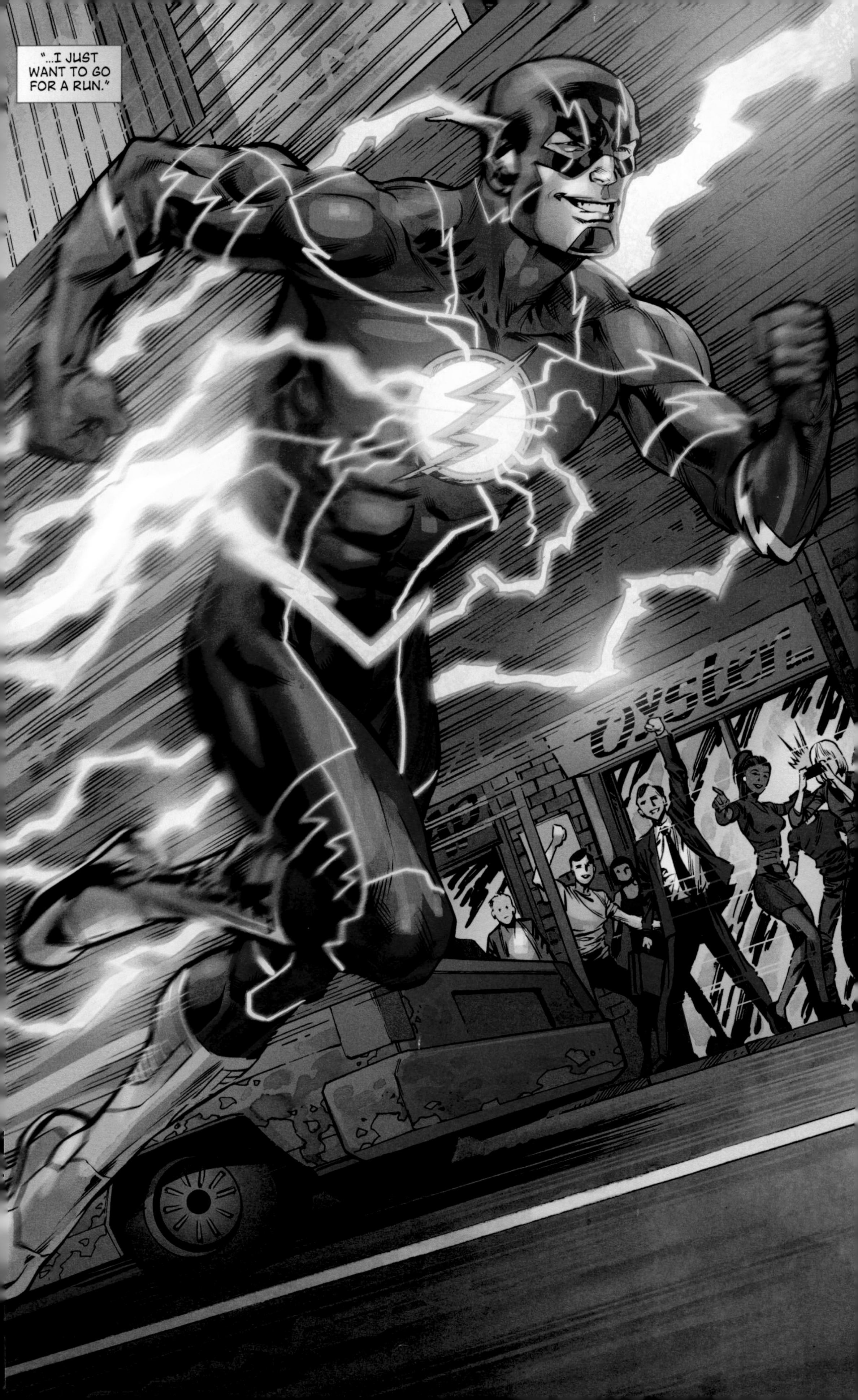
"...I JUST WANT TO GO FOR A RUN."
Oyster

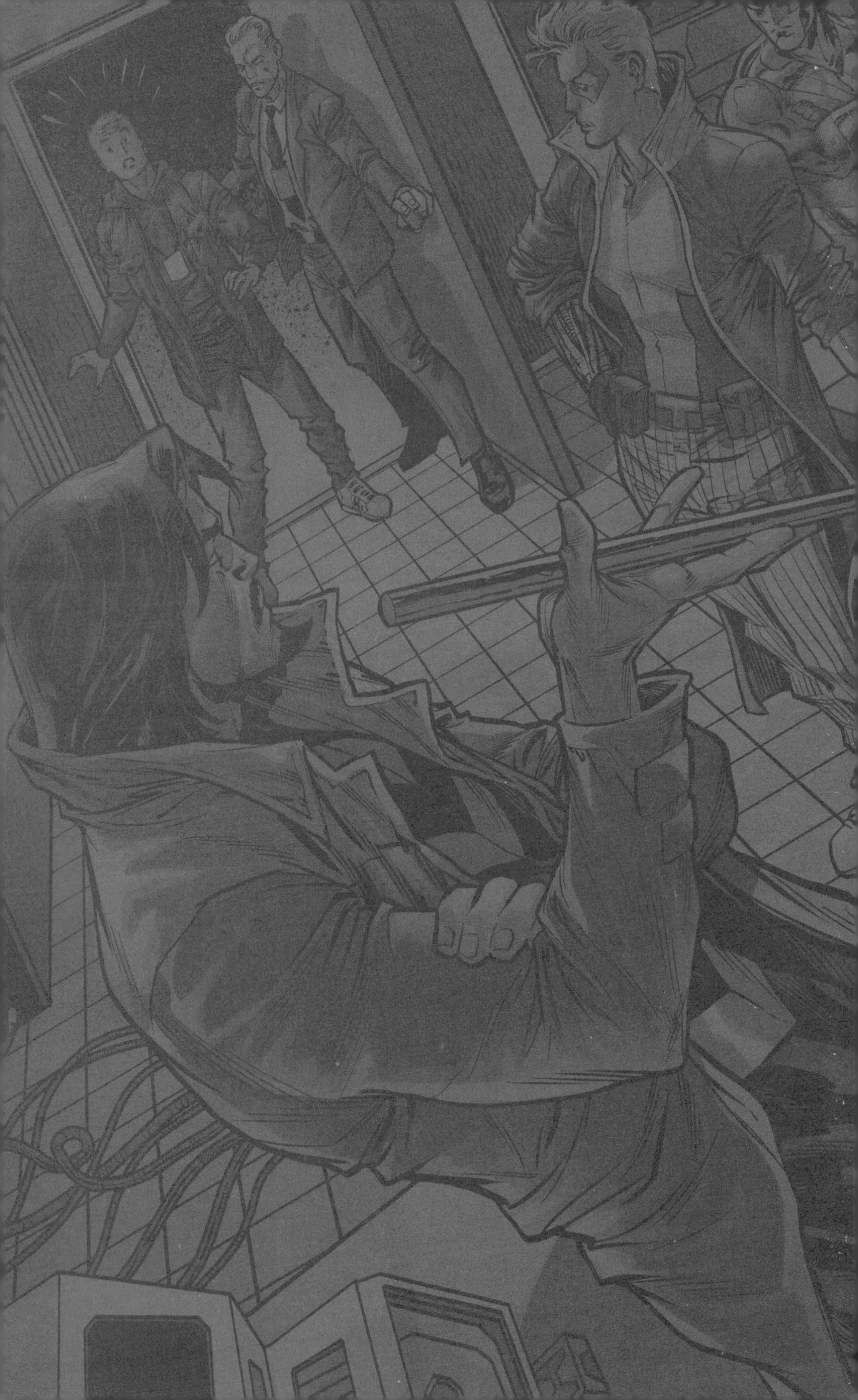

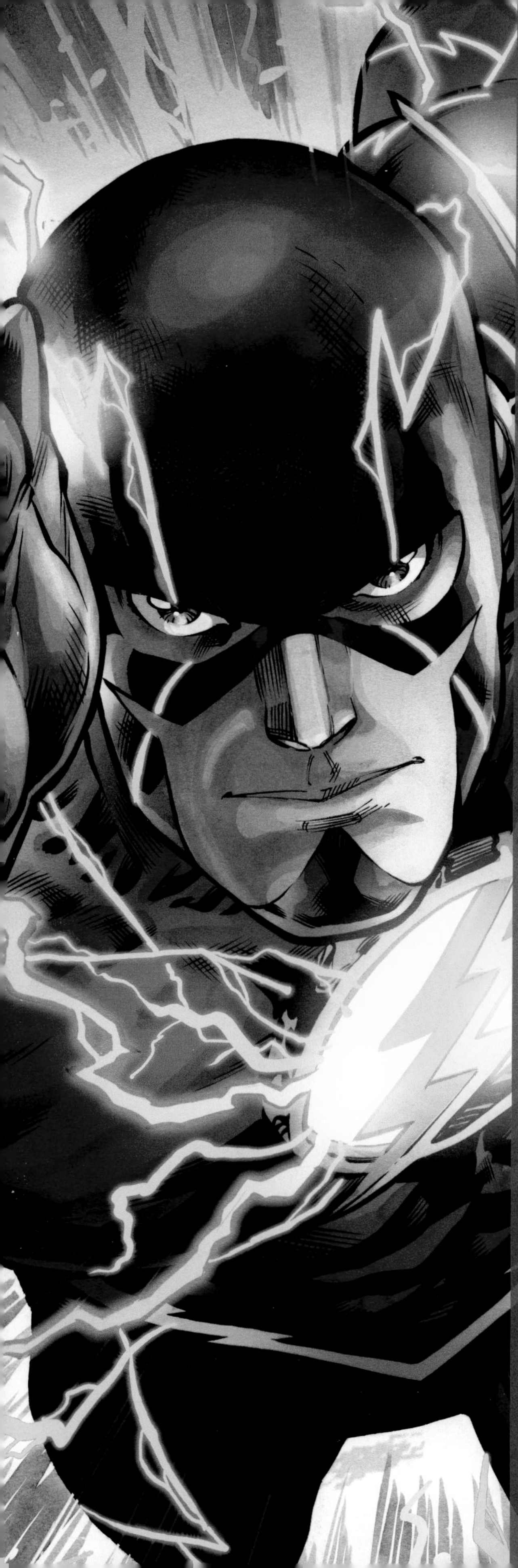

VARIANT COVER GALLERY

THE FLASH #48
COLORING BOOK VARIANT
BY DEREC DONOVAN

THE FLASH #49
NEAL ADAMS VARIANT
BY NEAL ADAMS
& FRANK MILLER

THE FLASH #50
BATMAN V SUPERMAN VARIANT
BY DUNCAN FEGREDO

THE FLASH #51
JOHN ROMITA JR. VARIANT
BY JOHN ROMITA JR.
DANNY MIKI
ALEX SINCLAIR

THE FLASH #52
THE NEW 52 VARIANT
BY JESÚS MERINO GUY MAJOR

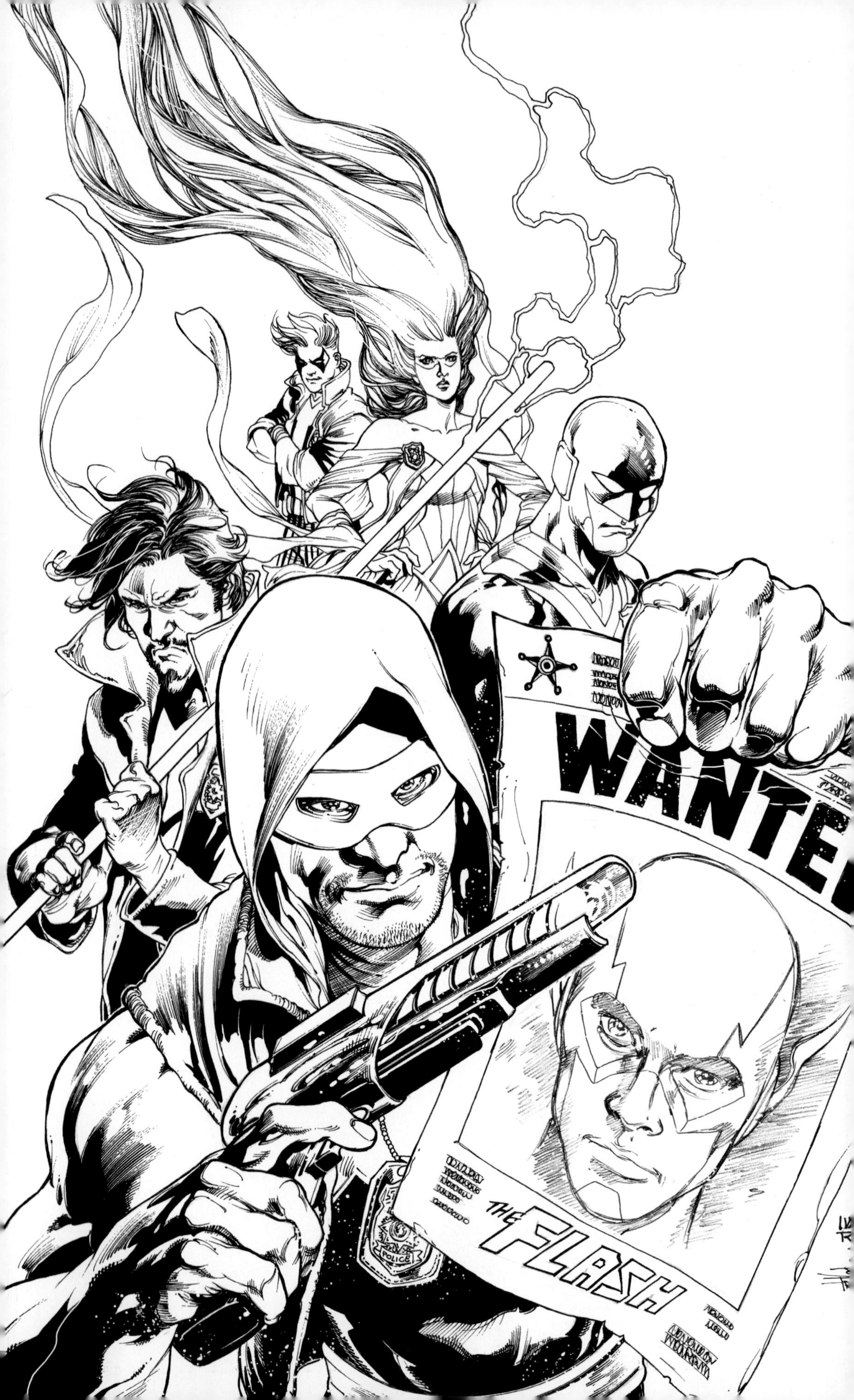

WANTE
THE FLASH

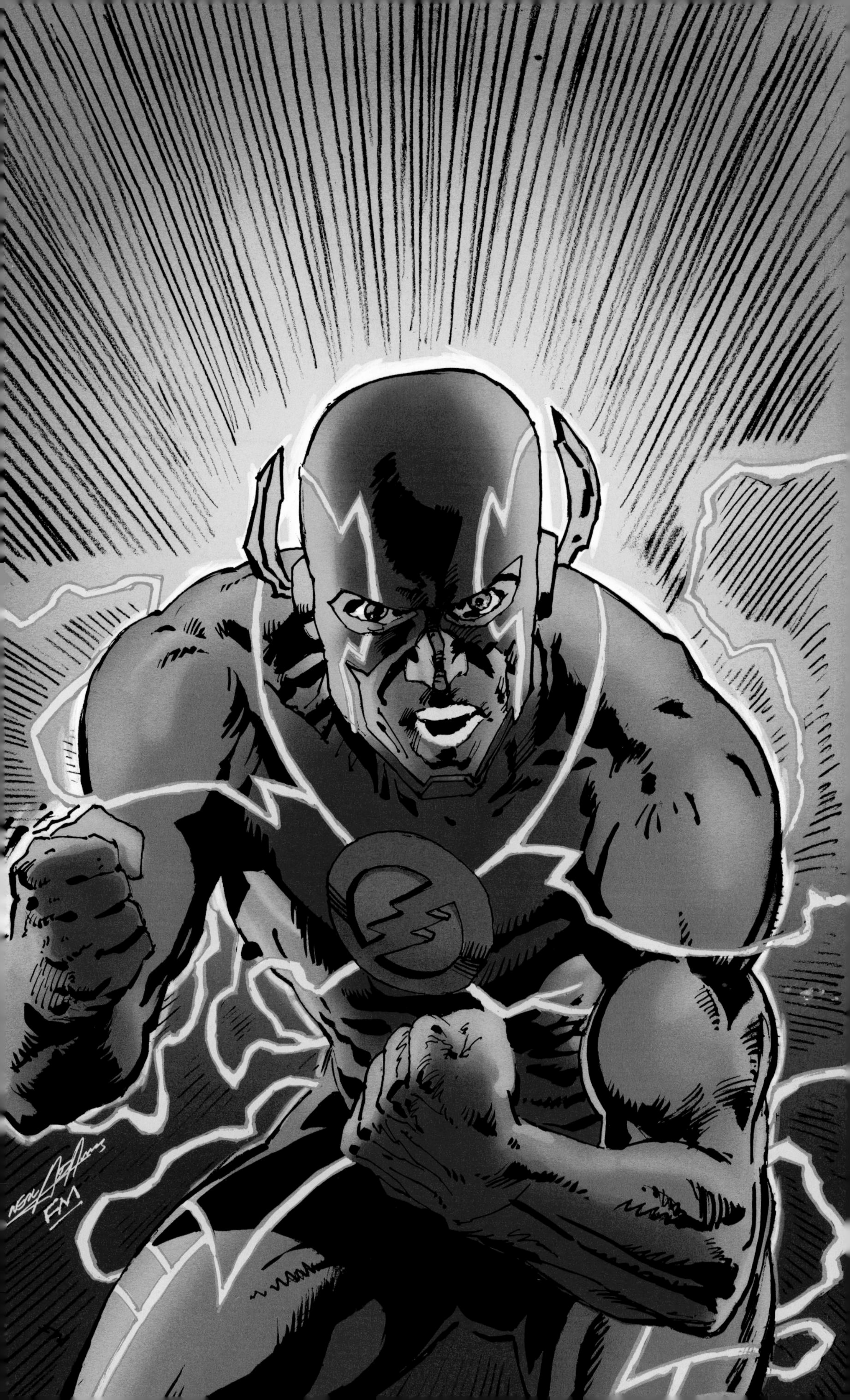

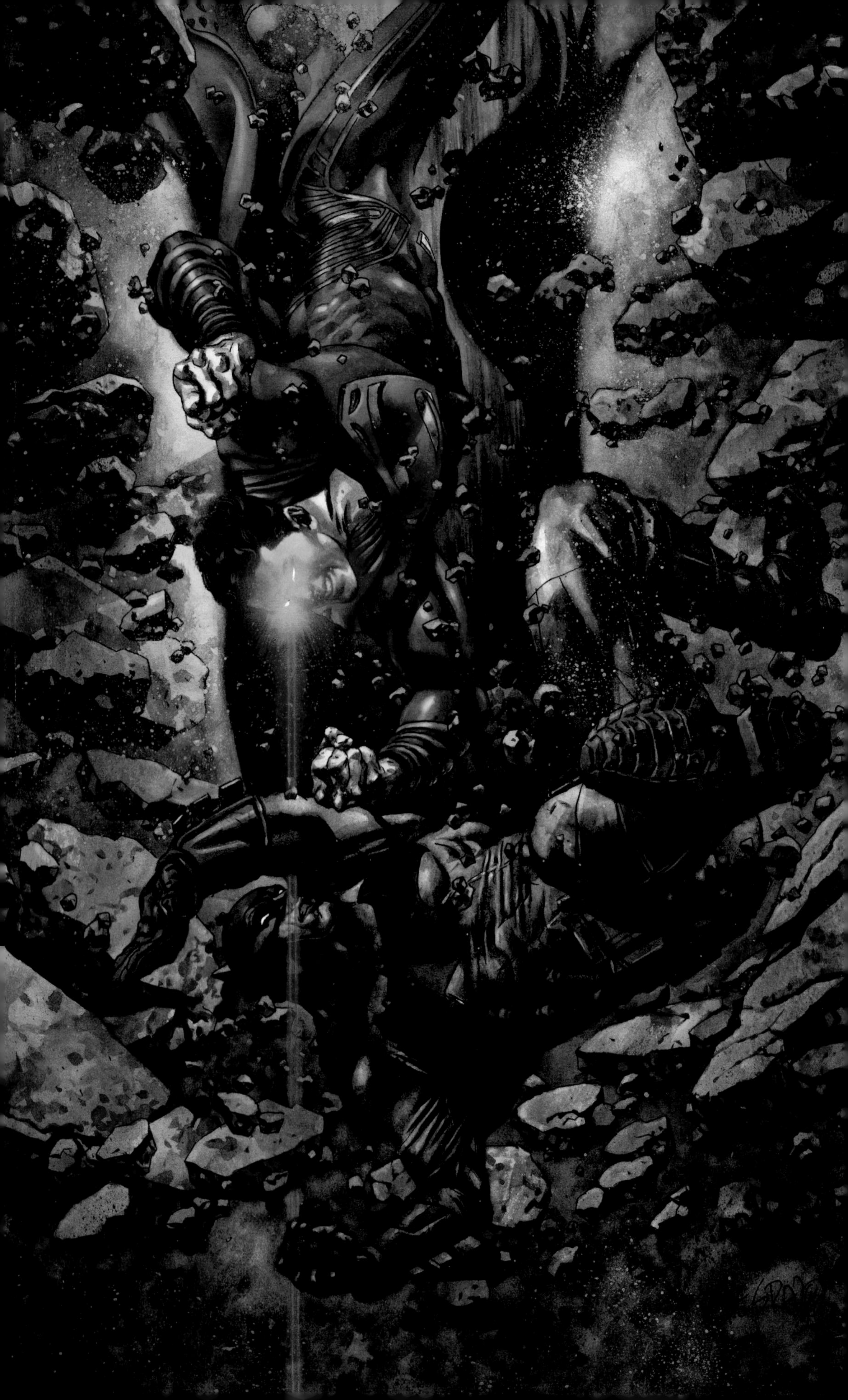

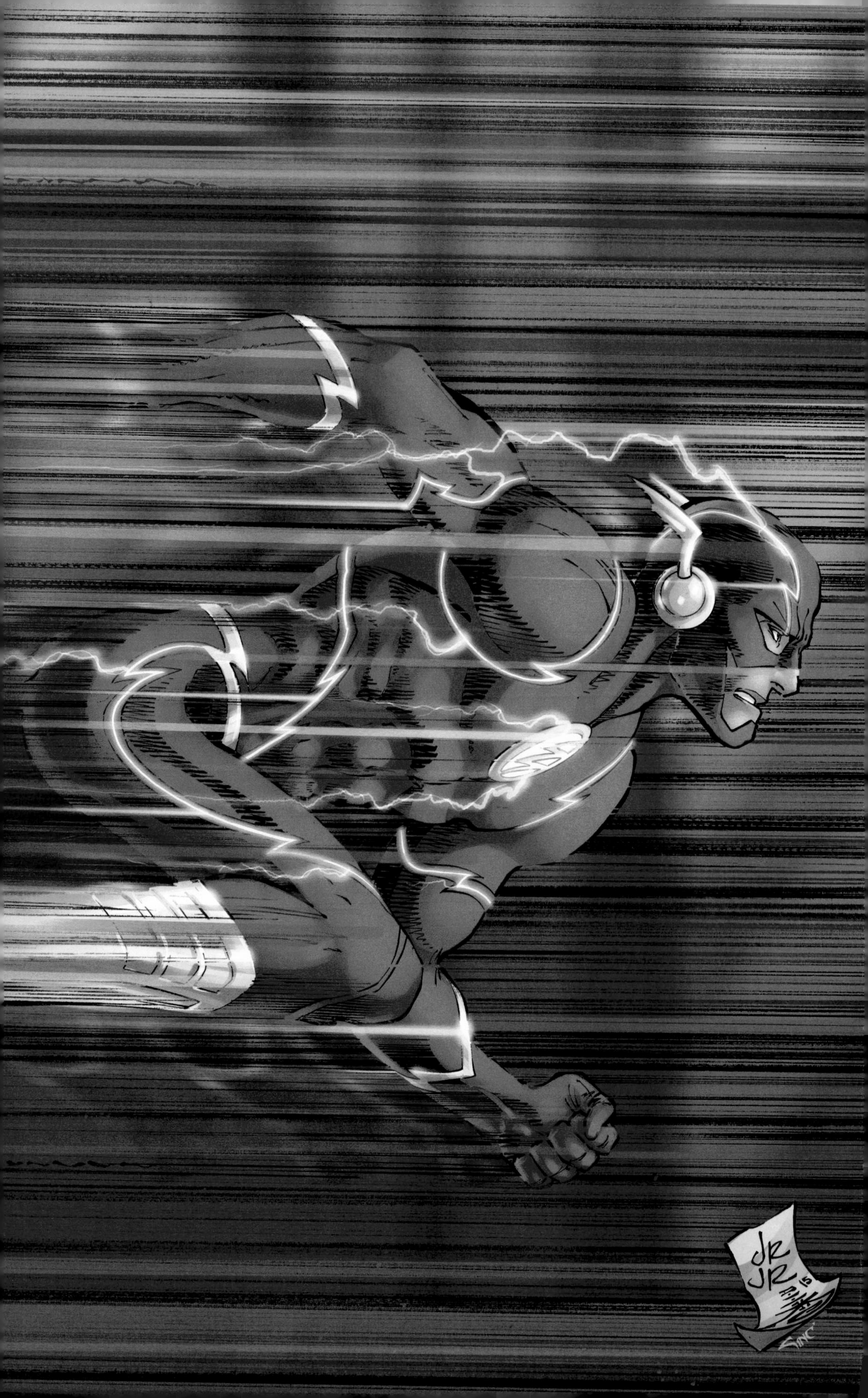
JR JR

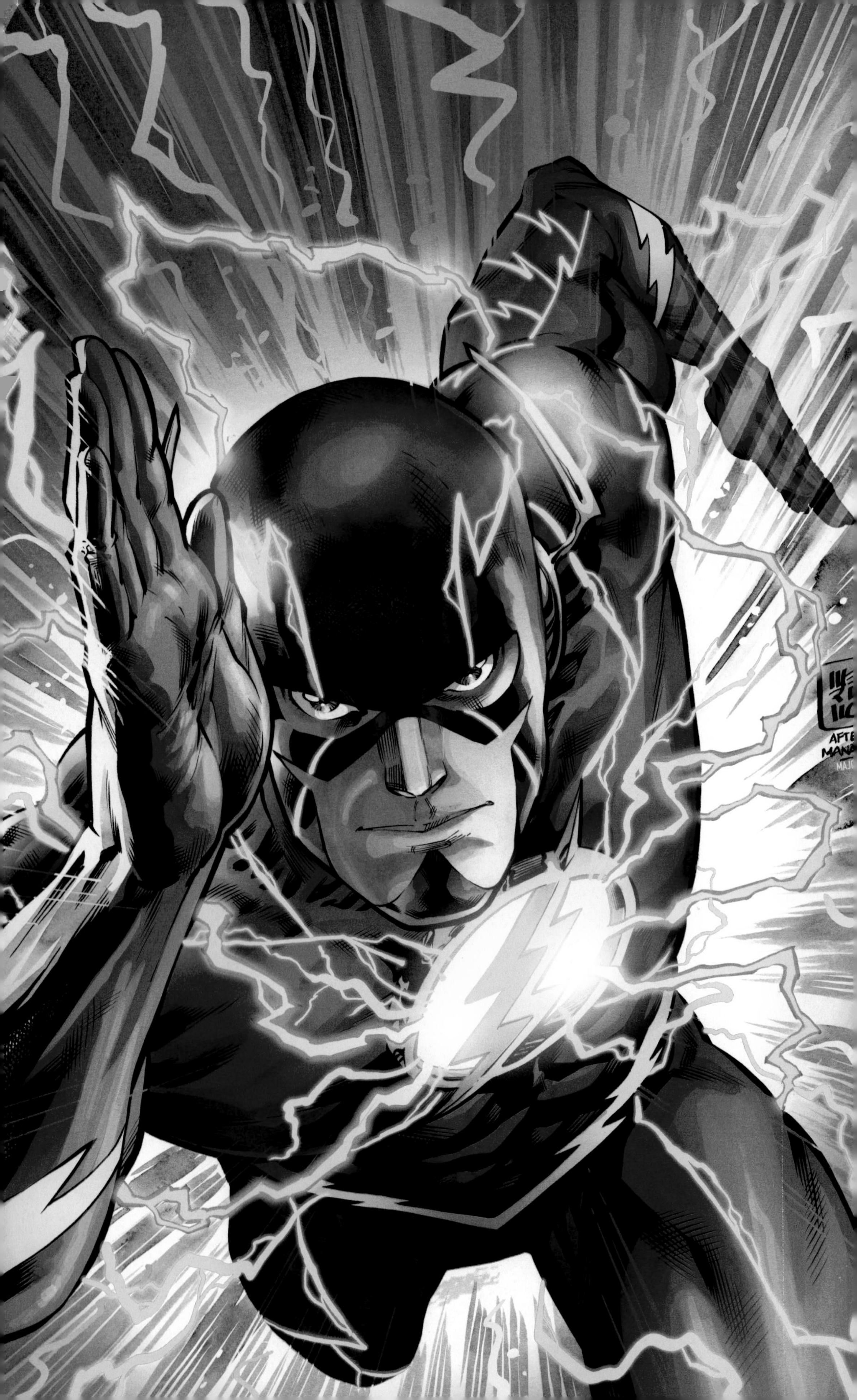

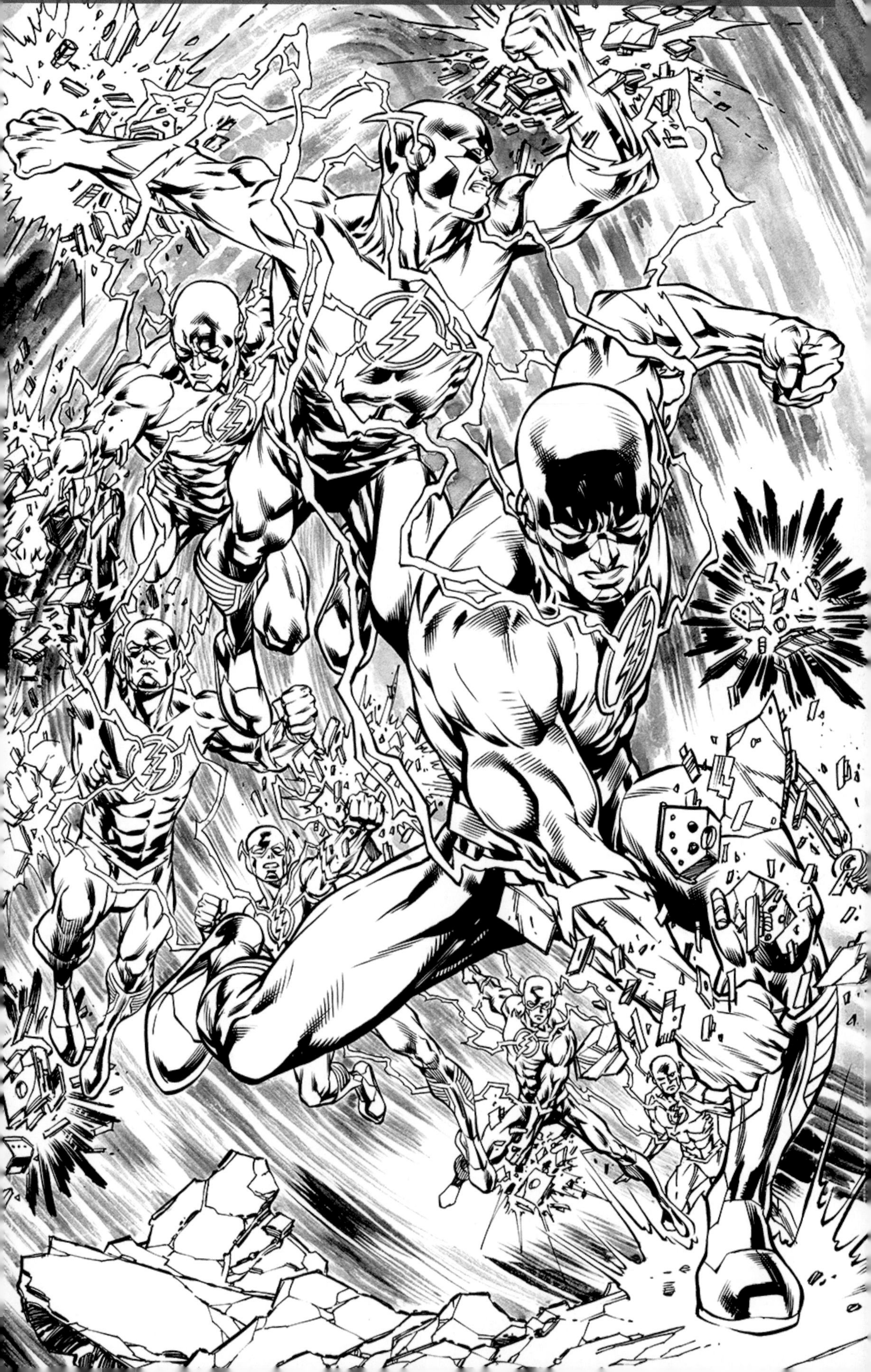

ART BY JESÚS MERINO FOR PAGE 135

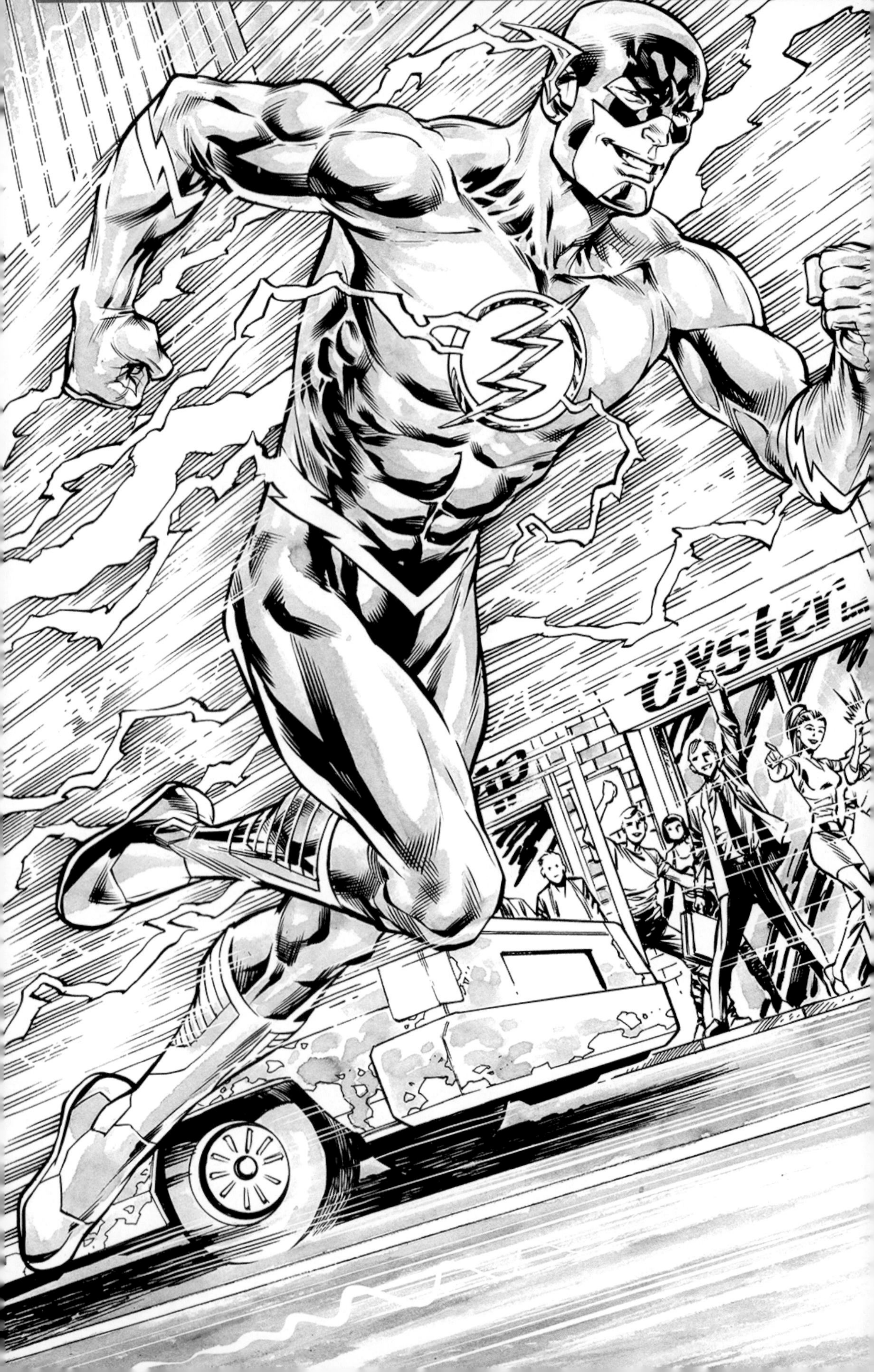

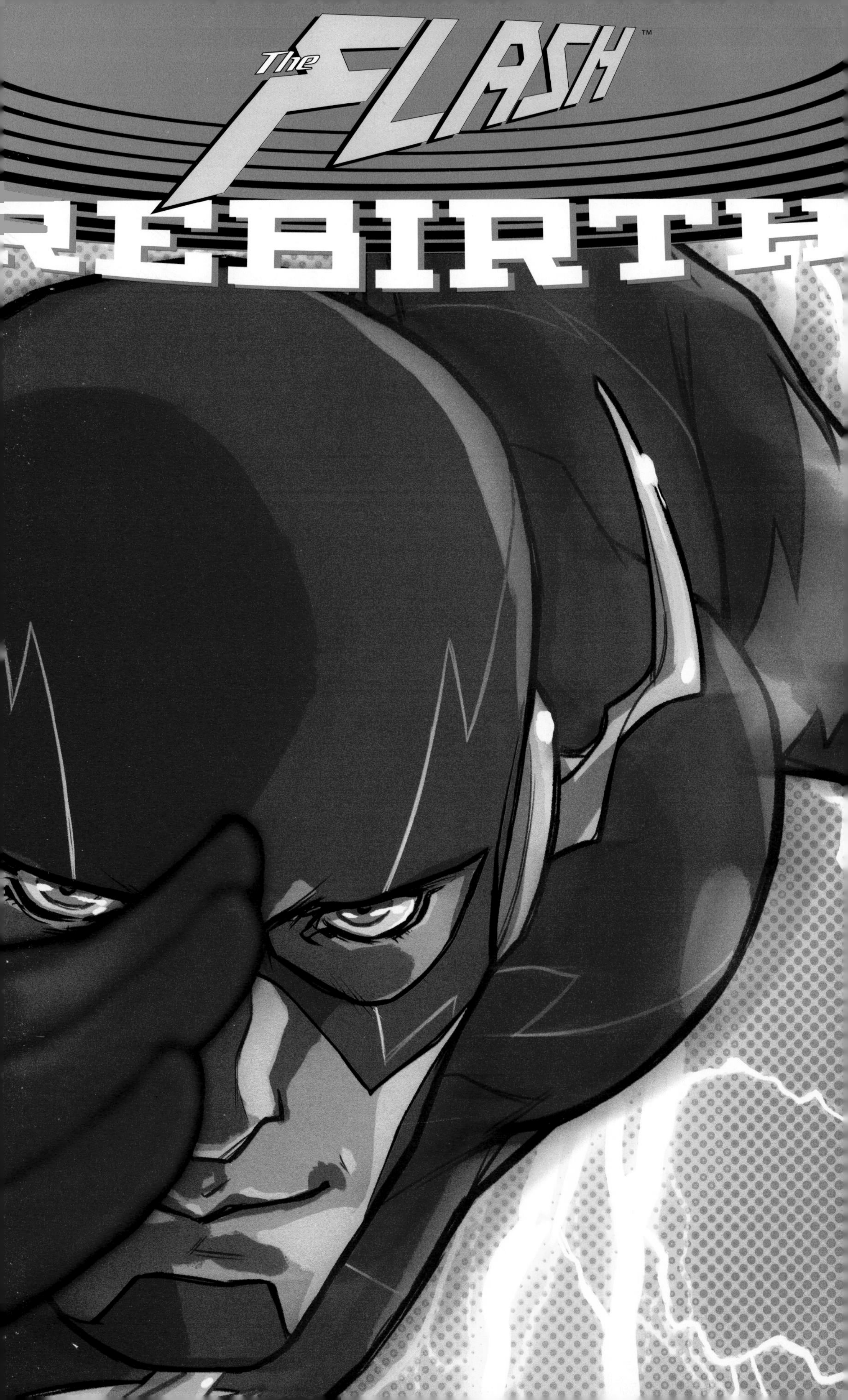
The FLASH™
REBIRTH

The future (and past) of the DC Universe starts with DC UNIVERSE: REBIRTH!

Explore the changing world of the Flash in this special bonus preview of **THE FLASH: REBIRTH #1**.

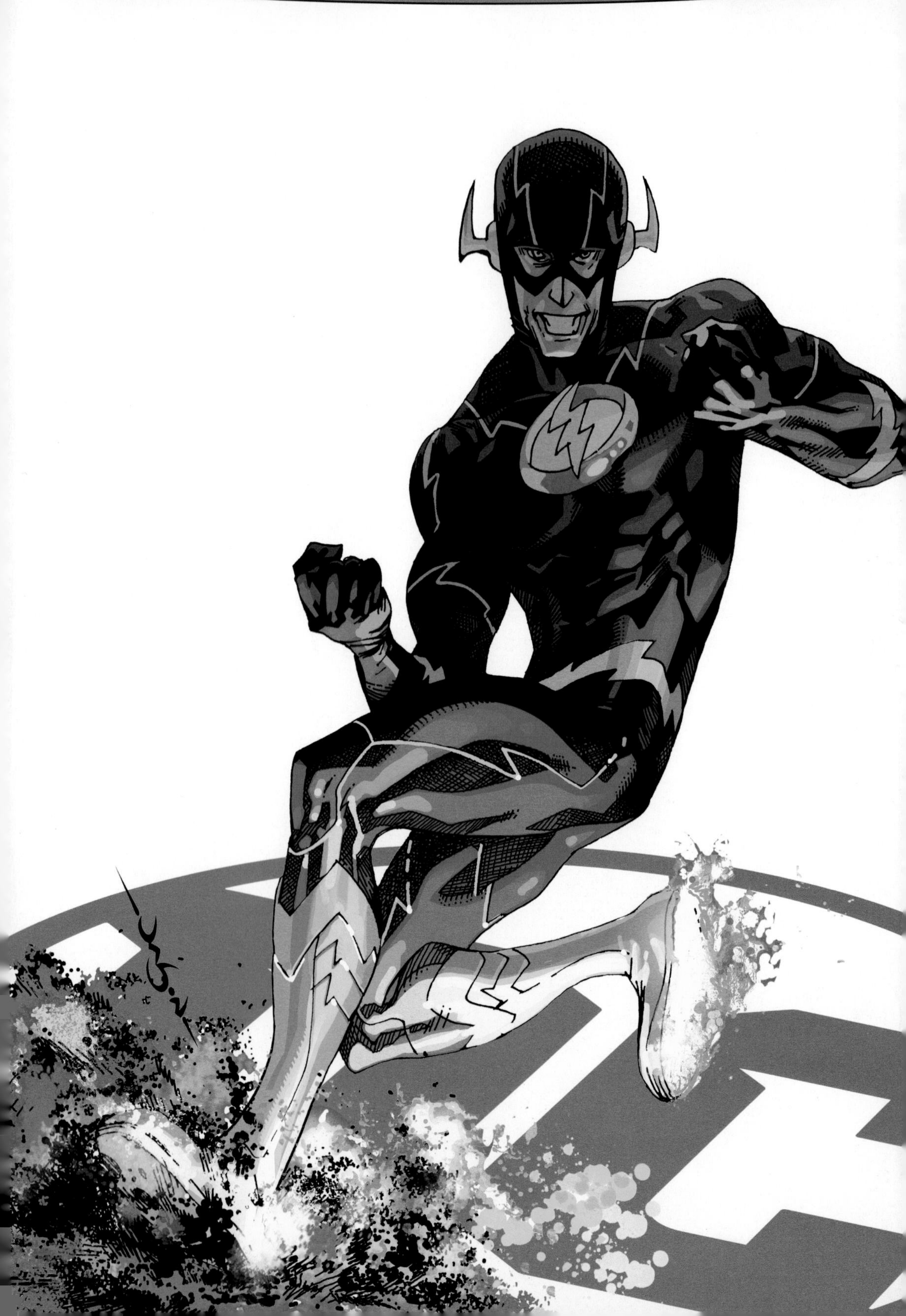

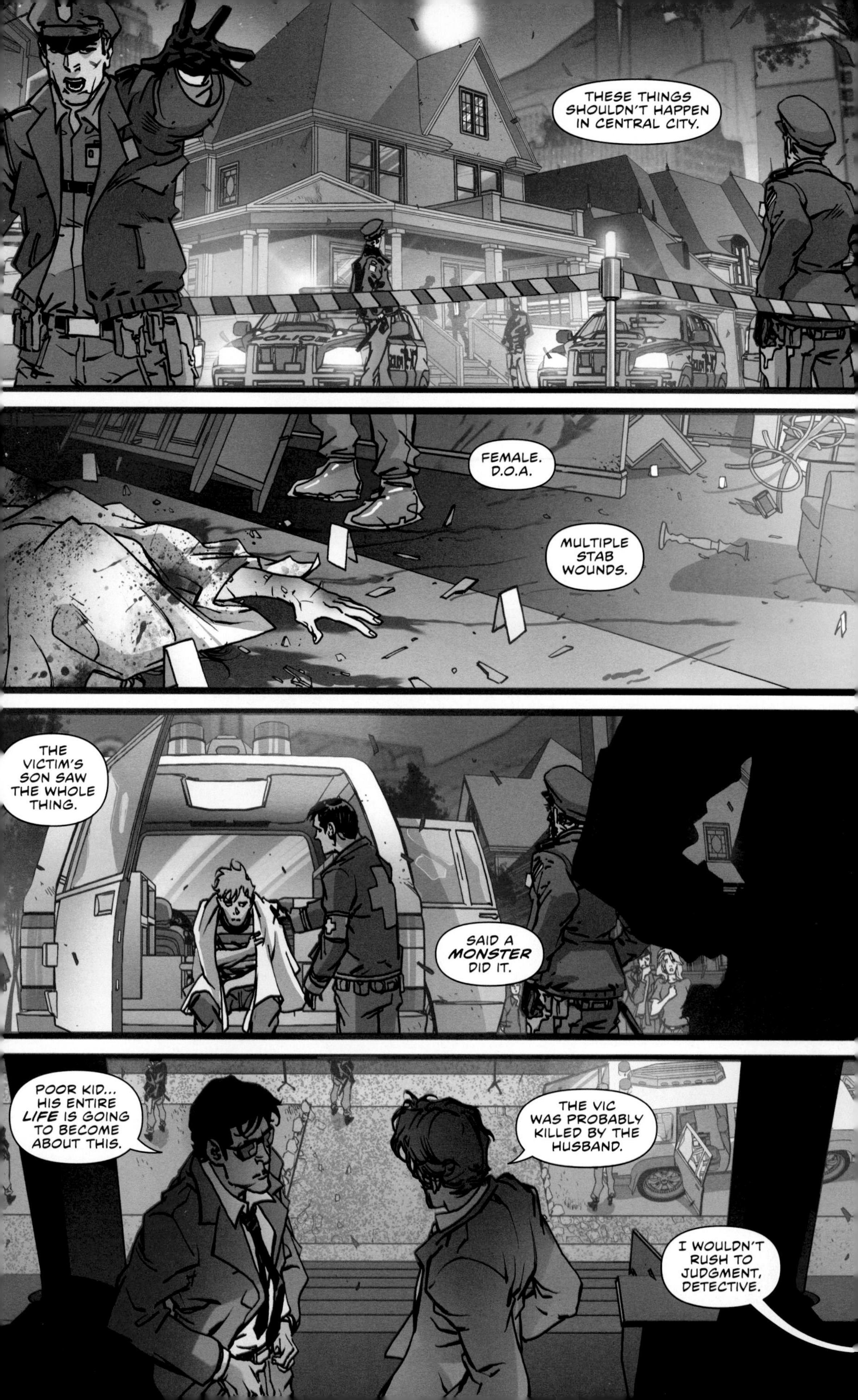
THESE THINGS SHOULDN'T HAPPEN IN CENTRAL CITY.
FEMALE. D.O.A.
MULTIPLE STAB WOUNDS.
THE VICTIM'S SON SAW THE WHOLE THING.
SAID A *MONSTER* DID IT.
POOR KID... HIS ENTIRE *LIFE* IS GOING TO BECOME ABOUT THIS.
THE VIC WAS PROBABLY KILLED BY THE HUSBAND.
I WOULDN'T RUSH TO JUDGMENT, DETECTIVE.

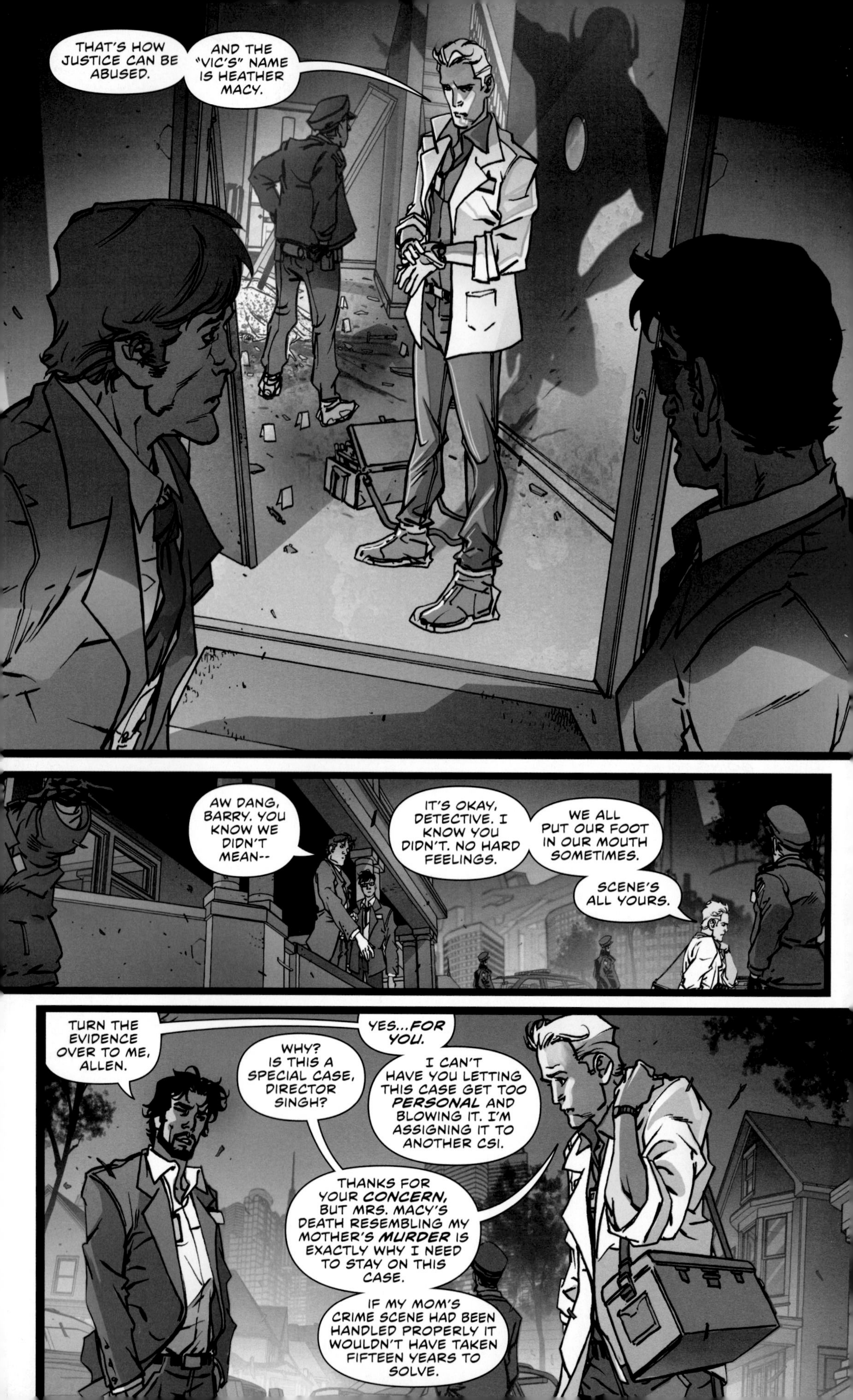
THAT'S HOW JUSTICE CAN BE ABUSED.
AND THE "VIC'S" NAME IS HEATHER MACY.
AW DANG, BARRY. YOU KNOW WE DIDN'T MEAN--
IT'S OKAY, DETECTIVE. I KNOW YOU DIDN'T. NO HARD FEELINGS.
WE ALL PUT OUR FOOT IN OUR MOUTH SOMETIMES.
SCENE'S ALL YOURS.
TURN THE EVIDENCE OVER TO ME, ALLEN.
WHY? IS THIS A SPECIAL CASE, DIRECTOR SINGH?
YES...FOR YOU.
I CAN'T HAVE YOU LETTING THIS CASE GET TOO PERSONAL AND BLOWING IT. I'M ASSIGNING IT TO ANOTHER CSI.
THANKS FOR YOUR CONCERN, BUT MRS. MACY'S DEATH RESEMBLING MY MOTHER'S MURDER IS EXACTLY WHY I NEED TO STAY ON THIS CASE.
IF MY MOM'S CRIME SCENE HAD BEEN HANDLED PROPERLY IT WOULDN'T HAVE TAKEN FIFTEEN YEARS TO SOLVE.

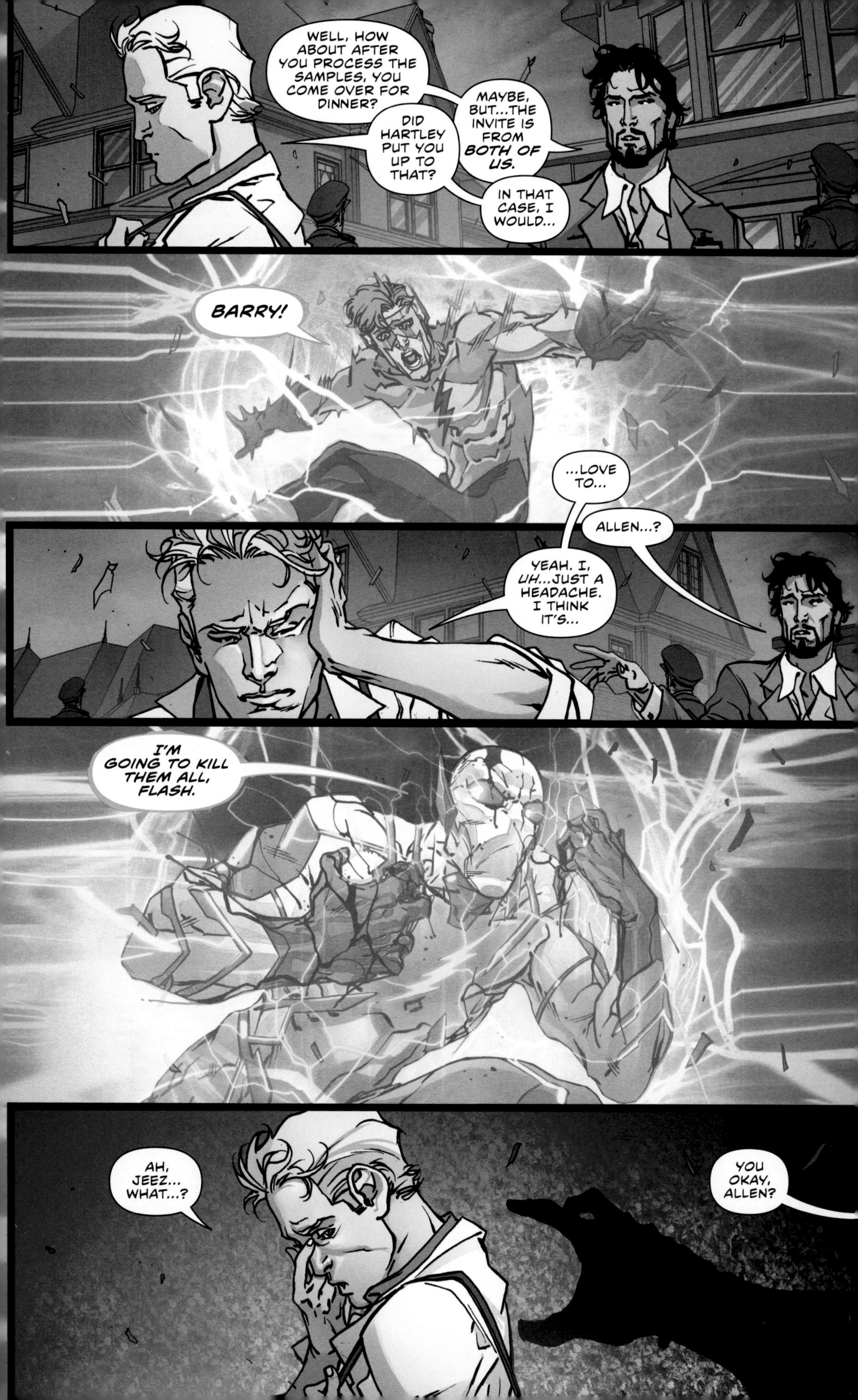
WELL, HOW ABOUT AFTER YOU PROCESS THE SAMPLES, YOU COME OVER FOR DINNER?
DID HARTLEY PUT YOU UP TO THAT?
MAYBE, BUT...THE INVITE IS FROM BOTH OF US.
IN THAT CASE, I WOULD...
BARRY!
...LOVE TO...
ALLEN...?
YEAH. I, UH...JUST A HEADACHE. I THINK IT'S...
I'M GOING TO KILL THEM ALL, FLASH.
AH, JEEZ... WHAT...?
YOU OKAY, ALLEN?

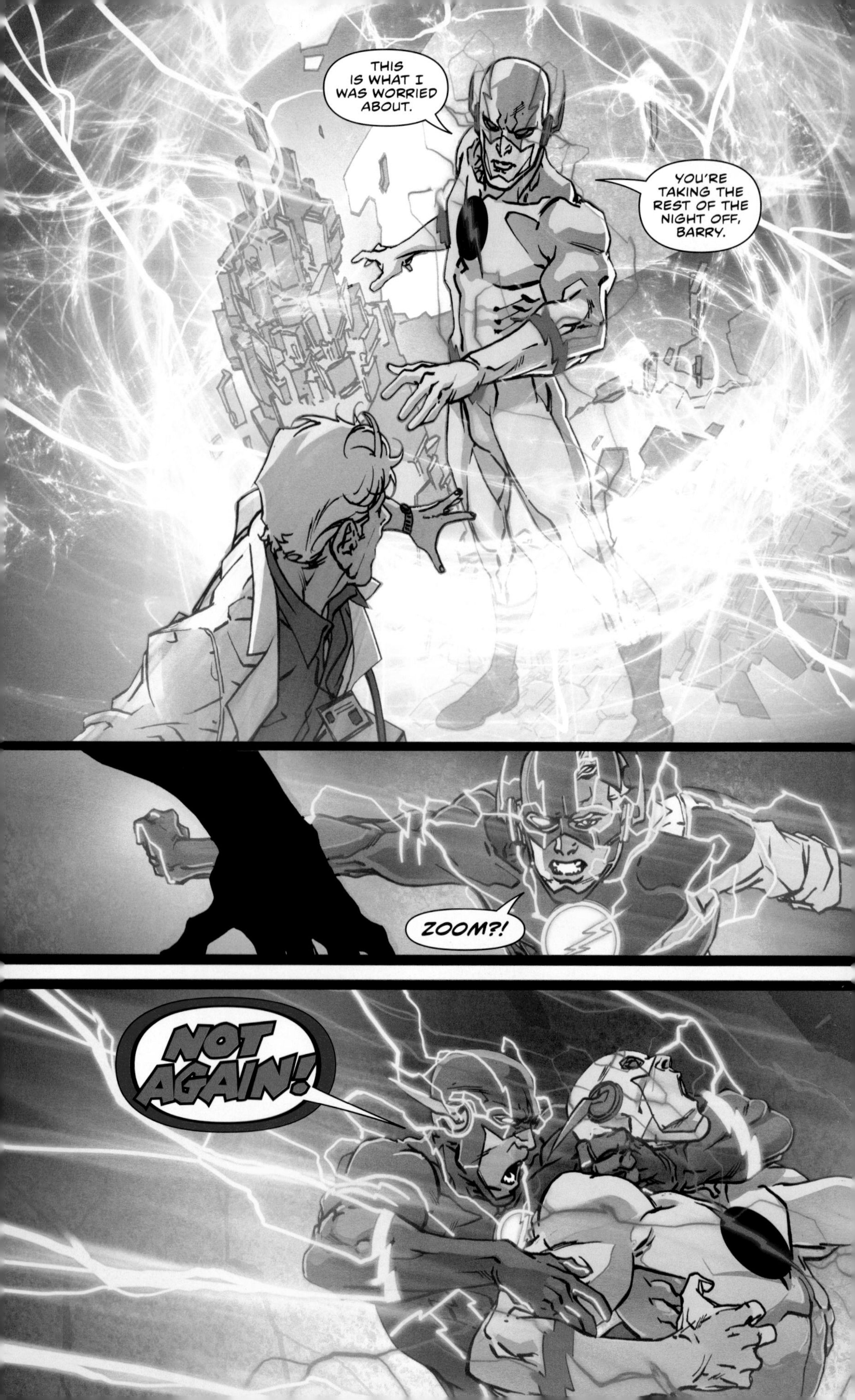
THIS IS WHAT I WAS WORRIED ABOUT.
YOU'RE TAKING THE REST OF THE NIGHT OFF, BARRY.
ZOOM?!
NOT AGAIN!

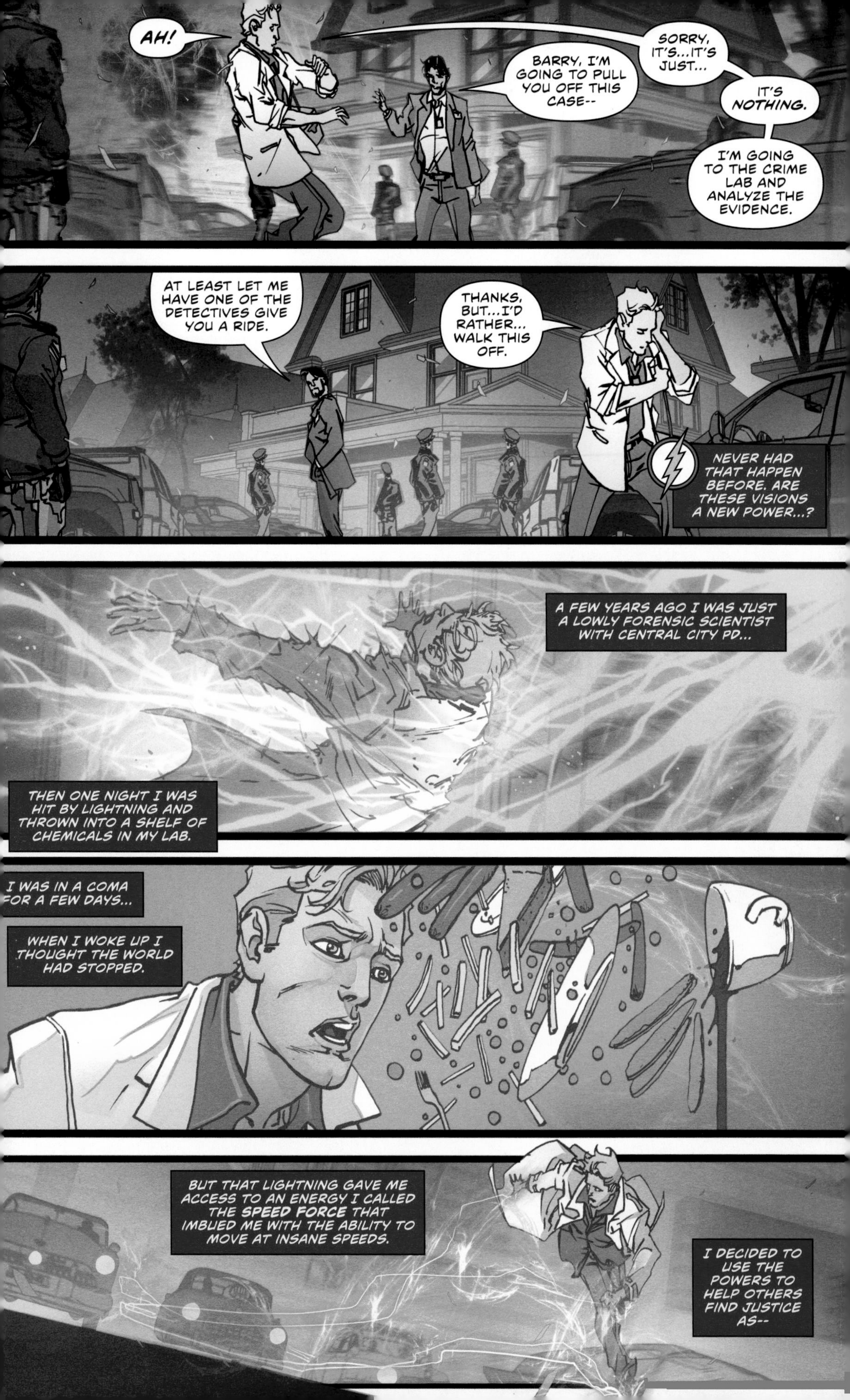
AH!
BARRY, I'M GOING TO PULL YOU OFF THIS CASE--
SORRY, IT'S...IT'S JUST...
IT'S NOTHING.
I'M GOING TO THE CRIME LAB AND ANALYZE THE EVIDENCE.
AT LEAST LET ME HAVE ONE OF THE DETECTIVES GIVE YOU A RIDE.
THANKS, BUT...I'D RATHER... WALK THIS OFF.
NEVER HAD THAT HAPPEN BEFORE. ARE THESE VISIONS A NEW POWER...?
A FEW YEARS AGO I WAS JUST A LOWLY FORENSIC SCIENTIST WITH CENTRAL CITY PD...
THEN ONE NIGHT I WAS HIT BY LIGHTNING AND THROWN INTO A SHELF OF CHEMICALS IN MY LAB.
I WAS IN A COMA FOR A FEW DAYS...
WHEN I WOKE UP I THOUGHT THE WORLD HAD STOPPED.
BUT THAT LIGHTNING GAVE ME ACCESS TO AN ENERGY I CALLED THE SPEED FORCE THAT IMBUED ME WITH THE ABILITY TO MOVE AT INSANE SPEEDS.
I DECIDED TO USE THE POWERS TO HELP OTHERS FIND JUSTICE AS--

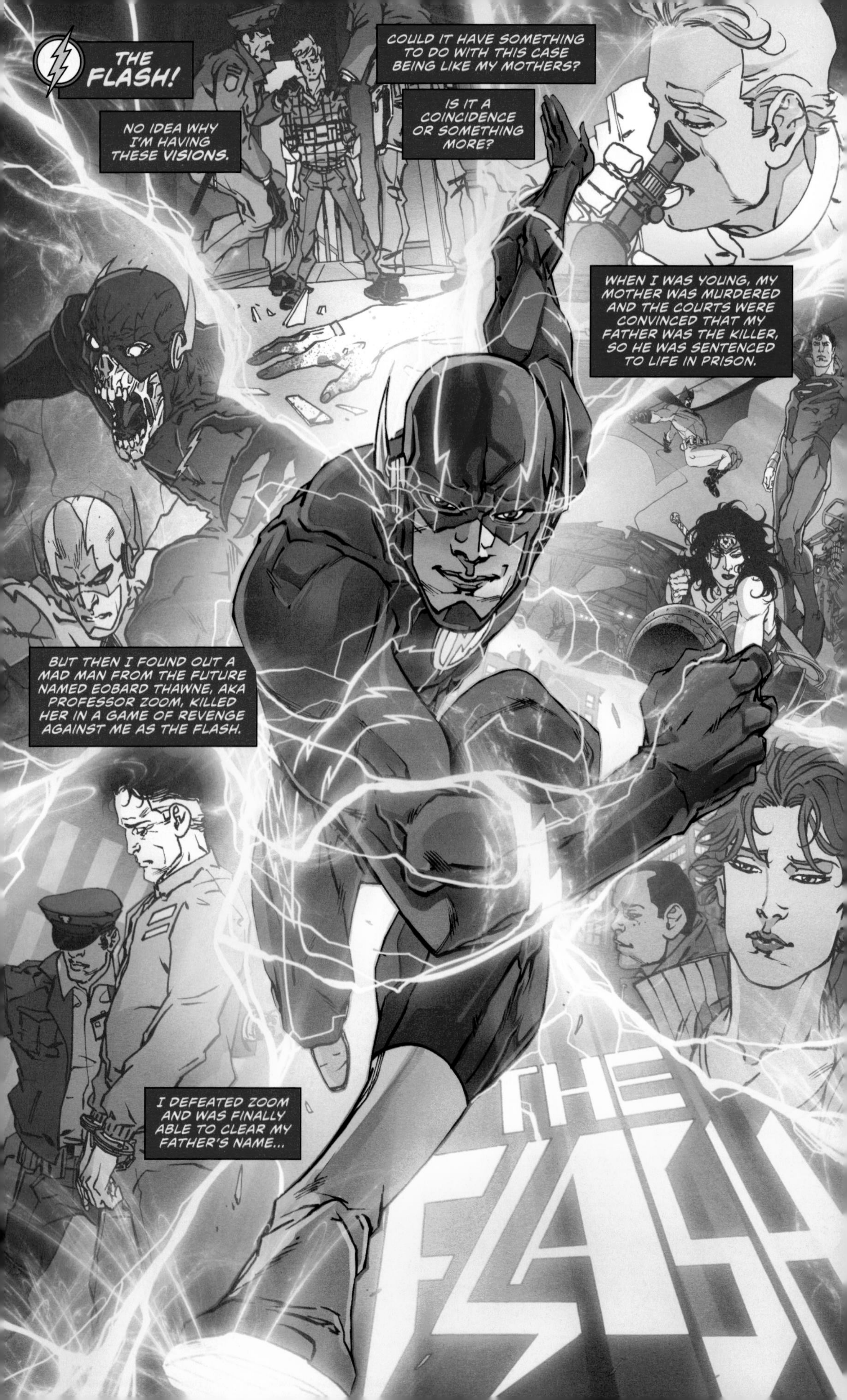
THE FLASH!
NO IDEA WHY I'M HAVING THESE VISIONS.
COULD IT HAVE SOMETHING TO DO WITH THIS CASE BEING LIKE MY MOTHERS?
IS IT A COINCIDENCE OR SOMETHING MORE?
WHEN I WAS YOUNG, MY MOTHER WAS MURDERED AND THE COURTS WERE CONVINCED THAT MY FATHER WAS THE KILLER, SO HE WAS SENTENCED TO LIFE IN PRISON.
BUT THEN I FOUND OUT A MAD MAN FROM THE FUTURE NAMED EOBARD THAWNE, AKA PROFESSOR ZOOM, KILLED HER IN A GAME OF REVENGE AGAINST ME AS THE FLASH.
I DEFEATED ZOOM AND WAS FINALLY ABLE TO CLEAR MY FATHER'S NAME...
THE FLASH

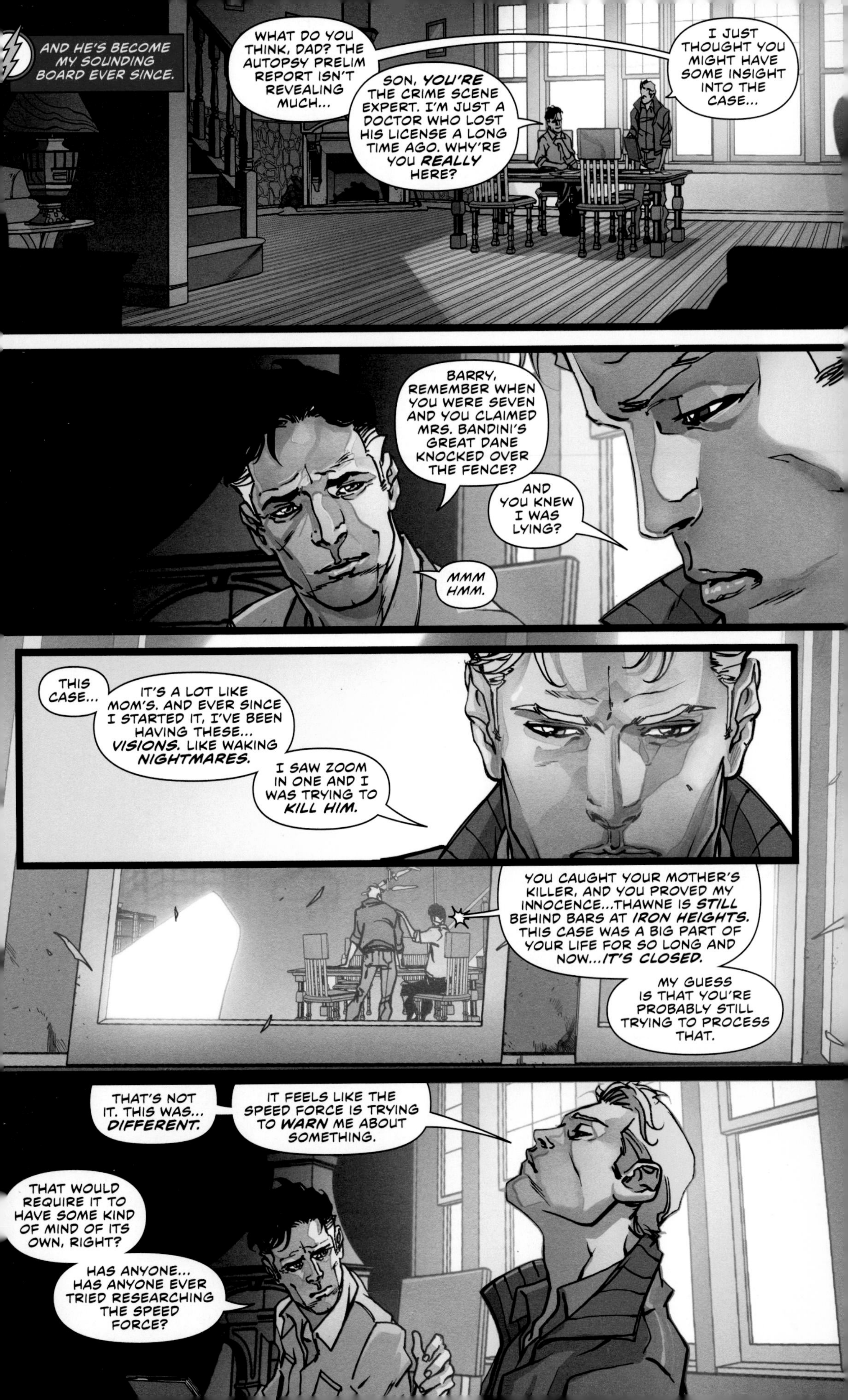
AND HE'S BECOME MY SOUNDING BOARD EVER SINCE.
WHAT DO YOU THINK, DAD? THE AUTOPSY PRELIM REPORT ISN'T REVEALING MUCH...
I JUST THOUGHT YOU MIGHT HAVE SOME INSIGHT INTO THE CASE...
SON, YOU'RE THE CRIME SCENE EXPERT. I'M JUST A DOCTOR WHO LOST HIS LICENSE A LONG TIME AGO. WHY'RE YOU REALLY HERE?
BARRY, REMEMBER WHEN YOU WERE SEVEN AND YOU CLAIMED MRS. BANDINI'S GREAT DANE KNOCKED OVER THE FENCE?
AND YOU KNEW I WAS LYING?
MMM HMM.
THIS CASE...
IT'S A LOT LIKE MOM'S. AND EVER SINCE I STARTED IT, I'VE BEEN HAVING THESE... VISIONS. LIKE WAKING NIGHTMARES.
I SAW ZOOM IN ONE AND I WAS TRYING TO KILL HIM.
YOU CAUGHT YOUR MOTHER'S KILLER, AND YOU PROVED MY INNOCENCE...THAWNE IS STILL BEHIND BARS AT IRON HEIGHTS. THIS CASE WAS A BIG PART OF YOUR LIFE FOR SO LONG AND NOW...IT'S CLOSED.
MY GUESS IS THAT YOU'RE PROBABLY STILL TRYING TO PROCESS THAT.
THAT'S NOT IT. THIS WAS... DIFFERENT.
IT FEELS LIKE THE SPEED FORCE IS TRYING TO WARN ME ABOUT SOMETHING.
THAT WOULD REQUIRE IT TO HAVE SOME KIND OF MIND OF ITS OWN, RIGHT?
HAS ANYONE... HAS ANYONE EVER TRIED RESEARCHING THE SPEED FORCE?

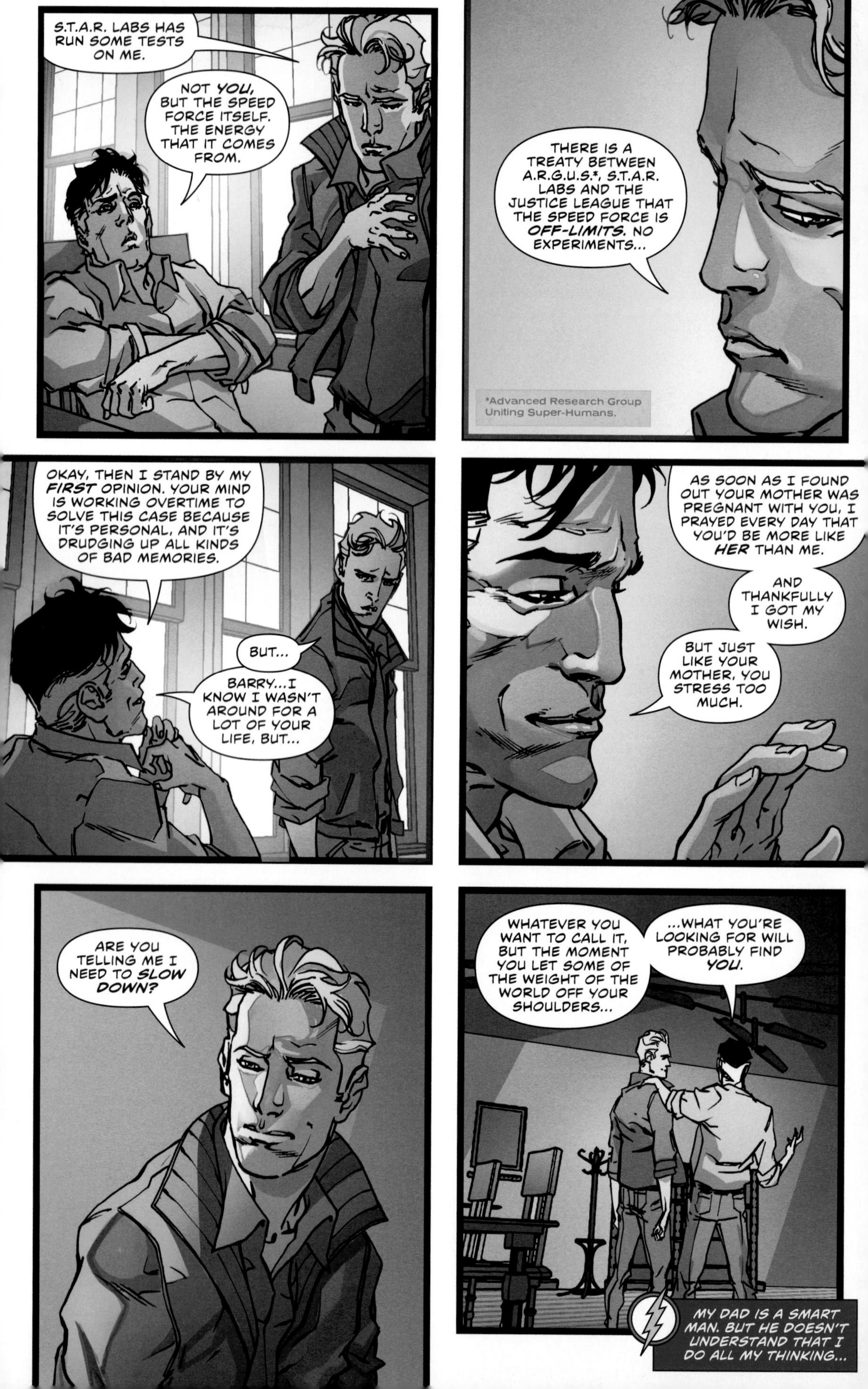
S.T.A.R. LABS HAS RUN SOME TESTS ON ME.
NOT YOU, BUT THE SPEED FORCE ITSELF. THE ENERGY THAT IT COMES FROM.
THERE IS A TREATY BETWEEN A.R.G.U.S.*, S.T.A.R. LABS AND THE JUSTICE LEAGUE THAT THE SPEED FORCE IS OFF-LIMITS. NO EXPERIMENTS...
*Advanced Research Group Uniting Super-Humans.
OKAY, THEN I STAND BY MY FIRST OPINION. YOUR MIND IS WORKING OVERTIME TO SOLVE THIS CASE BECAUSE IT'S PERSONAL, AND IT'S DRUDGING UP ALL KINDS OF BAD MEMORIES.
BUT...
BARRY...I KNOW I WASN'T AROUND FOR A LOT OF YOUR LIFE, BUT...
AS SOON AS I FOUND OUT YOUR MOTHER WAS PREGNANT WITH YOU, I PRAYED EVERY DAY THAT YOU'D BE MORE LIKE HER THAN ME.
AND THANKFULLY I GOT MY WISH.
BUT JUST LIKE YOUR MOTHER, YOU STRESS TOO MUCH.
ARE YOU TELLING ME I NEED TO SLOW DOWN?
WHATEVER YOU WANT TO CALL IT, BUT THE MOMENT YOU LET SOME OF THE WEIGHT OF THE WORLD OFF YOUR SHOULDERS...
...WHAT YOU'RE LOOKING FOR WILL PROBABLY FIND YOU.
MY DAD IS A SMART MAN. BUT HE DOESN'T UNDERSTAND THAT I DO ALL MY THINKING...

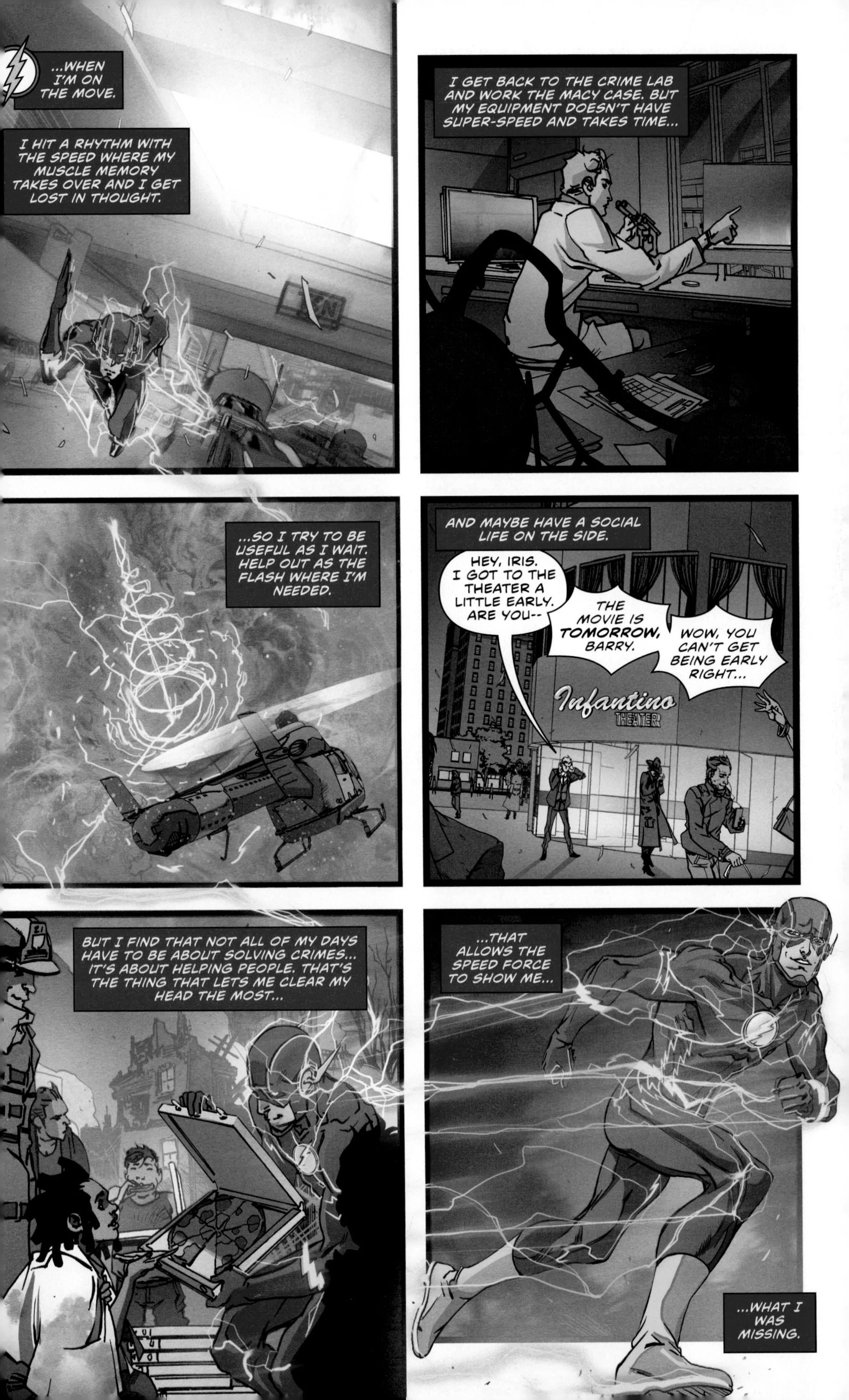
...WHEN I'M ON THE MOVE.
I HIT A RHYTHM WITH THE SPEED WHERE MY MUSCLE MEMORY TAKES OVER AND I GET LOST IN THOUGHT.
I GET BACK TO THE CRIME LAB AND WORK THE MACY CASE. BUT MY EQUIPMENT DOESN'T HAVE SUPER-SPEED AND TAKES TIME...
...SO I TRY TO BE USEFUL AS I WAIT. HELP OUT AS THE FLASH WHERE I'M NEEDED.
AND MAYBE HAVE A SOCIAL LIFE ON THE SIDE.
HEY, IRIS. I GOT TO THE THEATER A LITTLE EARLY. ARE YOU--
THE MOVIE IS **TOMORROW,** BARRY.
WOW, YOU CAN'T GET BEING EARLY RIGHT...
Infantino
THEATER
BUT I FIND THAT NOT ALL OF MY DAYS HAVE TO BE ABOUT SOLVING CRIMES... IT'S ABOUT HELPING PEOPLE. THAT'S THE THING THAT LETS ME CLEAR MY HEAD THE MOST...
...THAT ALLOWS THE SPEED FORCE TO SHOW ME...
...WHAT I WAS MISSING.

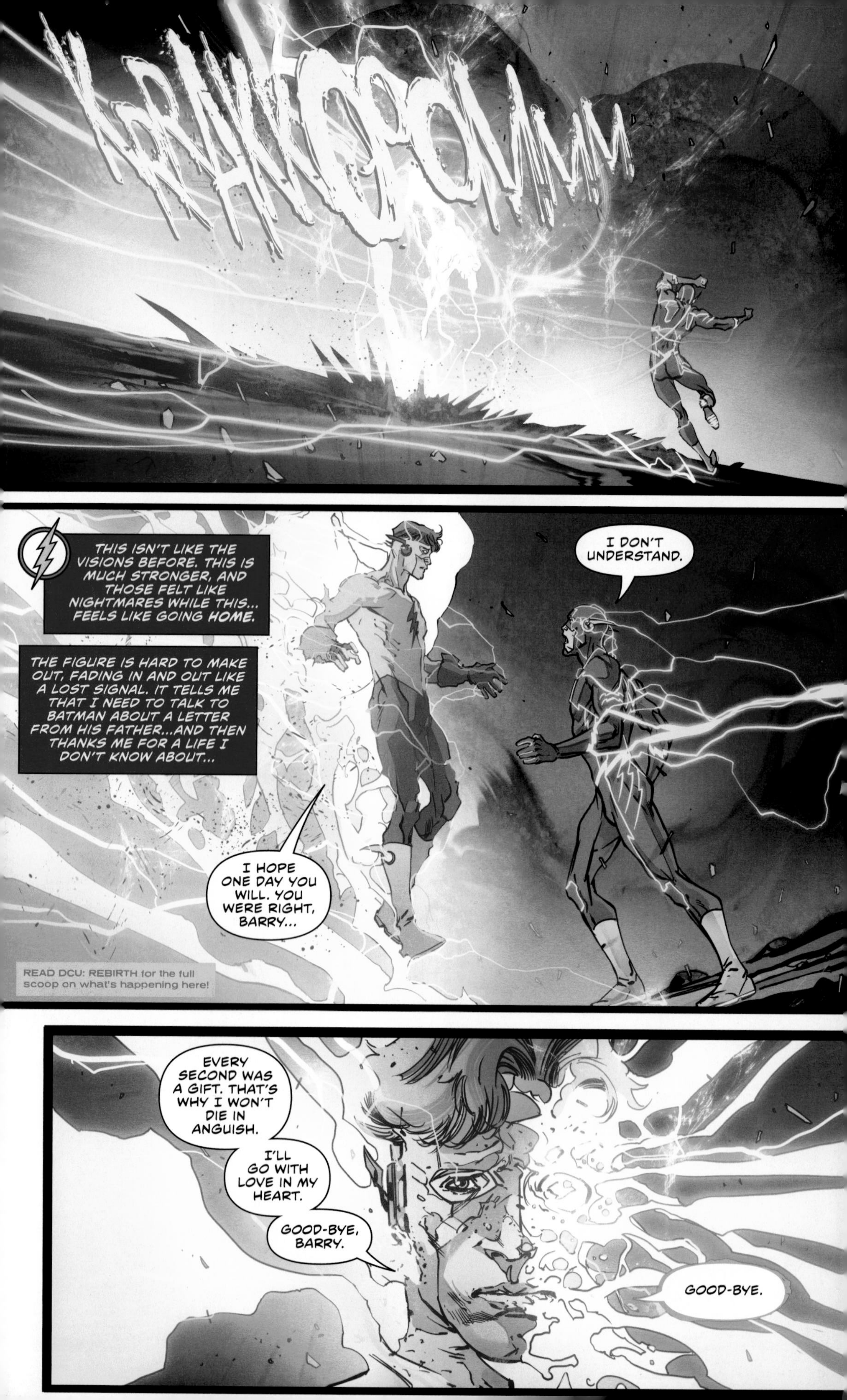
THIS ISN'T LIKE THE VISIONS BEFORE. THIS IS MUCH STRONGER, AND THOSE FELT LIKE NIGHTMARES WHILE THIS... FEELS LIKE GOING HOME.
I DON'T UNDERSTAND.
THE FIGURE IS HARD TO MAKE OUT, FADING IN AND OUT LIKE A LOST SIGNAL. IT TELLS ME THAT I NEED TO TALK TO BATMAN ABOUT A LETTER FROM HIS FATHER...AND THEN THANKS ME FOR A LIFE I DON'T KNOW ABOUT...
I HOPE ONE DAY YOU WILL. YOU WERE RIGHT, BARRY...
READ DCU: REBIRTH for the full scoop on what's happening here!
EVERY SECOND WAS A GIFT. THAT'S WHY I WON'T DIE IN ANGUISH.
I'LL GO WITH LOVE IN MY HEART.
GOOD-BYE, BARRY.
GOOD-BYE.

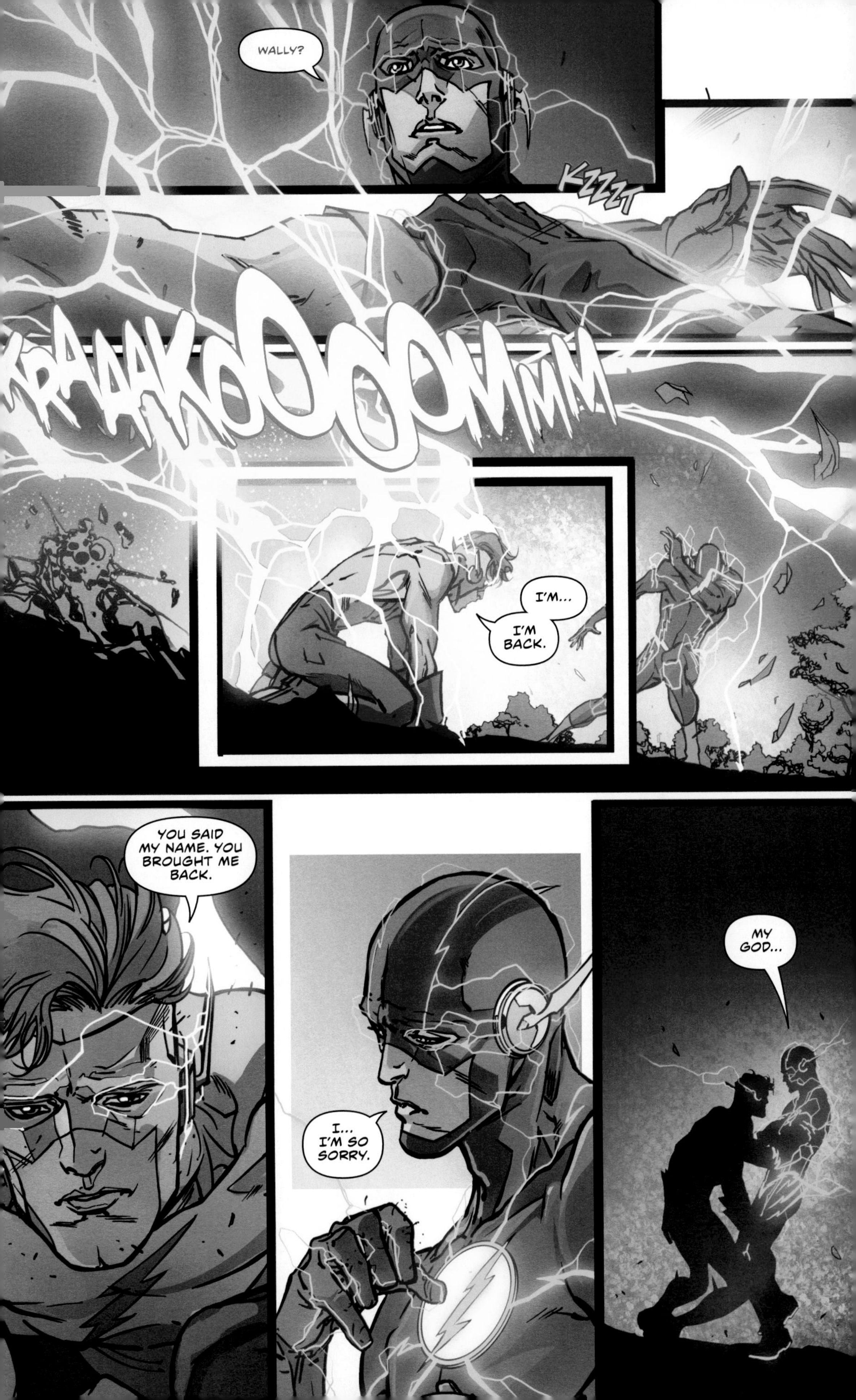
WALLY?
KZZZT
KRAAAKOOOOOMMM
I'M...
I'M BACK.
YOU SAID MY NAME. YOU BROUGHT ME BACK.
I... I'M SO SORRY.
MY GOD...

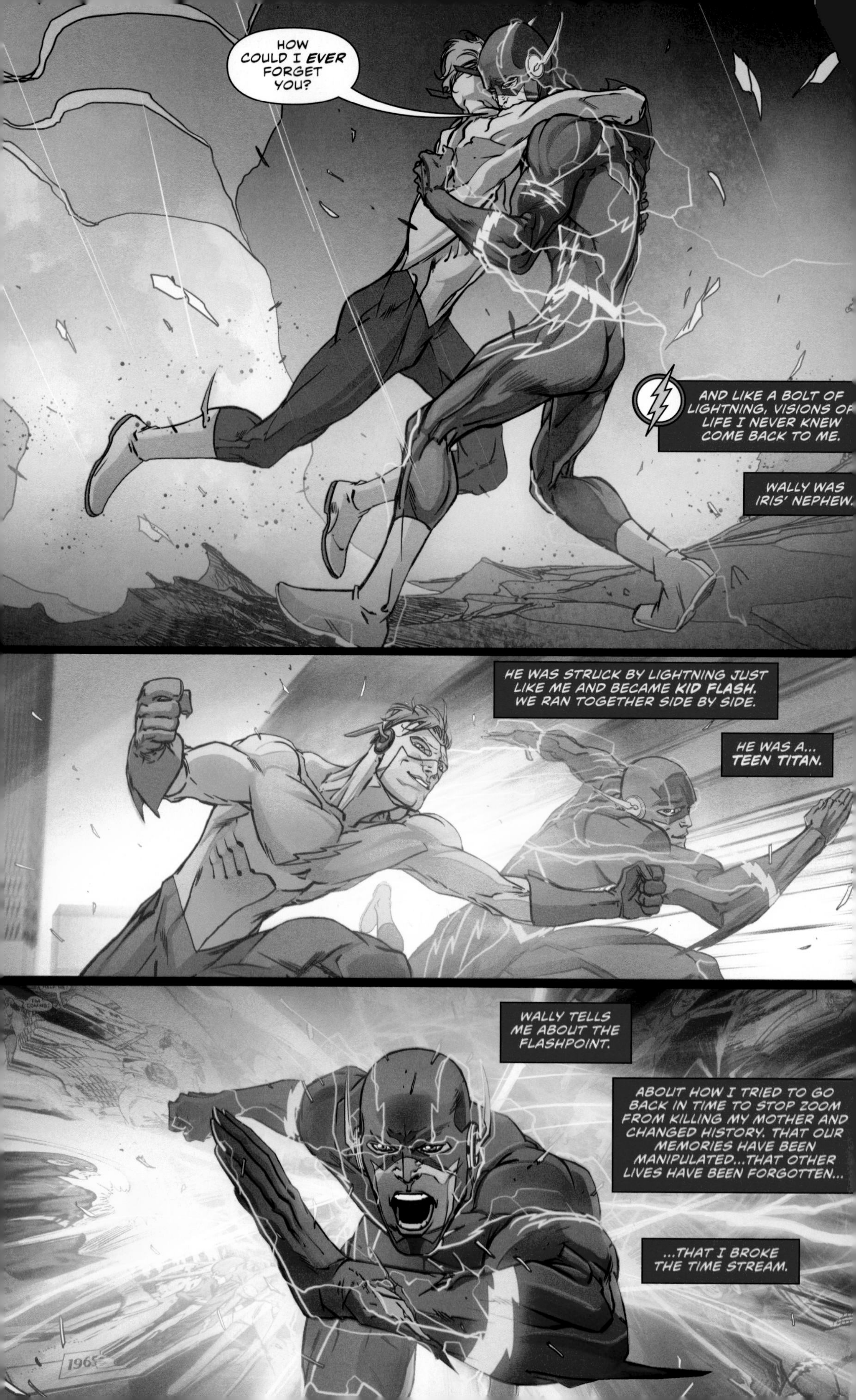
HOW COULD I EVER FORGET YOU?
AND LIKE A BOLT OF LIGHTNING, VISIONS OF LIFE I NEVER KNEW COME BACK TO ME.
WALLY WAS IRIS' NEPHEW.
HE WAS STRUCK BY LIGHTNING JUST LIKE ME AND BECAME KID FLASH. WE RAN TOGETHER SIDE BY SIDE.
HE WAS A... TEEN TITAN.
WALLY TELLS ME ABOUT THE FLASHPOINT.
ABOUT HOW I TRIED TO GO BACK IN TIME TO STOP ZOOM FROM KILLING MY MOTHER AND CHANGED HISTORY. THAT OUR MEMORIES HAVE BEEN MANIPULATED...THAT OTHER LIVES HAVE BEEN FORGOTTEN...
...THAT I BROKE THE TIME STREAM.

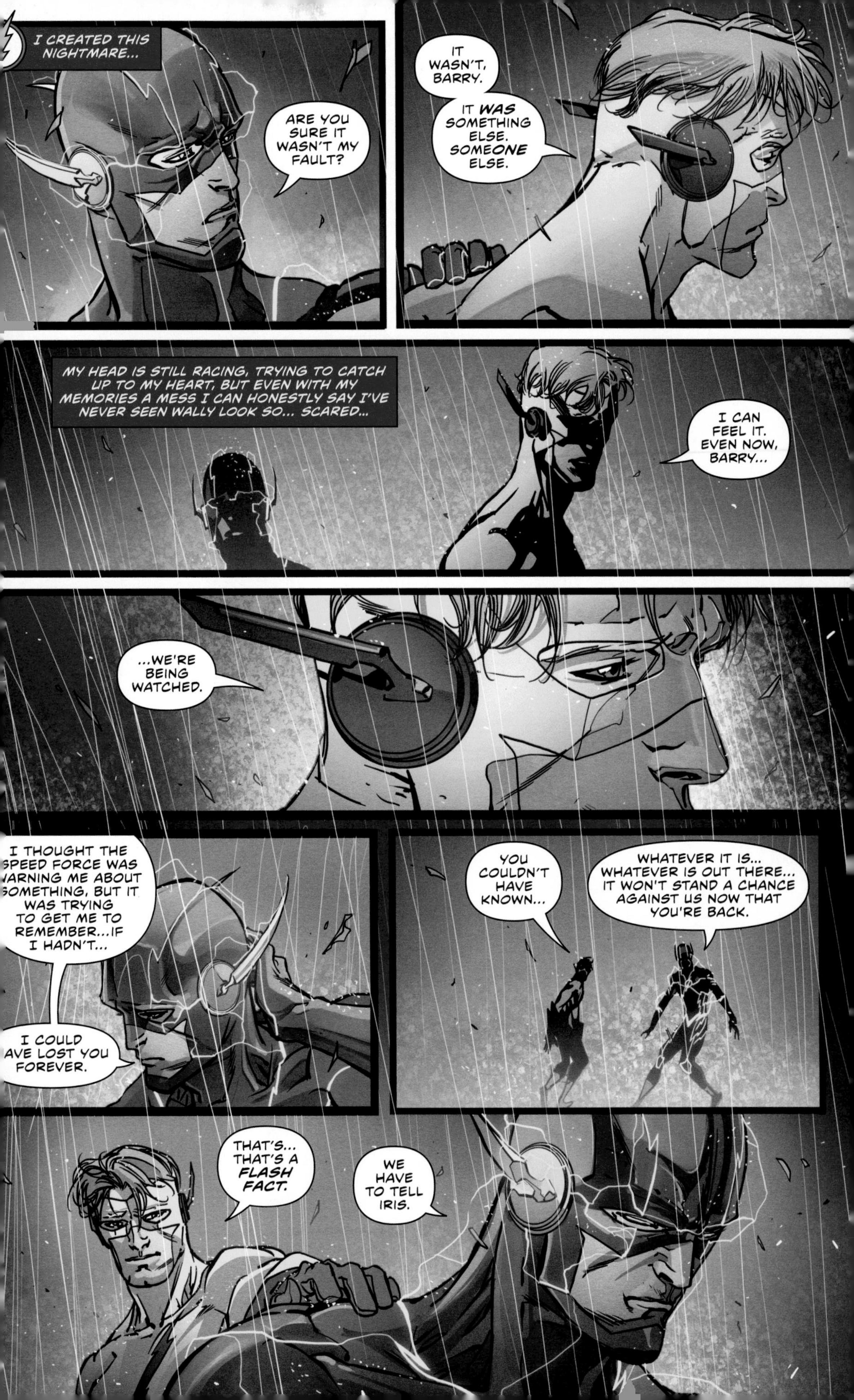

I CREATED THIS NIGHTMARE...
ARE YOU SURE IT WASN'T MY FAULT?
IT WASN'T, BARRY.
IT **WAS** SOMETHING ELSE. SOME*ONE* ELSE.
MY HEAD IS STILL RACING, TRYING TO CATCH UP TO MY HEART, BUT EVEN WITH MY MEMORIES A MESS I CAN HONESTLY SAY I'VE NEVER SEEN WALLY LOOK SO... SCARED...
I CAN FEEL IT. EVEN NOW, BARRY...
...WE'RE BEING WATCHED.
I THOUGHT THE PEED FORCE WAS ARNING ME ABOUT OMETHING, BUT IT WAS TRYING TO GET ME TO REMEMBER...IF I HADN'T...
I COULD AVE LOST YOU FOREVER.
YOU COULDN'T HAVE KNOWN...
WHATEVER IT IS... WHATEVER IS OUT THERE... IT WON'T STAND A CHANCE AGAINST US NOW THAT YOU'RE BACK.
THAT'S... THAT'S A ***FLASH FACT.***
WE HAVE TO TELL IRIS.

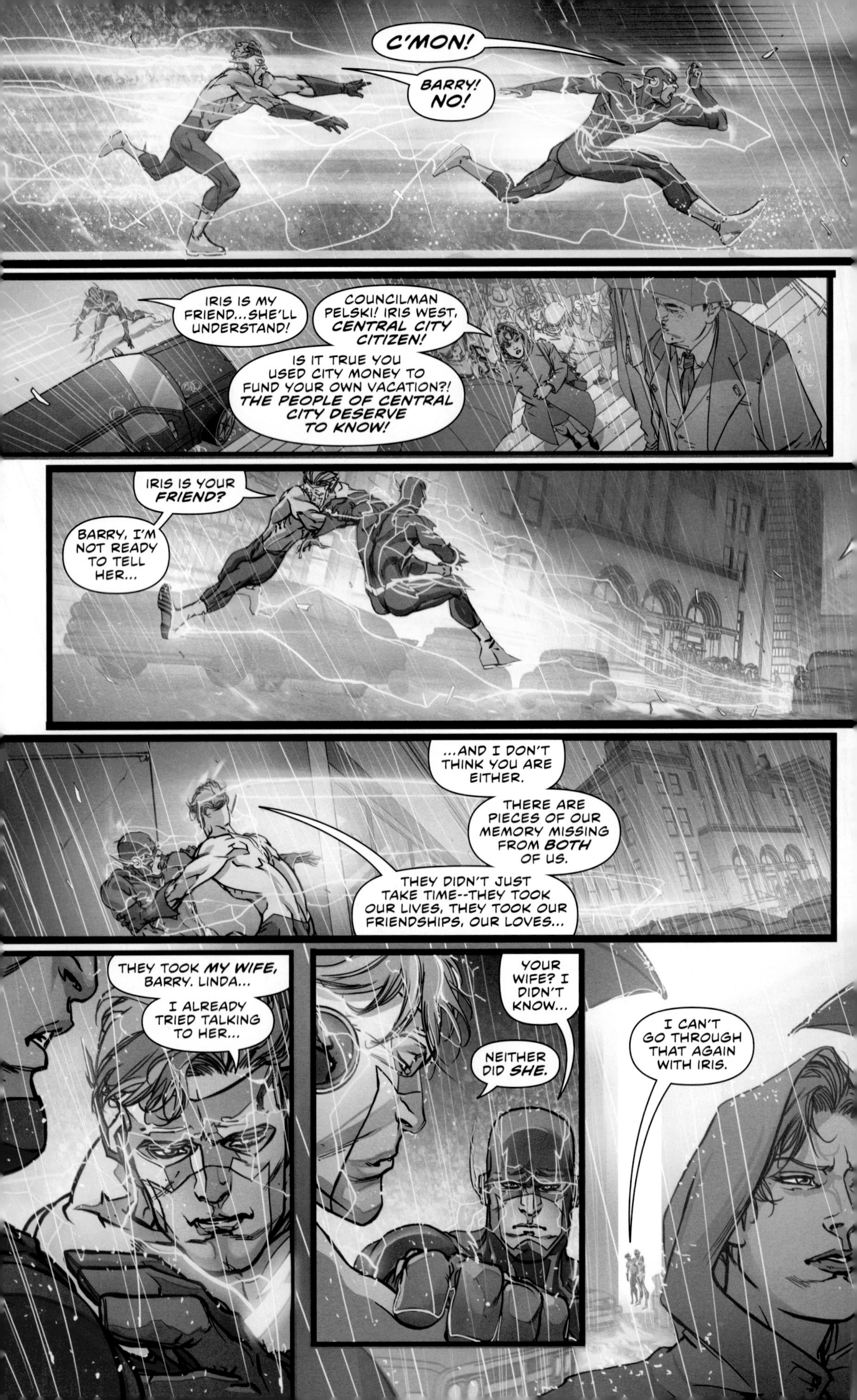
C'MON!
BARRY! NO!
IRIS IS MY FRIEND...SHE'LL UNDERSTAND!
COUNCILMAN PELSKI! IRIS WEST, CENTRAL CITY CITIZEN!
IS IT TRUE YOU USED CITY MONEY TO FUND YOUR OWN VACATION?! THE PEOPLE OF CENTRAL CITY DESERVE TO KNOW!
IRIS IS YOUR FRIEND?
BARRY, I'M NOT READY TO TELL HER...
...AND I DON'T THINK YOU ARE EITHER.
THERE ARE PIECES OF OUR MEMORY MISSING FROM BOTH OF US.
THEY DIDN'T JUST TAKE TIME--THEY TOOK OUR LIVES, THEY TOOK OUR FRIENDSHIPS, OUR LOVES...
THEY TOOK MY WIFE, BARRY. LINDA...
I ALREADY TRIED TALKING TO HER...
YOUR WIFE? I DIDN'T KNOW...
NEITHER DID SHE.
I CAN'T GO THROUGH THAT AGAIN WITH IRIS.

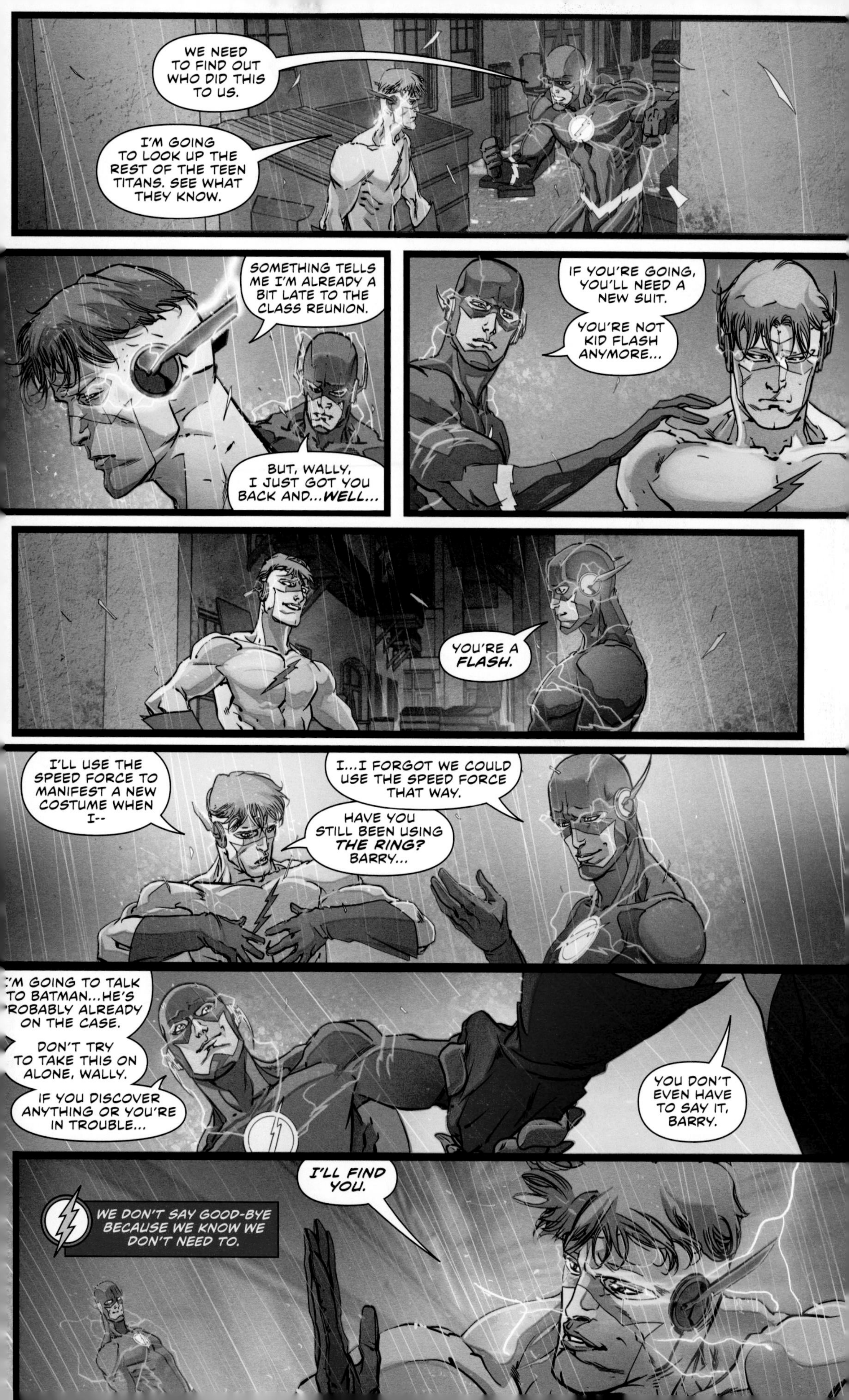
WE NEED TO FIND OUT WHO DID THIS TO US.
I'M GOING TO LOOK UP THE REST OF THE TEEN TITANS. SEE WHAT THEY KNOW.
SOMETHING TELLS ME I'M ALREADY A BIT LATE TO THE CLASS REUNION.
BUT, WALLY, I JUST GOT YOU BACK AND...WELL...
IF YOU'RE GOING, YOU'LL NEED A NEW SUIT.
YOU'RE NOT KID FLASH ANYMORE...
YOU'RE A FLASH.
I'LL USE THE SPEED FORCE TO MANIFEST A NEW COSTUME WHEN I--
I...I FORGOT WE COULD USE THE SPEED FORCE THAT WAY.
HAVE YOU STILL BEEN USING THE RING? BARRY...
'M GOING TO TALK TO BATMAN...HE'S ROBABLY ALREADY ON THE CASE.
DON'T TRY TO TAKE THIS ON ALONE, WALLY.
IF YOU DISCOVER ANYTHING OR YOU'RE IN TROUBLE...
YOU DON'T EVEN HAVE TO SAY IT, BARRY.
WE DON'T SAY GOOD-BYE BECAUSE WE KNOW WE DON'T NEED TO.
I'LL FIND YOU.

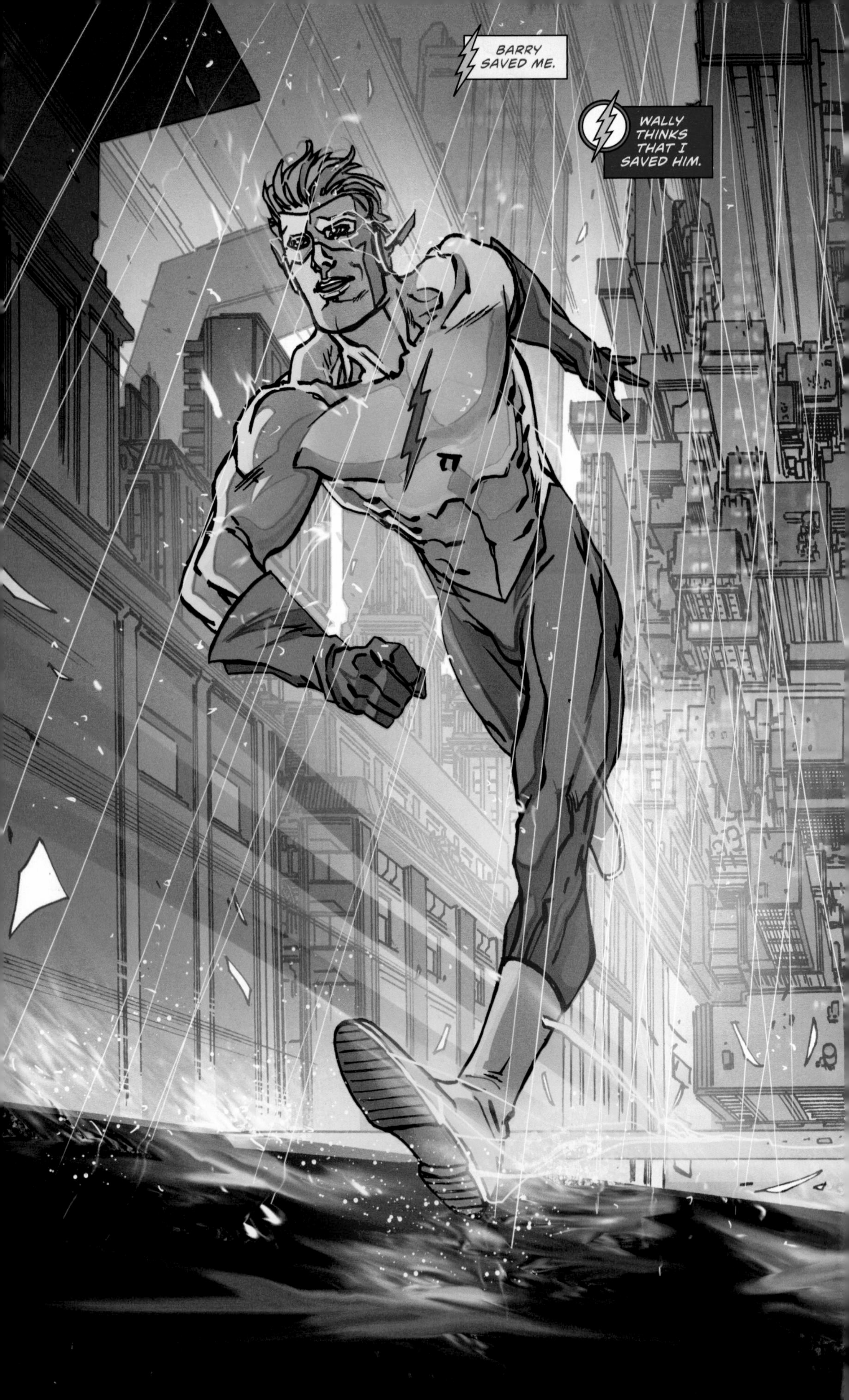
BARRY SAVED ME.
WALLY THINKS THAT I SAVED HIM.

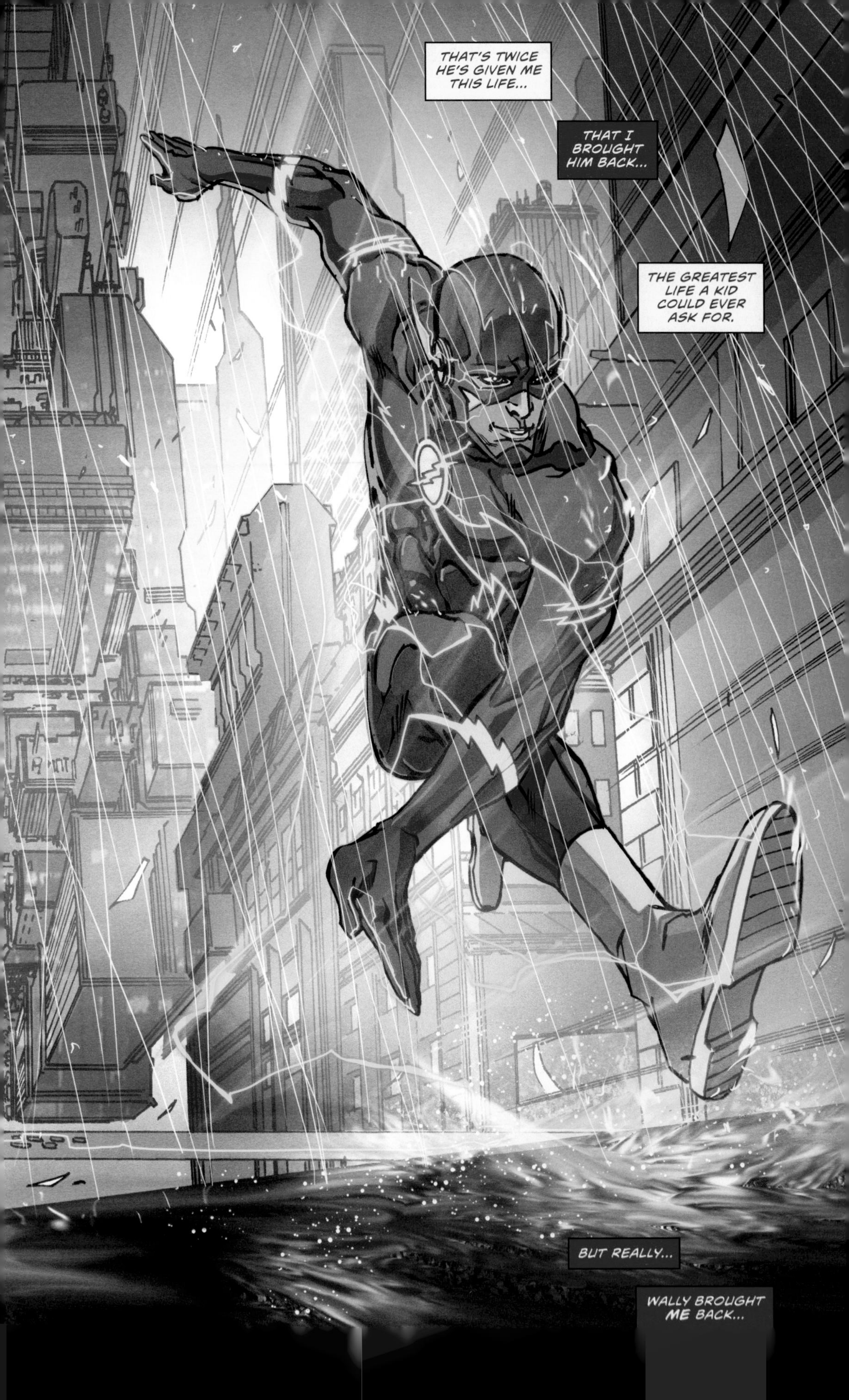
THAT'S TWICE HE'S GIVEN ME THIS LIFE...
THAT I BROUGHT HIM BACK...
THE GREATEST LIFE A KID COULD EVER ASK FOR.
BUT REALLY...
WALLY BROUGHT ME BACK...

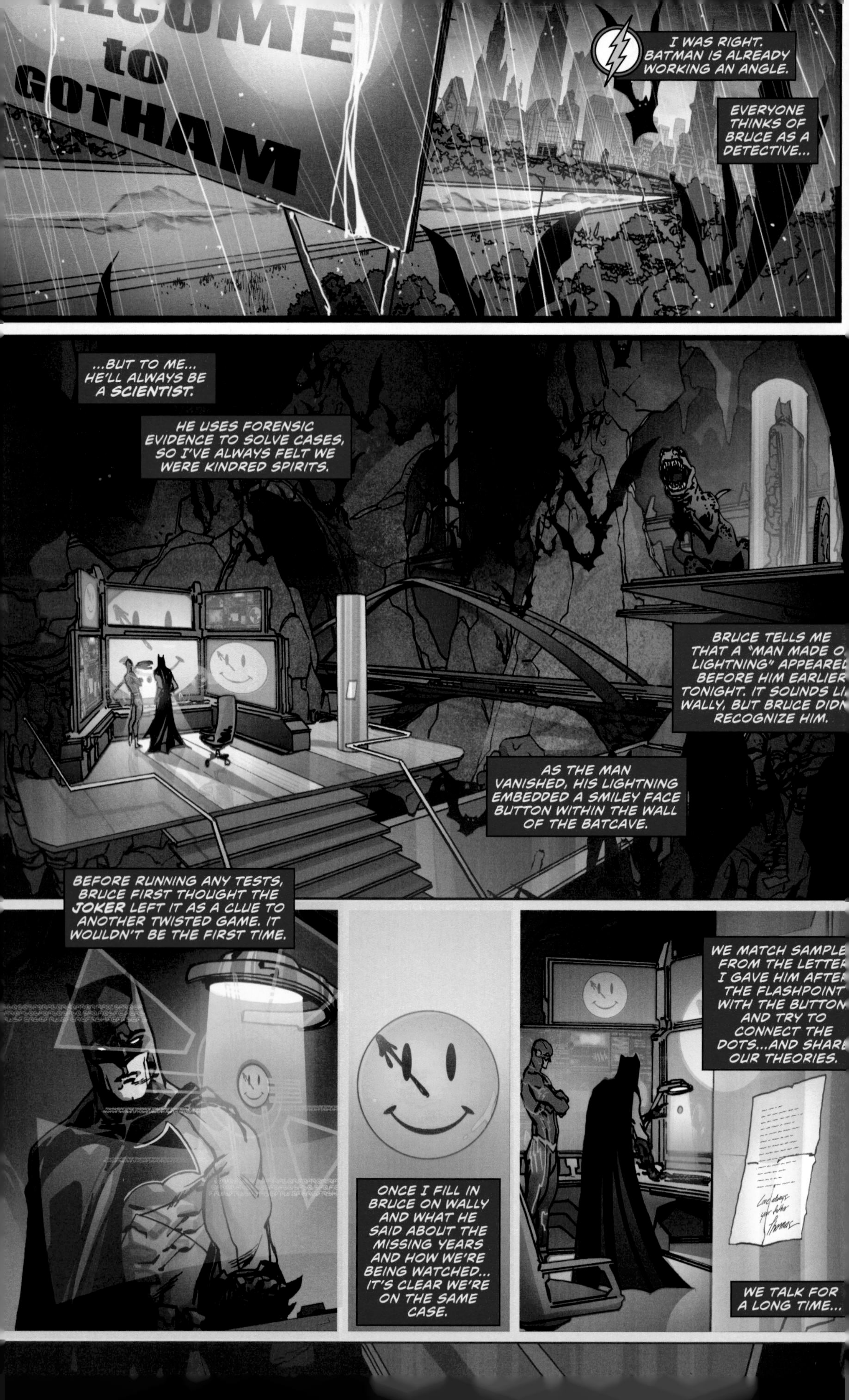
WELCOME
to
GOTHAM
I WAS RIGHT. BATMAN IS ALREADY WORKING AN ANGLE.
EVERYONE THINKS OF BRUCE AS A DETECTIVE...
...BUT TO ME... HE'LL ALWAYS BE A SCIENTIST.
HE USES FORENSIC EVIDENCE TO SOLVE CASES, SO I'VE ALWAYS FELT WE WERE KINDRED SPIRITS.
BRUCE TELLS ME THAT A "MAN MADE O LIGHTNING" APPEARE BEFORE HIM EARLIER TONIGHT. IT SOUNDS LI WALLY, BUT BRUCE DIDN RECOGNIZE HIM.
AS THE MAN VANISHED, HIS LIGHTNING EMBEDDED A SMILEY FACE BUTTON WITHIN THE WALL OF THE BATCAVE.
BEFORE RUNNING ANY TESTS, BRUCE FIRST THOUGHT THE JOKER LEFT IT AS A CLUE TO ANOTHER TWISTED GAME. IT WOULDN'T BE THE FIRST TIME.
ONCE I FILL IN BRUCE ON WALLY AND WHAT HE SAID ABOUT THE MISSING YEARS AND HOW WE'RE BEING WATCHED... IT'S CLEAR WE'RE ON THE SAME CASE.
WE MATCH SAMPLE FROM THE LETTER I GAVE HIM AFTE THE FLASHPOINT WITH THE BUTTON AND TRY TO CONNECT THE DOTS...AND SHAR OUR THEORIES.
WE TALK FOR A LONG TIME...

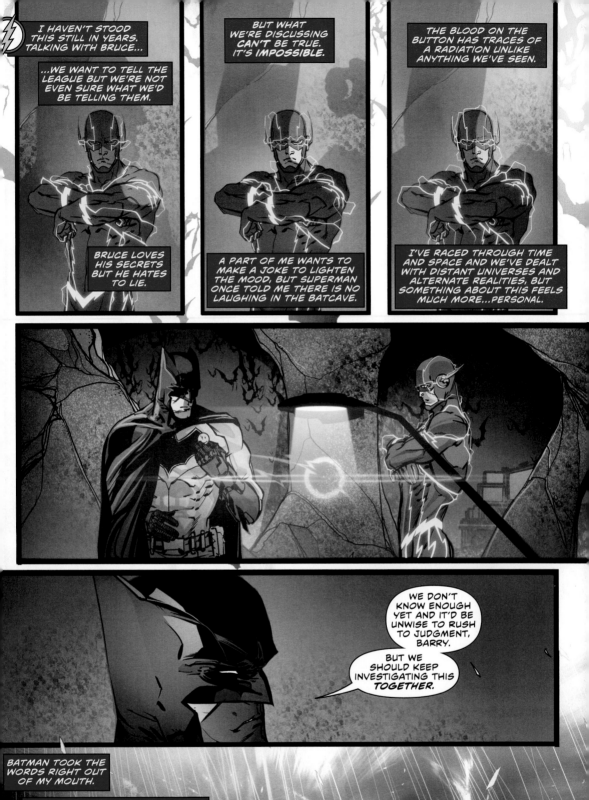

I HAVEN'T STOOD THIS STILL IN YEARS. TALKING WITH BRUCE...

...WE WANT TO TELL THE LEAGUE BUT WE'RE NOT EVEN SURE WHAT WE'D BE TELLING THEM.

BRUCE LOVES HIS SECRETS BUT HE HATES TO LIE.

BUT WHAT WE'RE DISCUSSING CAN'T BE TRUE. IT'S IMPOSSIBLE.

A PART OF ME WANTS TO MAKE A JOKE TO LIGHTEN THE MOOD, BUT SUPERMAN ONCE TOLD ME THERE IS NO LAUGHING IN THE BATCAVE.

THE BLOOD ON THE BUTTON HAS TRACES OF A RADIATION UNLIKE ANYTHING WE'VE SEEN.

I'VE RACED THROUGH TIME AND SPACE AND WE'VE DEALT WITH DISTANT UNIVERSES AND ALTERNATE REALITIES, BUT SOMETHING ABOUT THIS FEELS MUCH MORE...PERSONAL.

WE DON'T KNOW ENOUGH YET AND IT'D BE UNWISE TO RUSH TO JUDGMENT, BARRY.

BUT WE SHOULD KEEP INVESTIGATING THIS *TOGETHER.*

BATMAN TOOK THE WORDS RIGHT OUT OF MY MOUTH.

I'VE HAD CASES LIKE THIS BEFORE. NO REAL LEADS AND ONLY THE EVIDENCE TO FOLLOW. BUT IF THIS UNSEEN MANIPULATOR IS WHAT THE SPEED FORCE WAS TRYING TO WARN ME ABOUT, THEN I KNOW THAT BATMAN AND I WILL SOLVE IT.

"DID ALLEN EVER GET THE CRIME SCENE RESULTS BACK?"

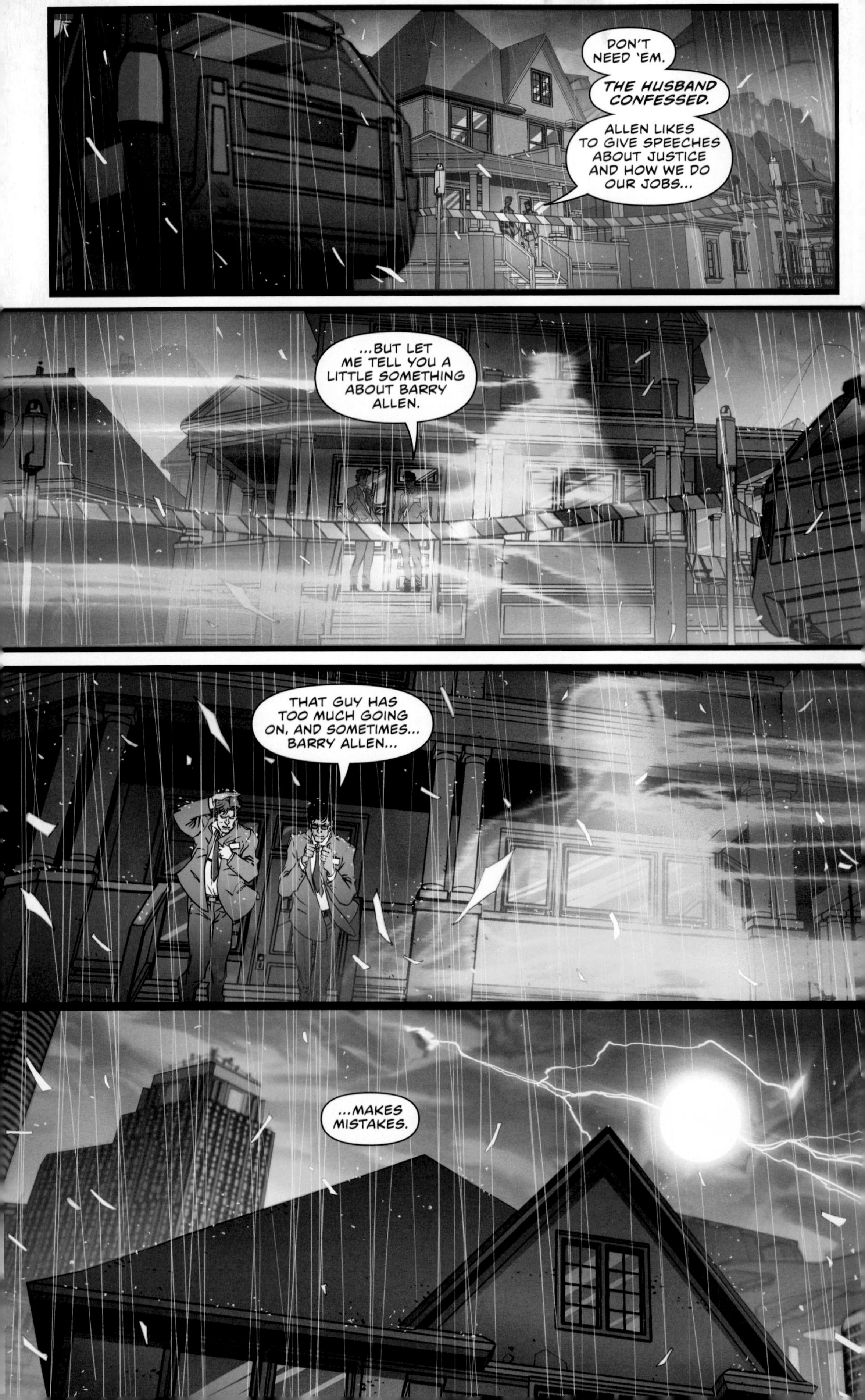

DON'T NEED 'EM.
THE HUSBAND CONFESSED.
ALLEN LIKES TO GIVE SPEECHES ABOUT JUSTICE AND HOW WE DO OUR JOBS...
...BUT LET ME TELL YOU A LITTLE SOMETHING ABOUT BARRY ALLEN.
THAT GUY HAS TOO MUCH GOING ON, AND SOMETIMES... BARRY ALLEN...
...MAKES MISTAKES.